CW00689159

Democracy WITHOUT Democrats?

This volume is part of the research programme on
energy and the environment in the Mediterranean
carried out by Fondazione ENI Enrico Mattei

Democracy
WITHOUT
Democrats?

THE RENEWAL OF POLITICS
IN THE MUSLIM WORLD

Edited by
Ghassan Salamé

I.B. Tauris *Publishers*
LONDON • NEW YORK

Reprinted in 2001 by I.B.Tauris & Co Ltd
6 Salem Road, London W2 4BU
175 Fifth Avenue, New York NY 10010
www.ibtauris.com

In the United States of America and in Canada distributed by
St Martins Press, 175 Fifth Avenue, New York NY 10010

First published in 1994 by I.B.Tauris & Co Ltd. Reprinted in 1995 & 1996

Copyright © Fondazione ENI Enrico Mattei, 1994

All rights reserved. Except for brief quotations in a review, this book, or any part
thereof, may not be reproduced, stored in or introduced into a retrieval system, or
transmitted, in any form or by any means, electronic, mechanical, photocopying,
recording or otherwise, without the prior written permission of the publisher.

ISBN 1 85043 866 8

A full CIP record for this book is available from the British Library
A full CIP record for this book is available from the Library of Congress

Library of Congress catalog card: 93-60686

Printed and bound in Great Britain by Mackays of Chatham

Contents

Part II: Cases

Contributors

AZIZ AL-AZMEH is professor of Islamic Studies at the University of Exeter. His books include *Ibn Khaldun* (1982), *Arabic Thought and Islamic Societies* (1986), *Secularism* (1992, in Arabic) and *Islams and Modernities* (1993).

JEAN-FRANÇOIS BAYART is director of research at the Centre d'Études et de Recherches Internationales (Paris) and professor at the Institut d'Études Politiques of Paris. He is the author of *Thermidor en Iran* (1993, with Fariba Adelkhah and Olivier Roy) and *The State in Africa: The Politics of the Belly* (1993).

PHILIPPE FARGUES is a demographer and director of the Centre d'Études et de Documentation Economique, Juridique et Sociale in Cairo. His publications include *Atlas of the Arab World* and *Geopolitics and Society* (1990) and *Chrétiens et Juifs dans l'Islam Arabe et Turc* (1992, with Youssef Courbage).

GUDRUN KRÄMER is senior research fellow at the Stiftung Wissenschaft und Politik in Ebenhausen, Germany and professor of Islamic Studies at Bonn University. She is the author of *Egypt under Mubarak* (1986, in German) and *The Jews in Modern Egypt, 1914–1952* (1989).

ABDELBAKI HERMASSI is professor of Political Sociology at Tunis University and Tunisian Ambassador to UNESCO. His publications include *Leadership and National Development in North Africa* (1976), *Third World Reassessed: Society and State in the Maghrib* (1980). His latest publication is *The Maghrib in the Face of International Transformations* (1993).

JEAN LECA is professor of Political Science at the Institut d'Études Politiques in Paris. He is the author of 'L'État et Société en Algérie' (in *Maghreb: Les Années de Transition*, ed. Basma Kodmani (1990) and 'L'Islam, l'État et la Société: L'Expérience Française' (in *L'Islam en France*, ed. Bruno Etienne (1991).

GIACOMO LUCIANI is an expert on the political economy of the Arab countries and deputy director, International Strategies, at ENI Spa in Rome. He is editor of *The Arab State* (1990).

ROGER OWEN is professor of Middle East History at Harvard University and author of *State, Power and Politics in the Making of the Modern Middle East* (1992) and *The Middle East in the World Economy* (reprinted by I.B.Tauris in 1993).

Contributors

VOLKER PERTHES is a researcher at the Stiftung Wissenschaft und Politik in Ebenhausen/Isar, Germany. His publications include *Staat und Gesellschaft in Syrien, 1970–1989* (1990) and *Der Libanon nach dem Bürgerkrieg: Von Ta'if zum gesellschaftlichen Konsens* (1994).

OLIVIER ROY is a researcher at the Centre National de la Recherche Scientifique (CNRS) in Paris; he is the author of *Islam and Resistance in Afghanistan* (1990) and *L'Échec de l'Islam Politique* (1992).

GHASSAN SALAMÉ is director of studies at the Centre National de la Recherche Scientifique (CNRS) and professor of international relations at the Institut d'Études Politiques in Paris. He is the editor of *The Foundations of the Arab State* (1987) and *The Politics of Arab Integration* (1989).

JOHN WATERBURY is William Stewart Tod Professor of Politics and International Affairs in the Woodrow Wilson of Princeton University. His publications include *The Egypt of Nasser and Sadat: the Political Economy of Two Regimes* (1983), *The Political Economy of the Middle East* (1990, with Alan Richards) and *Exposed to Innumerable Delusions: Public Enterprise and State Power in Egypt, India, Mexico and Turkey* (1993).

DEMOCRACY WITHOUT DEMOCRATS?

Introduction: Where are the Democrats?

GHASSAN SALAMÉ

With the end of the Cold War, the disintegration of the USSR and the declining appeal of left-wing ideas in the past few years, the hopes of a further expansion of representative democracy have, without any doubt, increased. Western countries have witnessed not only the collapse of a strategic counterweight to their influence in the world, but also the undisputed failure of a rival model of voluntary and authoritarian modernization which in the recent past has inspired, in variable measure, many a Third World experiment in state building. A new wave of universalism has filled the void: if democratization was feasible in Eastern Europe it might also take root in other regions. The ideological *caesura* demarcated by the Cold War is no longer a *summa divisio* and societies which have already borrowed the European model of the modern state might be expected to embrace democracy unhampered by the political alignments of superpowers or leftist condemnations of 'bourgeois' political practice. Representative democracy has quite suddenly become a kind of 'common good of humanity' or, at least, a mode of government widely considered as normatively superior.

Contemporary events in the Arab-Islamic region have meanwhile reinforced a contrary but widespread idea according to which that part of the world has been too slow in adjusting to this trend, somewhat resistant to a rapid democratization process. While Southern Europe and, later, large parts of Eastern Europe and Latin America were increasingly adopting forms of democratic government, the region stretching 'from Tehran to Marrakesh' has witnessed the uninterrupted rule of authoritarian leaders. While the limits to experimentation with representative democracy are tested and becoming obvious in most newly democratic countries, the islamic region in general and the Arab world in particular has not, it seems, even had the opportunity to experience this process. Elected governments have been toppled (Sudan), elections brutally stopped (Algeria), and when an authoritarian regime has been threatened, the fear of utter chaos (Somalia), of partition (Iraq) or of civil war (almost everywhere else) has been too common to be brushed aside.

The idea of an Arab and/or Islamic 'exceptionalism' has thus re-emerged among both western proponents of universal democracy and established orientalists, and this in turn has encouraged a great many local apologists of 'cultural authenticity' in their rejection of western models of government. Illusions concerning the rapid fall of some regimes have been reinforced by fears triggered by the undemocratic nature of most opposition groups as well as by the revival of clichés about deeply rooted cultural obstacles to democratization in this part of the world. Calls for democracy have remained too muted, too superficial, too dispersed to convince any observer that a push towards political participation is really sought in these societies.

It is precisely this presumed 'exceptionalism' that this book intends to question. Drawing upon a large number of national cases, the authors have engaged in a discussion of social change, of institutional evolution and of the prevailing political discourse. In doing so they have produced a complex picture. They do not refute exceptionalism out of hand: its existence as much as its causes are widely discussed (see in particular the chapters by Leca and Waterbury). Beneath the surface of continuity, societies have changed greatly during the past two or three decades and while leaders may remain in power, the nature of their power has been altered by incessant adjustments both to domestic, regional and international constraints. When accepted as a fact, the Arab/Islamic exception still has to be explained, and the reasons for its existence may not be the ones which are most frequently suggested: (in religion, as suggested by many), in culture, in a specific combination of socio-historical factors (Sharabi 1988) or in the permanence of intractable conflicts (and the ensuing militarization). Emerging from the discussion in this book is a clear idea that forms of political participation are there, though there are no compelling unifying factors triggering a unilateral political evolution towards democracy. More importantly, while calls for democratization may indeed be muted, and while the political discourse dealing with democratization may be only partly convincing, forms of political opening are increasingly viewed by the leaders themselves, if not by the society, as a precious instrument through which a rapid deterioration of law and order, if not of the collapse of the whole state apparatus, might be avoided or at least delayed.

'Pacts' on limited forms of political participation are in these situations negotiated between the ruling group and significant sectors of the civil society. O'Donnell, Schmitter and Whitehead (1986) have already suggested that such pacts could prove to be crucial to the survival not only of nascent experimentations with democracy but also of the state itself and have since been followed by many others, most notably Przeworski (1988; 1991). Where the Middle East is concerned, the idea, though alluded to by Lisa Anderson, writing on Tunisia, and Rémy Leveau on the Maghreb, needed further discussion. In some countries this 'pact' has been rather explicit as a para-constitutional *mithaq* (Jordan, Yemen, Kuwait, Lebanon, Tunisia), while elsewhere it is implicit (Morocco) though in all pacts, the informal part (as on the autonomy of the armed forces during the transitional phase, or the political impunity of royal families) is often crucial. The absence of such an understanding has sometimes proven fatal to a new experiment: the Algerian case is there to demonstrate that the electoral process is easily reversible when viewed as irremediably detrimental to some significant social or political factor such as the armed forces. If pacts have proved to be useful for a gradual, non-aggressive political opening, they are, of course, no guarantee for the success of the experimentation.

In this sense, democracy could be judged less by the attachment to its principles by some actor or the other, than by its common use as a means to avoid civil war or institutional chaos. Thus, forms of political participation are being sought by regimes which have come to believe that their old-style authoritarianism may be difficult to maintain or is becoming counterproductive. Others have arrived at the same conclusion because of their inability to adopt an IMF-inspired austerity programme without help from representative sectors of civil society. Still others have concluded that this is, after all, the only way to make a segmented society live together. Those who have engaged in the process may well be intolerant, repressive, dictatorial. The programme of some opposition groups may well be simply to replace an existing authoritarianism by one of their own. In all such cases, forms of democracy are defined and judged less by the identity of those who made them happen than by their efficacy in phases of transition. Democrats may not exist at all, or they may not exist in great numbers. Yet democracy can still be sought as an instrument of civil peace and hopefully, gradually, inadvertently, produce its own defenders.

Islamism and democracy

This is all the more true in the present situation in the region where old-type authoritarianisms are facing opposition groups gathered around a religious banner. Culturalists (those who think that a specific culture and/or religion could in itself be an obstacle to experimentation with democracy) generally concentrate their 'exceptionalist' views on Islam which they think of as organically different from all other religions. Since the Prophet revealed a religion and founded a state at the same time, his successors are unable to isolate these two elements without betraying his message. This view has of course its own weakness: a democrat, at least in the tradition opened up by the French revolution, can hardly accept a de-universalization of democracy without questioning the very essence of human rights and citizenship. He might be able to adapt his democratic expectations to the evolution of different societies at different tempos, admitting that access to democracy could not be achieved at the same time everywhere, but he could not accept a geographical, human or allegedly transcendental limit to the extension of democratic values. (Hence western governments' negative reaction, during the 1993 Vienna UN conference on Human Rights to calls for 'regional' charters of human rights: non-universally acceptable human rights simply cease to be 'human'). On the other hand, a Muslim would have difficulty in accepting that his religion legitimizes nothing but authoritarianism, even if he admits that Islam has in effect been taken as an obligatory point of reference by innumerable non-democratic regimes and parties throughout history. Someone who is both a good Muslim and a good democrat is not an aberration.

Culturalists may be on a more solid ground on other points which are susceptible of historical explanation. The first is that in western thinking, as Norberto Bobbio among others has remarked, dictatorship is viewed as a temporary and exceptional phenomenon, even in the face of historical evidence that is, to say the least, ambiguous. In the Roman tradition, the dictator was the magistrate to whom exceptional powers were legally entrusted, as a temporary measure, to deal with a foreign invasion or sedition; dictatorship was never taken to be a normal form of political organization. This could not be as clearly induced from islamic thought, in which, as Ridwan As-Sayyid, Charles Butterworth and Abdallah Laroui have demonstrated, authoritarian power is generally assumed to be the norm and democracy the exception, supposing that democracy is actually envisaged as a possible form of government, which is not the case for most authors of the islamic tradition (Salamé 1987a). Taking a trans-historical view, traditional islamic thought thus appears more realistic than its western counterpart, in that autocratic and more generally non-democratic regimes have been more numerous and more durable in world history, from China to Latin America, not forgetting Europe, and from classical antiquity to our own days. One needs to remember that authoritarian regimes, of various persuasions, have been the norm in world history and democracy has been and remains exceptional. Hence the basic intellectual effort should be to explain why democracy has flowered in certain countries at certain times rather than, as is usually the case, to try and discover the reason for its absence from most countries most of the time.

In the islamic tradition, more specifically, the opposition between order and chaos, state authority and civil war is stated vividly and continuously, as if there could not be an interstice between these two extremes. Who does not recall Ibn Taymiyyah's preference for a tyrant for a year rather than a single night without a ruler? What internal fragility in islamic societies has kept its thinkers on the alert in this way, triggering a continuous confusion between an understandable need for public authority and the mere surrender to authoritarianism? The answers given by students of islamic thought differ: some have noted an obsession with keeping the *umma* united, at any price; others insist on the confusion between political opposition and religious secession, itself triggered by the ambivalent nature of leadership in the caliphate; still others oppose islamic teachings to dynastic realities, or expose the wide Sassanian and Byzantine influences on the definition of islamic power during its formative years. Whatever the answer might be, the question remains: supposing that the sediment deposited by a long tradition really is such, what is the actual verifiable effect of that tradition on political behaviour today? Is written tradition being given a contemporary relevance which it does not normally have and for what purpose? Are we not exaggerating the impact of this tradition only because it is more familiar and in many ways more accessible to us than the actual evolution of Muslim societies? Are we not taking at face value the incantation of 'the Fathers of the islamic tradition' by today's islamists? What is the real political efficiency of that tradition?

To these questions different answers have been proposed; the idea that tradition is being reinvented remains the most convincing. But reinventing tradition is a project implemented by contemporary Muslims with contemporary objectives in mind, which of course explains the permanent selectivity with which the tradition is generally approached, usually dictated by political expediency. This does not prevent most islamists and many orientalists from maintaining the view that Islam as such informs political behaviour, or could or should do it to levels social scientists can hardly accept. In mainstream orientalism, the idea that democracy, human rights, political participation, ought to be understood according to each culture's values, or even entirely ignored in the study of some cultures, is quite prevalent. The opposition was already vivid, a few decades ago, between missionaries trying to export the West's values, customs (and religion) to the rest of the world and orientalists who considered this endeavour as sheer folly. A similar debate is perceptible nowadays in many a western society: while diplomats, NGO militants and pro-democracy institutions are actively trying to spread western values, 'experts' and 'analysts', not to mention revived orientalists, are insisting on some old clichés such as 'Islam is Islam and the East is the East'. This permanent tension in western culture between universalism and alienation from the world is well mirrored on the other side by the deepening cleavage now opposing old-style nationalists who adopt the West's models yet fight against its domination and islamists who seek to reject the West's model and influence altogether.

The 'culturalists' may be on even shakier ground when democratization is explicitly linked to secularization. Generalizations are common here, despite the fact that Muslims, supposed to be given to confusing *din* (religion) with *dawlah* (government), do not systematically confuse the two themselves, while societies ruled by democratic regimes have many clear cases of such confusion. Laroui has shown how historically political *fiqh* (jurisprudence) very quickly became part of an exercise in the idealization of islamic power, being content, in the context of the whole, to be subject to authoritarian power in the name of emergency or defence of national unity, reciting, like al-Mawardi among others, the qualities of a 'good' islamic power while knowing perfectly well that such a recital constitutes an incantation linked to the function of a *faqih* rather than an immediate exigency which could be opposed to the governing power (Laroui 1984). In fact it is difficult to think of the policy of the *fuqaha* as fundamentally opposed to the historical powers the islamic world has seen. It is more of a utopian representation, repeated, embellished or given slight differences of meaning, but not necessarily something whose practical incarnation was vigorously sought.

The present establishment of the islamic law *(shari'a)*, therefore, raises the very interesting problem of the status of non-Muslim minorities. Those putting the *shari'a* into practice have a reply which it would be wrong to reject immediately, namely that an islamic regime ruled by the *shari'a* easily admits the principle of plural legislations, particularly in the matter of personal status (covering a field wider than in other legal traditions), to the advantage of non-Muslims. We are, of course, faced here with a direct attack on the modern national principle of one law for all citizens. But for many minorities, it seems more acceptable to deny that principle than to relinquish the right to their own law. In fact it would be easier to get an islamist to exclude those who do not share his faith from the application of the *shari'a* than to make him admit western political principles of the protection of political minorities. In other words, if society really seeks a re-imposition of religious tradition, it might be easier to establish religious (and consequently legal) pluralism than political pluralism. This is a serious obstacle to efforts for democratization, since it presupposes that adherents of the islamic majority would be deprived of the right to withdraw from application of the *shari'a* (a god-defined and therefore un-amendable legislation), while members of non-Muslim minorities would have the advantage of being able to avoid it. But in such a system members of those minorities would be as much victims as members of the islamic majority, since they would be deprived of the support of a neutral and secular state against the possible excesses and inevitable closure of their own community law.

What then can be done to ensure that the islamic religion (of the majority) and the other religions and/or sects (of the minorities) play a part not only in the legitimation of political power but also in limiting and even contesting it? Put like this, the problem obscures the fact that militant islamism is in some ways playing that oppositional role today, even in Iran. We should therefore think instead of a path for islamists to take which would not entail their passing from absolute opposition to the power of others to absolute legitimation of their own. Rather than a ruthless shift such as occurred in Algeria at the beginning of 1992 which saw the islamic revolutions in Iran 'devour' a number of its moderate children, or which was forcibly installed in the Sudan with the military regime of General al-Bashir, it would be more relevant to seek a process of mutual accommodation that would operate both before and after a possible acquisition of power by the islamists. One of the most attractive ideas is that of pre-electoral pacts between the regime in office and the various component parts of the opposition, including the islamists, pacts which would clarify the nature of the shift in power, the function of the first elections to be held and those that followed, and offer guarantees of both the quality of the polls and a preservation of the electoral practice in future. It need hardly be said that such pacts fostering the gradual adoption of representative democracy would be possible only if the islamists agreed to consider the decisions they made once in power as democratically reversible, and their policies open to legitimate contestation. If on the other hand they saw themselves as carrying out meta-political, transcendental values and policies, immune to any possible later revision by other political and social forces, such pacts would become unthinkable, if not actually perverse.

Beyond the case of Islam itself, the relationship between religion and democratized politics remains problematical, to say the least. It is interesting to note that Alain Touraine, among others, readily puts islamism into the category of dictatorships, while seeing the Solidarity movement in Poland as an almost unique case of the triumph of a democratic movement in our time. His theory of 'subjectivation' is even more problematical in that democracy is defined both in terms of its opposition to the religious element, and then, on the contrary, in terms of the subject's capacity to counterpose a meta-policy, which might be religious in nature, to the state and the free market. Touraine thus wants 'subjectivation', i.e. the dissociation of the man from the citizen and the non-subsumption of the former in the latter, to be brought about by recourse to tradition 'for the individual separated from all tradition is merely a consumer of material and symbolic goods, unable to resist the pressures and persuasions manipulated by those in power' (Touraine 1992, 403). Yes, indeed, but then what is there to say that this 'subjectivation' by recourse to tradition will not be to the advantage of religion and the religious? Nothing, says Touraine, adding that 'subjectivation' appears where political and social power is actively limited by 'the religious or more widely speaking spiritual appeal'. The problem, then, is whether and how far the islamist movements correspond to this profile. In other words, we must determine whether the islamist trends of today are political movements like those against which they are struggling or whether, on the contrary, they aim to form an absolute or at least absolutist meta-political structure.

There is a widespread and predominant notion that the question is primarily one of political actors, parties and groups seeking to take power. All the ambiguity of islamism today may perhaps arise from its political nature on the one hand (being a sort of islamism without Islam) and, on the other hand, from its meta-political discourse – that permanent, opportunist and disturbing balancing act between its political nature and its religious discourse. But matters are not much simpler on the secularist side. In a work of luminous clarity, Aziz Al-Azmeh has shown that the modern state in the Arab world was secular to begin with, but that for reasons of political opportunism it progressively accommodated the islamist sectors of the population becoming an instrument of islamization itself, in a perverse process which led it to adopt the programmes of its critics (Al-Azmeh 1992a). Olivier Carré had already come to this conclusion through his study of school textbooks bearing the distinct stamp of religion, albeit in a country wearing the secularist badge of Nasser's Egypt (Carré 1982). Al-Azmeh shows that in Egypt this process of change was hastened under Sadat, and furthermore that such a renunciation by the modern state of its twin liberal and secular origins has been seen throughout the Arab world as a whole, notably in Iraq and to a lesser extent in Syria (and he might have added even more obviously the Algeria of the FLN). He also notes with sadness the resignation of the secularizing intelligentsias to the victory of islamism even before it has come about.

If that is the case, we can see that the Islam of the islamists may be nothing but a discourse, and the secularism of the modern state only a remnant already sacrificed on the altar of survival. But such a conclusion badly blurs our view of the two principal actors in current conflicts, and severely devalues the place of the spiritual factor in its links with politics. For the religious element no longer appears as a meta-political point of reference which may perhaps exert some control over authoritarianism, but as an instrument of discourse in an ordinary struggle for power between forces which at bottom resemble each other more than they would care to admit in their contempt for both democracy and religion. This would make the islamists different simply in their more systematic and politically more efficient use of a frame of reference to which regimes in office, and even supposedly secularist oppositions, do not hesitate to have recourse when they feel the need. It has been, for example, convincingly suggested that the opposition between the FLN and FIS in Algeria was not between two different ideologies but between two different networks and two different generations within the Algerian nationalist nebula. If this is the case, we should stop putting the question of the alleged uniqueness of Islam (whose similarity to eastern Christianity on the social and ritual level has often been observed), and ask a completely different one: why is the reference to religion politically useful? Such a question would bear less on theology or political thinking (not to mention religious sociology), than on analysis of the discourse and its effects. The beginnings of a reply to this (practical) question may perhaps be sought in the organic illegitimacy (and poor achievements) of dictatorial powers and consequently the fact that their nationalist discourse is no longer effective, and above all in a centuries-old segmentation of societies which turns the religious reference into a sublimated appeal to unity around the state, and to the state's advantage.

With the rapid spread of islamist contestation this work could not avoid such questions. Jean Leca rightly reminds us that the presumed Arab 'exceptionalism' is generally linked to that of Islam, but the connection is not unique: it may be, as Gellner notes, that the Arab world is exceptional (in a negative sense) in its relation with democracy because of historical factors that are unique but not necessarily instigated by the predominance of the islamic faith. But is 'eternal Islam' to be interrogated on this point, or the islamists of today? John Waterbury observes a genuine 'analytical dilemma', suggesting that democratization would gain more from circumventing that factor than using it in a more or a less opportunist way. Gudrun Krämer describes both the discourse and the practice of the islamists in the face of a policy of reaction on the part of governments in office which is made up of both accommodation and exclusion. The outcome remains uncertain and ambiguous, as though the time to draw up a balance sheet has not yet come. Aziz Al-Azmeh lays emphasis on the totalizing nature of an islamist discourse obsessed, to an overwhelming degree, by the uniqueness of history and a quasi-automatic correspondence between history, Islam, society and the power to be established, islamist 'democratization' actually being a means of translating an ideal of societal corporatism into the reality of a state corporatism. The latter, of course, repudiates all political pluralism of the western kind, retaining only confessional pluralism or that of 'world civilizations'. (Incidentally, a militant islamist would confirm (and be greatly comforted by) Samuel Huntington's more than debatable views on an imminent 'clash of civilizations' – Huntington 1993.) Other national cases are cited in this volume; Jean-François Bayart observes a revival of Turkish Islam which, in his view, may not endanger democracy at all but on the contrary encourage it to take root, just as parties owing allegiance to Roman Catholicism have done, almost despite themselves, in a number of South European countries.

Democracy, the prisoner of the asabiyyat?

If the non-discursive reality of politicized religion presents problems that it would doubtless be premature to settle out of hand, that is not so much the case with the organized *asabiyyat*, whose continued existence or new development should help to explain the prevalence of religious discourse as a supra-segmentary if not unitarian frame of reference, as well as delays in democratization. In such an investigation, we cannot remain within purely traditional parameters. Although a Khaldunian interpretation of the societies studied here is useful, it is impossible to ignore the limitations of such an interpretation at the end of the twentieth century: the *asabiyyat* exist, but they are as urban as they are rural and, even more important, they are more frequently constructed than inherited. The 'nations' created by Stalinist planning are as present in the landscape of Central Asian identity as the secular ethnic groups; the heterogenous Third Estate of the big cities can be identified as easily as the traditional ethnic, confessional or linguistic groups. Any simple reading of these societies is bound to become simplistic, for it seems that the ravages of modernity are found as inevitably as the remnants of identity from a more distant past. An un-statist interpretation of Syria in the manner of Michel Seurat should be complemented by another which sets out from and returns to the state, as Volker Perthes has done in his contribution to this book: the two interpretations are not mutually exclusive, but complementary and mutually enlightening.

The question of the continued existence of some *asabiyyat* and the rise of others actually presents a much more serious problem, i.e. the contemporaneity of, and to some degree the collusion between, the two concepts of the nation and of democracy in pioneering experiences such as those of France or the United States of America. The idea of the nation in fact derives from that of the individual who is its constituent element, and who acquires, through the democratization of the political regime, the right to contribute to the future of the whole. This triplet, nation/individual/democracy, constitutes a problem in those societies where one might look for democracy while the first two elements remain vulnerable, superficial and threatened and, more importantly, reversible. Those regimes which say that democratization could lead them not only to lose their

authoritarian ascendancy but to destabilize the entire state should be taken a little more seriously. This is not just propaganda: from the moment the dominated
asabiyyat decide that any sign of the opening up of authoritarian regimes actually signals weakness on the part of the hegemonic *asabiyya*, it is difficult for
them to avoid slipping towards centrifugal tendencies, from a simple questioning of the dictatorial regime to questioning the very existence of the state which
marks its geographical limits and provides its legal justification for existence.

If this question appears particularly acute in most islamic societies, it is less
because they are 'mosaics' (on many levels Europe looks far more of a mosaic
than the Arab world, which has a clear religious, confessional and linguistic
majority within it), but because the persistence of the ancient tribal, confessional
and ethnic *asabiyyat* and the existence of a social and political environment
favourable to the constitution of new ones (most notably because of the prevalence of neo-patrimonialism) have been factors militating against the emergence
of the triplet mentioned above. The 'nation' has suffered from the legitimacy of
these *asabiyyat*, recognized to a greater or lesser degree, throughout early
Islamic, Byzantine, Persian and Ottoman history, and the 'individual' has suffered even more. This is why the most interesting western democratic models
for this part of the world are not so much those founded on nation/indi-
vidual/democracy as those where a certain degree of community organization is
seen to be legitimate.

For this reason, the democrats of the islamic world cannot easily avoid a preliminary consideration of the place of the individual in their societies. This consideration is rendered yet more urgent by the mythologization of the
demographic factor, for democratization must also be regarded as a competition
between equals in an already largely post-patriarchal society, as indicated by
Philippe Fargues in a very original hypothesis presented in this volume. When
western sociology invites democrats to denounce extreme individualism along
with their more traditional struggle against authoritarianism, the South can take
that invitation up only circumspectly. There are two fronts here; one is the
(common) struggle against dictatorships, and the other is the necessity of keeping communities from confining individuals within them. The search for democracy thus becomes a four-pronged procedure beginning with the state rather than
the nation, going on to recognize communities, then to re-evaluating the individual, and ending in some experience of democracy. The task is arduous precisely
because one must think of democracy as both the defence of ascriptive groups
and the defence of the individual confronting the twin and rival authorities of
those groups themselves and of the state. In this authoritarian climate the emergence of the modern state appears both a blessing and a curse. While it has
allowed the individual, in imitation of the western model of the modern state, to
define himself outside the *asabiyya*, it has also shown him that in future individuals will have to suffer the double constraint of their *asabiyya* (even if the state
impels them to ignore or surpass or extract themselves from it) and of the state
to which they now belong. Individual liberty, when it is possible, is often the

fruit of a balancing act individually conceived and realized between these two constraints, in which each acts as a counterweight to the other. Individual liberty therefore means an ability to use the new state to relax the hold of the *asabiyya* so as to emerge from its system of values, to rebel against its established powers, while still parading the original *asabiyya* in an attempt to limit the growing ascendancy, authoritarian if not arbitrary, of the state apparatus in the process of being established.

That is why getting a process of democratization going from the starting point of an identification of the nation with democracy is a Sisyphean task. The nation, here, is basically an intellectual construct representing a plurality of groupings, and is in any case only precariously rooted. The word nation has been used for too many local human groups, large or small, well or not so well organized, for it to retain its lustre as a unique, exclusive or at least predominant reference. We must thus think about democratization without previously settling the question of national identity. A good Jacobin would say it is impossible to skip such a crucial stage: first must come the nation, then its democratization. However, decades after the establishment of present-day states, we are obliged to recognize that democratization cannot be indefinitely conditioned by a prior outpouring of nationalitarian and/or nationalist fervour, a fervour adding itself to the real existence of states claiming to be national, of machinery engaged in the construction (in Foucault's sense and not that of nation building), if not the voluntary formation of a nation which would embody the state and be the expression of its autonomous politicization to the people. Such is the dilemma which invites all observers to define democratization even more clearly by its instrumental virtues. It should not be a natural complement to the development of the individual/nation couplet, but a compensation for the inability, in practice, of bringing the two together with the rival but complementary reality of the state apparatus and the *asabiyyat*.

It is necessary to introduce another term into the equation – namely social classes. Here again, Touraine's propositions are problematic: 'Where class conflict has been strong,' he writes, 'democracy has been strong as well.... Democracy assumes a firmly structured civil society, associated with an integrated political society, both as independent as possible of the state defined as the power acting in the name of the nation' (Touraine 1992, 382). The prerequisite of a civil society has become the parrot cry of Middle Eastern (as well as eastern European) discourse on the subject of democracy in the immediate post Cold War era, the favourite catchphrase of anyone who wants to see, beyond the collapse of immense authoritarian machines, the password of politically timid intelligentsias calling on democracy without daring to name it. The correlation between the strength of the class conflict and the quality of democracy is a more original idea, notably because it opposes the partiality of social claims to the nation's bent for political arbitration which, because it has the means to transcend social divisions, becomes increasingly independent of the social factor.

However, what does civil society mean in the islamic cultural area? Let us note first that the population is not really what it is commonly thought to be, and is developing rapidly but not along the lines generally supposed (Fargues). Next, where are the classes whom one would like to see in struggle, so as to cast even more light on the role of the state as the personification of the nation, or at least as the mouthpiece of its 'interests'? A clear response, in the form of another question, is provided by Muhammad Abid al-Jabiri when he asks: 'Is it possible to see democracy unfolding in a society which is not "civil"; is it possible to see a civil society emerge by non-democratic ways?' (al-Jabiri 1993). This double question is based, of course, on a double denial: of 'civil' society and of democratic practice. Noting what I have described elsewhere as 'the first moment of liberalism' in the region (Salamé 1988), al-Jabiri attributes its failure, early and indisputable, to the fact that the 'democratic experience of the time was a state experiment being made on society with a view to controlling it, not an instrument whereby society could control the state'. This experiment would be followed by the military state, a state which would 'devour' civil society by forbidding the emergence of autonomous institutions. This kind of state would be even more authoritarian than its Soviet model, since the USSR was at least based on a party which gave rise to a state and an army, while in the Middle Eastern case the army creates both its state and its party. Returning to an explanation that I developed in my work *State and Society in the Mashriq* (1987b), al-Jabiri attributes the weakness of civil society to the vulnerability of the Arab and islamic *civis* confronting the stranglehold of 'rural and Bedouin society, with its institutions, values, customs and conduct'. Al-Jabiri closes with a normative conclusion affirming the therapeutic virtue of democracy; observing that local elites thought little of its advent, he calls for it to be introduced because it must be available as a 'remedy' even if the invalid has not really become aware of the gravity of his disease, a conclusion all the more interesting for our purpose in this volume in that the author has actually become famous on account of his search for theological, or at least jurisprudential foundations for political phenomena.

This is an elegant exit from a set of questions which are far from being solved by the prescription of the democratic 'remedy'. For whatever definition of civil society is adopted, it continues to present a problem once it is exported to islamic societies (and no doubt in its countries of origin too). If, following Hegel, we view civil society as primarily a factor in the process of state formation, how do we adjust that definition to situations where the state has indeed been 'imported', in the terms used by al-Jabiri and Bertrand Badie (Badie 1992) and when in any case that state has seen its bureaucratic apparatus set up even before civil society in its hegelian sense has come into being? Should we then follow certain hegelian and islamicist sociologists in distinguishing two civil societies, the traditional one which did in fact give rise to innumerable traditional states, and the modern one, dependent, westernized, brought into being by the modern state and born with the original sin of its colonial parentage? Can we really speak of the co-existence, even the superimposition, of the rivalry or the conflict of two societies, one 'authentic', the other artificially created? Falling back on Marx is no help, since he saw civil society as the society which a partic- ular actor, the bourgeoisie, historically produced. Looking for the Arab or Persian bourgeoisie at the origin of established states would not be a very useful exercise – from the perspective of Marx himself, if not of his local interpreters.

The state and its doubles

It is clear from the preceding remarks that the key element on the road that may lead to democracy is the state, rather than the individual, the community, the nation, class or the market; and moreover it preceded these other elements too. Political logic remains favourable to the state, the authoritarian state, and more precisely to those forces which have inherited the bureaucratic legacy of French or British colonialism or that of the former USSR. This will continue to be the case in so far as the national question remains open, and culture (for which Waterbury cannot find a convincing definition), frustrated of its blossoming as a whole, is still defined principally by its opposition to the adversary in nationalist or religious terms and, more commonly, in some mixture of the two. The seizure by the ex-communist *asabiyyat* in central Asia of the apparatus of the new states born, as if despite themselves, of the decomposition of the USSR (see the essay by Olivier Roy) is curiously reminiscent of the seizure of power in Iraq by Ottoman-trained officers on the eve of the 1914–18 war. It is in the very heart of decomposing empires that forces capable of making the transition from the imperial to the national are found; Ottoman officers yesterday, Brezhnev-trained apparatchiks today (re-islamicized military men tomorrow?). Once the transition has been made, the state, reinforced by the world tendency towards statism and the urgent need statist actors established in the West have felt to negotiate with their equals and peers, becomes both the crucial stake in the game between com- peting *asabiyyat* and the political actor par excellence.

The abrupt introduction of that statist machine, whether Pahlavi, Kemalist or Arab, has marked a profound watershed in a development which might have favoured democracy more. Not only were the modern heirs to empires usually the military, not only did their 'states' risk being nothing but complements to their armies; in imposing their authority they also disrupted a process of statist modernization and democratic evolution, slower and more endogenous, but also better adapted to local time schemes, which had begun in the nineteenth century. 'Skipping stages' was only a way of taking a swift hold on societies, authorita- tively defining their needs and aspirations and setting about the task of coming to their aid with a greater or lesser degree of success. Secularization too often meant the exclusion of those who, in the name of tradition, required this modern machine to be accountable. Nationalization was the reply to those who wanted to go on deriving some slight say from their comfortable economic situation. State nationalism meant the exclusion of all who were defined through sectoral identities, or who intended to oppose the state monopoly of contact with foreign countries and their powers and ideas. The modern state has thus generally been constructed on a series of exclusions and ostracisms, the combined effect of which was to multiply the number of political orphans and orphans of politics, for politics henceforward was the state and nothing but the state. Outside the state, there was a situation of assumed exclusion (depoliticization) or rejection, and then one closer to that of 'national' treason than legitimate opposition. In this the modern state was reproducing a highly traditional model, that of the *khuruj*, departure from the state, which was commonly presented by the regimes as sedition or rebellion, and which consequently incurred punishment. Prison and exile became the natural homes of all questioning of current policy, which was worn right down by the state apparatus; to oppose was to leave, to leave was to betray.

If nation-building was also, or even primarily, a wide operation of exclusion, the question of representation, crucial to all democratic experience, was first practised as the co-opting of forces and individuals, one of its essential functions being to obscure the fact that the state sought first and foremost to create a political desert around it; rump parliaments, submissive syndicates, associations created by and for the state. Populism subsequently turned out to be an ideal complement to this political desert; it established a unilateral political link based on the active initiative of some emblematic figure, as much as on the passive support of the 'masses', sometimes ratified by plebiscite. Society suffered an increasingly serious lack of representatives, and populism had the added advantage of doing away, in an authoritative manner, with the need for representation by using the easy subterfuge of direct communication, first by radio and then by television, between power ultra-personified in one man and the masses increasingly relegated to formless anonymity. Suddenly these societies were frustrated not only by the lack of representation, but also by a plethora of fake representatives chosen by the state. These personal charismas will have to be eroded, through military defeats and the perverse effects of all long-term populism, before the call for genuine representation of the people can again make itself heard. That rulers have for decades conducted experiments with illusory forms of representation burdens all forms of representation with deeply rooted scepticism which explains the wish, often concealed, for a change of faces, leaving actual programmes untouched; such a wish being paradoxically accompanied by a deep suspicion of any new ruler even before he displays his power.

Oil revenues will play a prominent part in the consolidation of these powers (and subsequently their downfall). If one had to identify something specific to the Middle East, it would surely be the prevalence of the rentier economy. Revenues (particularly from oil, but also from foreign aid, rights of passage through the Suez Canal, revenues deriving from the strategic function of this or that country, or from political cover for some western military intervention), have in fact reinforced the external and superimposed position of the state in relation to societies at the most opportune moment. Lavish military expenditure, rackets dexterously operated on oil-exporting countries by countries producing little or no oil, and bilateral security aid not entered in the national budget, have reinforced the autonomy of the state machinery, giving autocrats the means to modernize their instruments of control without burdening the population with duties and taxes. Oil has allowed these states to consolidate without making painful choices between expenditure on security, prestige and social services. Once a logic of allocation rather than production was firmly entrenched, oil generally assured the critical mass of financial inflow, permitting a postponement of questions about the financial system or any redefinition on the relationship between state and society with a view to better control of the latter over the effective expenditure of the former (see the essay by Luciani and the questions put by Waterbury in this volume). The present crisis of political regimes is therefore closely connected with the sudden fall in revenues and the inability of regimes to push through policies of adjustment to situations of new austerity.

Oil arrived like a *deus ex machina* in the political economy of societies that were not civil, or were inadequately so. Special attention should, therefore, be paid to the methods, particularly economic and financial, which allowed the authoritarian state (or its twin, the anarchic state) to last. Gangs, nepotistic privatizations, trafficking in influence, tolerance of drugs, militia, corruption, the so-called black or informal economy, and para-statist rackets have all been obstacles to democratization. But to remain at this level of ethical condemnation is inadequate precisely because these gangs are also the instruments of survival of groups marginalized by the state as well as forces maintaining those states; the FLN state in Algeria triggered the practice of *trabendo* (with the complicity of the Islamic Salvation Front FIS); the 'black boxes' of various regimes had their parallel in secret transfers of expatriates' savings, a black market in money, the so-called islamic investment companies, a sad reality for many ruined savers, and drug trafficking by militarized *asabiyyat*. Groups outside the state had a tendency to imitate 'the people of the state' in depending on trafficking outside the state in order to survive. Contraband, dealing in illegal substances, and similar practices were also ways of bringing modern adaptation to structures threatened by plunder, economic marginalization or excessive dependence on the redistributive system of a state often impotent and always unjust, or perceived as organically so.

Of course a genuinely national economy also developed in some of the more stable countries, less dependent on oil and where state authority was more firmly rooted, as in Turkey (see also the analysis of Syria by Perthes in this volume). But on the whole the 'national' economy is only the partial meeting place of political and social actors around a 'national' budget. Alongside their public budgets, regimes had at their disposal huge 'black boxes', and autonomous groups had 'informal' sources of revenue assuring their survival. Democracy as a mechanism for controlling expenditure, where taxation and representation arise together and mutually sustain each other, was obviously inadequate in this kind of political economy, where informal business ventures could do better than the classic kind and trafficking was sometimes bigger business than exchange, and where racketeering rubbed shoulders with commerce (if they were not in fact entirely indistinguishable).

Democracy in the political arena

The title of this work might lead the reader to believe that democracy is based on 'chance and necessity'; on the idea, put forward in most of the contributions to this volume, that when democratization occurs it does so without political forces really making it a programme in and for itself (see in particular the contributions by Leca, Waterbury and Salamé). Democracy in the western style, orphaned, is the end product of complex social phenomena rather than of a struggle for democratization carried out by organized groups. It is often conceded by a power which does not have the means of establishing complete authoritarianism, or which, having exercised such authoritarianism over a long period, finds itself compelled to loosen its grip at a certain moment (as Owen sets out to demonstrate in the case of Egypt and Perthes in the case of Syria). We may say that there is nothing original about such findings, since democracy in Europe has historically been the daughter of crises in authoritarian regimes which are unable to sustain themselves. Some writers have already commented on that fact, particularly in eastern Europe, where 'the fall of authoritarian regimes is more frequently due to their internal decomposition than to the success of popular opposition movements. This leads to the almost passive victory of a democracy reduced to a free political choice, whose superficial character is quickly revealed by the weakness of popular participation' (Touraine 1992, 397). Certainly, but what was a 'natural' phenomenon two or three centuries ago occurs today in societies where it was thought that elites, well informed about the world, had already made it their programme.

Banal as it may be, the statement remains valid; the fundamental political split in the societies studied in these essays (although not in them alone) is not between opposing democratic forces but between forces which are often equally strangers to democracy (or equally uninterested in establishing democracy). There are, notably, islamists whom it would be unjust to consider less democratic than many other rival forces; for example, that 'islamist versus democratic' cleavage propounded by anti-islamist Algerians is founded, at best, on an ambiguity, and quite possibly on a fraud. If the adoption of democratic elections by the islamists is considered opportunist, reversible and insincere, the regime as well as many 'secularist' forces certainly do not produce any more convincing professions of democratic faith. As Al-Azmeh notes, this is more in the nature of a clash (some would say collusion followed by collision) between equally populist variants.

But if the crisis affecting regimes is more relevant than the appeal of democratic forces, is not military defeat the most effective factor in bringing about the collapse of a dictatorship? That factor was seen in Argentina after the defeat of the generals, the fall of the regime of the Greek colonels after their misadventure in Cyprus, or the shaking of Salazarism following the liberation movements in the Portuguese colonies of Africa. However, on the other side of the Mediterranean this rule does not seem to apply. Some would even say that military defeats have the effect of strengthening dictatorships rather than weakening or toppling them, more particularly in the Arab world – another kind of exceptionalism. Perhaps the reality is not such a clear-cut contrast, and the effects of a defeat here need more time to make themselves felt. Thus the overtures to democracy in Egypt in the mid-1970s can be linked to the military defeat in 1967; the fall of Siad Barré can be connected to his failure in the Ogaden a decade earlier; the Algerian crisis can be linked to the failure of Algeria in the Saharan crisis; and the spectacular defeat of Saddam Hussein cannot ultimately leave his power entirely unaffected. The error frequently consists of a desire to derive immediate advantage from the defeat of a dictator, which results in prolonging his reign. For the first effect of defeat could well be to arouse solidarity. For while the national question is still far from being settled, to have defied the West will often compensate for the failure that may follow the attempt. The popularity of the challenge to the adversary often sustains the defiant regime even amidst the opprobrium of defeat. Questioning may come later, 'cold', at the moment when external pressure in fact seems to have relaxed; memories of defeat then return in force to discredit an already defeated regime. This temporal factor operates very differently from the western electoral accounts system, as George Bush discovered to his cost when he tried to destabilize Saddam Hussein during the two years from the defeat of Iraq to the 1992 American presidential elections.

This is all the more true in that it becomes very difficult to think of democratization in this part of the world while ignoring development in the international arena. Here again, however, explanation of the effects of global on regional and above all local factors must be made with care, avoiding hasty generalizations about global trends and exceptions to them. However, we may put forward a number of premises. First, the 'wave' of democratization, begun in southern Europe and continued in Latin America and eastern Europe, has not left the intellectuals of the Arab world unmoved. However, to say they have reached the conclusion that a great wave of democracy is breaking, from which they are clearly drawing encouragement, would indubitably be an exaggeration, for these intellectuals remain to a great extent prisoners of a role they define for themselves in terms of the state to which they belong, while politicized culturalism, which they have tended to amplify and exaggerate, immunizes them against automatic emulation. The abrupt collapse of the Soviet empire, on the contrary, was of great importance to everyone interested in public events, for its effects were immediate even if their conclusions are far from being uniform. While the states of central Asia have suddenly found themselves orphaned, and the marxists of the region have seen their Muscovite Mecca turn away from itself even more than from them, the islamists have shown an ambiguous reaction made up, on the one hand, of the fear of seeing the West, emerging victorious from the Cold War, extend and intensify its hegemony over their countries, and on the other hand, of the satisfaction of seeing the sudden collapse of the nationalist, secularizing or atheistic progressivism which, over several decades, had stolen their intellectual hegemony within their own societies. To the islamists, the fall of the Kremlin was translated into the fall and marginalization of their local ideological rivals whom the USSR more or less inspired or sustained.

These are events of universal importance whose indirect fallout and subsidiary effects upon these societies must be studied. However, the reactions and external policies more directly aimed at the Middle East itself call for study too. We should note here that in the region there is a prevalent idea, extending beyond all reason, that external forces have unlimited influence over internal affairs. Indeed the adversary, notably or even exclusively western, is credited with the means of causing local situations to develop in one direction or another, a notion which at the same time arouses opposition. The disclaimers of the western governments concerned, the genuine indifference of western public opinion to certain developments in the South, make no difference; think how many Algerians accused France of being behind the coup of 11 January 1992, after accusing Paris of being the mainstay of the FIS, or of all the explanations one has read and heard of ex-President Bush's desire to maintain Saddam Hussein in power, or on the contrary his desire to destabilize him. An extreme sensitivity to what the adversary in the West says or does about regional and local situations prevails. It functions as a useful way of obscuring the inability of local people to change their own situation, and also shows a kind of resignation to the will of the strongest, which paradoxically goes hand in hand with a nationalist antiimperialism nowadays degenerating into chauvinism and xenophobia.

In fact the outside world has more effect on the evolution of this region than it likes to admit, which reminds us of the point already made by Hicham Djait, that Europe and the islamic world are too close to each other, so relations are tense and impassioned. There is here another source of specificity if we are still looking for one; geographical proximity, centuries of commerce, exchange, alliances, struggles and conquests both one way and another give rise to a particular sensitivity in the relations of the Arab-Islamic area to a West which is at once too close and too different, too familiar and too strange. Ambient islamism may be a reaction to this particular situation, which links Europe and the islamic world while differentiating them. People cling to the absolute difference, the difference of faith, at the very moment when they feel especially weak confronting a neighbour who has become over-powerful. Adoption of the western model in the organization of power, with the ideology of human rights (not to mention the many 'rights to intervene' which the West has defined for itself since the collapse of the Soviet Union, in relation to other most frequently islamic countries), is bound to suffer because it is hard to dissociate it from the emotional charge aroused by this mixture of fascination and repulsion, proximity and otherness.

Other cultures which have less impassioned relations with the West are no doubt better able to make such a dissociation, separating the democratic model from the real or supposed ambition to dominate of the powers which are brandishing it.

The aim of this present volume is to take another look at the problems of democratization, linking them as far as possible to the social changes that have taken place during the last two or three decades. The balance sheet is not hopelessly pessimistic. We may indeed think that democratization had more chance of coming into being a few years ago when demography was still 'manageable' (the essay by Fargues in this volume relativizes the impact of this so-called 'bomb'), when chaotic urbanization had not yet created big cities that could not be properly policed, when opposition parties with secularist ideas had not yet been marginalized. But that moment has now passed; population growth has accelerated, governments have on the whole shown an inability to deliver the services and social protection promised by all authoritarian states in the 1950s and 1960s, and opposition groups have been worn down by exile or corruption, leaving the islamists firmly in the driving seat in most cities of the region.

In dealing with the Middle East in its widest sense, this book does not aim to produce the impression that the area as a whole, containing several hundred million people, will follow the same course. On the contrary, the dominant idea is that the countries considered here are not necessarily engulfed in a wave of islamization, democratization, or anything else, and might well pursue very different political paths during the years to come. Different levels of democracy may well take root, different attitudes to human rights may be seen, different kinds of authoritarian regimes may be maintained or established, and so-called 'islamist mobility' may even end up giving birth to political regimes with very different relations to democracy. At the end of the day, even if social constraints, inspirations and external pressures are similar, even if ideological orientations can be located from one country to another, real people, united in real associations and institutions, will have to make concrete decisions, and these will hardly be uniform. They never have been.

Above all, we must not trust appearances, that is to say, principally, the dominant discourse, whether the discourse of politicians or the better informed comments of innumerable 'observers' of the scene. Authors contributing to this work will invite the reader to cease thinking of Turkey as less islamic than Iran, of anti-stalinist ethnic groups as more powerful than the nations created by the 'little father of the peoples', to give up the idea that the alleged exceptionalism of Arab societies is a matter of verified fact, that peoples will fall back into their old *asabiyyat,* or that the regimes in power have lost all ability to make their hold on society last, even to reproduce themselves in some new avatar. None of these simple, 'obvious' ideas has seemed to us immune from criticism. That is why we offer the reader a work full of questions rather than a collection of statements above critical question. From chapter to chapter, questions multiply and complement each other; they are not the same, they are not presented in the same way, and no attempt has been made to transform this work of critical interrogation into a uniform account of the 'state of societies in the islamic world', still less a manual of democratization for formerly authoritarian societies.

One of the recurring themes in these studies as a whole (notably in the essays by Owen, Krämer, Perthes and Hermassi) is the attitude and conduct of regimes supposedly in crisis. That factor is to a great degree what permits the development, slowing down or burying of experimentation with electoral democracy. The outcome of the crisis may be peaceful or bloody, durable or temporary, effective or superficial, depending on the regime's ability to adapt to a radically different demographic, economic, fiscal and social situation, the evolution of oil prices, its responses to new internal and external challenges, the success or failure of its policies of austerity, the choice of its electoral law, the credibility it manages to re-create for itself by opening out rather than becoming exclusive, its mastery, effective or otherwise, of the political climate, and more generally the personal and visionary courage of its leaders. Objective situations can be elucidated, but concrete decisions in the face of concrete challenges frequently make all the difference between emergence from the crisis and plunging deeper into it.

There remains the role – central in principle, marginal in fact – of the intelligentsia. The *asabiyyat* may be modern or old, inherited or 'constructed', supporters or critics of the regime, but they can prove equally sterile; western sociology invites students of democratization to take less notice of social forces than cultural forces, the latter having shown their attachment to democratization, even their efficiency, better than the former. Who can forget that Chinese student trying to stop a column of armoured cars? Who can forget that the 'velvet revolution' was the work of Václav Havel and the dissidents? The question becomes a penetrating one: what are the intelligentsias of the islamic world interested in, if not throwing off the yokes that burden the political and social life of their societies? The intellectuals of this part of the world often have matters other than democratization on their minds, another sign that they too are products of the modern state, the state which excludes rather than innovates, the state of legitimation rather than vision. These intelligentsias often seem caught in a sterile, debilitating choice between the maintenance of states from which they came and the restoration of states whose memory they have childishly embellished. Democratization, however, will not rise from nostalgia for a reconstructed past or attachment to a jaded present. But if that is the choice, the 'cultural forces' of democratization are still a hope for the future rather than a reality in the present.

PART I

HYPOTHESES

1

Democracy Without Democrats?: the potential for political liberalization in the Middle East

JOHN WATERBURY

For the sake of argument, I am taking at face value the claim that the Middle East, or, more specifically, the Arab Middle East is exceptional in its resistance to political liberalization, respect for human rights, and formal democratic practice. The task is to examine the extent to which this claim is valid and the reasons that account for this regional resistance. I will argue that the claim is by and large valid.

The first part of this essay will explore standard explanations of the preconditions for democracy and the various, Middle East-specific reasons for their failure to exert their expected influence. The second part will explore the possibility of democratic transitions despite the obstacles identified in the first part; that is. can a democratic transition be successfully sustained without the participation of committed democrats?

Ends-oriented states and the bourgeoisie

The argument that high levels of literacy and urbanization, and substantial middle-income strata yield an informed middle class with a stake in how politics are conducted, a heightened sense of citizenship, and an insistence that public officials be held accountable, has been widely criticized but never convincingly refuted (Seymour Martin Lipset has been its most persistent contemporary proponent; on the Middle East, see Charles Issawi 1956). The fact that India and Sri Lanka, both ranking low on the standard indicators of 'socio-economic status' (SES), have followed democratic practices for long periods of time suggests that poor, agrarian, broadly illiterate societies can still aspire to some form of democracy, but our general sense is that *they* are somehow exceptional, not their typically authoritarian neighbours.

By contrast we see Taiwan, South Korea, Thailand, Mexico, Nigeria and others groping their way toward more liberal, civilian political systems at the same time as their prosperity and their middle classes have been fitfully growing. Such countries appear to conform to the hypothesis associating democracy with increasing SES, although the levels of SES vary significantly among them. Positive social science seeks thresholds, and it has been argued that outside the communist world, few countries whose per capita income has reached or exceeded $4,000 (in 1988 prices) has been able to avoid the development of competitive political systems, Robert Wade (1990, 375) states the logic thus: [1]

> [Above this threshold] the economic advantages of continued restrictions of civil and political rights – of continued consolidation of authority in the hands of the state – are probably offset by the costs of growing conflict, weak legitimacy, and overburdened state decision-making.

In the Middle East, the ascent of indicators of SES has been underway for some time. Keeping in mind the considerable variation among some 22 nations, it is the case that half or more of all Middle Easterners live in urban areas, half or more of adult males are literate (well below East Asian levels), and the ratio of university students to total population in several large Middle Eastern countries is similar to ratios prevailing in Europe. In income terms the ranks of the white collar, self-employed, professional, and upper-income blue-collar members of the middle classes have swelled prodigiously. Yet, to date, this rising SES has had no unambiguous 'democratic pay-off'. [2]

Indeed, it may have been Turkey that made the first major democratic breakthrough in the Middle East, in 1950, dropping its single-party, military authoritarian system for a free-wheeling, two-party contested democracy. It did so at a time when it was still largely agrarian, with a small middle class and high levels of illiteracy. The experiment did not last a decade before the military once again intervened, but the 1950 breakthrough was crucial to the much more viable democracy now existing in Turkey. SES has finally caught up with the political system.

Other early experiments in the Arab world, under colonial auspices or in the years immediately following independence, are not to be dismissed lightly simply because they were dependent upon a small and manipulable middle class. But with the exception of Lebanon, they collapsed easily and definitively.

Relatively high levels of SES in a general sense can thus be seen as merely facilitating political liberalization and accountability. Low levels cannot put up insurmountable barriers to democratic transitions (India, Turkey, and sporadically the Sudan) nor can high levels determine that a transition will take place (see note 1). High levels of SES are neither necessary nor sufficient to bring about democracy, but all other things being equal, they certainly do help. The problem in the Middle East is that other things are not equal.

How exceptional is the Middle East?

Until the 1980s, the Middle East was not exceptional. Only with the gradual redemocratization of Latin America and Southern Europe at the beginning of the decade, and the tentative democratization of South Korea and Taiwan towards the end did the Middle East begin to appear behind the curve. The strong popular pressure for greater democracy in several sub-Saharan African nations coupled with the collapse of the eastern European communist regimes cast the Middle East in an even more unfavourable light. Pakistan and Bangladesh also showed that under certain circumstances Islam and democracy could mix.

What is not yet known is whether or not the transitions begun elsewhere in the last decade are sustainable. Recently we have seen democratically elected governments overthrown in Peru and Haiti and strongly challenged in Venezuela and Cameroon. Few of us, I suspect, would wager heavily against a return to authoritarianism in, say, the Philippines, Argentina, Romania or Pakistan, to name but a few precarious democracies. Since 1950 Turkey has been a democracy subject to periodic military intervention. Is that a likely pattern elsewhere? Would one interpret General Pinochet's 17 years at the helm in Chile as an interruption of an older pattern of Chilean democratic government?

If the Middle East is exceptional, the question then is, relative to what? Democratic systems (like market systems) vary widely, and in some respects Taiwan's fledgling democratic system may resemble Ba'thi Iraq more than it does multi-party India. On the other hand, we must constantly distinguish what factors are peculiar to the Middle East and what characteristics it may share with regions or countries in which democracy is practised.

The socio-economic profile of several Middle Eastern societies does not differ markedly from that of the Philippines or Brazil. Moreover, the kinds of crises to which the region has been subjected are not unique although they are often cited as impediments to democratization. The Middle East shares with other regions economic adjustments and political systemic crises. Its involvement in wars and civil wars is not unique. Many societies, especially in eastern Europe, are undergoing severe conflict over values and norms.

Finally, it should be noted that there are exceptions to the exceptionalism. Turkey, Lebanon, the Sudan, Egypt, Jordan and the Yemen have periodically or cautiously undertaken democratic experiments. In no instance, however, can it be said that the broad base of the citizenry participated in any meaningful sense in the process of devising the rules by which the 'democratic' game was to be played.

Thus, to the extent the Middle East is exceptional (and developments elsewhere in the world may reduce that extent considerably in the near future), it is the result of the conflation of a number of characteristics that have produced an environment singularly inhospitable to legal pluralism and democracy.

The ends-oriented state and the burden of the military

Other regions of the developing world have experienced high levels of conventional and non-conventional warfare coupled with bristling truces and modi vivendi. It is, however, fair to say that with six conventional wars (four Arab–Israeli, Iran–Iraq, and Operation Desert Storm), a number of regional clashes (the former Spanish Sahara, Chad, Cyprus, the Israeli invasion of Lebanon in 1982), and a number of devastating civil wars (Lebanon, the southern Sudan, Iraqi Kurdistan, Shi'ite southern Iraq, North Yemen), the region has experienced so much armed conflict, that this may in itself be peculiar. Whether the extraordinary burden of arms and outsized militaries has resulted from or been the cause of these conflicts, the fact remains that Middle Eastern praetorians have dominated the political scene to a degree and with a technological impregnability that 'tin-pot' African dictators or Latin American caudillos could seldom boast.[3]

The praetorians, in a context of war, tensions, and civil strife have consistently claimed to rule in order to carry forward a sacred mission. Emergency laws are the norm rather than the exception, and habeas corpus is routinely suspended in the name of the quest. I can think of no region in the world in which the rhetoric of governance has been more ends-oriented, moralizing and patronizing. Because the mission is sacred – anti-imperialism, liberation, socialism, islamic justice – debate over ends or means is immediately seen and characterized as subversive or blasphemous. Wars, missionary government, and political repression move in mutually re-enforcing ways. Of course it has been said since 1967 that few ever believe the rhetoric any more, although the mission, as an abstract entity, may still resonate strongly among Middle Eastern individuals. What is puzzling is that as the gap between practice and rhetoric widens, as alienation and indifference spread among non-enfranchised citizens, the demands for accounts are still so weak. When the Argentinian military led their nation into the fiasco of the Falklands/Malvinas war, they lost their ability to rule. Neither the débâcle of 1967 nor Saddam Hussein's even more colossal strategic blunders caused him or anyone else in the Middle East to lose power.

What is going on here? Repression and terror are to authoritarian states what reserve requirements are to a bank. They are only effective if there is no run on them. Once a majority of the citizens challenge the system, it cannot find enough terror, jail space, or sheer brutality to meet the requirements of control. This is what happened in eastern Europe but did not happen in the People's Republic of China. In the Middle East the only two entities in which there was the beginning of a run on the repression bank were the West Bank and Gaza in the course of the *intifada*, and Algeria, starting in 1988 and gathering momentum in 1990 and 1991. The abstract logic of the situation is that if authoritarianism is justified in the name of the mission, and if the authoritarians have patently failed to achieve any of the goals of *the mission*, then authoritarianism can no longer be legitimized but only imposed. Is that the case in the Middle

East today, or is the chemistry of legitimacy and acquiescence more subtle?

Until the major causes of regional armed conflict in the Middle East have been dealt with, the military establishments of the region will continue to combine with ends-oriented government to suppress pluralism and debate. India, however, and now South Korea, have shown that real external enemies and a powerful military do not totally block the path to democratic practices.

The ambivalent bourgeoisie

The Middle East is not unique in having a bourgeoisie, and, more broadly speaking, a middle class that is very unsure whether or not it wants democratic procedures. What is peculiar to the Middle East is that such a large proportion of the middle classes are directly dependent upon or employed by the state (*inter alia*, Richards & Waterbury 1990; Bakhash 1991). Manfred Halpern saw this phenomenon early on and, in his analysis of the new middle class, described the bureaucrats and the military as two wings of the same class entity. In may respects Middle East intelligentsias are state intelligentsias, a fact long noted by Turkish intellectuals. The coincidence of interests of the intelligentsia and the state goes beyond emoluments, employment, and professional licensing to include a strong sense of identity and shared goals. The intelligentsia has frequently been the rhetorician of the state mission. Thus, in many ways, the intelligentsia has never become the catalyst to new, critical associations within civil society but rather has seen incipient pluralism as a kind of *fitna* within the revolution.[4]

The private-sector bourgeoisie likewise has entered into a pact with the state which has impeded progress toward democracy. Years ago Clark Reynolds, writing about the Mexican state and the Mexican bourgeoisie, described the arrangement as an 'alliance for profits' (a play on words referring to John F. Kennedy's initiative toward Latin America called the 'Alliance for Progress'), and Ghassan Salamé (1987b) saw much the same thing in the Arab world. The tacit understanding has been that the bourgeoisie would renounce any overt political role and that it would follow the broad economic directives of the state, in exchange for which it would be allowed to make significant profits. The state would keep labour docile through a combination of welfare benefits and political repression.

In this way encompassing labour confederations and their leaders, the private-sector, bourgeoisie, and the leaders and managers of the state, develop interests that could be threatened by a democratic opening. Labour and the owners of capital, most of the latter being concentrated in the public sector, rather than constituting the nuclei of an emerging civil society, link together to maintain authoritarian controls. None of this is peculiar to the Middle East. Argentina or Mexico exhibited similar alliances. But for a transition to begin some segment of the bourgeoisie, with substantial resources, has to be ready to ally with forces outside the state's patronage network. It may be that Islamic business groups, most prominent in Egypt, have begun to make such a move. But there is equally compelling evidence that Islamic business interests are thickly inter-twined with state economic interests, state functionaries, and the military.

Both Leonard Binder and Lisa Anderson see the role of the bourgeoisie as crucial to any democratic opening. For Binder (1990, 68) the challenge is to dis-cern if a liberal interpretation of basic islamic doctrine can be wedded to the material interests of an islamic bourgeoisie to sustain a broadly tolerant and lib-eral islamic polity. Anderson (1992), by contrast, sees the weakness and subor-dination of existing bourgeoisies as a major cause of continued authoritarianism. In so arguing, she distinguishes between the existence of middle classes and what she calls an underdeveloped bourgeoisie. It is underdeveloped because it was stunted in its growth by the colonial powers, and then overwhelmed by an overdeveloped state inherited from the colonial era.

If what Binder and Anderson are concerned with is the expected political preferences of an entrepreneurial bourgeoisie, then, given the highly inconsis-tent behaviour of such bourgeoisies just about everywhere in the developing countries, one must question whether or not they will play any major positive role in promoting democracy. Anderson, for example, implies that a bourgeoisie with a liberal mission should be one that is entrenched and with interests pre-dating the emergence of the heavy state systems of the twentieth century. Perhaps only in Morocco and Iran was there an indigenous, non-minoritarian bourgeoisie that would fit this requirement, and in both countries it is better associated with nationalism than with liberalism. In inter-war Egypt, parts of the small indigenous bourgeoisie aligned with all political factions, including the throne, and it was the business leader Isma'il Sidqi who suspended the democra-tic process in 1930.

Elsewhere, it has been the state itself which, wittingly, or unwittingly, has fostered the development of an entrepreneurial stratum. Nowhere has this been more striking than in Turkey where the state, after 1923, set about quite deliber-ately to create a national bourgeoisie. By the end of the Second World War it had succeeded in doing so, and by 1950 parts of this bourgeoisie had aligned with the anti-state forces of the Demokrat Partisi to bring about a change of gov-ernment through the ballot box. Since then, however, prominent businessmen have avoided siding publicly with any party, although private interests do con-trol some of Turkey's press. The importance of the bourgeoisie lies in the resources it controls. If they are significant and beyond the reach of the state, then the mere possibility that the bourgeoisie might confront the state is enough to create political space.

There is also a long-term democratic logic to the development of a capitalist class. The alliance for profits can work for a time, but not all private interests will prosper, and sooner or later the fact that the regime unilaterally determines all parameters of economic life – interest rates, discretionary credit, tariffs, prices, etc – will be intolerable for some private actors. Groups will begin to lobby to protect themselves. If concessions made by the government involve the transfer or creation of real private wealth, real power will be transferred as well. Private interests may move from lobbying for their specific advantage to trespass into foreign affairs (we need good relations with 'X' to protect or open markets) or into the affairs of state (the government must do something about inflation; the central bank should be autonomous). The expansion of the private-sector agenda requires no explicit demand for democracy, but it is rooted in a demand for accountability on the part of those who own wealth and capital. Accountability is a public good, and once it is available to some, it may be hard to deny to others. It may then be that someday the Middle Eastern bourgeoisies will work their alleged democratic magic, but it is by no means clear where on the road to the long term the bourgeoisies are now.

No taxation without representation?

Lisa Anderson is not alone in asserting that in recent Middle Eastern history '... there was little taxation, and there was little representation'. The notion is simple; governments that extract significant resources from their own subjects or citizens will sooner or later be held accountable by the taxed. Again, citing Anderson, 'the taxed devise ways to be represented'. The logic is compelling, but tax regimes need to be disaggregated and the empirical record carefully examined.[5]

Peter von Sivers (1991) arrives at conclusions similar to Anderson's noting that the Middle East is undertaxed relative to advanced industrial nations. However, if we compare the Middle East to other developing regions, it is not undertaxed. In fact it is the most heavily taxed of the developing regions, while Latin America, with several democratic experiments underway, is the least. World Bank figures (1988, 82 and 84) show that over the period 1975 to 1985 tax revenues as a proportion of GNP averaged 25 per cent for Middle Eastern countries while Latin America averaged about 12 per cent. This reflects not merely the effect of the preponderant weight of captive petroleum corporations in several Middle Eastern countries, which can be easily and heavily taxed. On average 19 per cent of total tax revenues in the Middle East came from corporate profits tax while the corresponding figure for Africa was 20 per cent, for Asia 19 per cent, and for Latin America 10 per cent.[6]

The point is that the relative absence of conventional institutions of accountability in the Middle East cannot be attributed to a weak tax effort. The effort has not been, in historical or comparative terms, weak, but neither historically nor in the twentieth century is there much evidence that taxation has evoked demands that governments account for their use of tax monies. Predatory taxation has produced revolts, especially in the countryside (Kazemi & Waterbury 1991), but there has been no translation of tax burden into pressures for democratization.

What seems to be at the heart of the disjuncture between tax burdens and political demands is the nature of the taxes. First, Anderson is quite right to point out that several Middle Eastern states live more from rents than from direct tax revenues (see also Beblawi & Luciani 1987), and the reliance on rents means that governments are not obliged to develop those organic, albeit adversarial, links with their citizens that taxation is believed to bring about. Second, typically the greatest source of tax revenue is indirect; from tariffs, excise and sales tax, and flat fees. For instance in the mid-1980s, 65 per cent of Egypt's total tax revenue came from indirect taxes (World Bank 1990, 81). More invisible to the payee are differential prices that lower, say, the price of agricultural goods and raise the price of manufactures. The least visible of all is the inflation tax that, for the government, costs nothing to collect and falls implacably on all citizens. It is hard to demand accounts for taxes one is hardly aware of paying.

Direct taxes fall on personal income, corporate profits, and property. In the Middle East the latter is typically low, especially in agriculture while corporate profits taxes, often generated by publicly owned entities like petroleum companies, tend to outweigh income tax by a considerable margin. Even then, there is widespread evasion especially among the self-employed and the liberal professions. In Egypt, curiously, the captive civil service is not heavily taxed, paying in recent years only LE 200 million of total tax revenues of LE 5.5 billion (Ibrahim, 30/12/91).

The relation of taxation to political demands is not at all straightforward. On the one hand, there are the 'hard' states of East Asia which tax their populations heavily, but only recently and grudgingly have made any concessions to demands for accountability. On the other hand, if, as Anderson suggests, declining oil rents will force states to develop those missing organic links to taxable populations that will yield accountability, one wonders why this has not worked in Indonesia.[7] Finally, there are anomalies that require attention. The developing world's oldest and largest democracy, India, has traditionally relied upon indirect taxes (excise and tariffs) for three quarters of its total revenues and the proportion has been growing in the last decade (see *The Economist*, 23 May 1992). In Turkey, the tax burden as a proportion of GNP has declined from 17 per cent in 1982 to 14 per cent in 1988, a period corresponding precisely to Turkey's most recent democratic transition (see Tüsiad 1989, 23). We may conclude that there must be a number of intermediate variables between levels and kinds of taxation and demands for accountability, and until we are able to specify those variables we will have only an intuitive, and often inaccurate, appreciation of the dynamics at work.

Islam and patriarchy

I argue above that Middle Eastern intelligentsias for many years were rhetoricians of the authoritarian order. In the Arab world, at any rate, that is no longer the case. In recent years there has been a spate of self-criticism of such vehemence that, had it come from any other pens, would have been dismissed as stereotypical Orientalism. The general tenor of these critiques is to suggest that cultural factors explain the region's persistent authoritarianism. The critics have greater difficulty in situating Islam in their critiques, stumbling over the problem of whether to treat Islam as an independent cultural and ideological variable or as a credo that has been suborned by a pre-existing culture.

Hisham Sharabi's *Neo-Patriarchy* perhaps puts the case for a kind of cultural flaw the most forcefully, but he is not alone. He argues that traditional patterns of gender relations and the typical forms of the exercise of power and authority within the family, have produced patriarchal patterns of political authority in the Arab world. The traditional patriarchy has been wedded to the powerful state apparatus imported from Europe, and in the hands of petty bourgeois Muslim fundamentalists represents the most reprehensible form of governance possible: obscurantist, anti-scientific and repressive of women.

Similar analyses have been undertaken by Saad Ibrahim who emphasizes the stress in Arab culture on the need for obedience and deference to authority, which then usually evolves from fear to terror and then to worship.[8] In his writings on civil society Ibrahim reinvokes in a positive light themes and values reminiscent of Pye and Verba's work in *The Civic Culture* some three decades ago. Similarly, Abdellah Hammoudi has plumbed the cultural roots of sainthood (the *marabouts*) in Morocco to find the dynamics of political leadership and followership as well as the characteristics of subordination.

All of this leads me to wonder whether or not we should reassess an earlier, discredited literature out of the modernization school. Take for example David McClelland's comparison of Turkey and Iran in the early 1960s. In what I always regarded as a simplistic content analysis of children's stories and folktales, he concluded for Iran (McClelland 1963, 164):

> On the basis of findings for other countries, one would have to predict a bloody future for Iran. The mood is an authoritarian one. Either the Shah will succeed in suppressing opposition by force, or he will be 'suppressed' by a revolutionary force.

Almost a quarter-century later, Roy Mottahedeh, in *The Mantle of the Prophet*, summarized another cultural disposition in writing about Iranian attitudes toward Mosaddeq (Mottahedeh 1985, 125):

> He had long fulfilled an essential need in the moral drama that Iranians expect to see performed on the political stage. This drama allows Iranians to obey, and sometimes even to admire, the ruling autocrat, but requires that somewhere there be a man of standing who selflessly and tenaciously says 'no' to the autocrat. Many Iranians believe that as long as they quietly, almost surreptitiously, admire the antihero, they need not feel that their inner soul has been bought by power, and they hope that the autocrat, aware of this hidden division of allegiances, will be more cautious in dealing with his subjects.

There are two orders of questions we need to ask of such analyses. First, if accurate, do these depictions set the Middle East apart from other world cultures? I suspect not. One has only to peruse the vast literature on clientelism to find *zu'ama* (political bosses) reincarnated in *cacciques* and African tribal chiefs recast as heads of state. But, we must remember that McClelland's argument went further to suggest that there was an unusual correspondence, specifically in Iran and Iraq, between the values and expectations of the led with the style of rule arrogated by the leaders.

The second question is far more difficult and involves the very essence of what we mean by culture. Some observers of the current political scene in the Middle East appear to take culture as a kind of epiphenomenon that is produced by 'objective' conditions ranging from poverty and income disparities to the institutions of political domination.[9]

This latter question poses particularly difficult problems for understanding political Islam in its twentieth-century manifestations. Binder is not alone in trying to liberate Islam from the grip of the followers of Ibn Taymiyyah. The general proposition is that political Islam has been hijacked by a peculiarly puritanical and rigid understanding of the scriptures that does not represent either their essence or the preferences of most Muslims. Specifically, the hijackers reject liberal democracy as more than an unnecessary addendum to the political tolerance already inherent in Islam to depict it as part of a western strategy to destroy Islam. In addition, the purists argue that all sovereignty flows from God, that the notion of popular sovereignty is therefore a pernicious aberration, and that men cannot arrogate to themselves the right to make law (Sayyid al-Qutb saw such arrogation as the hallmark of the new *jahiliya*).

The intelligentsia once again faces an analytic dilemma with real implications for its future. Many want to believe (and they may be right) that the Islam that is so implacably hostile to what the secularists among them stand for, that puritanical Islam cannot be what it appears to be. Rather it is the invention of opportunistic 'islamic' leaders, orientalists, and western powers in search of new evil empires. As the editors of MERIP wrote in a recent special issue on democracy in the Middle East (1992, 5):

> The high profile of Islamist groups today owes more to the character of state repression in the past than to the exceptional religiosity of Muslim societies.

Therefore change the character of state repression and militant Islam may go away. To take militant Islam at face value, however, means either joining it or fighting it with the same passion, and perhaps the same methods, it has already displayed or used.

Conclusion

I have argued that there is something exceptional about the degree of authoritarianism that prevails in the Middle East today. It does not derive from any single factor but rather from a combination of factors that have been detailed in the subsections above. Despite the growth of the literate, urban middle classes in the Middle East, there has yet to be the predicted pressures for greater political liberalization. Part of the problem is that the middle classes in the Middle East may be particularly dependent upon or absorbed by the state and therefore unable to create space beyond the control of the state. More specifically the private-sector bourgeoisie and the intelligentsia have, to a great degree, been suborned by the state and have made little contribution to the creation of a civil society able to bargain with the state.

Second, and partially explaining the first point, the Middle Eastern state has been forged in and based its claim to legitimacy on the conduct of a sacred, often violent mission. The Middle Eastern state claims a *telos* and has demanded that all of society rally behind the quest. The instrumental values that might evoke broad-based demands for governmental accountability may be strengthening in the region as state after state fails monumentally to make progress toward its goals. But, at the same time, the islamic groups basically claim that they can revivify the spirit of mission and better lead the crusade.[10]

The hypothesis that heavily taxed populations will sooner or later demand accountability of those who spend their taxes cannot be empirically confirmed. Middle Eastern populations are not undertaxed nor have they been historically. The tactics of the taxed vary according to their wealth and power and have ranged from resignation and migration, to evasion and lobbying for favours once the basic allocation of tax revenues has been determined. I can think of no significant protest or movement in the Middle East (outside Israel) that has questioned the devotion of extraordinary amounts of national savings to defence and preparations for war.

Whether or not Islam and Middle Eastern 'culture' are separable phenomena, the two work in ways that do not augur well for democracy. I believe that basic tendencies in regional culture and in religious practice must be overcome rather than utilized in any efforts to promote pluralism and democracy. Moreover, Middle Easterners have not shown much explicit concern for democracy. In 1980, according to Saad Ibrahim, only 5.4 per cent of the respondents in a sample drawn from ten Arab countries cited democracy (or its absence) as a major problem in the region, and while that figure more than doubled to 11 per cent in 1990, it is still very low.

With these summary remarks in mind, the question then becomes: can the Middle East move toward democracy in the face of these obstacles?

Democracy: a bargained equilibrium

The aborted elections in Algeria provided the focal point for a debate about Islam and democracy that has far wider implications. On the one hand there were those, including Lahouari Addi, who argued that democracy can only be sustained by committed democrats, and that because the Islamic Salvation Front (FIS) had proclaimed its hostility to democracy, the game could not be played in Algeria (inter alia, Lahouari Addi).[11] This put the defenders of the new regime in the awkward position of pre-empting a democratic transition because they thought it could not be sustained. For those of this persuasion, criticism of the coup was confined to the observation that it would have been better for the armed forces to have waited until after the FIS had inevitably violated the constitution and mismanaged the economy to intervene. Either way, a substantial segment of the Algerian middle classes and intelligentsia preferred military, secular authoritarianism to what they were convinced would be islamic populist authoritarianism.

Against this view were those who felt that democracy is doomed if it does not follow its own rules. If the majority supports non-democrats, the majority's will must be respected.[12] Besides, denying an electoral victory to a popular choice will discredit democracy for years to come and drive the thwarted victors into clandestine and extra-legal channels to seize power. A possible alternative to islamic rule in Algeria would thus not be secular, technocratic authoritarianism but rather an islamic dictatorship, based on an alliance with parts of the military, as has existed in the Sudan since June 1989.

John Entelis believes that the very participation of the FIS in the elections represented the victory of the moderates within the movement and that they would have honoured the rules of the game had they been allowed to govern. Presumably they have been discredited and legitimacy shifted to radicals who will fulfil the worst fears of the secular opposition. Going beyond Entelis's conjunctural analysis, François Burgat, writing before the coup, has charged that claims of the incompatibility of Islam with democracy are in essence ideological. Referring to Rashid Ghannushi in Tunisia, he submits that Ghannushi's professions of democratic values are sincere and not merely tactical. Ghannushi's embrace of Saddam Hussein during the Gulf War must raise some doubts about his understanding of democracy but even more about his sense of tactics.

Democracy as a second-best solution

In this subsection, I shall use the propositions of Dankwart Rustow and Adam Przeworski to explore the possibility of democracy without democrats. Both authors essentially see democracy as a second-best solution to intractable conflicts of interest. Both suggest that democratic practices may flow from bargains arrived at by parties with no experience and little philosophical commitment to democracy. I have argued that both conditions prevail in the Middle East.

Dankwart Rustow over 20 years ago laid out a scheme for the initiation and sustaining of democratic transitions, based on the historical experience of Sweden and other countries. The transition consists in three phases. The first involves a long, inconclusive political struggle that mobilizes new political participants. Positions tend to be polarized, and democracy is espoused tactically, as a means to other ends. Then comes the decision phase in which the major antagonists recognize a no-win stalemate and negotiate compromises (or what in the *Transitions* studies are treated as pacts). In this phase democratic rules and various quid pro quos are agreed upon. In the third phase, repeated plays of the democratic game produce habituation and, presumably with time, a positive identification of most citizens with the democratic rules.

Obviously not every country need pass through every phase. Turkey never passed through the first, negotiated no explicit pacts in the second (although there was an implicit one that allowed the transition from military rule in 1983), but has, since 1950, accumulated democratic habits that may be fairly robust. India in its peculiar way has gone through all three, with the destructive bloodshed of partition serving as an example of what might happen in what remains of India if democratic compromises were not reached.

In Rustow's view, the building of democracy is carried out by non-democrats who had hoped to win everything, but learned through painful experience and stalemate that the *possibility* of winning something was better than the possibility of winning nothing at all or, indeed, losing everything, including one's life.

It is very much in this spirit, but with much more formal reasoning and games theory, that Adam Przeworski, 20 years later, analysed the prospects for democratic transitions in marketizing economies in Latin America and eastern Europe (Przeworski 1991). His argument is worth examining in detail, and I shall hold up pieces of it to the light of Middle Eastern experience.

Przeworski employs rational expectations assumptions. Political actors seek to maximize their power and material strength and will choose the means most appropriate to achieving those ends. The hope for democracy is that under many circumstances it provides those means in a Pareto-superior manner. One need not be a democrat, but one must be rational. Przeworski stresses the importance of history and culture in shaping preferences, but for most of his argument he ignores both to privilege economic interests in shaping preferences and in protecting institutional power. As we shall see, this limits the force of his arguments when applied to the question of islamic political associations and democracy in the Middle East.[13]

Democracy, he argues, allows today's losers to look ahead and entertain a future in which they have the possibility of winning. The possibility of winning something in the future may outweigh the possibility of losing everything in the present. The transition to democracy must result from a negotiated pact, or a bargained equilibrium that at once assures that no parties to the pact will be eliminated (part and parcel of winner-take-all politics) and that the rules do not preclude the victory of any party in the future.

If this is to be the beginning of what Rustow sees as the second, decision, stage, progress may not be made in the Middle East. In most states in the Middle East 'religious' parties are not allowed. In Turkey, where they are allowed, no party can reject the constitutional provision that Turkey is a secular state. As a result, the islamic Refah Party (Welfare Party) must remain silent over the issue of applying the *shari'a* as the law of the land. In Egypt religious parties must ally with non-religious parties in order to offer candidates for election. In Algeria, where the FIS was authorized *qua* religious party, it was not allowed to win. Only in Jordan were the Muslim Brethren allowed to run their own candidates. If it is crucial that all major actors have the legal right to participate and the possibility of one day winning office, then islamic groups have not been granted the opportunities that might assure their loyal adherence to democratic procedure. Moreover, what most concerns islamic groups is not control over material resources or bettering the material welfare of their followers, although both are important, but rather maximizing their control over value systems and the institutions of mass culture. Seizing control of the political apparatus is a means to this end and not an end in itself (I shall return to this theme below). Przeworski's scheme does not handle any of these factors well.

The gamble of the accommodationists is that if one lets the islamic groups into the democratic process, they will, with time, begin to behave according to the utility maximizing assumptions of Przeworski. They will prove human, enjoy power, find satisfaction in the approbation of the electorate, learn the importance of the mundane, and grant grudging respect to the system that allowed them to be politically recognized.

The fact that constitutions and other fundamental documents of the existing order so forcefully prohibit organized religion from participation in politics means that in the democratic struggle, if it ever begins (as it did in Algeria), the documents themselves become the prize in the struggle. Non-incumbents will want not merely to displace incumbents but to shred the documents of their adversaries and write their own. If the legal clauses were not there, if the constitution and other documents were mute on the subject of politicized religion, the stakes of electoral contests would be lowered.

I would add here that if I were an incumbent prince, I would want my minister of the interior to manufacture a certain kind of electoral outcome. As no one knows what the size of the islamic vote might be, one must guard against two outcomes. The first is that the islamic groups do so poorly that they are humiliated and decide the ballot box has nothing to offer them. Unlike secular parties with instrumental programmes, religious parties will not question their premisses merely because the electorate is uninterested. Hasan al-Turabi and the National Islamic Front in the Sudan showed just that after the elections in 1986. The second is that the islamic groups win outright, as appeared to be the likely outcome in Algeria. Had the Algerian government paid greater attention to the modalities of the elections from the very start, the FIS might have been induced to endure a fairly long apprenticeship as a minority participant in a new Algerian democracy. The period of habituation cannot be completed without the partial marginalization of participants who still harbour a winner-takes-all mentality.

In the manoeuvring towards a negotiated pact there are generally four positions, two for the incumbents and two for the challengers, as rendered below.

Incumbents	*Challengers*
hardliners	radicals
reformers	moderates

Some degree of co-operation is assumed between hardliners and reformers on the one hand, and radicals and moderates on the other. The only likely alliance that might join the two clusters is that between reformers and moderates, but it is very hard to achieve. Przeworski explains why. If reformers seek alliance with moderates, the latter will move closer to the radicals in order to increase their bargaining strength vis-à-vis the reformers. This would be the worst possible outcome for the reformers. Note that this is what happened in Iran in early 1979 as the Bakhtiar government sought understandings with Bazargan, Bani Sadr and moderate ayatollahs. It may not be fair to say that Bazargan et al. turned to the radicals (i.e. Khomeini), but they were certainly absorbed by them. The moderates among the Shah's incumbents paid a fearful price.

For that reason, Przeworski argues, reformers will ultimately align themselves with the hardliners and the status quo. 'Reformers have no political strength of their own and thus no prospect of being politically successful under democracy' (Przeworski, 1991, 70). We can run these roles against the FIS and the Algerian government: [14]

Incumbents	*Challengers*
Benjedid (reformer)	Madani (moderate)
Hamrouche (reformer)	Belhadj (radical)
Ghozali (hardliner)	
Nazzar (hardliner)	

Benjedid and Hamrouche did seek, perhaps not convincingly, an accommodation with the moderates of the FIS. It was not so much a question of the latter turning to the radicals of the movement as of the movement splitting over strategy in June 1991. Within weeks incumbent hardliners and clandestine radicals could each claim to have been vindicated in their initial assumptions. The Przeworski schema seems once again to work.

But it leaves something very important out. The reformers, and also the moderates, are not without political power. Przeworski does not explicitly ask why there are reformers in the first place. There would be none, or few, unless a threat to the incumbents worse than reform were not perceived. Hardliners and reformers both perceive the same threat but differ on how to deal with it. But if both agree there is a system-threatening menace, then the reformers may have leverage over the hardliners. If the hardliners have self doubts, or internal divisions, the reformers can exploit them.

The military is the key component of most hardline blocs. Here again, I think

Przeworski oversimplifies. He treats the military as having a single position or as a single unit.[15] Unlike other political actors, however, a single military faction can impose its view on the rest of the establishment if it moves by surprise and maintains superior fire power relative to other factions. It may be that Khalid Nazzar had the full backing of the Algerian military, but it is difficult to know. In the Sudan one can be almost sure that General Bashir has not spoken for all, or perhaps even most, of the Sudanese military.

The point is that one of the ways to begin a pacted transition is for challengers to guarantee not to try to settle accounts with the military once they come to power. This solution is what Przeworski calls 'democracy with guarantees', but it does not take the entire military establishment to wreck a pact, rather just a few determined officers. That is nearly what happened in Spain in February 1981. By the same token, if the hardliners are divided, especially in the military, then the reformers have a chance to reach out to moderates on the other side.

There are several possible bargained equilibria, but I will deal only with a few. There is one in which the negotiated equilibrium is arrived at by antagonists whose strength is known to one another. Lebanon offers two examples of this. In the first, the national pact laid down the rules for a democratic system with reciprocal guarantees (no resort on the part of the Christians to soliciting western protection; no attempts on the part of the Muslims to pull Lebanon into a larger Arab unit). The numerical strength of the contending sides was known and the system of representation built on that knowledge. The military was not autonomous, at least not until 1958.

The second example is embodied in the Taif Accords which seek to re-establish Lebanese democracy and to adjust the system of representation in the light of new knowledge. In both instances the object was to avoid civil war, in which everyone loses. No faction was clearly predominant so that the pacts reflected a 'no winners, no losers' principle.[16]

We may contrast this equilibrium (and I hardly need say that these equilibria are obviously very unstable) with those of Israel and the Sudan where the relation of forces is also known (Jews versus Arabs; Northerners versus Southerners) but unbalanced. In these instances the rules, or the pact (Israel has no written constitution), resemble a treaty drawn up on the terms of the victor. It establishes a regime, but its legitimacy is likely to be challenged by the 'losers'.

In Algeria we encounter a situation in which the real strength of the contending parties was not known, and a transition was begun without any pact at all. The incumbents acted as if they represented the bulk of Algeria's citizenry and thus could impose their own rules on the challengers. In June 1991, there was a feeble attempt on the part of the hardliners (Nazzar and Ghozali) to negotiate with the FIS, but the effort went nowhere and came after the acquisition of new knowledge stemming from the local elections. I agree with Przeworski, however, that perhaps the fairest pact will be one negotiated when the parties are unsure of their relative strengths. Not knowing this means that each party has an incentive to agree to clauses that give maximum protection to losers in any democratic contest.

There are two ways in which the military can relate to pacts. The first, as already mentioned, is democracy with guarantees, in which the challengers (principally the radicals) accept certain guarantees for the military and other adversaries in the event the radicals come to power. Once in power, if all parties honour the pact, winners can begin the habituation phase, gradually learning by doing and internalizing the norms that make the system function. In the Middle East, the closest thing we have to this is the position of the Ikhwan in Egypt, although I think it fair to say that the Ikhwan know they will not be allowed an outright electoral victory. Otherwise in Iran in 1978–79, and in Algeria in 1991, neither the forces of Ayatollah Khomeini nor the FIS accepted any guarantees for the military or any other adversaries in the event of their victory.

The second way in which the military can act in a transition is as an autonomous force. There can be no stable democracy so long as the military remains autonomous from civilian political control. At the same time, an autonomous and well-disposed military can protect the moderates as they pursue a pact, and allow them to escape the 'structural' dilemma mentioned above by which their best option is alliance with hardliners and defence of the status quo.

Turkey exemplifies the best and worst of the autonomous military. Three times since 1960, the Turkish military has intervened to interrupt temporarily the democratic process. By the same token, it was an autonomous military that allowed the civilian 'reformer' Turgut Özal to pursue a carefully staged process of redemocratization after 1983.

Islam and pacted transitions

In Poland, the seizure of power by General Jaruzelski in 1981 may be seen as the first step in the transition to democracy. Nearly a decade of stalemate followed, in which the armed forces and the police were pitted against Solidarity. During those years large segments of Polish society were 'mobilized', and civil society began to create political space for itself. Could the aborted elections in Algeria and the seizure of power by the military and technocrats signal the beginning of a similar transition?

I believe that the answer is no, primarily because the FIS, aside from its popularity, in no way resembles Solidarity. As mentioned above, the FIS and many other islamic organizations elsewhere in the Middle East do not oppose, or wish to replace, incumbent power blocs because they are undemocratic but because they have no sense of mission. Moreover religious political groups (islamic and non-islamic) are non-democrats of a peculiar kind. Non-religious, non-democratic groups, primarily ethno-nationalist, may alter their prejudices over time and in the light of experience. The same is of course true for messianism but there the time frame is very long. Where the scriptures are both holy and explicit, as is the case in Islam, pragmatic compromise will be very difficult. It is usually the off-shore scholar or pundit who takes the long view, who cites the long centuries of gradual change in western Christianity to the point where pluralism and secular government were not only accepted but, in a sense, blessed.

Thus there are many who ask the secularists of the Middle East to gamble, to ensnare the fundamentalists in the democratic process and to wean them gradually off their messianic quest. When Ghannushi, or some other Muslim leader, professes his commitment to democratic ideals, we should, we are told, take his words at face value and not as a tactical ploy. When a Belhadj says quite the contrary, we should take his words as electoral posturing and demagoguery that will give way to flexibility and pragmatism once the heat of electoral battle has died down.

I do not reject such near-sophistry out of hand, but I am profoundly sceptical that it is at all responsible. The sporadic democratic experiments of Pakistan, Bangladesh and Malaysia suggest that a certain kind of political Islam can be made compatible with a certain kind of democratic practice (both need to be specified). But I also recognize that islamic parties, once in power, would not entirely rewrite the rules of the game. The countries mentioned above aside, Muslim groups have participated in electoral politics only in countries where they have not shared in writing the rules – e.g. Turkey, Sudan, Algeria, Jordan, Egypt, India (and now, I suppose, Bulgaria). Frequently, Muslim groups have suggested that they accepted the rules only under duress and that they would change them if given the power to do so. This, for instance, has been a consistent pattern in the Sudan. Between independence in 1956 and the Abbud coup of 1958, both the Umma Party and the Khatmiya sect called for the application of *shari'a* in all of the Sudan. The National Islamic Front revived the call in 1985 and allied with the military to depose Sadiq al-Mahdi of the Umma Party when it was rumoured that the latter was considering modifications in existing laws to guarantee rights to minorities (Fluehr-Lobban 1991), Ikhwani candidates in the Jordanian elections of November 1989 invoked neither democracy nor the constitution, but rather Islam as the religion of state and the application of God's law (Duclos 1990, 50). The similar and more vociferous declarations emanating from the FIS have been well-documented (Kapil 1991; Camau 1991; Leveau 1991).

At the risk of a facile analogy, the dilemma for democracy resembles that confronting Europe in the two decades following the Second World War. Most European nations contained powerful marxist-leninist parties that commanded a substantial portion of the electorate and which espoused ideological goals fundamentally at odds with existing democratic laws. Over time, as Przeworski or Rustow would have predicted, persistent failure to win outright majorities led the communist parties of Europe, not to resort to extra-legal means, but to adopt eurocommunism, acknowledging the legitimacy of 'bourgeois' democracy and agreeing to play by the rules before and after elections.

Political Islam in the Middle East presents the same sort of challenge, and, as was the case in Europe in the late 1940s and early 1950s, there is the possibility that Muslim groupings could win majorities. As Michel Camau rightly notes, to exclude the *intégristes* from electoral politics is a delusion; to include them without prior conditions is to invite the destruction of the democratic process and of the territorial state. Therefore, a transition with negotiated guarantees may offer a solution, or at least a goal. Muslim groups, in order to participate legally and as religious parties, must formally accept the rules and laws of a constitutional order that may well reflect islamic values but which will be quite explicitly secular. No democratic system could merit the name if the rights of women and minorities were in any way distinguished from those of men and Muslims.

I am not sanguine that this relativization of sacred texts can take place easily if at all. Even Leonard Binder's cautious assessment (one that nonetheless implies a certain inevitability) may be too optimistic (1990, 82 and 359):

> In itself, the normative structure of Islam is unusually open to adaptation to the political and cultural needs of a liberal bourgeoisie in maintaining social peace, protecting private property, and attaining a measure of freedom of choice. Until the circumstances *render the concept self-evident* – emphasis JW – to mass and elite alike, the prospect for Islamic liberalism will remain dim.

One recalls the efforts of the French in Algeria in the 1930s to make French citizenship contingent on Algerian Muslims formally renouncing their islamic personal status law. The Project Blum-Viollette of 1936 brought about the 'conversion' of no more than a handful of Algerian Muslims in almost two decades preceding the beginning of the armed revolution in 1954. Negotiated, contingent participation of Muslim groups in electoral politics may be a more reasonable expectation than Algerians abandoning religious law to become French citizens. But no matter how improbable, some attempt at contingent, pacted participation of Muslim parties in electoral politics will be the only way to reduce the immense risks faced by secularists in the Middle East.

The best face that can be put on the current situation in Algeria is that it may be the first of many inconclusive confrontations between fundamentalists and secular authoritarians. There may be a long and painful learning process ahead stemming from stalemate and repression. In this sense Algeria could resemble Poland. During the period of stalemate, liberals, myself included, would argue that careful accommodation of the Islamic forces would be the best line to follow, both tactically and normatively. In his unflamboyant manner, Husni Mubarak has shown how this game can be played (Lesch 1989).

However, it is not at all self-evident that repression will fail. Here too Mubarak has been exemplary. Detention and imprisonment have regularly separated the true believers from the faddists. Here, the hardline approach divides the ranks of the Muslim opposition, creating some space for moderates who offer hope to those not yet willing to die for their beliefs. The reformers among the incumbents can then co-opt various of the moderates. The FIS in Algeria is divided, and Sa'id Gueshi, expelled from the FIS in August 1991, was brought into the Boudiaf–Ghozali government. The regime can play along other fissures in the islamic movement, represented by the Nahda Islamique and Hamas. Similar splits, fissures and possibilities of co-optation can be found in Tunisia and Jordan as well. This sort of probing and testing of the resolve of the adversary is a two-way street, and may be part and parcel of a transition to pacted democracy.

The battle to control education

Most Muslim groups and much of the more secular middle class are struggling not so much over seats in parliament, cabinet posts, or patronage but rather over control of education and the values that will be imparted to the next generation of Middle Eastern youth. The contest may be misplaced: it is not obvious that schools, public or private, necessarily shape the values of the young, but the protagonists in this contest believe that they do. Leveau (1991, 98) argues that for Algeria's military and technocracy, losing control of the educational system is as frightening as losing power.

Turkey's Muslims may be more acutely aware of what is potentially at stake than is the case for their co-religionists in other Middle Eastern societies. Kemal Atatürk demonstrated dramatically what control over the national education system could do to indoctrinate entire generations in the (for Muslims abhorrent) values of republicanism, secularism, and populism. Atatürk froze Islam and Muslims out of the educational system, and in the 1960s when the so-called *imam-hatip* state schools to train preachers were integrated into the national education system, Muslim groups used the graduates of the schools to infiltrate the state teaching corps, the ministries, the police, and the military.

In the last Turkish elections in 1991, the islamic Refah (Welfare) Party focused a major part of its campaign on what it called the 'democratization of the university'. It called for opening up admissions to nearly anyone of university age and with high school training, the expansion of the teaching profession, and the right of students to be represented and to cast votes in all administrative bodies of the university. Departments run by student-faculty committees should vote into office all deans and rectors, who in turn would be the executors of departmental decisions. The party did moderately well in the elections, but was not made a coalition partner of the True Path Party of Süleyman Demirel.[17]

Elsewhere, I believe, the same hope is harboured by Muslim groups that, as in republican Turkey, a cultural revolution or value transformation can be engineered from the top through control of educational institutions, but I suspect that this is something of a delusion. The youth of the Middle East cannot be sealed off from the outside world, because of television, video cassettes, and worker migration. It is quite possible, of course, that the exposure of rival values and modes of comportment may actually reinforce the adherence of many young Middle Easterners to their faith, but for large numbers the opposite is as likely.

In Algeria, the FIS could not see in the FLN and its control of national education for three decades an exemplar of what could be done to change the hearts and minds of young Algerians through the school and university system. It is fairly obvious that Algerian youth came away from their schooling neither respecting the FLN as an organization nor sharing its increasingly amorphous values. Nonetheless, Abbas Madani has consistently stressed societal and value reform through education, and he managed to place his adepts throughout the national education system (Cheriet 1992, 9–14).

Thus, the strategy of religious parties may be to enter into the electoral game, if permitted, to try to win control of the state apparatus the better to control education and the mass media, but, simultaneously, to build support within the educational system itself among teachers and students and in the educational bureaucracy. From there, whether or not elections are ever held, whether or not Muslim parties are allowed to compete, the islamic organizations can slowly infiltrate the cadres of the administration and of the military and the police. Hasan al-Turabi and the Ikhwan in the National Islamic Front played on both registers in the Sudan from 1983, and when the electoral process was not kind to them, they turned to their allies in the military to seize power by coup.[18]

For Islam or against the status quo?

It was often said that the communist vote in Europe was a protest vote, not an endorsement of marxism-leninism. Similarly, many, like the editors of *Middle East Report*, see the Muslim vote in the Middle East as an expression of hostility toward politically bankrupt regimes rather than as an endorsement of islamic government. Can we move any closer to an assessment of the validity of these positions by identifying the members of the movement?

In principle, yes, but the fragmentary evidence at our disposal allows no sure characterization. What does appear to be the case is that, contrary to what the European and Latin American literature suggests, the challenge in the Middle East is not mounted by radicals with an extensive, state-centric, redistributive agenda. Rather, as Michael Fischer (1982) and others argue, radical Islam is the creature of the small-scale entrepreneur. The latter have never been treated well by the interventionist states which they now oppose. They appear to want an islamic state that protects cultural and religious values but stays out of the economy except to support private endeavour.[19] Time and again, the leadership of the islamic movements has fallen to well-educated technocrats from provincial backgrounds (Necmettin Erbakan of Turkey's Refah Party and Abbas Madani of Algeria's FIS are typical).[20]

Nonetheless, the islamic movements are very heterogeneous. In Algeria the FIS ran very well in urban areas and had strong appeal among the poor, the unemployed, and the populations of the *bidonvilles*. These constituents would surely put great pressure on any islamic government to use all the state's resources for social purposes and to intervene in the economy to create jobs.

The Islamic Republic of Iran has shown over the last 13 years all the contradictions that are likely to emerge within the ranks of Muslim radicals. Iran's is a big state in economic terms, and it is still highly interventionist, owning vast amounts of property and productive assets. Like many secular states in the region, it has placated the petty bourgeoisie and the merchant class through an islamic 'alliance for profits' in which shortages, black markets, smuggling, and drug trafficking allow the 'bazaaris' to prosper despite the state.

It is much too early to assess what it is the islamic vote represents. Those who say it is a protest vote probably do not have to live wth the consequences if they are wrong. If they are right, however, one would expect protest voters to hold islamic governments accountable for poor economic performance. Something of the sort appears to be at work in Iran. There, however, no one can contest the islamic nature of the regime, nor can women or non-Islamic minorities exercise full political rights.

Conclusion

Democratic procedures make political sense. They lower the stakes of political competition allowing players to live to play another day. They help resolve disputes that deadlock political factions and paralyse societies. They do not require committed democrats to put them in place. That said, some contexts will be more favourable than others in nurturing democratic experiments, and the Middle East today offers a non-nurturing environment.

We do not know, for example, where the Middle East is located in the process of economic development and societal transformation. Samuel Huntington argued years ago that as economic growth accelerated, the likelihood of political instability would grow in a curvilinear fashion. That is, in the middle stages of growth, instability would peak and praetorian government would spread in order to repress the demands of an increasingly mobilized civil society. As growth continued, he argued, these material demands would be increasingly met, the causes of instability would diminish, and the need for authoritarian repression would disappear. We could call this the Korean pattern. To the extent the proposition has empirical validity, we do not know whether the Middle East is climbing the curve, with the implication that there are years of praetorianism and repression ahead, or whether it is descending the curve, with the implication that the days of praetorians and authoritarians are numbered. We can be sure that the Middle East is, by and large, in the middle stages of economic growth and development.

According to how one assesses this relationship, radical Islam could either be seen as the wave of the near authoritarian future or as the last heroic stand against the overwhelming forces of liberalism, markets, and pragmatic politics. Binder, I think, in the passage cited above, endorses the latter.

The Middle East offers some unique characteristics that block transition to democracy. Powerful states with suborned intelligentsias and dependent middle classes have pursued great quests and messianic visions. Society has been harnessed to these quests, and while the regimes themselves may have lost their legitimacy, the quests have not. The major challengers to the incumbents in the Middle East do not therefore offer democracy as the alternative to authoritarianism but rather an untarnished instrument to pursue the great cause.

These quests are not quixotic. The region has been riven by wars and civil strife in a manner rivalled only in the Asian sub-continent and now in the Balkans. But India has shown that even in such conditions democracy can survive. Here, political Islam must enter the equation as a unique force. It is not like any other religion in that its very heart lies in its sacred texts. For the present there does not seem to be much room, in practical political terms, for interpreting and relativizing those texts insofar as they bear on the organization of government and the definition of political rights. That brings us back to the curve. Perhaps this re-interpretation of the texts will come soon, or perhaps not for a generation or more. We must be very careful, therefore, in advocating democracy at all costs. Rather, a period of confrontation and bargaining may be what is needed to hasten the process of re-interpretation so that a pacted transition to democracy can begin, in which all parties accept the logic, if not the spirit, of the rules.

Notes

1   Wade notes that Singapore is the exception in East Asia. If we turn to the Middle East we find 11 countries with per capita incomes near or exceeding the $4,000 threshold. Nine of these countries manifested no or very few of the institutions conventionally associated with democratic practice (universal suffrage, competitive elections, freedom of the press and assembly). Kuwait's restricted suffrage election in autumn 1992 altered this picture only partially. The per capita income levels of these nine countries ranged from $3,500 in Iran and Iraq to $19,400 in the United Arab Emirates (UAE). The remaining two countries were Israel (per capita income, $10,800) and Turkey (per capita income, $3,900), both of which did manifest institutions of a conventional democratic variety. Algeria, which flirted with a democratic transition, had a per capita income of $2,470 prior to the flirtation. All figures are expressed in 'parity purchasing power' and are taken from UNDP, *Human Development Report* (New York, Oxford University Press, 1991) pp.119–20.

2   For evidence of rising SES, see Richards & Waterbury (1990) Chapters 5 and 10.

3   *On average* in the late 1980s Middle Eastern nations spent 8.8 per cent of GNP on their militaries, as opposed to 1.3 per cent in Latin America, 2 per cent in East Asia, 3.8 per cent in South Asia, and 4 per cent in Africa. Of the 12 countries worldwide that devoted the highest proportion of GNP to military expenditures, ten were Middle Eastern. Oman was, in 1990 number one with 23 per cent and the Yemen Arab Republic (Yemen AR) number 12 with 9.6 per cent. Israel, Saudi Arabia, Jordan, Iraq, Yemen People's Democratic Republic (Yemen PDR), Egypt, Syria, and Libya fell in descending order between Oman and Yemen AR. See 'Arms Race or Arms Control', *Middle East*

Report, vol. 22, no. 4, 1992, pp.6–7; and Richards & Waterbury (1990) Chapter 13.

4 John Entelis, in remarks at a conference in Princeton in February 1992, noted a 'deep authoritarian streak in Algeria's secular opposition', and Saad Ibrahim in recent writing on Arab civil society has pointed to the typically authoritarian leadership styles prevailing within parties that preclaim their faith democracy.

5 Implicit in this argument is the notion that owners of fixed assets will have the greatest stake in whatever political regime prevails and will generate the most effective demands for accountability in the use of the taxes they pay. By contrast, Bates and Lien (1985) argue that it may be the owners of liquid assets, who can threaten the regime with the flight of their wealth, who will generate the most effective demands for accountability. Jill Crystal's study of the merchant class in Kuwait bears this out. In 1909, in response to new levies on merchant wealth by the Shaykh, Kuwaiti merchants 'exited' to Bahrain and Iraq. The Shaykh backed down, and during the 1920s there took place the gradual enfranchisement of the merchant class culminating in the Majlis movement and Legislative Assembly of 1938. Confirming the arguments of Anderson, and Luciani and Beblawi (1987), however, the merchant class was politically marginalized once oil rents came to dominate state revenues. See Crystal (1990, 24–5 and 47–8).

6 Various empirical studies bear out fairly high rates of direct and indirect taxes country by country. See Askari & Cummings (1982).

7 Algeria would seemingly confirm Anderson's thesis: declining rents, the riots of 1988, democratic opening in 1990. My own understanding is, however, that Benjedid was not so much responding to popular demands for liberalization as he was exploiting a crisis to discredit the FLN and, through elections, to distance himself from it.

8 In *The Republic of Fear* (1989) Samir al-Khalil lays out in detail the same process in Ba'thi Iraq. He also takes apart Michel Aflaq's writings to show their deep authoritarian and intolerant foundations. However, Khalil almost never invokes culture *per se*, as opposed to political structures and the personalities of those who run them, to explain what is going on.

9 It is only fair to note that Richards & Waterbury (1990) take this position with respect to many of the basic issues of contemporary Middle Eastern political economy.

10 In this respect political Islam has adopted a message that secular leftists proffered in the 1970s. Salah Issa, in his 1974 article 'The Future of Democracy in Egypt', declared the bankruptcy of nasserism, but saw the democratic future lying in the constitution of a national front to carry on the struggle with zionism and imperialism. The best general synthesis remains Malcolm Kerr's 'Arab Radical Notions of Democracy' (1963).

11 Sid Ahmed Ghozali, the prime minister before and after the coup, compared the FIS to the Nazis in the Weimar Republic (*El País,* 19 February 1992).

12 It is very important to note that the majority referred to here is really a plurality. The two-round electoral system in Algeria favoured the FIS even though its total vote had declined by a million since the local assembly and municipal elections of June 1990.

13 Economistic explanations of the first steps in possible democratic transitions work in sub-Saharan Africa. Bratton & Vandewalle (1992) show that African neo-patrimonial regimes lose control of rent-seeking clients in periods of economic adjustment

and austerity. The visible rent-seeking, when the pie overall is shrinking, provokes corporate, white- and blue-collar interests, experiencing absolute declines in standards of living, to demand accounts from neo-patrimonial rulers.

14   The four player schema cannot be taken too literally; Madani and Belhadj cannot be clearly distinguished in terms of moderation and radicalness, but I do so anyway for the sake of argument.

15   When Przeworski turns to empirical analysis he shows his sensitivity to these same issues. For example he points out the striking fact that in eastern Europe, the military was not part of the hardline bloc, unlike the police, and was prepared to back the reformers' steps towards a transition.

16   In Rustow's phasing, Lebanon may now be in phase two, one of recognized and fruitless stalemate, in which a second-best compromise may appear desirable (Rustow 1970). The problem is that one could argue that Lebanon has been in this phase since the 1850s. Rustow also stipulates that for the compromise to come about there must be a sense of national unity.

17   In alliance with the right-wing nationalist party of Alparslen Turkes, the Refah Party won 17 per cent of the national electorate, about double its vote in the 1987 elections.

18   See Hasan al-Turabi, 1992. It is alleged in Egypt that al-Turabi is currently targeting Muslim populations among the numerically dominant Oromo in Ethiopia and among the Eritreans in order to register a large 'Muslim' vote in forthcoming elections in both Ethiopia and Eritrea (*al-Wafd*, 11 March 1992 9).

19   Przeworski observes that in eastern Europe '...most groups other than unskilled workers and party bureaucrats...opt for capitalism' (1991, 102).

20   In 1987 in Turkey, a poll was carried out that showed that only 7 per cent of a national sample was in favour of the application of the *shari'a*. The majority of those in favour were young, rural males with good education and of lower-income backgrounds.

2

Democratization in the Arab World: uncertainty, vulnerability and legitimacy. A tentative conceptualization and some hypotheses

JEAN LECA

The voters' discontent is not a sufficient reason for imperilling democracy. We are progressing step-by-step toward democracy; it is a difficult process. But Algeria is not some sort of boy wonder and democracy is not the natural outgrowth of human actions. Therefore, we must stop the electoral process in order to safeguard the democratization process.

anonymous Algerian official quoted in *Le Figaro*, 10 January 1992

The first free and pluralist parliamentary elections ever organized in Algeria took place on 25 December 1991. The Islamic Salvation Front won an overwhelming majority of the seats attributed in the first round of balloting and was expected to obtain a sizeable parliamentary majority after the run-off election on 16 January 1992. President Chadli Benjedid resigned on 11 January, probably under pressure from the government and military establishment. It is likely that the second round of balloting will be called off.

Le Figaro, 12 January 1992

By way of introduction: variations on political pacts

The aim of this chapter is not to detail social and political conditions prevailing in the 'Arab world', that is the area ranging from Morocco to Iraq. Rather, the Arab region will be treated as a case study with the aim of highlighting a few basic issues raised by theories of democratization. The most intriguing of these is the notion of 'political pact', which was revived by the *Transition from Authoritarian Rule* series (O'Donnell, Schmitter & Whitehead 1986, IV, 37ff) using Kirchheimer's and Rustow's insights (Kirchheimer 1969; Rustow 1970). In that work, a 'pact' was defined as 'an explicit, but not always publicly explicated or justified, agreement among a select set of actors which seeks to define (or better, to redefine) rules governing the exercise of power on the basis of mutual guarantees for the 'vital interests' of those entering into it. At the core of a pact lies a negotiated compromise under which actors agree to forgo or underutilize their capacity to harm each others' corporate autonomies or vital interests' (O'Donnell et al. 1986, IV 37, 38).

As I understand it, a 'political pact' is not a coalition organized to propose a definite 'political supply'. It sets rather the preconditions for different political supplies to be self-restrained and compatible enough not to be considered by the other party, or parties, as an unacceptable threat that would justify the breach of 'democratic rules'. The meaning of 'democratic rules' usually takes on, prima facie, a legal-organizational dimension: the legal existence of political parties and interest groups and their integration into a constitutional legal order. But it also has a normative dimension, the core of which is pluralism (*ta'addudiyya*, Ibrahim 1989), that is to say that no single group or party enjoys a monopoly on the political truth. Pluralism thus entails tolerance, acceptance of majority rule, limited government, and protection of basic rights. The term 'democratic rules' also has a power dimension: the sharing of power within the system, the emergence of different centres of power, and the accountability of power-holders to elected representatives and to public opinion.

It should be noted that this definition of 'political pact' is not theoretical, but merely descriptive of a more or less shared world view. It does not form a concept, but merely puts together various features identified by Arab and other intellectuals. O'Donnell and Schmitter's definition is much more ambitious, as it is based on the double assumption that citizenship, as a set of rights and obligations, must be allotted to each *individual* so that he can make individual, and participate in collective, choices; and that, moreover, democratization is the process by which citizenship is either applied to political institutions previously governed by other principles or *expanded* to include those not previously enjoying citizenship (from women, youth, illiterates to foreigners), or *extended* to cover issues and institutions not previously subject to citizen participation, which implies that nothing is immune from politics as a self-creating process (O'Donnell et al. 1986, 80). In part I, below, we shall try to arrive at a definition that attempts to avoid weighty metaphysics. Short of being a mere tautology – a regime always works *as if* there were a pact of some sort among relevant forces, for if not the regime would not persist; but does it follow that this pact is a prerequisite for the regime? – the political pact hypothesis gives rise to a number of misgivings.

If society is not fully incorporated into the state, or the policy, that is to say if there is a struggle not only between organized interests for the monopolization or the sharing of power, but also between actors competing for the articulation of 'legitimate interest' and for the construction of the legitimate social world (i.e. the transformation of grievances into ideologies and political demands through the construction of specific worlds of shared meaning), a pact may be unlikely, unless one of the contenders gains the upper hand in the struggle for hegemony. In the Arab world, there is no cultural hegemony in the field of politics, which might explain, along with foreign interference, the continuous 'search for legitimacy' (Hudson 1977), not only the legitimacy of the political authorities and regimes but also that of the political communities (to cite Easton's familiar division, Easton 1965). Arab countries are not likely unique in this respect; indeed, the social fabrication of moral conventions of consent that legitimize systems of subordination can be found everywhere (Beetham 1991), though in the Arab world they exhibit pronounced characteristics (see the essays edited by Salamé 1987). It is always possible to reply that politics is not about meaning but rather about power, and that a pact is apt to be 'signed' by people having nothing in common except a willingness to compromise (all other solutions being still worse) and perhaps an abstract feeling of belonging to a common *umma* (community of believers). But then the question becomes: how is such a compromise likely to be durable between 'parties' that are not self-contained units, like states or armies, but whose various salient identities – as Syrians, Palestinians, Iraqis, or as workers, shopkeepers, believers, members of a region, a city, a lineage, a class, a patron-client network, an ideological group, and so on – are not ranked according to stable functional criteria, but according to subtle situational shifts? The system may work smoothly as a way to deal with social change (Geertz, Geertz & Rosen 1979) but, in order to work, it has to have been working for a long time. Which brings us to the tautology that the pact works when the system is working and the system always works as if there were a pact between competing 'parties'.

Once again, the Arab world is not unique in this respect, and even members of the so-called 'stable democracies' were never reduced to the identity quartet: citizenship, occupational group, religious or ideological affiliation, party affiliation. Still, there the identity and substance of parties can be ascertained more securely than in the Arab world, which incidentally to some extent explains why the various political labels – 'islamic', 'islamist', 'Muslim socialist', 'liberal', etc – can get rather jumbled when manipulated carelessly. In this chapter, I will try to avoid becoming bogged down with labels by setting down a set number of designations, irrespective of the way the actors may wish to describe themselves. First, by *conservative islamic groups* I mean those who advocate classical sunni or wahhabi Islam, support 'traditional' rulers (as in, say, Morocco or Saudi Arabia), and oppose authoritarian nationalist rulers. Second *radical islamists* are those who advocate a 'political' Islam opposing 'traditional' rulers, authoritarian bureaucrats, military leaders, as well as 'westernized' democrats (or liberals). This label covers two sub-groups: 'islamic democrats', who call for pluralism and free elections; and 'revolutionary islamists', who are reluctant to recognize the legitimacy of party pluralism while at the same time rejecting single party rule. The *democrats* (with more or less pronounced islamic, socialist, nationalist, liberal ideologies) are those who accept pluralism, free elections, and constitutionalism. Finally, there are *nationalist (or socialist) authoritarians* of various persuasions (nasserist, Ba'thist, National Liberation Fronts). They consider the state or the government a secular power (meaning 'autonomous in relation to religious authorities'), as well as a guiding force of the national economy and ideology (which may incorporate many religious themes). Some of these labels may partially overlap, individuals may belong to two groups (or to none), and affiliations to patron-client or other 'particularist' networks may bear no relations to the political attitudes connected to the labels (the radical islamists being a partial exception).

It is possible that these labels could be used to identify future parties to 'political pacts', since the political supplies extended by 'elites' that are supposedly representative of 'groups' (or more precisely, groups of political entrepreneurs trying to create constituencies) are not aimed chiefly at proposing policies based on expressive beliefs in order to give shape to ordinary people's experiences. This logic calls for the emergence of *partis identitaires* whose function is not a competitive struggle for power according to established rules but to promote alternative forms of socialization and mobilization and proclaim a collective political identity different from the official one (Badie 1992, 237). In such a situation, 'politics is not coups and constitutions, but one of the principal arenas in which [these structures of meaning] publicly unfold' (Geertz 1973, 312). As Geertz puts it: 'For a state to do more than administer privileges and defend itself against its own population, its acts must seem continuous with the selves of those whose state it pretends it is, its citizens – to be in some stepped-up amplified sense, *their* acts.' Which makes the problem of legitimacy ('How do some men come to be credited with the right to rule over the others?') all the more acute (Geertz 1973, 317).

A political pact requires that each 'party' sufficiently trusts the others and the 'system' to give precedence to the binomial 'incomplete victory (benefit) – provisional and relative defeat (risk)' over the binomial 'total victory (benefit) – absolute defeat (risk)'. It is therefore necessary that the first binomial be worth a try: if one thinks that an incomplete victory is tantamount to a total defeat, and that a relative defeat can always be transformed into an absolute defeat, distrust reigns and democracy does not work. The only options left are 'Freedom or Death' (in our part of the world, it is rather 'Justice or Death'). For democracy to work, the motto 'Freedom or Death' must be discarded, yet it is not enough to proclaim in good faith the value of democracy to ward it off. That means that the major parties (i.e. the parties most endowed with powers of coercion, retaliation or mobilization) must be already convinced that their best interest is to show forbearance. As people must have good reasons for acting on moderation, they must construe their situation as one whereby their basic interests are not irredeemably jeopardized. That amounts to saying that a political pact is the precondition of a political pact.

That is not as tautological as it sounds: if the parties do not feel too vulnerable, they may agree on a pact guaranteeing that something will *not* happen (they do not have to agree on a specific and substantive outcome). If one party thinks it is almighty, it will not envisage a pact. Conversely, if all feel vulnerable they will not envisage a pact either, since mutual distrust will be much stronger than the willingness to let the other(s) control significant resources. Both situations are conducive to what Adam Przeworski has called 'risk insensitiveness' (Przeworski 1986), that is to say an unwillingness to modify one's stance despite the risk. In the second instance, where the risks are *maxima*, the situation presents something of a paradox. Democracy can prosper if, and only if, the uncertainty that is its mechanical output (Przeworski 1986 and 1991) does not for the concerned parties presage their certain extermination (or condemnation to a gentler form of 'final solution': unbearable stagnation, or, for the lucky ones, definitive exile).

Vulnerability is not necessarily felt in the same domains by the various parties: an islamist movement may think it is religiously so in the right, and that its appeal to the masses is so great, that nothing can threaten its righteousness or its cultural legitimacy; yet at the same time the movement may feel politically vulnerable, and its social base support (jobless youth, petty civil servants appalled at a ubiquitous corruption) may feel hopelessly vulnerable as well. Secular democrats may feel secure as workers or senior civil servants and yet vulnerable as women, or as parts of an 'alien', 'western' culture, and so on. Diverse vulnerabilities can strengthen one another and so become cumulative, stifling any attempt to bargain with the enemies. People in a situation of vulnerability perceive available resources as being fixed, and thus competition for them is seen as a dangerous and potentially destructive exercise (Waterbury 1977, 337): either one eats or one is eaten. If the dominant image depicts the resources as permanently fixed (Foster 1965) or if the patterns of resource-allocation are perceived as immutable ('If you have something you'll get something else, if you have nothing you'll get nothing else', as more that a few sceptical peasants and poor city dwellers used to say in eastern Algeria during the 1972 'agrarian revolution'), it strengthens specific forms of solidarity, particularly patron-client networks (Waterbury 1977; Leca & Schemeil 1983). If, on the other hand, the relevant goods are perceived as provisionally fixed and potentially expansive (on condition that either the patterns of allocation or the dominant morality and, in any case, the distribution of power are changed), the leninist question is thus revived: 'Kto kogo?' ('who eats whom?'), a question characteristic of what Sartori calls 'warlike politics' (Sartori 1987, 41–4). In both cases, vulnerability is averse to the solidarity born from a common citizenship binding together people who have in all other respects every reason to oppose one another.

If Islam poses problems in this respect, it can no more be said of democracy that it 'is the solution'. Neither are 'political pacts'. It is nonetheless necessary to elaborate upon these gloomy outlooks, first by defining democracy in the Arab context and then, secondly, dealing with 'Arab exceptionalism' (in short, 'democracy is problem-solving but Arabs are unable or unwilling to solve their problems'). Finally, we shall review and update the basic theories of democratization as they are applied to the Arab world.

Defining democracy in the Arab context

Since democratization is nothing other than the process leading to democracy, one cannot avoid the obligation of defining democracy, be it at risk of giving the impression of depicting a natural entity already 'out there' and waiting to be discovered by reasonable people freed from ideological deceptions. Unfortunately, when a word is used to convey the ideas of self-evidence, self-explanation, historical or natural (or supernatural) necessity and universal goodness, reason (and in particular social-scientific reason) is in trouble. Such is the case when a concept (however vague and sometimes *because* it is vague) is taken for granted and is considered as expressing a conventional wisdom which it would be indecent to question. That is why the average contemporary political scientist would regard Sir Robert Filmer – for whom *patriarcha* (the identity of patriarchal and political power, kingship, and fatherhood) was precisely such a self-evident concept – as an alien thinker belonging to a long-lost world. He would be viewed as perhaps a topic for a discussion on the history of political thought, but certainly not as a fellow scholar. By the same token, one (or at least I) might feel inclined to laugh at those who, not so long ago, used to write extensively about the (necessary?) 'transition to socialism'. Likewise, one might feel more than uncomfortable with the crowds that chant 'Islam is the solution'. 'Socialism' and 'Islam' should be treated, like *patriarcha,* as practical concepts used for the sake of ideological persuasion by social and political contenders involved in a struggle to legitimize beliefs, organizations and regimes (as such, objects of inquiry for political scientists), not as 'scientific' concepts used as a part of political scientists' kit for the sake of understanding and explanation.[1]

The problem is that 'democracy' may be in precisely the same predicament when used both as a practical and 'social-scientific' concept. Small wonder: social scientists are also social beings involved like anybody else in practical conflicts over power and meaning, and the scientist's cognitive world has no pre-eminence over that of the 'common man', all the more so since the scientist is also a common man. Quentin Skinner was no doubt right when pointing out that the use of the term 'democracy' is twofold: it is both a denotation and an evaluation. We use these twin concepts in two ways: first, to gather a set of empirical characteristics and to classify an object endowed with these characteristics (or some of them, and which ones?); second, to engage in a speech-act involving an evaluative assessment of the object (Skinner 1973). It might not be the 'plague' that Skinner seemed to think it is, yet we should keep in mind that democracy is not some kind of good and self-evident order that emerges from the failures of authoritarian regimes, like Minerva from Jupiter's thigh (a recent version of the Enlightenment and Whig outlook).[2] Democracy can be seen as 'problem-solving', but is first and foremost 'problem-raising', as even a cursory reading of Tocqueville and Schumpeter, among many others, will remind us. Actually, democracy is not a 'natural' regime, but a sophisticated artefact the transition to which should never be taken for granted and whose conditions should be scrutinized regardless of what we wish as citizens or of what the people committed to a specific endeavour (deemed 'democratic') might believe, and lead us to believe. 'Waves' of democratization are not like the waves of the sea: they break more easily and the undertow is even more powerful and less predictable. Arab public opinion is sometimes acutely aware of that phenomenon when it chides the rulers and their intellectuals for justifying a facade democracy *(dimuqratiyya shikliyya)*, that is to say an authoritarian government masquerading as a 'people's democracy' embodied in personalist and/or single-party rule, or as a 'desert democracy' embodied in the tribal *majlis* system of consultation or rule subject to the guidance of a council of islamic jurists, to cite two familiar versions of the argument, respectively nationalist 'leftist' and traditionalist 'rightist': 'to each culture its democracy', which is nothing other than the adaptation of the 'naturalist argument' to the 'specificity' of societies and cultures.

We must try to avoid the traps of definitions that can be rejected for applying alien and ethnocentric standards (the standards merely varying with each scholar's ideological persuasion or social location), or for being so imbued with relativism that they encompass almost any regime. To avoid this danger, it is insufficient, however useful it may be, to look for what specific contenders actually mean when they advocate, or combat, 'democracy', and for what purpose; for the various positions and strategies are connected by the political scientist to different social, structural and situation variables within the framework of a general hypothesis, generally functionalist or marxist.[3] As the same contenders usually say different things – or say few things (I cannot remember any significant supporters of Latin American 'bureaucratic authoritarianism' caring to articulate his values, except law and order, 'national security', and anti-communism) – we are obliged to define 'from the outside' the regime, democratic or authoritarian, whose advent or failure we are endeavouring to predict or explain. We shall have to take into account the profound historical transformation of democratic concepts and practices (Dunn 1992) without putting comparative analysis in jeopardy by excess of 'conceptual stretching' (Sartori 1970). Our exercise will be both a deductive definition of abstract characters and an inductive interpretation of specific discourses and practices.

It might be relevant to start with a specific problem and then to move to a definition. Why, in the Arab world, are people who call themselves 'democrats' frightened by the possible coming to power of other people who are also fighting for 'democracy', even if it is an islamic one? Why do imaginary coalitions, potentially unified by the hatred, or distant contempt, for the prince (sometimes bureaucratic and military dictatorships, or single- or dominant-party rule, and sometimes traditional rulership) break down to the point that the democrats are terrified at the prospect of 'democracy killing democracy', and sometimes find themselves on the verge of throwing themselves into the 'hated' ruler's arms (or going into exile) rather than playing by the rules of 'pluralism' and majority rule? Why is no political pact thinkable, not between reformist rulers and moderate opponents (such pacts seem at times more likely, as the accepted practice of patron-client networks facilitates them at the risk of the participants being accused of getting 'bought off' by the rulers), but rather between people whose common opposition to the incumbents is an established fact? The situation looks somewhat like the French one in the 1960s and 1970s, when it was impossible to conceive of a stable alliance between communists and socialists, with the double difference that France's rightist rulers were not accused of being against democracy, while such is usually the case in all the Arab countries (with the usual exception of Lebanon and to a lesser extent of Egypt and Yemen); and secondly, there is no state playing the same role vis-à-vis the 'islamic democrats' as that played by the Soviet Union vis-à-vis the French Communist Party (there may be several candidates, say, Saudi Arabia or Iran, but this plurality still makes a big difference).

It is too easy to give the apparently obvious answer to that trivial enigma: 'islamic democrats' are not democrats at all and their 'radical' and 'revolutionary' views are no more democratic than those of their religiously and politically conservative counterparts with whom they share the same intellectual structure.[4] They are fighting with the single aim of imposing total control on society. A significant minority of them hold that there cannot be any accommodation, not only with 'godless rulers' but also with alien 'western democracy'. The West is seen as embodying a set of principles that Muslims should reject; first, ideas of people's sovereign will (contrary to God's sovereignty); second, parliaments 'legislating without reference to Allah' (contrary to the completeness and perfection of *shari'a*, the Quranic Law;[5] third, the equality of believers and non-believers on behalf of tolerance (thus ignoring the search for the good and the war against evil); fourth, equality between men and women, leading to the disintegration of Arab society and its penetration by the western virus; fifth, political pluralism, putting on an equal footing the true 'party of God' (the only occurrence, incidentally, where the term 'party' may legitimately be used) and the parties emanating from state-engineered political 'participation'; and finally, an objectionable concept of majority rule based on the false idea that issues of right and justice can be quantified and that greater numbers of votes can be translated into greater moral positions.[6] The point is well taken, and it may be that the only Arab democrats are those resembling the average western scholar of liberal persuasion, which exposes them to the criticism of being out of tune with the people, in other words of being too elitist and not sufficiently democratic. The argument thus becomes circular, yet there is some way to go forward.

Both 'democrats' and 'islamic democrats'[7] can be used to exemplify the two core characteristics of democracy in contemporary political theory: they are contradictory to each other, yet equally essential when defining democracy. On the one hand, the 'islamic democrats' exemplify *populism*, while on the other hand the 'democrats' exemplify *constitutionalism*. They do not see themselves in these terms, which are used by political scientists as descriptive and stipulative concepts. Yet these two concepts capture rather adequately what the two groups are all about, even though they do not necessarily tell the whole story and leave out other important layers of meaning.

Populism is linked to the access of the masses – temporarily or, more frequently, permanently – to politics.[8] The urban bourgeoisie, landowners, tribe leaders, and palace officials are no longer the only *legitimate* contenders for political positions. Moreover, the state is legitimate only in so far as it enables every citizen to get his ('her' is more problematic) due. It is the duty of the state, based on the will of the people, to fight poverty and help the citizens.[9] The democratic state has duties because its citizens have rights, not because the prince is benevolent and god-fearing. Admittedly, most contemporary islamists don't believe in a state-run economy and nor do they expect salvation from economics, which differentiates them from marxists, from 'socialist bureaucratic' rulers (of the Ba'thist, nasserist, or Algerian Liberation species, a point made early, in 1962, by the Algerian association of *ulama*, or doctors) and even from the 'democrats', and brings them closer to their conservative counterparts. It is doubtful, however, that the social basis of the elites would induce them to take the easy way of 'traditional fundamentalism'. Indeed, it is not a likely prospect that they would demand very little of the state beyond the enforcement of divine law and the institution of the social order necessary for the believer to abide by the law in his everyday life. The well-to-do shopkeepers and perhaps the small land-holding peasant may go along, but what about the petty bureaucrats and the new urban underclass? It is more plausible that the legitimacy of the state and the government, or simply their durability, would depend on the volume of resources allocated to mobilized (or mobilizable) social groups: collective goods, consumption goods, jobs, housing, means of production and reproduction, access to entitlements and, finally, rights to make choices. These expectations entail demands for political participation in order to make sure that the rulers take care of their constituency. As resources are never fairly allocated, and as society is never fully incorporated into the state, the rulers and their institutions and norms are simultaneously eyed suspiciously and subject to continuous demand pressures. Hence the two guiding principles of populism: first, the will of the people to be identified with justice and morality prevails over any institutional norm; and second, the leaders are good only to the extent they are directly related to the people, over and above the intermediary elites (intellectuals, experts, technocrats).[10] It does not follow that the islamist figure of populism is the natural offspring of 'popular Islam' whose longstanding persistence is common knowledge (Gaffney 1992). Like their nationalist predecessors, his ideological bearers strive to capture the social base of popular Islam whilst fighting off its supposed archaism and particularism (Babeair 1990). Organization and hierarchy are not neglected in practice; they are in fact extensively utilized, but are always justified as the necessary expression of the organic unity of the people. So representation is both required and despised because it can always be manipulated by the 'elites'. Likewise, populism is both the politicization of everything, as it stems from a mass involvement in politics and an attempt to change society through politics (understood as a quest for cultural revolution or regeneration and not as the routinized management of public affairs), and the rejection of factional politics since the minority can be only blind or alien to the community.

Constitutionalism refers to the 'rule of law' protecting specific spheres of life against arbitrary power, making possible a competition between plurality of values and interests as well as a polyarchic compromise between strategic elites more or less representative of important social demands. Constitutionalism is closely allied to the notions of pluralism and limited government (Friedrich 1950 & 1968; Sartori 1962; Elster & Slagstad 1988), which are themselves related to the notions of divided society and evolutive society: not only must society be protected against the rulers but individuals must be protected against society itself to protect their learning capacity and their ability to rectify their mistakes: 'to preserve voluntariness, voluntariness must itself be restricted' (Holmes 1988, 239). 'The true institutional enemy of constitutionalism is the state, as its true cultural enemy is ideology' (Arjomand 1992, 79). Constitutionalism requires less discussion than populism since it has long been closely associated with the notion of a liberal republic in which a limited set of players recognize that the rules of the game are more important and deserve more respect than their own specific interests as players: as long as the relevant political forces act as though they are convinced they would lose less in losing while abiding by the rules than in winning by violating them, constitutionalism is safe. Such an outlook implies, in turn, that the 'winners' do not take all and that the 'losers' still keep a significant amount of rights and assets – or 'trumps', so to speak – and thus stand a fair chance of winning, or at least participating meaningfully, in the next contest. For the game to be played out smoothly, cleavages must not be so deep that the plurality of civil and political associations limit politicization, or expand it to the point that it cannot be kept under control (Sartori 1968a).

Why should constitutionalism be an essential dimension of democracy? And should the concept of constitutional government be used as a synonym for plural democracy or polyarchy? (Dahl 1971) The usual answer is: first, that democracy requires governmental accountability (if not, what would the people 'rule'?) and accountability requires the rulers to be accountable not on their own terms but according to rules they are not at liberty to change at will; and, second, that democracy requires free, non-violent and regularly repeated competition between groups organized to gain power, as well as participation of all citizens in the choice of leaders and policies. A constitution is therefore needed to guarantee a fair competition and true and free participation since every player may be suspected of making and changing the rules to control participation or to gain a decisive advantage. And, finally, if there is no constitutional guarantee for the minority, 'the real world implication', as Giovanni Sartori puts it, 'is that a part of the people becomes a non-people, an excluded part' (Sartori 1987, 32), which mutilates the population and thus destroys the very basis of democracy.

But those classical arguments, however well-grounded, do not go far enough since the basic issue – both in the Arab world and elsewhere – is not about the legitimacy of competition and accountability, nor even about the right to disagree, but about what one is allowed to compete for and disagree about. Which brings us to the question of 'we, the people'. Is it a community held together by some morally based identity (or 'authenticity', *asala*, derived from a cultural and religious patrimony, *turath*), from which no moral exit is thinkable? Or is it a collection of individuals eligible for new contractually based identities?[11] A watershed separates communitarians from liberals (Walzer 1990, 15–16), as well as populists from constitutionalists. For the latter, freedom consists in escaping from groups and forming new groups; for the former, freedom is to achieve 'identity of characters with his fellows', that is to say 'not to be different or to change' (MacRae 1967, 160). As an Egyptian philosopher put it in an eulogy, now rather forgotten, of the Iranian revolution: '*Tawhid* (God's unity) is a process of unification in the future of something revealed and accomplished in the past. It means freedom of thought, rejection of fear, the end of hypocrisy and of dual personality. "God is great" means the collapse of despotism' (Hanafi 1982). So 'freedom' is the populist freedom to re-enact something already enacted and brought to perfection in an ideal realm. Whatever the intrinsic value of that kind of argument may be,[12] it helps us to grasp its opposite, namely the connection between constitutionalism and democracy. Without constitutionalism of some sort, democracy leaves the individual with no chance of escaping his (current/actual or ideal) community's social tyranny. 'The people' eats up the individual, while the opposite is never true. To come to that conclusion we have to admit that 'it is within the nature of democracy that no one's interest can be guaranteed' (Przeworski 1986, 59), which means that no interest, or value, can triumph forever, except the rules guaranteeing the possibility of new choices. If the substantial outcome of a democratic process is always uncertainty (meaning not only that the democratization may not succeed, but more importantly that the future is not written because only the strategic interaction of people can write it), then constitutionalism is the only way to give a limited chance to real people (populists and communitarians included), whereas populism leaves no chance to 'constitutionalists' and 'liberal' people. That does not mean that constitutionalism is democratic by itself, which is why it needs populism as a counterpoise to its elitist bias. We maintain only that it is an indispensable part of democracy.

The fact that both populism *and* constitutionalism are the specific components of democracy has no bearing on the fact that each of them may be an aspect of a variety of political structures and cultures. For example, a regime combining a chiliastic, or millenarian, ideology with authoritarian organization and practices may be imbued with a strong populist culture. Also, in a regime averse to mass enfranchisement and careful to restrict politics to a plurality of closed elites, a strong constitutionalism is likely to take root. The uniqueness of the democratic combination results from the contradiction opposing the two components, which makes it particularly fragile despite the formidable pull it may get from nationalism (since 'self-determination' is inherently democratic[13]) and from the provisional wane of authoritarian regimes. The analysis of the contextual conditions accounting for the phases of expansion and contraction of democracy is thus more delicate than it would appear at first glance, since social forces and sociological factors underlying and explaining democracy may not be the same depending on which component we are considering; we are looking not for the conditions of either populism or constitutionalism, but rather for the conditions of their combination. And it will not suffice to examine the constitution of a 'civil society' of some sort as the main explanatory variable. The concept of civil society indeed is a precious tool to help us fully comprehend a complex society of which democracy is a part (see Keane 1988 and Gellner 1991), and it may be usefully revisited and adapted to Arab cultural and intellectual paradigms or debates (Zghal 1991a; al-Alawi 1992 and Norton 1993). But we still have to look for other crucial elements, such as the requisites of, and the forces behind, a viable civil society. The third section of this chapter is devoted to setting forth the main theories that have been elaborated to account for the making of democracy and civil society. But we must first dispose of one particular argument that has marred scholarly debates and turned them into an ideological shambles: 'Arab exceptionalism'.

An Arab exceptionalism?

Is the Arab world 'out of step with history' (Heller 1990) and immune to the trends affecting other parts of the world? A recent survey on democracy in developing countries excludes most of the islamic world and all the Arab world because those countries 'generally lack previous democratic experience and most appear to have little prospect of transition even to semi-democracy'. The authors assert that 'democracy is the only model of government with any broad ideological legitimacy and appeal in the world today' (a nice example of an empirical statement, plausible but disputable, utilized as an implicitly normative one about democracy as a law of nature) with the exception of 'that large portions of the world from Indonesia to West Africa where Islam is the major dominant religion' (Diamond et al. 1989, Preface). It is always permissible to reply that 'democracy' and 'democratization' deserve a more elastic conceptualization than they often receive in studies using an excessively elitist, liberal and western approach,[14] and that the core of democracy is the involvement of 'average people' and the 'many ties between leaders and mass public' (Levine 1990, 385 criticizing O'Donnell et al. 1986). Which brings us back to first base; democracy as an essentially contested concept. It is also possible, and more accurate, to suggest that democracy may come in bits and pieces (Sklar 1987). The following examples, however, are mine: in some countries, competitive elections without any decisive influence on the government (as in Morocco, Kuwait before 1990, and Jordan, see Eickelman 1986 and Layne 1987, but on Egypt see Iman Farag's stern assessment, Farag 1991); in other countries, flowering associations (as in Egypt, Bianchi 1989); and still elsewhere the incorporation of significant groups of elites into parliament or various advisory boards (as in Syria, Perthes 1990 and 1992a). But the trouble here is that by sorting out various 'democratic features' disconnected from one another, we give up any hope of putting together the core elements of a 'democratic regime' (not to mention a 'democratic society'), which incidentally allows autocratic rulers to parade as 'true democrats'. It may well be that 'real history' works precisely this way and that democracy makes headway under a mask, but the mere fact that, to paraphrase Marx, men make history without knowing the history they are making, should not exempt political scientists from trying to know what they are talking about.

Finally, it is always possible to argue on behalf of Islam by portraying it as the paramount democracy thanks to three concepts; *shura* (consultation), *ijtihad* (independent reasoning), and *ijma* (consensus). Moroccan thinkers add the concept *bay'a* (contractual acceptance of the ruler by tribes and urban corporations, al-Jabiri 1988), and specialists of 'oriental empires' emphasize the significant degree of autonomy enjoyed by diverse communities endowed with 'unexpected democratic' features (Springborg 1987). It is thus not far-fetched to claim that 'Islamic political thought is rescued from the charge of autocracy by the need of the rulers to consult widely and to govern on the basis of consensus' (Esposito & Piscatori 1991, citing Asad 1980). It is also true that 'the exertions of some Muslim writers in devising a theory of islamic democracy, or in demonstrating the democratic temper of Islam, cannot be dismissed as an unfounded and desperate presentation of Islam' (Enayat 1982, 120). It is always a good polemical device to turn an essentialist and ahistorical argument against its exponents. This argument remains nonetheless ahistorical, and is thus devoid of any contextual substance. It says nothing – or at least no more than the major religious texts of the great religions and cosmogonies – about the problem of pluralism in a disenchanted world where the legitimacy of basic values does not depend on a given truth revealed to the believer but depends rather on the confrontation of equal members of the same political community who hold different opinions on those values and their implementation. In other words, most modernist Muslim thinkers, as well as contemporary theorists of democracy, simply avoid the problem of the connection, conflictual or not, between historical forms of 'Islam' and 'democracy' (Enayat 1982, 135).[15] As long as 'Islam' is not analysed within specific social contexts as a symbolic resource used to justify, condone, or blame specific institutions and behaviours,[16] it remains *to the political scientist*[17] something empty of social meaning, lending itself to variable interpretations.[18] Thus the retorts to the 'exceptionalist argument' are rather feeble. Be that as it may, most mainstream political scientists, while finding fault with the 'orientalists' (here chiefly the scholars studying the Arab area) for not making any contribution to the comparative study of democratization, still hold that the Arab countries are so unpromising in terms of democratic transitions that studying them – even as 'counter-cases to help validate or invalidate hypotheses about the success of democratic transitions elsewhere' – would be 'an unprofitable use of scarce academic resources' (Hudson 1990). This is a rather contradictory indictment, for how can we include Arab countries within a comparative global framework if we keep them out of the picture?

The 'exceptionalist argument' must be dealt with in a different way. We must recognize at the outset the value of the partial findings lending some support to the argument. True, there may have been three 'liberal waves' in the recent history of the Arab world; the nineteenth century 'liberal age' (Hourani 1967), the liberal era in Egypt, Iraq and Syria under the British and French protectorates, and the current erosion of national authoritarian regimes in Chadli Benjedid's Algeria, Ben Ali's Tunisia, and Husni Mubarak's Egypt (Salamé 1991a), or the opening of Jordan and Morocco (Ibrahim 1993). But Arab politics is still dominated by the dual image of traditional kingdoms fuelled by oil resources in the Arab peninsula with Yemen as an exception since oil was found there only recently and the regime is republican and partially constitutional (Hudson 1990 and 1991a; Ibrahim 1993) and of a *mukhabarat* (national security) state, which may be oil-rich like Iraq or Algeria or a state like Libya in a category of its own (Davis 1987). This type of state is an 'authoritarian-bureaucratic Leviathan whose stability derives more from fear than from legitimacy' and whose growth has been charted from the 1960s through the mid-1980s in terms of budget, numbers of employees, internal security capabilities and the like (Hudson 1991a). It has been put forward, more boldly, that the Arab states are distinguished by a particularly socio-political structure described as 'neo-patriarchy', an offspring of corrupted traditional patriarchy wedded to distorted modernity, the midwife (and the real cause) being continuous economic and cultural dependency (Sharabi 1988). According to Sharabi, neo-patriarchy's main attributes are: (i) social fragmentation, meaning that the family clan and religious or ethnic group, as opposed to the nation or civil society, constitutes the basis of social relations and organization; (ii) authoritarian organization in which all relations, from the micro-structure of the family to the macro-structure of the state, are characterized by domination, coercion, and paternalism as opposed to co-operation, mutual recognition and equality; (iii) absolutist paradigms, that is to say a closed, absolutist consciousness grounded in transcendence, metaphysics, revelation and closure rather than in difference, plurality, openness, and so on; (iv) ritualistic practices, or behaviour governed by ceremony, custom and ritual, rather than by spontaneity, creativity and innovation.

Mustapha Kamil El Sayyid has, more soberly, pinpointed the main 'dilemmas of democratization' in Arab countries (El Sayyid 1991). The first is the coincidence of the democratization process with an economic crisis. Harsh economic measures, though needed, are difficult to implement since the legitimacy of a democratic government does not depend only on the practice of democracy but above all on what the people get from the rulers. 'No representation without allocation' or 'what is representation for if there is nothing to allocate?' The second dilemma is the totalitarian bias of certain opposition groups, mainly the islamists, Aziz Al-Azmeh observes that 'these groups postulate that the accomplishment of democracy can only be signalled when an Islamic state is installed, thus making for the full correspondence of state and society', itself based on 'a sort of pre-established harmony, located in the proposition...universally stated by Islamist authors, that the Islamic order is primeval, in conformity with the predisposition of societies at all times and places, a sort of natural law, or even a cosmic order' (Al-Azmeh 1991c, 9, also 1991a and 1991b). Third, the exacerbation of inter-ethnic tensions in situations of political pluralism and majority rule within a nation-state. It might be added that it is precisely *because* of majority rule that political pluralism fails, and that cultural pluralism calls for another kind of democracy, which Lijphart has called 'consensual' (Lijphart 1984 and 1991). That is only sensible; the problem is that, in the kind of situation mentioned in the introduction to this chapter, in which confrontations involve either 'ethnies' or 'world views' and sometimes *both,* an enormous dose of civil virtue is required of the elites for them to accept the delicate balance of proportional representation and constitutional guarantees, unless they are convinced they have no other strategic choice. The other alternative would be quite mad, as in mutual assured destruction – no stalemate between opposing forces, no prospect of 'consensual democracy'. Lastly, international and regional politics are problems of their own. Not only did the Gulf War contribute to the weakening of the legitimacy of all Arab political regimes unable to defend their borders, to institute an effective collective security system, and to prevent 'foreign' (i.e. non-Arab) intervention, but it also exacerbated nationalism and deepened the cleavages between Arab regimes in a region where the interference of Arab brothers[19] in the 'national' political systems often takes place through patron-client networks, financial aid, racketeering, direct threats, secret police, and electronic surveillance devices – none of which could be said to be conducive to a democratic political process. A chord of fear has been struck in most of the Arab regimes more or less involved in the Gulf War, and the process of reform has been blocked almost everywhere, both in the traditional monarchies as well as in the authoritarian states (Salamé 1991b), with Algeria as the highly visible exception (at least until 12 January 1992).

It should be noted that these characteristics may be found elsewhere, the fourth being perhaps truly exceptional. If each of them has distinctly 'Arab', and sometimes 'islamic', connotations, most are not 'purely' Arab or islamic (need it be recalled that famous islamist authors such as the Egyptian Qutb and the Iranian Shariati were entranced by Alexis Carrel, a French Nobel Prize laureate in 1912, who was a supporter of fascist regimes in the 1930s? – Al-Azmeh 1991c). Their combination, however, makes an impressive history. It may be tempting to pile up arguments pertaining to different disciplines and periods to complete an apparently alluring picture. In order to emphasize the lack of political representation, for example, one could recall the traditional political weakness of the cities (Gellner 1981, 54) and point out that 'the classical *umma* lives under a divine law whose protector is the *umma* itself; the ruler, on the other hand, is neither the source nor the guarantee of the law; he is only the executive power. Thus the state becomes a superstructure with which the population does not identify itself' (Von Grunebaum 1962, 137). Or, to explain the failures of party pluralism, one could draw on a whole range of anthropological research. Richard Antoun, for example, examined the notion of *hizb* ('party' or 'faction') as a term of religious, moral and political reference by analysing the weekly sermons of a Muslim preacher in a comparative perspective. Noting a pattern of contradiction in the overlap of its secular and religious force, Antoun argues, not surprisingly, that the term is evaluated negatively, and he identifies the persistence of a popular ethos that rejects partisan politics as represented by *hizb* in its modern denotation. Thus political pluralism is perceived as disruptive and culturally alien (Antoun 1989). To explain why 'citizens in Arab countries do not protest very much against the non-popular regimes under which they live', one careful historian of political thought stressed the dominance, throughout the last five centuries, of jurists and theologians whose primary concern has been less that the political community be well-governed than it merely continue to exist. Even those who praise democratic principles and call for popular rule 'have failed to consider how they may be brought about', since they have not addressed the central issues familiar to western political thought from Machiavelli onwards; not 'a speculation on what is the best regime as defined by some vision never known to have existed', but an inquiry into what really happens in the political arena and a reflection on how the citizens should direct their own actions accordingly (Butterworth 1980 and 1987), Arabs, then, may know how to play politics like everyone else, but they wouldn't know how to think about politics. They give precedence to the legitimacy of good government over prudence in the management of politics and the search for procedural devices guaranteeing that the most admirable aims are not achieved at excessive cost of freedom and toleration (Butterworth 1982 and 1992). This is not so derogatory as it might seem if we keep in mind that Leo Strauss wrote about the derailment of modern political theory since Machiavelli. Political Islam raises deeper problems, and challenges western political thought more concerned with safeguarding freedom than with providing for citizen virtue. This raises the question of whether moral improvement is the proper concern of government (Butterworth 1992, 36–7). Such a situation may have something to do with the relative weakness of public law and institutions as instruments of political and social regulation. As long as individuals are far more constrained in their daily lives by social conventions and time-honoured traditions than by political laws or regulations, that intellectual approach is not likely to change (Butterworth 1987, 110); no political thought without an efficient and accountable state, no democracy without regulation and taxation. Other explanations, more cultural or sociological, have insisted on the status of the law, viewed more as an instrument of submission or protest than as a means of regulation of political conflicts (Badie 1986 criticized by Zubaida 1989).

Many other examples could be cited, including the famous *summa divisio* between the two modes of domination, tribal and patrimonial, whose regional figures are the Khaldunian and Ottoman models (Gellner 1981). More recently, the late French sociologist Michel Seurat explained the Syrian case by using Ibn Khaldun's concept of *asabiyya* (group feeling): 'The game consists of keeping one's own confessional cohesion (one's *asabiyya*) by having the others forget theirs under the pressure of the ideology of nation-building, which implies that everybody gives up his own difference as a condition of the achievement of equality for all in the civil society. In such a game, the "majority" is always defeated since it is defined by a lack of group feeling' (Seurat 1989, 31).

Each of the above points has been carefully researched, yet the conclusions we are invited to draw – though not always by the authors themselves – are not altogether convincing. It is not only that one can find counter-arguments by drawing on other, or the same, disciplines (particularly, and not surprisingly, economics and political economy, Richards & Waterbury 1990, but also political science, Binder 1988, Zubaida 1989, sociology, Farsoun 1988, and history, Hourani 1981 and Lapidus 1987); or that the Arab regimes are so diverse and Islam so multiple that even such widespread phenomena as islamic revivals or radical islams cannot lend themselves to a single interpretation[20] or be reduced to a single model, all the more so as people react to specific political contexts (Hudson 1980) and within complex political traditions (see the example of an influential Tunisian leader, Zghal 1991b). It is rather that, for a case to be truly 'exceptional', its history must be unique, not likely to change, and it must 'confirm the law of the universal path towards democratization'. It cannot be doubted that the history of the Arab world is unique (if there is indeed such a thing as 'one' history of 'one' world). But the two other conditions can be met only by some trick of our imagination. There are already enough reasons for being cautious about the prospects for democracy in the region without getting overburdened by dubious hypotheses.

It must be said, however, that there is at least one theory that accounts for an Arab – or, in fact, Muslim – exceptionalism while not emphasizing Islam's essential otherness.[21] Ernest Gellner, far from regarding Islam as a unique religious type, treats it as similar to other religions, in particular with respect to the contrast between its two social forms, anonymous-centralized and communal (which leads to the Humean conflict between 'enthusiasm' and 'priests of communalism'). Gellner stressed the historical uniqueness of Islam by insisting on the interplay of functional and sequential processes (Gellner 1981 and 1991).[22] The story he tells goes something like this; in a traditional islamic society with a relatively stable and complex system of ascribed social roles, the two social forms of religion, while by no means perpetually locked in overt conflict, were in a latent tension which from time to time could erupt with force. The anonymous-centralized form with its unitarian, individualistic, puritanical, magic-free, nomocratic and scripturalist features was impersonated by literate and qualified urban scholars, legitimizing and challenging in turn the rulers of the central states on behalf of a law offering a universal (trans-ethnic and trans-polity) salvation to individuals. The communal form, with its saint cults and religious orders, centered on shrine and festival and magical practices, and provided the semi-autonomous rural groups with a 'Durkheimian religion' mirroring the social order and confirming the local society without transcending it. Revivalism – the re-affirmation of the central, unitarian and universal values exemplified by the first social form – was more suited to the rise of the new social movements. But those movements were never able to achieve a permanent and definitive success because of the resistance of the communal religion, which was better-suited to the needs of rural society and much of urban society. Yet both forms were necessary to societies needing 'to identify with a unitarian scripturalist transcendent world religion', and at the same time 'to evade its requirements and live by a socially incarnate, customary and communal one' (Gellner 1991, 508).

In modern conditions, marked both by an erosion of communal units and all-encompassing collectivities and by a highly unstable and mobile system of modern specialized occupations that presuppose literacy and the ability to communicate in a context-free code, the 'swing of the pendulum' between the two religious forms is likely to come to an end and 'revivalism can achieve a definitive and lasting success'. The high tradition of the anonymous centralized and egalitarian religion has won over the folk and low tradition of the communal religion since it meets the same functional needs as nationalism elsewhere; a literate, school-acquired high culture is a man's most important possession, for it – and not any participation in restrictive rites – accords him *droit de cité*. Thus nationalism provides the ability to enter the modern world of capitalist societies and international relations. Better still, nationalism and fundamentalism may go hand in hand[23] since Islam enables Muslims to escape the familiar dilemma of many Third World nationalists confronted with colonial powers and more advanced industrial nations; either 'westernization' (i.e. the search for international equality at the humiliating cost of endorsing the foreigner as a valid model) or some sort of populist romanticism that idealizes the alleged virtues of a folk culture at the cost of never achieving any progress towards modernization. Islam, as a high culture, is both modern (unitarian, magic-free, individualistic, puritan, scripturalist, with a rule-ethnic) and genuinely indigenous, as 'the re-affirmation of High Islam does indeed require the repudiation of folk practices, but in the same name, not of some extraneous ideology, but of one which was always most revered locally!' (Gellner 1991, 509 and 1981, 68).

Where does all this leave us, so far as the future of democracy is concerned?[24] The answer is surprisingly harsh: nowhere. The victory of high Islam has conspicuously failed to lead to any kind of civil society. On the contrary, it has led to either a co-existence of the sacralization of daily life in the name of a high religious moralism and a kind of political cynicism triggered by a 'state' that is nothing more than a source of conflict between rival patronage networks and personal loyalties; or a search for 'democracy' understood as a fusion of secular sovereignty and absolute Truth – what Bassam Tibi aptly calls the 'repoliticization of the sacred' (Tibi 1990, 123). Actually, the term 'politicization' would be more apposite since strictly speaking this is a new phenomenon, contemporary with the emergence of the state and modern politics on a national scale. The consensus over the 'religion of the state' has not worked out a social compass pointing at liberal constitutionalism, the most plausible reason being that there has been no *stalemate* between puritan enthusiasm and priestly superstition. Whereas the puritan Protestants – who according to Hume were inimical to liberty – were forced, when partially but not wholly defeated, to abandon the aspiration of imposing that absolute truth on the entire society, in Islam the direct transition from communal priests to universalistic unitarian enthusiasts has not favoured the emergence of a civil society, all the more so as the enthusiasts tend to capture the deepest social grievances and resentments. Here perhaps has been the reason why, despite the similarities in the structures and orientations of islamist and calvinist belief systems (Goldberg 1991), one may doubt that islamism, in the historical sense where it operates, may lead to a civil society whose basic value is that nobody possesses the 'right answer' (Shils 1991).

This may be too parsimonious an explanation of such a complex and variegated process, and it would be tempting to dismiss it outright for its excessive simplification. Tempting but wrong, for Gellner's account helps us to identify two basic features of the sociological analyses of the democratization process, namely the functional and the strategic. The reference to the functional needs met by the two social forms of religions illustrates the first feature. The 'stalemate thesis' illustrates the second (since a situation of stalemate calls for strategic innovation of relevant actors). So Gellner's story – if it is the story of an 'exception' – far from removing the Arab world from the mainstream of democratization studies, should bring it back in. Indeed, are we not witnessing today various kind of stalemates, ranging from relatively peaceful equilibriums to protracted or open civil wars? Endeavours to look for their functional explanations, to explore the possible outcomes to which their social and political conditions may lead, and to reflect on the prospects for democracy, must be undertaken as urgently in the Arab world as elsewhere, exception or no exception.

Some theories of democratization applied to the Arab world

At this point we can consider three theories from the starting point of the definition of democracy provided in the first section of this chapter, leaving aside 'democracy' viewed as a total remoulding of the social fabric in accordance with what authentic people really want. We can call these three theories, in order to emphasize the main feature of each: 'rational strategic', 'functional', and 'systemic'. The first sees democracy as the output of social interactions between groups or individuals with interests and values that they try to further by making choices and pursuing strategies. The second theory is more macrosociological, seeing democracy as a possible consequence of functional requisites and structural preconditions. Over and above the general theories of modernization, the class approach will be dealt with as a specific approach among the various types of explanations based on political economy (Leca 1988a). According to the third theory, democracy is viewed as a system of exchange, possibly conditioned by the international system in which it is embedded. The functional and systemic theories have in common that they both allow for the intervention of specific policies and choices.

Hirschman's 'tunnel effect' provides an excellent example and a good starting point for the 'rational strategic' thesis (Hirschman 1973). Picture two trains going in the same direction but blocked in a tunnel on two parallel tracks; if the people in the train whose carriages are not moving see the carriages of the other train start moving in the right direction, they may realize that something is going on and thus anticipate that they, too, will start moving soon. In other words, that bit of information brings about a gratification which annihilates, or suspends, envy. This is all the more so as the passengers left behind have a feeling of empathy towards people who are ahead, such as after a successful national revolution or a liberation war. Hirschman stresses this point, emphasizing that 'the most homogenizing agent is perhaps an intensive historical experience that has been shared by all members of the group'. So the rising expectations which usually come with the introduction of mass politics may be curbed and tamed provided that, firstly, the first train does not move too fast, and, secondly, that the second train starts moving, too, and does not slow down and include a growing number of 'passengers'. The *first* tunnel effect could have paved the way for a first wave of democratization from above in the 1950s and 1960s in Egypt, Syria, Algeria, Tunisia – not to mention the attempted bourgeois liberalization of the 1930s in Egypt and Syria – had the prevalent nationalist mood not favoured authoritarian systems of mobilization under the guidance of the army-bureaucracy-party trio. But much more important for our problem is the *second* tunnel effect, occurring as a result of worsening economic conditions suffered by people whose numbers and expectations have increased tremendously. As Hirschman puts it: 'The tolerance for inequality may decline simply because those who are excluded from advances no longer perceive such exclusion as temporary bad luck but as an inevitable or even calculated effect of the "system"'. If, after gaining speed for a while, the overcrowded second train slows down or stops, regardless of what happens to the first train, the passengers are likely to change their anticipations and to shift from empathy and trust to envy and suspicion. The more centralized and bureaucratized the incumbent political system is, the more likely it is to be rejected (Leca 1990, on Algeria).

That may be a blessing in disguise, since the rulers do not seem to have any choice other than proposing or accepting a 'democratic bargain' aimed at opening up the political process. By granting new elites some access to power, the rulers try to retain legitimacy by convincing the passengers on the second train that it is still worth hoping against the odds for a future improvement of their condition, and convincing those on the first train that they will have to accept some sacrifices at the very moment a sizeable number of them do not feel so privileged. Such a bargain would be modelled on the local conditions and historical patterns specific to each country; is it unthinkable, for instance, that in Egypt 'the state will exchange some of its autonomy in decision-making for access to some of the abundant resources held by its citizens'? (Springborg 1989, quoted by Hudson 1991). On the other hand, the Gulf regimes may have to cope with the second tunnel effect, which in their case would be the only one since the oil resources and the traditional patrimonial system have rendered the first irrelevant; facing tight financial conditions, they could have difficulty in covering their investment budget and, in some cases, even their current expenditures (Luciani 1992). In such a situation, in which increasing resources are diverted to defence spending, the rulers might have to trade political liberties for fewer economic handouts (Abd El Khalek 1991). But there are other ways of handling the problem; a moderate pace of industrialization benefiting a set of merchant families, bound together by 'traditional' or regional ties and linked to the allocation state, is not likely to favour demands for more formal political participation (Luciani 1990, on Saudi Arabia). In the post-Gulf War period, the control over industrial, and not merely financial, assets abroad through integrated oil companies operating downstream may be 'an excellent insurance policy against domestic enemies', rendering democratization measures less germane, at least in the short run (Luciani 1992). Another problem, illustrated by the cases of Algeria and Tunisia, is not the difficulty in working out a bargain between conflicting symbols, as it has been argued above, but that the parties are manifold and hence what is likely to satisfy one may antagonize the others. To give more leeway to islamist activists would threaten the rulers and the democratic or 'secular' minorities; and to recognize human rights and political pluralism may be of little consequence in the eyes of the islamists. Finally, as Michael Hudson, and common sense, remind us, the same forces that unleash social upsurges and are conducive to mass mobilization – thus leading to democratic bargaining as a much-needed solution – could prove to be a hindrance to that very solution since they may also prevent stable democratic practices from taking root (Hudson 1991). Instead of an exercise in the 'political economy of patience' – as Offe (1991) characterized Hirschman's approach – achieved through a control of the temporal structure of the process leading to a mutual state-market economy-democracy reinforcement, we may be faced with the sociological impossibility of having both economic reforms (price and property) and political reforms (constitutional guarantees and widening of participation), however complementary they may look from an abstract logical point of view. In the real world the opposite effects can be cumulative; economic and political reforms are both blocked, as they are in Algeria (Leca & Leveau 1993).

Hence the case for possible confrontation. The most frequent interpretation of islamic – or islamist – protest movements is that secular nationalism supported by the new strata (new middle-class intellectuals and the working class) is no longer a dominant force, and islamic ideology offers serious competition as it both recuperates and dialectically expresses a desire for autonomy from foreign imperialism, which is felt as a yoke of cultural aggression and material exploitations; a revolt against the state, which is seen as manipulative, corrupt and corrupting; and an affirmation of a personal and collective identity, a merging again of the spheres that bourgeois society separates (public/private, religious/political, economic/moral). This ideology generally takes hold in the small towns, among those of a rural background, and also among relatively well-educated and politically informed young people living in areas of rapid urbanization. These groups, however, are not the only ones to use such language. All islamic intellectuals do not come from the periphery (see, for example, Kepel & Richard 1989 and, on Shi'ism, Cole & Keddie 1986) but the relative importance of peripheral groups gives their discourse a specific function of 'vindication of frustration' (Roy 1992, 79), thus transforming their self-deprecation into self-esteem. Necessity is made virtue.

This contemporary islamism, whatever its social content – for example, whether or not it is favourable or hostile to the private ownership of the means of production – has certain characteristic traits; for example, an all-embracing ideology, egalitarian in the abstract and anti-individualist in practice, whose religious code is its very root source and not simply an instrument used for political ends. Such a common experience of resentment and frustration – in the economic and intellectual spheres, giving two homothetic social categories – could be considered as progressive (Davis 1984) or, conversely, as a branch of the fascist family tree (Arjomand 1984b), which is by no means a contradiction in terms. It does however form a relatively identifiable social unit through its symbolic content and by its organization. It rejects partisan or institutional intermediaries and favours recruitment via family bonds or personal contact in loosely organized and often very fragmented groupings. This does not prevent the unleashing of vast social movements making urgent material demands – frequently in the form of protests against rising food prices directed against close-at-hand symbols of corruption such as 'western' shops and bourgeois districts – in the name of a religious code of justice calling for an islamic 'moral economy' (Burke 1986).[26]

These movements are sometimes described as the revolt of the petty bourgeoisie (Fischer 1982). According to this interpretation, members of the educated lower-middle-class seek to ascribe a meaning to their fears and grievances by searching for a 'sameness' and homogeneity of some sort which will provide society with a solid moral and material armour to shield them against outside aggression. This is likely true in certain specific cases. But the essential point is elsewhere; the redistributive state, with its ever-increasing social weight, has created the structural conditions that lead to a calling into question of its own power as well as that of the elites and the groups and classes who seem to benefit the most from these conditions. When there are no longer sufficient resources to satisfy those expecting a minimal gratification (the impoverished peasantry, the urban sub-proletariat, unemployed skilled workers, those with decreasing spending power), the state becomes the target of manifold discontent which no class ideology can express. Thus the excluded of various classes reject the system that no longer has the means to integrate them into the allocation process.

But this is too big a picture, and the 'democratic bargain' versus 'total confrontation' dichotomy is too rigid for a theory whose basic tenet is to pay close attention to the processes involving strategic actors able to play various games according to the resources supplied by ideological and organizational legacies as well as contextual opportunities and constraints. In Algeria, for example, I would argue that the gains achieved by the Islamic Salvation Front have more to do with the persistence of the dual image of the Association of Ulama and of the Parti du Peuple Algérien than with the complete rejection of organizational politics. The outcome of the game depends on three main variables: (i) the non-negotiable parts of the bargain (what the key actors have determined *not* to put on the bargaining table); (ii) the actual opportunities offered to groups and individuals by the social, economic and political contexts; (iii) the trust placed in the openings offered by the different parties. If coercive repression 'succeeds' in convincing oppositional groups that nothing is to be achieved through total confrontation and manages to insulate 'radical militants' from their social base while extending social and political advantages to the islamist social movements' supporters, it is always possible to move from total confrontation to an updated democratic bargain. Still, it can be wondered whether such a prospect is but the daydream of the advocates of 'democratization from above'.

To go beyond these rough estimates would require for each political unit a much more careful assessment of key actors, goals, preference distributions, thresholds, processes of coalition-building, and perceptions of costs and probabilities of success (Collier & Norden 1992). We will return to these issues in our conclusion.

The second thesis will be treated more briefly since it brings us back to basics: that the functional need for the emergence of an autonomous class structure paves the way for democratic politics. This theory, itself part and parcel of a more general approach based on political economy, uses the usual class-based explanations in reverse; instead of emphasizing the class conditions that account for authoritarianism, patrimonialism or clientelism (see examples provided in Leca 1988a, 27–32, and in the less systematic but more balanced essay by al-Naqeeb 1991), the class-based democratization approach is cast in the same mould as the familiar marxist theory of the French 'bourgeois' revolution. It is usually applied to the evolution of the 'socialist authoritarian states' previously based on a 'social compromise' fuelled by oil revenues; these oil revenues and access to foreign loans permit the generalization of salaried employment, and the reinforcement of managerial and bureacratic activities but without any corresponding creation of value. When a distribution crisis, coupled with the ideological collapse of a socialist economy, looms large on the horizon, the state must either retreat or give some leeway to the private sector. This may lead to political democratization in order to meet the demands of both the new businessmen and the exploited classes.

This logic is implicitly bound to the fact that the creation of classes leads to class action, which is led by groups politically identifying themselves in terms of class and demanding political autonomy vis-à-vis the state. Thus, along with the economic market opened up by the establishment of a private sector, there should be a corresponding political market opened up by the establishment of class groups or factions. I have discussed such an hypothesis elsewhere (Leca 1988b), and I still maintain that it is not supported by any conclusive empirical evidence, although the relevant literature is expanding (Harik & Sullivan 1993; Niblock & Murphy 1993; Suleiman & Waterbury 1990). A private sector growing up in the shadow of the state – and thanks to the public sector – certainly has an interest in gaining freedom of economic action, more access to credit and fiscal advantages, and the freedom of cross-border traffic. But why should it have to undertake open political action when it can try to obtain all this at less cost to itself by playing the more discrete game of bureaucratic and palace politics dominated by informal networks of family, regional, and factional solidarity?

It is true that the private sector can, by virtue of its very existence, provoke class conflict and drive the workers and the excluded to demand freedom of political action which the bourgeoisie itself may not need. But the structural conditions for such class mobilization exist neither in the agrarian nor the industrial sectors (given the rural classes' composition and the size of private enterprises in industry). Moreover, like the bourgeoisie the workers also have their demands (jobs, housing, subsidized low-price consumer goods, free medicine, educational opportunities), which are likewise gained not through any autonomous politicization but through bureaucratic and palace politics, or sometimes through local strikes or riots in towns. The same could be said of the middle classes' liberal role prognosticated by Halpern some 30 years ago (Halpern 1963). It has been noted that they 'may want direct responsibility for governance, not merely cooptation by praetorians and authoritarians', but that 'there is in any case no reason to expect them to be committed liberals' because 'authoritarianism of various kinds may find favour with them as long as they have a meaningful role in it'. This is all the more true as the middle classes can be kept under control by a strong military and police apparatus (Richards & Waterbury 1990, 437).

The notion that class structure, observed from the outside (that is, without reference to specific social and historical contexts) might by virtue of simply existing in the body politic destabilize populist-authoritarian regimes, is related to the bourgeois society paradigm (erroneous in my view), whereby economic and social relationships are mediated by citizenship and represented by political relations in the public arena. In a society where social and economic relations are determined by political ones, and where the citizen does not enjoy autonomous political rights but only the possibility of putting pressure on the bureaucracy through membership in a community or power group, it is not certain that the class structure would bind the regime's roots, however strong international constraints might be and regardless of the resentment they may create or the strategies (accommodation or confrontation) they may give rise to. In fact, behind the embourgoisement and the apparent homogeneity of the productive private sector there is a fragmented and heterogeneous social structure – with a weak industrial bourgeoisie and weak working classes, plus a highly stratified middle class the members of which occupy several class positions – which favours a scattered social consciousness and mediating institutions which 'instead of being the mechanism for mobilizing the people and acting as centers for checking the authority of the State have become a means of control of the people by the State' (Farsoun 1988, 231). Iraq is a good case in point, for the private capital that has flourished in that country over the past 20 years has remained subordinate to and dependent on the state. In fact, the social basis of power, in a rentier state in general and in Iraq in particular, remains very narrow. The channels of access to resources do not pass through the public sphere, but rather through personal relationships with an elite which determines how resources will be allocated. It seems, then, that unless there is a basic change in the political structure, even a renewed economic liberalization would not be able to bring about the rapid emergence of an entrepreneurial middle class that was independent of the state (on Iraq, see Sluglett & Farouk-Sluglett 1990 and Farouk-Sluglett 1991). Curiously enough, though with compelling reasons, the same line of argument has been applied to the modernization of traditional oil monarchies (Luciani 1990 and 1992).

From this point of view, the emergence of the private sector has a triple social significance, over and above the necessity for increased production (always a reason to justify a productive, non-parasitic, private sector). It is, first of all, the strategy for advancement of an upper-middle-class associated with the state. It is also, perhaps, an expression of the state's wish to indemnify itself by putting in place intermediate targets for social protest movements. But this renders the social structure and social inequalities more visible. The 'statification' (in French, *étatisation*) of society and the privatization of the state (Camau 1984) are criticized together. The private sector, instead of coming to the aid of the authoritarian state, can in this way make it more fragile. Yet this does not provide sufficient evidence for viewing its development as a prodrome of democratization.

The functional theory of democratization has so far been exposed as logically and empirically faulty. There is, however, a modest, and more justifiable, variant: for the market to work, the rule of law is necessary, and only democracy can sustain and strengthen it (Corm 1993; Richards 1993). It is an instrumental theory which makes an autonomous political participation a necessary tool for building up Arab capitalism, yet it does not predict that things will happen that way. If it did, it would presuppose that the actors *understand* that such a move is necessary and act accordingly, and by doing so prove the very necessity of democratization. Such an argument confuses the 'necessity' pointed out by the social scientist (as a topical or desirable process) with the 'necessity' experienced by the agents themselves. What the social scientist may find necessary is not predictable, nor even probable, as long as the functional requisites he has isolated are not vindicated by actual decisions observed in the actors' behaviour.

The third, systemic theory, could be summarized by the classic formula, slightly modified here: 'No representation without taxation' (Huntington 1991, 65). If a government does not need its population's resources to carry on its job, whatever it may be, a democratization process is unlikely. Thus there is link between extraction of resources and democracy in a modern state; if the government is powerful and ruthless enough to extract resources by sheer force, or if it does not need to resort to that device, no actual process of conflict or (more or less) balanced exchange can prepare the way for a democratic, or institutional representative, regime.[27] As Peter von Sivers puts it: 'In a development process under the auspices of autonomous governments[28] (that is, governments based on oil revenues, external grants, foreign aid and low taxes) rulers set as the benevolent (?) [*sic*] autocrats without needing the consent of their populations. As long as the price of oil stays moderately high, those rulers do not need to ask for high taxes and thereby can largely dispense with the participation of the population' (von Sivers 1991).

A relevant counter-example could, according to Dankwart Rustow, be provided by Turkey. His argument is twofold: first, the political parties have had increasingly to act according to the logic of democratic competition since they have to get votes and thus represent interests, or at least promise services; and second, the political divisions have been between material interests, not between ethnic or cultural groups, and 'those divisions have been attenuated by the processes of economic devèlopment and social mobility which democracy itself has done so much to accelerate' (Rustow 1988). In a comparable vein, albeit dissimilar and distinctly less optimistic, John Waterbury has shown how, in a period of structural adjustment and export-led growth, a 'centre-right coalition' may enable a government to survive politically by relying on one-third of the electorate (Waterbury 1992). The process he describes, however uncertain and fragile, bears witness to the mediation and management of conflict of interests through a complex combination of state patronage, policy making, and electoral politics involving parties reflecting different economic interests. It is only fair to recall that Waterbury pays much more attention to the use of public expenditures to promote exports and maintain a winning electoral coalition rather than to the level of resources extracted through the tax system. But we may safely consider these issues as two sides of the same coin.[29] Besides, the whole process evolves in a regime in which, despite authoritarian coups, moderately free and pluralist elections and some kind of part system have been for some time part of the political routine. Finally, this arrangement, which may collapse at any moment, centres on a core combination (the 'centre-right coalition') supporting private property, private enterprise, and state intervention in the economy, but not political liberalism, or at least not obviously so. Even as a counter-example, the Turkish case is not quite convincing; and it would be all the more hazardous to treat it as one with respect, say, to Algeria or Tunisia.

If most of the 'autonomous governments' have a low or non-tax base while investing in infrastructures, industries, education and health, they possess the means of postponing accountability as long as there are enough other resources; but as soon as they are burdened with expenditures no longer covered by these resources, 'structural adjustment' looms large; subsidies will have to be decreased as well as taxes on international trade and transactions. A sizeable part of the population will suffer more while being expected to contribute more to public resources through direct taxation. Only Turkey, and to a lesser extent Syria, seem to have fully practised this method of structural adjustment, and it is only in these countries that the direct-tax share of government resources has risen, thus predicting (if the theory is accurate) a moderate weakening of government autonomy (von Sivers 1991, 22–3; von Sivers' estimates for Syria are not confirmed by Ayubi 1993 and Hinnebusch 1993). The other governments have been reluctant to adopt full-fledged policies of structural adjustment since they would lose their autonomy and therefore their capacity to keep their populations under control. As is often the case, the constraints of temporal sequences contradict the logical requirements of abstract process: the necessity of accountability may require the democratization of the political system, but democracy, by making the governments accountable, also renders them more vulnerable and hence unable to keep a firm enough grip on the process in order to facilitate a peaceful transition to democracy. We thus end up with the vicious circle which we stressed at the outset: rulers, feeling vulnerable, will be tempted to postpone or block a process which, though in purely abstract terms would make the government both less vulnerable and more accountable, would in fact put the current rulers and any government in jeopardy. Only legitimate rulers can afford to run the risk of a democratic process required by structural adjustment: since groups opposing an autonomous government cannot act as legitimate 'interest groups' entitled to make demands in exchange for what they give to the government, they have to claim a higher legitimacy and to proclaim the government's illegitimacy in order to escape the impotence and clientelization of *l'opposition de Sa Majesté*. Hence the relevance of Islam as a global ideology of protest and the continuous struggle for the political use of this central resource.

This last point is worth underscoring: the third theory seems to explain fairly well why the radical islamists demand, in von Sivers' terms, 'full cultural monism', while most of the governments insist on a 'minimal cultural pluralism'. The struggle over cultural monism is an essential ingredient of the struggle for legitimacy in systems where the competition of interests is not sufficient to lay the foundation of the political competition. For governments, a modicum of cultural pluralism is a way of downgrading powerful oppositional groups by denying their claim to the monopoly of religious legitimacy, just as the opposite holds true for the islamists, who portray the government as sheer naked force and cannot grant it even a scrap of religious, and hence political, rectitude. In between, there is of course plenty of room for intermediary strategies that should be explored by using the tools provided by the first theory. The third theory also has something in common with the second, as it claims that 'private entrepreneurship' in manufacturing is the sole base from which regime autonomy in the Middle East and North Africa can be challenged with any chance of success, now that structural adjustment has been imposed by international financial organizations and the industrialized countries (von Sivers 1991, 29, an important addition not usually made by the second theory).

Summary and conclusion: democratization between strategic, cultural and structural analyses

My main purpose in this chapter has been to bring the 'Arab world' back into comparative studies of democratization, while not taking for granted that democracy is everywhere and always the necessary output of a universal process as well as the best and only way to 'solve problems'. Is this exercise altogether futile? Not quite if we try to combine the 'political pact' approach – which by itself is insufficient to provide a full account of the process but should be utilized more extensively as a part of the rational strategic theory – with macro-sociological approaches to carry out historically-grounded research. After all, the challenges are very similar inside and outside the Arab world, and we have pointed them out at the outset and throughout this essay by emphasizing the dilemma of vulnerability and uncertainty in a context characterized by three paradoxes: (i) behaviourally, the parties do not act only to satisfy their own interest, or even to assert their own identities, but also 'define rules and procedures whose configurations will determine likely winners and losers in the future' (O'Donnell et al. 1986, 6). Therefore, the 'subjective probability' of the outcome of a move – i.e. 'the perception of the likelihood of its success' and of its long-term consequences – becomes of crucial importance at the very moment the actors are the least-equipped to assess the value of the probability (Collier & Norden 1992, 235); (ii) structurally, democracy requires, if the second and third theories are correct, a certain type of pluralism and a civil society whose content and validity are hotly contested, and whose probability of development depends on the achievements of the process of democratization; (iii) normatively, democracy (and beforehand, democratization) require, as do most political regimes, that certain normative choices should be ruled out, not as individual preferences but as collective rules worth considering. When the content of public morality is itself at stake in the process of democratization we may be facing a dead-end since the process's prerequisite is also its outcome. The problem may become intractable when the three paradoxes go together instead of following one another (two being frozen while the third is managed) or balancing one another (a provisional pact may lead to a restructuring of the economy which may relieve the normative tensions in the cultural sphere, or any other combination).

From these very general problems, more specific ones may derive in historical situations. In this respect, what happened in Algeria in 1991 offers a good example by way of conclusion. The intriguing issue in Algeria was the overwhelming importance of electoral legitimacy. Everyone everywhere was saying, along with Prime Minister Ghozali, that 'free and faultless elections' were the main condition for the crisis to come to an end; yet no significant effort was made on the part of the government to build a viable coalition able to get through the first round of balloting. It was as if it were already taken for granted that the Islamic Salvation Front would not capture an absolute majority, and that the three weeks between the two rounds of voting would be enough to mobilize people who had been left behind during the campaign. Very little political campaigning was done in many electoral districts, and only the FIS worked systematically at the grassroots level. It is clear today that a part of the military establishment had already decided before the first round of voting to stop the electoral process. As for the others, they probably thought that palace politics was, as usual, more important than appealing to the people, and they had good reasons for believing so given the persistence of deep cleavages among the members of the political establishment and the failure of professional politicians to provide voters with a well-delineated political map to replace the now-exhausted ideology of the 'National Charters'. Voting is not a natural and self-evident process: it is an obscure rite whose practice requires some learning and, above all, a myth of some sort to transform 'crowds' into 'constituencies', that is to say, a way of helping citizens find their way through the amazingly complex network of party lines claiming to connect grievances, demands, and forms of behaviour to a single piece of paper to be dropped into a ballot box. If the function of a myth is to reduce complexity and to provide the voter with a cognitive map making the rite meaningful, mythmakers are badly needed.[30] Moreover, one may ask how democratization may work when the incumbent elites and their challengers have been socialized for more than 30 years by authoritarian politics. A process of democratization engineered by a segmented elite without a strong leadership is likely to backfire and the 'conspiracy' of various clans (including the secret police) may regain pre-eminence under a new guise. If we move to the level of basic economic structures and class interests, it may appear obvious that a strong market economy needs a competent public bureaucracy to implement the rules of fair competition; but it is not enough to proclaim the necessity of freeing the initiative of private entrepreneurs (a slogan religiously repeated since the early 1980s) if a weak bureaucracy lets the so-called competitive firms become mini-monopolies exploiting situational rents. A true market economy 'requires a superhuman effort of officials'[31] and they have no reason for making it unless there is already a class of entrepreneurs eager, and able, to put some pressure on the state to change the rules instead of using them to acquire rents. Once again, the expected outcome of the process is also its prerequisite.

Such dilemmas help us to understand why studies of democratization tend to turn towards more micro-sociological and strategic approaches in order to overcome structural contradictions brought out by more macro-sociological studies. Hirschman's 'possibilist approach' (Hirschman 1971, 29–35) emphasizes three elements: first, 'blessings in disguise' which are 'conditions or actions that appear to obstruct desired changes but prove instead to facilitate such changes'; second, 'unintended consequences', or actions which do indeed have the direct effect of blocking directed change, but have the secondary effect of encouraging it; and thirdly, the 'accommodation of attitudes to actions', through which 'attitudes and beliefs, often seen as prerequisite for desired change, instead emerge as a consequence' (Collier & Norden 1992, 240). Such a way to escape the vicious circles we have outlined is a tool both for knowledge and for action. But it demands many more detailed studies of specific situations in order to escape the all-too-familiar binary opposition between islamic thought and liberalism, 'Islam' and 'democracy' or, more precisely, islamist ideology and constitutionalism.

Above all we should keep in mind that the processes of democratization do not take place by virtue of an 'invisible hand' unknown to concrete human beings, deemed 'rational' whether they like it or not. After all, democracy needs democrats – in other words, not only 'rational' but also 'reasonable' agents. But rationality may still have the last word, for structural and cultural reasons: in a period of crisis of legitimacy and of intense resentment, an unequal exchange of resources leads to 'rational' behaviour akin to a gigantic prisoner's dilemma, 'the pulverization of society into myriads of rational-opportunistic agents' acting at highly disaggregated levels, with extremely short time horizons and with assumptions that everyone else will do the same. In such a situation, 'when it becomes clear that many violate the law and the costs of doing it are usually nil, the lesson learned further erodes the predictibility of social relations'. Therefore, an irrepressible anger about a situation which all – and hence apparently nobody – seem to cause is directed against a major culprit: the state and the government (O'Donnell 1993).[32]

In many Arab countries, this anger has still to find an idiom which would express, trigger and control the grievances. A great tradition is available, and islamism fights to monopolize it.

Notes

1   I am not by any means implying that we should get rid of these words (as if social realities were to disappear by a decree of the scientist's will). I am pleading for pre-

cisely the opposite: we should use them to define in a better way what we are talking about instead of treating them as self-explanatory concepts (for valuable attempts to do this regarding Islam see Gilsenan 1982, and Talal Asad's critical survey, 1986). The analytically distinct yet closely connected problem of where we are talking from is the subject of a whole library of inquiry in the western social sciences. Regarding islamic and Arab social sciences, see the most interesting essays of Ahmed 1986 and 1988 and Zghal 1982, and the seminar held in Abu Dhabi in April 1983 orginized by the Arab Regional Center for Research and Documentation in Social Sciences (Cairo) on the topic 'Toward an Arab Social Science.'

2   It is always useful to keep in mind Giovanni Sartori's caveats: if the term 'democracy' signifies a set of ideals as well as a political system, the more it 'has come to be a universally accepted honorific term the more it has undergone verbal stretching and has become the loosest label of its kind.' 'Democracy...does not describe a thing [like in Aristotle's typology], it prescribes an ideal' (Sartori 1968a). Hence the familiar issues: is 'democracy' the 'rule of the people' or the 'rule for the people'? Is 'the people' an organic whole, a plurality of autonomous individuals, a collection of airtight communities? What does the notion of 'self-governing people' have to do with these concepts of representation, majority rule, competition, protected opposition, alternative government, rule of law and the like? What are the standards used to label a polity 'democratic' or 'undemocratic'? Is it the absence of outright dictatorship (tyranny)? The existence of a constitutional government? The political and social enfranchisement of the 'masses'? Though written at a time when the main problem was the contest between 'liberal democracy' and 'popular (socialist) democracy' (with 'guided democracy' as a Third Worldist contender), those statements still hold true at a time when the notion of 'islamic democracy' is making its way in the 'shadow of God' after the collapse of socialist ideologies and authoritarian rulers. 'Ninety-five per cent of the people are for the Islamic Salvation Front and the remaining 5 per cent are the French party,' said a supporter of the Algerian islamist party after the Front's breakthrough on the first round of voting in the December 1991 legislative elections (the first contested elections to the legislature held since 1962). Actually, the Islamic Salvation Front captured 48 per cent of the ballots against 52 per cent for all the other candidates (including minor islamic parties), with about 40 per cent of voters abstaining.

3   Lipset's study (1960) remains a towering example, like O'Donnell's attempts to work out a theory of bureaucratic authoritarianism in Latin America through the notion of 'coalition group' (O'Donnell 1973; Collier 1979). Both Lipset and O'Donnell were careful to provide preliminary definitions of the regimes whose coming or continuation were to be explained. They had to do so for obvious reasons that are made clear in the text.

4   For a careful analysis of 'radical Islam' as a counter-society and of its relation with its 'conservative periphery', see Sivan (1987). Note that Sivan, while emphasizing the current pregnancy of this kind of Muslim world view, does not entertain essentialist fancies and makes clear at the outset that he has written 'an essay in the history of ideas viewed and interpreted in their social context'(p. XI). One may disagree with his interpretation, but one cannot accuse him of confining the real Muslims in an 'eternal Islam'. For more on this issue, see Part. II, below.

5   On the apostasy of people who hold that parts of the *shari'a* are valid only in relation to their original historical context see An-Naim (1986) and Mayer (1991 182,

183).

6   A sensible criticism, as any constitutionalist thinker will readily admit (Elster 1988). In an important but very specific sense, separation of power is inherent to Muslim thought, far ahead of Enlightenment political theory in this respect: 'Legislation has been pre-empted by the deity, and so cannot be usurped by the mundane political executive power, or by the people either' (Gellner 1991, 506). But the similarity is very abstract: note that majority rule is also criticized by the 'democrats' afraid of the obnoxious consequences of an islamist majority (if they knew Riker's work, they would probably name it a 'populist democracy', Riker 1982, 211–22), but they tend to emphasize the individual's right to have his/her beliefs recognized and guaranteed (Mayer 1991, 50 ff), not the right of the bearers (whether or not they are clerics) of the (supposedly) highest (common?) values to carry them out at any cost. In other words, some 'islamic democrats' are against 'majorities' because they are also against 'minorities' (except ones endowed with a status ascribed to protected religious minorities) and they advocate the unity of the community under God, against deadly divisions (*fitna*). Democrats 'tout court' are against *unlimited* majority rule because they want to preserve their effective 'right to have rights' in the present and their power of becoming a majority in the future (on democracy as the opposite to the exclusion of minorities, cf. Sartori 1987, 31 ff).

7   I readily admit that they may be regarded as caricatures (or, in a more dignified way, loose ideal types). Likewise, it would be preposterous to portray all Arab rulers as being at war with their societies, Sadat's assassination notwithstanding. Nevertheless, the legitimacy problem pointed out by Hudson (Hudson 1977) is as real as the dual nature of oppositions to authoritarian regimes, the islamist groups leading in Algeria and Jordan, winning in Sudan and being more or less harshly repressed almost everywhere else.

8   On populism, the best collection of essays available is still Ionescu and Gellner (1969), unfortunately too little-known by orientalists, who fail to see, firstly, the distinctly populist connotations of the 'new islamists' ('Populist Islam' is mentioned by Bill 1984, cf. Dekmejian 1985. 'Religious populism' is cited by Ibrahim 1988); and, secondly, the continuity of populism from the nationalists to the more or less radical islamists (Al-Azmeh 1991a and 1991b). The articles by Donald MacRae and Peter Worsley are particularly relevant. Worsley is perfectly right when he states: 'Populism as direct participation is thus a dimension of the democratic and socialist traditions' (Worsley 1969, 246). I would go a little further and say that it is a constitutive dimension. The fact that, as Worsley reminds us, 'the most inhumane and authoritarian regimes in modern times have, at least verbally, rationalized their authority in terms of some reference to the will of the people' does not really matter. Likewise 'constitutionalism' has been used to justify oligarchic politics. Complexes of thought and behaviour are always manipulated, that is to say institutionalized and/or corrupted when embedded in various social niches and contexts. For example, one may consider Egyptian religious populism a 'functional equivalent' to nasserism (Ibrahim 1988, 684) and the Tunisian islamist movement a component of the nationalist ideology and dynamics (Zghal 1991b, 206).

9   The point was made for the first time by Barère, a member in 1793 of the French Convention Nationale's Comité de Salut Public. Gellner (1967) considers that this official duty is one of the dominant features of modern political systems. The politicization of social protest means that the lower classes fought both for citizenship and

for social rights. On the relation between citizenship and social rights see Marshall 1973 and Bendix 1961.

10 This is not inconsistent with the challenge to majority rule (see note 6). The community is much more than a majority (that implies pluralism): individuals' judgements are free but coincide since there can be only one Good (MacRae 1969, 160). Whether the people (as a community: *umma*) are made, or permitted, by the recognition of a transcendental truth or by some natural process is a secondary issue.

11 Note that the quest for authenticity may be the mark of an extreme individualism, either romantic or post-modern, when 'It is taken to be that which a human being possesses, only when all the artificial accretions of society, and all the barriers of social restraints are removed'. I owe that definition, obviously inspired by Rousseau, to Elie Kedourie's conservative essay, 'Diversity in Freedom', *Times Literary Supplement,* 10 January 1992. Kedourie seems to put down that search for authenticity to 'Liberalism', at least to the view that the body politic is made up of individuals, each of whom is endowed with natural rights. Much more important, in my view, is the fact that the two 'authenticities' suppose that there is nothing to bargain about. Authenticity, whether it is traditional-communitarian or innovating-individualist, presupposes that nothing is to be negotiated or to be learned, everything should be rediscovered in its original purity (a similar distinction has been made between 'law-making' and 'law finding' in Arjomand 1992). Either the community or the individual (or, better, *both* of them) are the perfect good. The 'imperfect' social networks, which are the historical output of evolving artificial arrangements, are downgraded. Alienation is evil unless it is alienation from the community, and in such a case, as Rousseau would tell us, it is not alienation at all. On authenticity in recent western philosophy see Taylor (1992a and 1992b). In the Arab world the term, almost unknown during the period 1920–50, sometimes refers to a combination of individualism and communitarianism: individual innovation cannot occur without an inclusion of the individual into the collective personality (Boullata 1990, 14–15).

12 It is a blend of authentically islamic and, more broadly, religous arguments (note the biblical reference to 'do not fear', dear to Václav Havel and Pope John Paul II) modernized and historicized with the help of more conventional revolutionary arguments, a wonderful illustration of MacRae's thesis on populism as an ideology (with the marxist addition that 'the intellectuals think the Revolution and make it a theory'). Hence its 'constant ambiguity' (Al-Azmeh 1991a, 52) close to logical inconsistency: 'For on the one hand they [Hanafi and others] advocate transformation of society, political and culture that could have been advocated by any Latin American marxist political economist, while on the other they assimilate this to the notion of an independent and invariant historical subject as elaborated in *al-Urwa al-wuthqa* journal published in Paris in 1884 under the influence of Afghani. (On the connection of islamic revivalism, social darwinism and populism, see Al-Azmeh 1991a, 48 and *passim*.) But it is only fair to recognize that the opposite 'liberal' thesis has its own ontological shortcoming: a tendency toward instability and dissociation, the spreading of the free-rider problem (Walzer 1990), It remains to be seen whether modern neo-communitarian regimes are free-rider-less), and, as Hanafi reminds us in terms Michael Sandel would not disavow, a fundamental non-recognition of the constitution of the self as the embodiment of social values (Sandel 1982).

13 For want of space, I cannot dwell on the two faces of self-determination, based on a

given *collective* identity supposedly recognized and expressed by *individual* preference. Nationalism may be considered as 'a rather unclear mixture of ideals about cultural identity and individual liberty' (Breuilly 1985, 373). On the philosophical dilemmas raised by such an articulation see Barry (1983) and Buchanan (1991).

14 'The use of the terms "democratization" or "democracy" should not be interpreted as an endorsement of any one model, for example, the separation of power in the United States or the Westminster parliamentary system' (Esposito & Piscatori 1991). All we are left with is Sartori's three standards....

15 The late Hamid Enayat was somewhat exaggerating; one has only to mention the important works of Mohamed Arkoun and Abdallah Laroui, although the two scholars are more concerned with the history of knowledge than with political theory (for example, Arkoun 1984 and 1986; Laroui, 1967, 1974, 1987).

16 I am not implying that any set of symbols is merely an instrument manipulated as discretion by its bearers, for it is a constraint as well as a resource. Besides, it cannot be picked out at will: individuals guided by their self-interest may do so, but not social groups whose collective consciousness contributes to construct and define the individual's interests and values.

17 ...And only to the political scientist. To the believer (in God, socialism, democracy etc.) living in the life world (*lebenswelt*), his beliefs and values, whatever they are, are so meaningful (and rightly so) that they cannot be construed as a resource or a constraint but as a part of himself, since he lives within a social context and is a part of it. To him, his beliefs cannot be contextualized. They *are* their context since they make it by making it meaningful.

18 For interesting panoramas of the many islamic ideals, besides Enayat (1982), see Donohue & Esposito (1982), Esposito (1983), Carré (1991) and Butterworth & Zartman (1992). For a brief and insightful comparison between various religious strategies see Anderson (1991). For a recent call to an islamic '*aggiornamento*' see An-Naim (1990).

19 And outside parties as well, both distrusted and required to intervene by Arab parties, which they are all too willing to do (if they are interested and strong enough) given their past imperial interventions and current 'national interests'. See on these points an historian's sobering reflections in Brown (1984), the detailed historical analysis of Laurens (1991), the excellent overview by Noble (1991) and Hudson's assessment (1991b).

20 Except the now-received interpretation that they do not have much in common with classical Islam (for example, Al-Azmeh, 1990, and on Shi'ism, Arjomand 1984a and 1988). It would, however, be unwise to ignore the fact that they are part and parcel of a long-standing historical tradition (Lapidus 1992 and Butterworth 1992).

21 I am not considering here Kedourie's thoughtful essay (Kedourie 1992) as a case for exceptionalism, although it looks like it at first glance. He insists on the failure of the constitutionalist grafting and the success of another western idea, 'millennialism', incorporated into 'ideological politics' (p.268) and so capturing what I chose to call the 'populist' component of democracy. But it does not follow that the Arab world is truly exceptional since Kedourie does not believe in any such thing as a universal democracy or democratization: only historically evolved innovations from inside are able to adapt the 'old ways' to changing conditions. So-called universal concepts (e.g. 'constitutionalism' or 'millennialism') are historical, nothing is exceptional – except the unnatural attempt to implement so-called universal models (such

as 'nations' or 'constitutions'). This unnatural move is so widespread that it is not an exception anymore. The disease is everywhere.

22 To complete the picture, see works in which Gellner does not focus his attention on Islam (Gellner 1983 and 1991).

23 The link between *salafiya* Islam and nationalism was always conspicuous in North Africa, though the two ideological schemes must be kept analytically distinct. Moreover, the activist groups as bearers of specific competitive ideologies and strategies, especially when suspected of being allied to 'communists', should be distinguished (for a Jordanian example see Duclos 1990, 70–71).

24 Gellner seems to consider democracy more as a societal state than as a political regime. Hence his emphasis on the concept of 'civil society'. It is not just a set of plural institutions capable of acting as a kind of countervailing force to the state, it is a set of *specific* institutions 'established by a sober and limited and specific contract rather than by status, let alone by heavily ritualized status' (Gellner 1991, 500). How can such a system come about? Gellner's answer is very Durkheimian: through the combined effects of economic growth and 'civic spirit', that is to say abstract observation of the law unlinked to clan and the respect for abstract constitutional principles as such and not only for the groupings operating within it (p.501). This comes close enough to the 'constitutionalist' part of our definition of democracy.

25 Richards and Waterbury (1990, 437) hold a similar and complementary view: 'Implicating strategic middle-class interests in the austerity measures through cautious democratization may be the wisest political course, and Egypt, Tunisia, Morocco and Turkey seem to be following it.' (They could have added Algeria in early 1992.) See also Richards (1993, 226): '...the cry of the era of structural adjustment may be "No subsidy cuts without participation".'

26 The term 'moral economy' may have two meanings according to its status and the contexts of its usages. As a social scientific concept, it implies that rational actors operate within an ethical context providing them with cognitive and evaluative maps (Scott 1976, Hyden 1980). It is the commonly accepted meaning. But as soon as 'moral economy' can be conceived as an outcome of ethical and cultural drives (such a view is not held by all the moral economists), it becomes possible to use the term in an evaluative and practical sense, to point out more human economic systems embedded in specific cultures based on altruistic solidarities, as is the case with the search for an 'islamic economy'.

27 This thesis is outlined by Lisa Anderson (1991) and expanded by Peter von Sivers (1991). It overlaps with the growing literature on the 'rentier states' (Mahdavi 1969; Beblawi & Luciani 1987) and the allocation states (Luciani 1987, 1990 and 1992).

28 'Autonomous government' in this limited sense must be distinguished from the more familiar notion of 'autonomous state' in liberal democracies (Dunleavy & O'Leary 1987).

29 According to the IMF tables compiled by Peter von Sivers, only Turkey comes close to most industrialized countries with respect to the share of taxes on income and profits as a percentage of total revenue (43 per cent in 1989, but Syria made a great leap forward from 5 per cent in 1975 to 32 per cent in 1987, the consequences of which for the political regime should be scrutinized).

30 I am not saying that people are unable to be rational or reasonable when they vote. Far from it. I maintain only that in mass democracies they need a cultural system (or a cognitive map) giving some meaning to the rules of the game and the identity of

the contenders (Bon 1979; on ideologies as cognitive maps during modernization, see Geertz 1964).

31 I am quoting the governor of the Algerian Central Bank in an interview (March 1992). Our interlocutor was careful to add that the international environment was not of any help: the market is not trusted as a way out of the crisis since the underdeveloped countries do not participate in identifying the players in the markets. In July 1992 the governor was ousted by the then prime minister.

32 I am deliberately quoting a student of Latin America whose statements are wonderfully suited to large parts of the so-called 'exceptional' Arab world.

3

Small is Pluralistic: democracy as an instrument of civil peace

GHASSAN SALAMÉ

> How many things which are difficult to unite does this government [democracy] not assume? Firstly, a very small state, where the people can readily be assembled, and where every citizen can easily be acquainted with all the others.
>
> Jean-Jacques Rousseau, *The Social Contract*[1]

For a long time 'small' Arab countries have been regarded as more hospitable ground for democratic ideas and practices than their 'large' neighbours. Because they are small, they have appeared to derive a kind of additional raison d'être as sovereign states from the democratic regimes they harboured. With their powerful neighbours menacing them from close by, sometimes laying claim to all or part of their territory, they have found in their democratic practice a justification for their existence as sovereign states which they hope will arouse support at home and also abroad, notably in the West. If the West recognized itself in its local emulators (who also adopted a capitalist economy, competitive elections and a free press), it would protect them against outbursts of greed and violence on the part of their mighty neighbours. There is great awareness in this part of the world of the advantages to Israel of its claim (rather disputable) to be 'the only democracy in the Middle East', and without actually admitting it, other countries would like to share these benefits.

This is most notably the case with Lebanon and Kuwait, and more recently, in varying degrees, in some other Arab countries which have been trying to adopt sets of policies to avoid the anathema of being considered 'undemocratic' by the only surviving superpower. Lebanon and Kuwait have been practically the only Arab countries to hold legislative elections (sometimes at regular intervals fixed by their constitutions), in which genuine competition between candidates could be discerned, despite some tough limitations and more or less justified accusations of malpractice. These two countries have also had long periods when the press was 'free' in the sense that it was the property of private groups or individuals (not government-run), and could express opinions relatively different from those of the rulers of the country. These two countries have never been governed by military dictatorships, were not affected by the great wave of single-party regimes, or by the punitive nationalization of recalcitrant bourgeoisies, and they have only rarely held prisoners of conscience. In spite of some notable differences – the existence of a large body of Christians within the Lebanese population, the considerable oil wealth of Kuwait – it has been possible to regard these two countries as in a category of their own in the authoritarian nebula which has been typical of most Arab countries immediately after they became independent. Recently, these two countries have been joined by Jordan (1989) and post-unification Yemen (1993). More limited experiments with competitive elections also took place in Algeria (1991), Morocco (1993) and Mauritania (1992). The most evident case of democratization as a device to seek the West's protection by its emulation, as much as to organize domestic segmentation in a hostile environment, has been Iraqi Kurdistan, where truly pluralistic elections have been held with these two objectives clearly stated by Kurdish leaders.

Although there has been critical evaluation of the democratic experiments of Kuwait and Lebanon, it has been inadequate, and has not been done in a comparative context. It seems to me, however, that the emergence of democratic practices in these two cases, and later in certain other 'small' states, allows us in general to think of them as the exception which illuminates, that explains and contextualizes the rule of the absence of democracy in other Arab countries. For it is difficult to think that the political culture prevailing in the 'small' countries is fundamentally different from that of their neighbours, or that the socio-economic structures of Lebanon and Kuwait are so peculiar to them that they can explain their special experiments. The 'exceptionalism' of Lebanon in the Levant, and to a lesser degree of Kuwait in the Gulf, has been taken at face value for too long, and their relationship with their regional environments has seldom been studied except for the tautological purpose of 'pointing out the difference'.

It would be inadequate to seek this exceptionalism only in imitation of their tutelary powers. Lebanon and Kuwait have certainly lived in the shade of pro-western regimes, and both have tried, like innumerable peripheral countries, to reproduce the mode of government of the mandatory or protecting power which created them as states or brought them to the baptismal font of political modernity, France in one case, Great Britain in the other. However, we might turn this argument around, or at least show its limitations, by recalling that at the moment of their independence, other countries in the area had elites even more westernized than that of Kuwait or perhaps even of Lebanon, for instance Algeria in 1962 and Egypt in 1952, where western-style democracy has not been victorious. In the case of Kuwait, the democratic constitution of the country was worked out with the aid of Arab (notably Egyptian) experts, who had not had any genuine democratic experience in their own countries. The importation of the western democratic model is in fact a very widespread practice in the Third

World, albeit in a very ephemeral manner in most cases, since coup d'état which is nationalistic in its discourse and authoritarian in practice soon intervenes to bring it to a speedy end. In any case, it does not explain why the model has endured in certain countries rather than in others.

The hypothesis we shall be exploring here is that the principal attraction of the democratic system in these two countries (and in some others sharing a similar logic) has been that it is the only system in a position to organize peaceful power sharing in a society where a hegemonic group could not establish an exclusivist or, at least, an openly dominant position. Democratization, when it is gradually brought about, has therefore been neither the product of a struggle conducted by 'modern' democratic forces, nor the modern reformulation of traditional democratic practices (like the so-called 'natural democracy' of the Bedouin). It is originally a mechanism which is not deeply rooted in culture and has no social and political forces to defend it in and for itself, a mechanism justified by its utility much more than by the values it is supposed to embody. This hypothesis disputes the validity of the valorizing discourse of democracy, and incidentally of those who claim to have been its creators, a kind of discourse generally produced *ex post facto* and having little effect on actual practice. It also distances itself from the sanctifying ideologization of democracy which runs through today's western societies, assured of their success in the Cold War and seeking ideological means to sublimate it.

My approach therefore sets out from the cyclical and instrumental function of institutions which are more or less democratic at a given moment; there is nothing new about this if we refer back to the non-mythological (but rather neglected) accounts of the birth of democracy in the West itself. It is a valid approach, if not a current one, to re-valorize the analysis of democracy as the involuntary result of relations between yet to be defined forces rather than the idealized incarnation of philosophical thinking. In other words, we have here a democracy without democrats, which is not to say that somewhere along the road democracy will not succeed in engendering forces to defend it. For this regime, like any other, favours some while claiming to be open to all. And beside those who, to use the familiar cliché, will say, 'I disapprove of what you say, but I will defend to the death your right to say it,' democracy is also and undoubtedly first and foremost the product of some social hegemony which is insufficiently dominant in a particular political configuration.

If this hypothesis could be confirmed we would be able to take another look at the current problems of the Third World as a whole in finding a peaceful way of reconciling the social divisions typical of the great majority of African and Asian countries with the political pluralism which the practice of liberal democracy implies by its very definition. What is most often perceived as an 'obstacle' to the democratization of these societies could, on the contrary, be tackled as an opportunity beneficial to that democratization, the initial form of pluralism (tribal, ethnic, linguistic or religious) which prohibits authoritarianism and opens up the way, first in instrumental logic and then in a more ideal dynamic, to the voluntary pluralism of open political competition. From this we may deduce that democratization is to a great extent brought about through a recognition of this ethno-cultural pluralism, rather than by its rejection; and, furthermore, that this rejection, so common since states became independent, is the classic soil in which authoritarian powers take root, using the permissible aim of national integration not only to justify the establishment of ostensibly integrationist/assimilist powers which in fact are strongly marked by the social origins of the rulers, but also to exclude any overtures to democracy. Two logics are thus in opposition: one that takes into account the basic social pluralism and tries to organize its political expression into consociative institutions, and another – more common – logic that ignores this basic pluralism in the name of national unity. It seems that the first logic has more easily prevailed in those small countries where no mission-oriented regimes are convincingly established, where cordial relations with the West are sought, and where the management of liberal/confessional pluralism (rather than its negation) is viewed as an asset in the permanent adjustment to a hostile regional environment.

The democratic deficiency among the 'large' countries of the region can, on the contrary, be connected with their claim to be playing a regional role beyond the frontiers of their own state. The regimes established in Egypt and Syria, Iraq and Algeria have thus developed 'historic missions' for themselves, ranging from the 'liberation of Palestine' to 'the achievement of Arab unity', not to mention the political and economic emancipation of the Third World or even the defeat of imperialism. The real function of these self-proclaimed missions seems to be to establish a 'nobler' legitimacy than would arise simply from the acceptance of these regimes by their own populations, a question which appeared at best trite to the supporters of Nasser or the admirers of Boumedienne. To ask for it was to act like a traitor, or at least an unwitting accomplice of all those external enemies who would question the role of a leader entirely committed to the universal struggle against imperialism. The 'small' countries could hardly lay claim to roles such as these, and without legitimation to be won by great deeds abroad, they had to find it at home. As they could not establish undisputed if not indisputable political hegemony at home, they were reduced to the necessity of power-sharing among the various segments of their societies, a key used almost unwittingly to open the door into the world of democratic practice and then democratic customs.

Lebanon: an incomplete confessional hegemon

In all probability, Lebanon as a state would not have existed but for the progressively forged alliance between the nationalitarian Maronite Christian movement and France. The Druze emirate of Mount Lebanon (seventeenth to eighteenth centuries) had been a landmark showing the way to the project of the creation of a state, but it was the Maronites, notably towards the end of the nineteenth century, who managed to make it a political project and find for it the necessary diplomatic support. The 'organic settlement' of 1861 thus sketched the profile of the future entity, whose present frontiers were sanctioned by the disappearance of the Ottoman Empire and the resolute stand taken by France in 1918–20. It was natural for the Maronites, the local group involved in this operation, to be its first beneficiaries. They thus progressively acquired political authority, sanctioned according to custom during the next two decades in the emergence of a presidential regime which was sometimes inclined to authoritarianism while formally presenting itself as a 'parliamentary democracy', though one in which the presidency and the reality of political power were given to members of that community.

But the Maronites were not alone in the 'Greater Lebanon' proclaimed by General Gouraud on 1 September 1920, whose frontiers form the content of the first article in the 1926 Constitution. In 1913 Mount Lebanon had a clear majority of Christians (nearly 80 per cent) and even of Maronites (58 per cent of the total) out of a population of 414,963 inhabitants. The Greater Lebanon of 1932, its territory now enlarged by the addition of the coastal plain and the Beka'a had only 50 per cent Christians (and 28.8 per cent Maronites out of the total) among its inhabitants. This Christian–Muslim parity would henceforward be inclined to evolve unilaterally towards the Muslim communities as a result of inequalities in birth rates and more emigration by Christians. Moreover, the Maronites who established their political hegemony over the new entity could not repeat this feat in the economic sphere: the modern (capitalist) sector of the Lebanese economy was largely concentrated in the hands of far more urbanized confessions such as the Sunni Muslims and the Byzantine Christians (Orthodox or Catholic).

This is why Maronite political hegemony seems at first to be founded much more on the undeniable historical part played by the Maronites in the emergence of the modern Lebanese entity than on the contemporary factors of that emergence. Demographically, the enlargement of Mount Lebanon by the addition of urban zones (such as Beirut and Tripoli) and rural areas (Jabal Amel, the Akkar and the Beka'a) deprived the Maronite elites, even though they had striven for this extension of the Lebanese domain (Zamir 1985), of the chance of legitimating their political hegemony by right of numbers. Any mention of that argument thus became taboo, and after the 1932 census, which showed demographic parity between Christians and Muslims as well as a higher rate of growth among the latter, the Lebanese state took good care not to resort to such an exercise. Unable to show that they were the economic driving force or had a superior cultural level, the Maronites could scarcely present themselves as the initiators of Lebanese prosperity. They were left with nothing to justify their political supremacy but the memory of their contribution to the existence of the state, and later the argument *a contrario* whereby, as the neighbouring countries (except for Israel, but Israel was even more clearly marked by its religious identity) were all dominated by Muslims, Christians had the right to maintain their precedence (or at least a politicized community identity) in at least one state in the region.

This demographic, economic and cultural deficit was not to prevent the Maronite elites from maintaining and even strengthening their predominance over the regime. If the election of a Protestant or a Byzantine as head of state or the candidature of an observant Muslim to that position could still be envisaged during the first two decades, when the state remained under the French mandate, that was no longer the case after the adoption of the unwritten 'National Pact' of 1943, the year of independence, as if the Maronite elite were even more jealous of its predominance once the protecting power left. In fact, at least between 1943 and 1964, the country went through a phase shaped by three Maronite presidents who transformed the semi-presidential, semi-parliamentary system into a presidentialism of a zealous, quasi-authoritarian nature, reinforced by the Maronites' effective seizure of the most important posts in the state apparatus, notably those of commander-in-chief of the army, head of the judiciary and the heads of the civil and military secret services. The state therefore appeared to be benefiting the Maronites by institutionalizing their hold on the apparatus (and consequently on the indirect advantages that any group derives from having a stranglehold on the state in an atmosphere of clientelist and nepotist practices, very widespread between 1943 and 1958, more discreet under Fuad Shehab 1958–64), even though their relative demographic weight was constantly falling. Moreover, the republic, first under French mandate and then independent, allowed the Maronite community to increase considerably its members' access to private and public education. There followed a movement of rapid urbanization which, while not peculiar to the Maronites, had the effect in their case of increasing their quasi-hegemonic pre-eminence in politics. For a long time the country appeared to be divided in two, a bipartisan split which merely passed a split in the Maronite community on to the whole of Lebanon, dividing those who had supported the Maronite hegemony, under the leadership of Emile Eddé and the National Bloc, and those who, with Bishara al-Khuri and the Dastur Party – and its successors – thought the survival of Maronite pre-eminence depended on concessions made to local Muslims and neighbouring Arab governments. The Maronite elite had thus become influential to the point of defining the splits in both the regime and the opposition, inviting the other confessional components to position themselves in line with its own divisions.

None the less, this hegemony could and indeed would be disputed. Critics of the Maronites blamed them for having created a state at the very start by separating it from 'natural Syria', a mythical entity but a common point of reference just after the First World War. Later the Maronites were blamed for having been the tools of France and thus being favoured by her. Others would demand another census to show the decrease in the Maronite position and the injustice of the 'privileges' (a word carrying strong political overtones) they enjoyed within the state. It is in the context of this Maronite predominance, unjustifiable by non-ideological arguments, that the democratic experiment in Lebanon took off. It aimed to arouse attachment to the statist entity in Islamic circles which were not adequately represented there, and to co-opt leaders whom within their various groups, would be advocates with an interest in the survival of that entity, but would not make exaggerated demands concerning the part they might play in conducting its business. Hence the electoral practice reputed to establish a 'parliamentary democracy', the adjective being supposed to form the basis for a confessionally pluralist administration of the state apparatus, one which would add shades of complexity to the predominance of the Maronite political elite and if possible justify its existence. The Maronite elite had gone too far in identifying itself with the state born in 1920, an identification which triggered in non-Maronite circles, a dangerous mixture of two basic strands: the disputation of Maronite predominance within the Lebanese context itself, and the (moral radical) rejection of the new entity as such.

So far, no community group seemed more anxious for democratization than any other. On both the clerical and the secular level, communities usually pursued time-honoured authoritarian practices within themselves, justifying these practices by the necessity of unfaltering unity and survival in a hostile environment. When the debate finally unfolded it bore immediately on a more equitable distribution of benefits connected with the state (in particular education, the powerful vehicle of social mobility and access to public office, the customary dream of any member of the lower middle class in search of promotion). That is why, confronted with the hegemonic tendency of the Maronite leaders, the keyword of the dispute was to be *musharaka,* literally 'sharing', which meant a new deal. The non-Maronite part of the political elite, taking into consideration the fact that the newly born entity is likely to last, was all the more insistent on being part of it and on securing a larger say in its government. Hence a strategy by which, instead of looking for a precocious death of that entity, they tried to coalesce as much Arab support as possible in order to secure a better position in the domestic arrangement. They will be partly successful in translating Nasser's influence in the Arab world into sectarian gains within the Lebanese system in the aftermath of the limited civil war of 1958. They will not stop asking for more after that first 'corrective' measure. When, however, the regime finally allowed the involuntary birth of a more radical, more democratic or simply a trans-confessional opposition, the leaders of the different communities were to be seen uniting to end it before Kamal Junblatt, followed by other Muslim leaders, could move from an alliance with part of the Maronite elite to radical opposition, with the support of these new radical forces (the predominantly islamic Third Estate) and then of the troops of the PLO.

Kuwait: an incomplete tribal hegemon

Kuwait had its founding act: the arrival there in the seventeenth century of a number of families from the Najd, and the establishment of a port which would thrive and prosper to the point of giving birth to an independent state in 1962. The city of Kuwait was most likely built around 1716. Some forty years later, thanks to the weakening of the tribal power of the Banu Khalid who controlled the eastern province of the Arab peninsula, the representatives of those families who had emigrated to Kuwait elected one of themselves – Sabah bin Jabir al-Udhbi – to be the administrator of justice and law and order in what was already a relatively prosperous port. This man (Sabah was his forename) does not appear to have had any legitimate family claim to his function, since no difference between the families could be discerned either when they first emigrated *en masse* or after they had settled in Kuwait. He was simply, as Abu Hakima (n.d.: 8) notes, 'the man with the required wisdom to settle conflicts'. It was at the same period, too, that the inhabitants of the little port chose their first *qadi*, one Muhammad bin Fayruz).

This event, which is not accurately dated, gave rise to two political practices. The first was that the Kuwaitis native to the interior of the peninsula thereafter regarded themselves as the only legitimate citizens of the emirate, the others being citizens only because their presence was tolerated by the first. A highly symbolic mark of their original appurtenance to the country was the presence of their ancestors inside the famous wall which the families who settled in Kuwait built around their city around the year 1760, both to defend themselves against Bedouin attacks and also, no doubt, to distance themselves from the Banu Khalid who were still the recognized masters of the whole of Hassa province (practically the whole of eastern Arabia), even though they were being steadily weakened.

The second practice began when the aforesaid Sabah was succeeded in the polysemous position of *shaykh* (not emir) by one of his sons, Abdallah. The nucleus of a dynastic system was thus indisputably outlined, but that system was still a weak one, since it was Abdallah's personal virtues ('bravery, wisdom, justice and generosity,' says Abu Hakima) and not his family background which seem to have led to his choice; moreover, he was only the youngest of Sabah's five sons, so that traditional dynastic rule of primogeniture was not in force. Furthermore, it appears that the head of another of the families who had emigrated to Kuwait wanted to replace the city's first *shaykh* on his death, trying to introduce the rule of alternation between the founding families. When this rival, whose name was Khalifa bin Muhammad, saw that the Kuwaitis preferred Abdallah, he and his family emigrated again, to Bahrain, where he founded a dynasty of emirs which has governed the archipelago from that time (1766) until the present day.

Abdallah governed the emirate of Kuwait for more than half a century, during which time it experienced increasingly prosperity, first because the port of Basra was beleaguered by the Persians, so that British mail boats on their way to and from India put in at Kuwait from 1775 on, and then because the emergence of a Saud-Wahhabite territorial power at almost the same time made other Gulf ports like Qatif unsafe. In the tribal and regional conflicts of this period, Kuwait managed to remain neutral because of the development of an internal consensus whereby the founding families refused to place their own interests above the common interest of the city. The effect was to confirm the identity of the city itself and the internal cohesion of its inhabitants. A city state not unlike the Venetian Republic was being born, one in which the political neutrality proper to a mercantile ideology prevailed. Its population was described by a British traveller of the period, J.S. Buckingham, as 'brave and freedom-loving'. Another visitor, J.H. Stocqueler, notes that the *shaykh* has no armed forces at his disposal and, more significantly,'the exact uniformity of costume among all ranks and ages, and the fact of there being no natives of any other country resident in the place' (see Abu Hakima n.d.). This observation on equality of dress, demographic introversion and rule by consensus, confirmed by other sources, is a clear enough indication of Kuwait's mercantile-egalitarian propensities. A third traveller reports that although political affairs were run by the *shaykh*, he was subject to the decisions of the *qadi*. More significantly, Pelly, who had visited all the other Gulf ports, notes that in Kuwait 'punishment was rarely inflicted. There seems to be very little government interference anywhere and little need of an army' *(ibid.)*, which seems to confirm the consensual and easy-going if already dynastic power of the Sabahs.

With no princely title, and no army to impose their will, but presenting themselves as a family *prima inter pares* in a city that was becoming a state, the Sabahs clearly distinguished themselves from the imperial Ottoman power working in successive military campaigns to pacify a naturally rebellious hinterland and make a satellite of it, as well as to repress the conquering, violent, proselytizing and proto-royal power of the Saudis. Kuwait, on the other hand, was a harbour city of merchants which prospered by depoliticizing itself, playing a limited and preferably financial part in the conflicts which shook eastern Arabia violently throughout the nineteenth century. This situation was to be changed on the eve of the twentieth century by the association of the Sabahs with an external force, the British. Once again, the external power did not content itself with transforming this proto-entity into a project for an autonomous state, but like the French in the Lebanon, it co-opted its local partner and thereby underwrote its authority. The statist project outlined in Kuwait, as in Lebanon, thus comprises both the fact of greater dependence on the protection of a colonial power and a programme of established internal domination to the benefit of some local hegemon.

In this case the process of change was principally the work of one man – Mubarak ibn Sabah, who' governed' Kuwait between 1896 and 1915 – rather than that of a confessional (clerical and political) elite as the Maronites of Lebanon. Mubarak's eldest brother had been killed in mysterious circumstances and replaced by a younger brother, but Mubarak killed him and a fourth brother and proclaimed himself *shaykh* in 1896, taking the Bedouin districts that lay outside the city wall as the base from which to assert his personal ambition, rather than the city itself. In other words, Mubarak's first act while he was still a young pretender to the position of *shaykh* was to de-urbanize himself, seeking support from those outside and even opposed to the city-state, before he committed his two (or three) assassinations inside it. Some historians speak of his being exiled from the city by his own family at the demand of the city merchants, in particular the most influential of them, one Yusuf al-Ibrahim. The latter was not a member of the founding families, but had acquired rights of citizenship through his vast wealth and his marriages with daughters of the Sabah family (the fact that they gave their daughters in marriage to the sons of the other families and even outsiders like al-Ibrahim was another sign of the lack of distinction between the Sabahs and the other inhabitants).

The chrysalis of a merchant city with republican-oligarchic traditions was abruptly shattered by Mubarak's authoritarian-Bedouin attempt to seize power in it at the expense of the mercantile oligarchy. Yusuf al-Ibrahim was the quintessence of mercantile power, noted for his wealth as much as for his urbanity. Mubarak, for his part, was a Sabah defending his family's title to political power, but he was weakened by the illegitimate nature of his bloodstained arrival in the seraglio and his recourse to extra-mural Bedouin forces to assert his power over the city. The two rivals were the depositaries of two opposing claims to legitimacy: in the case of the former, an oligarchic claim weakened by its representative's recent establishment; in the case of the latter, a Bedouin claim weakened by alienation from the mercantile 'establishment'. In the end Mubarak carried the day, at the same time making heavier the previously consensual government of Kuwait by the Sabahs, emphasizing the Bedouin element at the expense of the urban-mercantile factor, and above all strengthening British influence at the expense of all others, notably Ottoman. The moment of their founding and independence as modern states saw almost all contemporary Arab powers, from Iraq to Libya and from Syria to Tunisia, exhibit a similar rise in importance of rural non-urban (peasant or Bedouin) groups at the expense of the city itself. Here, that is to say in the fact that the moment of state emancipation saw rural clans acquiring power,[2] neither Lebanon nor Kuwait was really any exception.

On 23 January 1899, in fact, an exchange of letters took place between Mubarak and the British political Resident in the region, with the former giving up his political independence in return for a British undertaking to protect Mubarak and his successors. The essential point at issue was that the political and diplomatic autonomy of the city was exchanged for the protection of Mubarak's person. Accordingly, when the Saud-Wahhabites attacked Kuwait in 1920, the British intervened to help the people of the small port who had been defeated. The effect of this intervention was to strengthen the ascendancy of the Sabahs, who had negotiated a protection agreement with Britain. The defeat of the Kuwait volunteers and the success of the British intervention had a similar result: they cast light on the development of a proto-entity whose survival depended henceforward less on the bravery and spirit of independence of its united families than on British protection and on the Sabahs' astuteness in securing it. The effect of this change was to marginalize the role of the founding families even further, and to speed up the emergence of the power of the Sabahs as an authoritarian force on the spot, depending on foreign support (al-Naqeeb 1990, Ismael 1982).[3]

The families were not going to take such a change lying down. Towards the end of the 1930s they loudly reclaimed their former place in the government of the city, demanding that elected representatives of the population should share the conduct of affairs with the *shaykh*. This was the beginning of the 'Assembly Movement' *(harakat al-Majlis)*; the assembly sat for six months, and was then dissolved and replaced a few weeks later by another to which five Sabahs and nine representatives of the other founding families were nominated. The Sabahs were quick to employ a classic argument: they claimed that the supporters of an elected assembly were agents of a neighbouring power (from now on it would be Iraq and not the Saudis, whose expansionism had been moderated by several interventions on the part of the British RAF), while the Sabahs were the defenders of Kuwaiti independence. However, the British attitude, no doubt with an eye to stability in a country which had become interesting for its oil riches, gave a green light to this attempt on the part of the mercantile elite to recapture a vote in the city-state government, a fact which induced the *shaykh* to decide to set up a consultative assembly. It is notable, though, that the merchant families defined their aim in terms of *musharaka* (sharing), thus confirming an elitist definition of democracy, a word hardly ever uttered by their representatives at this period. Another interesting point is the fact that the Sabahs resisted their claim, arguing that any power sharing would lead to the diffusion of a power and hence a weakening of the nascent entity's means of resistance in a hostile environment. In Lebanon as in Kuwait, the political debate turned on power sharing, seen as a source of national vulnerability by the clear inheritor of colonial power but as a legitimate right and affirmation of national unity by the groups opposing him. The same procedure, sharing, was in turn a means of defence against foreign powers and a Trojan horse working to their advantage, depending on whether one was part of the prevalent *asabiyya* or not.

The establishment of the assembly was thus a sign to the families of a restoration of the balance of power that Mubarak had shattered. A return to the principle of the mercantile oligarchic city might well have been possible at this point but for the advent of oil like a *deus ex machina*, providing the Sabahs with a valuable tool for the re-establishment of their hegemony. The Sabahs used what looked like nationalization of the oil sector (public finances had in fact become the prerogative of the Sabahs) to neutralize the political ambitions of the founding families and set up an advanced welfare state, which won them the loyalty of the Third Estate outside the oligarchic families. The game thus became triangular instead of binary, giving the Sabahs the necessary tools to set two very distinct social strata against each other: the co-founders defending their privileges against what they saw as the unjustifiable authoritarianism of the Sabahs, and the rest of the Kuwaitis (Shi'ites, Sunnis from non-Najdi origins, Bedouins who had given up the nomadic life) who disputed oligarchic practices even more than the Sabahs' authority. The Sabahs suddenly became supporters

of a 'national integration' which would be the civil counterpart to their strengthened hold on power (and the riches deriving from it), an integration which both
leading families, still attached to their largely illusory privileges as 'co-
founders', could not back. At once the Sabahs seemed more 'modern' than their
oligarchic rivals: they had become authoritarian, assuming the title of emirs and
reinforcing their dynastic cohesion by a judicious mechanism of alternation on
the throne (between the two branches founded by the sons of Mubarak, henceforth called 'the Great'), but they showed concern for social egalitarianism
within so-called civil society as well as preserving the distinction between their
now dynastic family and that society.

It was in this context that Kuwait became independent. The Iraqi dictator of
the time, General Qassem, was making claims on Kuwait which foreign protection (western and Egyptian) had already frustrated. At home, the Sabahs could
not take the risk of seeing their own fears realized if they pushed the leading
families, thwarted in their wish for power, to siding with the Iraqi claims.
Independence was thus accompanied by the adoption of a consensual constitution in which Kuwait distinguished itself from its neighbours by establishing a
partially elected parliament and a written constitution guaranteeing human
rights. Like the Maronites who feared seeing their Muslim fellow citizens echo
Syrian claims to the Lebanon, the Sabahs seem to have understood that the loyalty of the merchant families to the new and now independent entity derived
from their participation in the government of the country. An incomplete hegemon, confessional in Lebanon, family in Kuwait, each of which had judiciously
acquired the support of the dominant foreign power (France in Lebanon, Great
Britain in Kuwait), understood that it could not ensure the new state survival
without co-opting representatives of the social spheres which might move from
internal opposition to questioning the state entity itself. In both cases, the price
of independence and the survival of the hegemon was a certain measure of a
democratization which contained concessions and limitations, but promised
development towards a regime of effective power sharing. Both the Lebanese
'National Pact' and the Kuwaiti constitution, which were contemporaneous with
and collateral to independence, pointed in this direction. In both cases, overtures
to democracy acted as an instrument of political cohesion within a newly established state entity; they clearly responded to a desire to limit the centrifugal tendencies within those tribal or confessional *asabiyyat* which were allowed a
limited position in the system and therefore were disposed to cash in their backing for the prevailing *asabiyya* and *its* state in return for a more or less homoeo-
pathic dose of participation in power, and the nepotist redistributive advantages
that implicitly went along with it.

Other examples

Bahrain pursued a similar path. A dynasty (related to the Sabahs) had succeeded in installing itself in power in this little archipelago. If Syria was the chief threat to the Lebanon, and Iraq to Kuwait, here Iran was a permanent threat because Bahrain had long been part of the Persian empire, and most of the inhabitants of the archipelago, before the arrival of the Khalifas in Bahrain, were Shi'ite, some of them even Persian-speaking. When Great Britain decided to withdraw from the Gulf, therefore, the Shah of Iran claimed that the archipelago belonged to his country. A referendum was organized under the auspices of the United Nations, which showed that a huge majority of Bahrainis favoured independence.

However, this referendum had been organized with a promise on the part of the Khalifa rulers that it would be followed by power-sharing through free parliamentary elections. The referendum was therefore simply part of a total deal, including, as was the case in the Lebanon in 1943 and in Kuwait in 1962, an unwritten agreement to introduce some level of power-sharing (here again power means not only positions in the state apparatus, but prestige, influence, visibility and resources for nepotism which go with it, all of which make it so attractive). Elections were indeed held, but the assembly was dissolved a little later. The hegemonic segment was even less assured here than elsewhere because of the weakness of a Sunni dynasty in a country with a Shi'ite majority and relatively modest oil revenues. That is why, under pressure from a relatively well organized civil society, the Khalifas restored their authoritarian power by turning to their neighbours: when they allowed neighbouring Saudi Arabia to make a quasi satellite of it in 1975, Bahrain had a crucial ally in its restoration of authoritarianism at home, which was accompanied by a partial sacrifice of its independence.

In each of these three cases, therefore, we see a regime of limited power-sharing installed in a more or less durable fashion, responding less to a genuinely democratic expectation than out of concern on the part of the ruling *asabiyyat*, whose statist plans were too vulnerable to the pressures and claims proceeding from the immediate regional environment, to neutralize those segments of the population tempted to move from political claims at home to questioning the political entity at the head of which the ruling clan had succeeded in installing itself, with the help of a tutelary power and against the wish of some powerful neighbour. None of the Lebanese confessional communities can claim to have had a more clearly democratic tradition than the others; the oligarchic families of Kuwait cannot claim to be more democratic than the ruling dynasty (they share a culture, and are even more firmly opposed to women's suffrage or the naturalization of the hundreds of thousands of expatriates who made the construction of Kuwait possible), and the Bahrainis are not necessarily any more democratically minded than their rulers.

One may even extend this comparison to the United Arab Emirates, where the system of confederation installed at the time of independence in 1971 was meant to manage an inter-tribal form of power-sharing among unequal emirates, notably between Abu Dhabi and Dubai, in a game for seven, strongly reminiscent of the inter-confessional game played in the Lebanon, the result of a permanent act of balancing between Abu Dhabi's attempts to impose its will and the other six emirates' resistance to these attempts. Abu Dhabi cannot afford to see the other emirates (some of them very poorly endowed with oil riches) becoming the satellites of Oman, Saudi Arabia or Iran without having Abu Dhabi's independence brought into question. The confederal (formally egalitarian) structure put together in 1971 is therefore a *sui generis* form of power-sharing, specifically meant to remedy the centrifugal tendencies which are the common feature of any tribal coalition. Abu Dhabi has also to redistribute some of its oil-generated wealth in order to cement a confederation permanently threatened with disintegration. Power- (and wealth-) sharing is therefore a prerequisite to keep a decent level of unity among these formally 'United' emirates. Once more: state survival and domestic formulae for power-sharing are intimately linked, clearly demonstrating that the emergence of the modern nation-state in that part of the world has had complex effects on power structures, pushing for excessive authoritarianism in some large polities and triggering the institutionalization of *sui generis* forms of power- and resource-sharing in other, smaller units. Kuwaiti constitutionalism, Lebanon's national pact, the UAE's confederation are hence the *quid pro quo* of state survival, a protective stratagem on the part of the ruling segment to ensure the state survival as well as its own permanent rule, by catering to the centrifugal trends among the non-ruling segments who are equally part of the modern state.

In all these cases, the overture to 'democracy' is the result of a decision to maintain civil peace and so-called 'national unity' as well as the fear that the nascent entity will be absorbed by some more powerful neighbour. The instrumental nature of the constitutional arrangement (to which 'democracy' was reduced at the start) is as clear as its contemporaneity with independence (an independence formally acquired at the expense of the colonial power, but which practically meant compelling recognition by an expansionist neighbour claiming that this independence was really just covert secession). 'Democracy' was established all at once, without democrats, as a power-sharing formula within the framework of new frontiers, for fear these frontiers might disappear entirely by means of collusion between dissatisfied internal segments and an expansionist neighbour(s).

It is this ambiguous origin, with the 'democratic pact' being strongly induced by the fragility of the state entity, that largely explains how overtures to democracy occur and in some cases persist in small rather than large countries in the region. In Egypt, in Syria, in Algeria and elsewhere, the same constraints do not operate. In such countries other configurations of ruling elites have been able to make a cleaner break with the so-called liberal model, discrediting it as an 'import' and basing their legitimacy on a nationalist discourse stuffed with 'historic missions' and a planned economy, both of them assumed to build powerful nation states even if the power is consequently exercised more at the expense of the society those states control than in confronting enemies abroad. Such a development could occur only because there was no opposition to the entity on the part of its new citizens. There was no need to 'hold' the various segments of the population, or even to recognize the latter's diversity. There was no need constantly to persuade them not to be seduced by the siren voices of a neighbouring country. Populist mobilization was, in large state units, a much more potent vehicle for legitimization than *sui generis* forms of power-sharing. Hence, while the Maronites, the Sabahs, the Bani Yas and later the Hashemites in Jordan were recognizing the segmentary fabric of the societies they were ruling, others were negating this fabric, hiding behind the concepts of state, national unity, citizenship, and later socialism, a social fabric not really dissimilar from that of the smaller units. The basic strategy was, in the smaller countries, inward oriented: recognition of segmentarity, power-sharing among the segments and prevalence of the leading segment in its position. In the larger units, on the contrary, legitimation strategies were basically outwards oriented or even expansionist. Nasser's pan-Arabism, Algeria's Third-Worldism, Iraq's expansionist policies (at the expense of Syria, and later of Kuwait), Syria's attempts to coalesce Lebanon, Jordan and the Palestinians under her control, Saudi interference in many Arab polities, were all symptoms of an outward-oriented legitimation strategy, of which the domestic preliminary was the almost absolute negation of segmentary (religious/ethnic/tribal) pluralism and the ideologized rejection of political pluralism as well.

'Democracy' between oligarchy and authoritarianism

Internal consensus in the small countries discussed above tended to be unstable from the first. To quote Rousseau again: 'No government is so subject to civil wars and internal unrest as the democratic or popular government, because no other is inclined to change its shape so much and so continually, and no other demands more vigilance and courage to maintain it in its shape' *(The Social Contract)*. To sum up, the ruling clan was obliged to associate other social segments in the exercise of power while avoiding pure and simple devolution of that power to their advantage (a process summed up by Ibn Khaldun in one word – *iltiham* – meaning at the same time loyalty, submission and coalescence with the dominant clan on the part of segments assigned minor status in association with the ruling *asabiyya*). This involved the pursuit of two series of conservatory measures at once. It was necessary first to keep power-sharing within control by imposing restrictive barriers which would assure the maintenance of the ruling clan's prevalence at the expense of its associates. It was also necessary to keep the Third Estate, the involuntary beneficiaries of the democratic overtures (who would elsewhere be called 'the people'), from questioning the consitutional arrangement as a whole, that is to say, constructing a genuine democracy of the western type or becoming the breeding ground and mainstay of a military dictatorship like those that were to dominate the rest of the region.

In Lebanon, several conservatory measures were therefore progressively adopted by the Maronite elite. A fundamental point was to place the armed forces under Maronite control (so as not to let them be manipulated by the other groups), and also to refrain from developing the army (so as not to allow a group outside the original arrangement to seize power at the expense of both the ruling confession and the traditional opposition). Thus the 'weak state' became a cliché for the elites in power aiming to fend off the emergence of a state apparatus, and above all of an army which might be tempted to a coup d'état, both of which would escape the will of the founding clan. It was therefore necessary for the state to remain dependent on its historic confessional origin, marked by it and conditioned by its decisions. If it became really abstracted from that heavily confessional origin it would be anonymous, and would thus become a stake for which clan *asabiyyat* and modern groups would compete. The confessional origin had to be emphasized so that the state would remain its appendage. The state was thus deprived of its functions of regulation, even of arbitration. With the capitalist development of certain sectors of the economy, this weakness assumed by and programmed into the state also served to allow the development of a non-statist, even anti-statist laissez-faire capitalism, a constant feature of mercantile republics.

Another conservatory measure consisted in establishing parliamentary representation but on a strictly confessional basis. The aim of pre-distributing parliamentary seats to the different communities was both to demonstrate the phenomenon of co-optation, making it very visible, and on the other hand to limit political influence of modern groups triggered by the capitalist transformation of the society (parties, syndicates and associations) and prevent their being the ultimate beneficiaries of the overture to democracy after they had been its involuntary beneficiaries earlier. The stipulation that every Lebanese citizen should return to vote in his village of origin rather than voting in his place of residence (which in 1975, on the eve of the war, was Beirut or its immediate surroundings for more than 50 per cent of the population), was evidence of the same concern. E. Rabbath spoke of 'Lebanese confined in their confessions', individual subjects who had been forbidden to exist politically outside their confessional groups, since the lasting nature of these groups was the only effective instrument for maintaining Maronite quasi-hegemony and the political survival of its co-opted allies from the other confessions. The system was thus a democracy to which the concept of citizenship was foreign, since civil peace between groups (and incidentally the predominance of one of them) and not the emancipation of individual citizens, was the central aim of the mechanism. In fact emancipation became a positive menace to the system from the moment it was manipulated by Muslim groups, ostensibly to introduce the concept of democracy by right of numbers, in fact to replace one historical hegemony by another.

The Maronite quasi-hegemon thus found itself facing a situation where the co-opted representatives of other communities could no longer 'hold' the people they were supposed to represent, whether because the latter were demanding a greater share of power and political visibility on behalf of their leaders, and

more posts in the administration in the name of confessional logic, or because
they were engaged in a more radical dispute with the system, demanding a re-
examination of the original arrangement as a whole. The attitude of the Muslim
leaders whom the system had co-opted became very problematic, since they
were in turn the allies of the quasi-hegemon in the face of radical opposition
(leftist or religious) to the arrangement, and its enemies when it was possible to
extract concessions of a confessional nature from the quasi-hegemon by threatening that it would have to deal with far more hostile masses. The Maronite elite
thought of the oligarchy uniting it with the co-opted islamic leaders as a
makeshift way of asserting a predominance it might have wished was stronger;
but socio-demographic evolution, on the contrary, impelled it to make a more
painful choice between even less predominance within the inter-confessional
oligarchy in power and radically democratic overtures to the 'islamo-progres-
sive' Third Estate, as the vocabulary of the civil war was to call it. A typical feature of the crucial pre-war years was the tacking back and forth of Muslim
confessional leaders between loyalty to an inegalitarian oligarchic regime which
had helped them into existence, and denunciation of it under pressure from 'the
street'. With the addition of the Palestinian factor from 1967 onwards, the second of these two options would eventually win out, opening up the way to civil
war.

In Kuwait, the Sabahs faced the same dilemma: they had both to instil identification with the regime into the co-founding families, without succumbing to
the temptations of the merchant republic, and also to 'protect' those families and
the ruling family against the formation of groups which did not identify at all
with the first arrangement and would have liked to put an end to it: Arab nationalists, naturalized Shi'ites, Palestinians seeking recognition. The Sabahs hesi-
tated between discreet complicity with the co-founding families, in order to
preserve the interests of both groups, and a populism which attempted to mobilize the Third Estate against the oligarchic families.

When it leaned towards the oligarchy, Kuwaiti 'democracy' functioned in a
manner which to some extent recalls Athenian democracy. As Moses Finley
(1963) has noted, 'The final paradox of archaic Greek history is [the] march
hand in hand of freedom and slavery,' in that without slaves, the Athenians
would hardly have had the time or the means to participate in the direct democracy offered to them. The immigrant workers in the oil emirate, whose proportion was not unlike that of slaves in the Athens of Pericles, dealt with that
emirate's business so that its 'citizens' would be able to engage in politics. We
might even take the analogy further and say that the Palestinians who settled in
Kuwait kept the state apparatus functioning like the metics of Athens (foreigners
who had been living in the city for a long time but were neither citizens nor
slaves), to allow the Kuwaitis to indulge in their passion for the city's affairs.
Like the Athenian democracy described by David Held, Kuwait was 'a tyranny
of citizens', with the *demos* consisting entirely of male adults of incontestable
Athenian (Kuwaiti) descent (1987, 22).

The history of independent Kuwait thus consists of constant tacking back and forth between a tribal authoritarianism similar to those which are predominant in the Gulf petro-monarchies, and an oligarchic republicanism which is truer to the origins of the city. Constitutionalism, free elections, the preponderant weight of the chamber of commerce and industry, a free press, are the demands of the merchant families, and they are sometimes granted. On the other side, suspension of the constitution, dissolution of the assembly 'because it threatens national unity', appointment rather than election of representatives, the retention of key posts by members of the Sabah family, a press muzzled 'because it reflects on national security', are the current practices of the Sabahs when they can manage to impose their will. From 1962 to the present, Kuwait has alternated between these two models, living most of the time under the rule of Sabah authoritarianism modified by overtures which the oligarchy would quickly exploit with a view to establishing a merchant republic, whereupon the Sabahs would instantly clamp down again to prevent such a change.

This tension, inherent in the regime, might of course have been influenced or even circumvented by the effective introduction of citizenship. But the two rival groups (the ruling tribe and the oligarchic families) seemed to have agreed to exclude that possibility by limiting suffrage to men, and to the descendants of the original residents of the emirate. Moreover, naturalization remained very much the exception in Kuwait and did not bring with it the right to vote. That has not prevented the emergence of radical groups opposed to both the authoritarianism of the emirs and the oligarchy. Such was the case with the Arab nationalist movement led by Ahmad al-Khatib and Jasim al-Qatami, the Sunni islamist religious movement which formed around the weekly *al-Mujtama* and the Shi'ite minority in the country. This composite Third Estate, the leaven of a 'civil society', has at times played a part useful to the oligarchic opposition, with which it associated itself by demanding a return to the constitutional system, and at a times one useful to the assertion of the emir's authority, through verbal onslaughts so offensive as to make the dissolution of parliament and the suspension of press freedom almost legitimate.

In Bahrain, the experiment was more promising because the authoritarianism of the Khalifa emirs confronted not so much an oligarchy clinging to ancestral privileges as a population which had a more convincing claim to be called a 'civil society'. Several factors peculiar to the archipelago, including a relatively high level of literacy, modest oil revenues, small numbers of immigrants and a history of syndicalism unparalleled in the region, gave a clearer social content to the democratic claim. That claim suddenly became even more radical, going so far as to elect avowed marxists in the only legislative elections, of 1974. The quasi-hegemon had no solution but to give up its political autonomy in exchange for Saudi participation in the repression of a movement which was questioning the regime in a manner more 'democratic' than oligarchic. The threat was graver and the remedy more costly than elsewhere (in terms of internal repression as well as dependence on 'Big Brother' in Saudi Arabia), but the

Khalifas had no other, internal, solution: they were directly confronting not so much a powerful oligarchy, a buffer between the hegemon and society, but society itself, and strong-arm authoritarianism struck them as both possible and inevitable. The bridge built between the Bahraini archipelago and Saudi Arabia was the visual sanction of this regional denial of democracy, called 'normalization'.

The consociative system which has been a feature of many small Arab states does therefore go into cyclical crises. The balance on which it is founded is so delicate and, most importantly, interference from mighty neighbours is so common, that it sometimes seems a miracle that those small states can keep an enviable level of democratic practice in such a hostile environment. Confessional democracy in Lebanon survived for half a century despite the dissatisfaction of the Muslim confessional elite, the attempts of the ruling confession to concentrate as much power as possible in its own hands, the overt rejection of the system by new radical forces triggered by modernization, and the constant interference by regional forces in the country's domestic affairs. Kuwait's parliamentary system survived, on and off, for some 30 years despite the absolute exclusion of immigrants from it and the overt opposition of Saudi Arabia, Iraq and Iran. The UAE inter-tribal confederal consociation is also surviving despite very strong centrifugal tendencies. The existence of a free press in all these small countries allows for these crises to be expressed and publicized, which is not the case in the larger units where the press has been kept under strict control. This control, in denying to anyone the right to mention crises, has given the entirely false impression that the large Arab units were forever crisis-free.

The auto-reproduction of the system

Survival of these delicately designed regimes depended largely on their ability to adjust to changing circumstances. Regional policy thus meant that Saudi Arabia, a country openly hostile to the democratic overtures of its neighbours, would be the place where the restoration of an oligarchic balance of power could occur, to the detriment of authoritarian trends both in Kuwait and in the Lebanon. The ruling elite, having had to face crises which endangered both its own survival and that of the country it aimed to control, would be led to attempting an operation of the re-foundation of its power through an historical compromise with the oligarchy (and to the latter's advantage). In the face of the choice between invasion from outside and democratic overtures at home, the Sabahs had no other real way out but to make new concessions; in the face of an ever higher price to be paid for its privileges, the Maronite political elite could no longer cling to them.

This is particularly clear in the case of Kuwait. On 2 August 1990, the emirate was invaded and then officially annexed by its powerful Iraqi neighbour. The oligarchic families pushed into opposition by the authoritarianism of the

Sabahs, which had reached a peak on the eve of the invasion (with government by technocrats who were not on the whole the 'natural' representatives of the oligarchy, and a parliament formed entirely by appointment after the constitution had been suspended), were not going to move on from their thwarted demands for more power-sharing (and petrodollar-sharing) to a collaboration with the occupying power. Confronting Iraq, the Kuwaitis were unanimous in showing patriotic support for 'their state', an attitude which, paradoxically, forced the Sabahs to recognize that the emirate was not their own exclusive property. The Sabahs would hardly have solicited such support for the state on the part of the Kuwaitis, since there would of course be a price to pay for it. Their ideal, had the invasion not occurred, probably would have been a moderate link between the Kuwaitis and their country, something which was not total patriotism but did not go so far as collusion with foreigners, a clever formula, but difficult to preserve when an invader is desperately seeking quislings among your citizens.

Accordingly, a new deal had to be offered if resistance to Iraq was to be organized. The idea of general national assizes gained ground, and was in fact organized in October that year in the Saudi city of Jeddah. The Sabahs needed to show their western allies that they really were the legitimate holders of power. It was therefore necessary for the oligarchic families to renew their recognition of that legitimacy, and this gave them a strategic opportunity to push their own demands through. The families thus drove a profitable bargain: their support for the emir in exchange for the Sabahs' solemn promise to bring the constitution back into force. In this way, the Iraqi invasion restored the balance of oligarchic power, by allowing the oligarchy to cash in on its support for the Sabahs without being accused, as it had often been in the past, of being a tool of foreigners.

The Kuwaiti elections took place in October 1992 , after the liberation of the country, even though the Sabahs tried to renege on their promise by exaggerating the foreign coalition's part in liberating their emirate, so as to make less of the part played by a resistance which they could not master and which had been demanding a rendering of accounts ever since the liberation. Underneath it all, an old debate revived, on the respective role played by the Sabahs and other Kuwaitis in the creation of Kuwait and the respective role played by foreign and internal forces in its liberation. The Sabahs emphasized their ability to ensure British secret protection in 1899 as much as the formidable western coalition in 1990. The Kuwaitis, on the other hand, emphasized the unity of the population and its participation in the resistance. These two claims to legitimacy are still at odds. The 1992 elections did not settle the question; on the contrary, they weakened both the ruling family and the oligarchic families by showing that the Third Estate, most notably because of its role during the occupation and its partial political islamicization, was more active than expected in what had hitherto been basically a game for two, played between the *asabiyya* in power and the oligarchy. The future of the regime, from the internal viewpoint (which was not necessarily the crucial factor of the international stakes now at play) seems henceforward to depend largely on any move made by this Third Estate towards an association with the Sabahs, an alliance with the oligarchic families in a 'wider constitutional front', or the development of an even more autonomous position on the local political chessboard.

The Maronite hegemon in the Lebanon experienced attrition over a longer period before it too had to make concessions at the assizes held in Taif, another Saudi city. The war that had made Lebanon a bloodbath since 1975 finally eroded the reality of the hegemonic power, although it continued successfully clinging to the texts that formed the legal organization of its incomplete hegemony. The inability of the Maronites, in the summer of 1988, to provide continuity in the presidency of the republic, for decades the emblem of their primacy, brought General Aoun to the front of the stage. Aoun was a populist leader who assumed the attitude of a 'saviour' but ended, in view of the balance of effective forces on the ground, by hastening the collapse of the Maronite hegemony rather than restoring it. The traditional representatives of Maronite hegemony, particularly the deputies elected 20 years earlier, therefore went to Taif to accept what they had hitherto managed to avoid: written confirmation of their loss of hegemony. The rival groups were strongly divided in themselves, and there was no devolution of power from one confession to another, only a constitutionally organized diffusion of the power of the former hegemon. Article 17 of the 1926 constitution, which gave executive power to the president of the republic and which had become the emblematic basis of the Maronite predominance, was amended so that the executive branch of government was devolved to the council of ministers as a whole. The council itself was seriously weakened by the exorbitant power granted to the parliament and to its speaker.

The institutional diffusion of the former hegemon's power is such that the concept of representation will henceforward prevail, in a most debilitating manner, over the necessity for government. The logic of acceptable representation of the confessional groups, not to mention the different tendencies within each of these groups, brings with it almost complete paralysis of the state apparatus. The state now seems to be ruled not by a president but by a troika (the Maronite president, the Sunni prime minister and the Shi'ite speaker of parliament). This troika has no legal foundation and decisions are officially taken by majority vote in a council of ministers made up of 30 members representing the internal tendencies within each of the groups (the troika is supposed to represent the groups as a whole). The council is itself supervised by an assembly of 128 deputies elected in haphazard fashion. The troika and the council, moreover, were supposed to appoint people to the 120 highest posts in the administration, the fundamental criterion of selection, yet again, being representation of the various confessional clans as well as the ever-growing number of nepotist clienteles.

The Taif Agreements, by thus systematically diffusing the old quasi-hegemonic power of the Maronites, presented a series of problems which were both practical and theoretical. The paralysis of power intensified the Syrian stranglehold on Lebanon, in the sense that the elimination of an effective decision-making structure (which had been systematically sought by Damascus) handed decision-making powers, at least in the first phase following the Taif Agreements, to the Syrian government, which itself was centralized, not very much interested in confessional representation, and frankly authoritarian. In this sense, Taif is a handicap to Lebanese democracy, since it gives power de facto in Lebanon to a government which is neither democratic nor Lebanese, i.e. Syria. The other problem, this time a domestic one, has been one of persuading the non-Maronite *asabiyyat* hitherto accorded a secondary status in the system, that the Taif Agreements cannot end in the replacement of one hegemony by another, not so much because the other confessions (for instance, the Sunnis or the Shi'ites) have no right to repeat the Maronite experiment in 'soft hegemony' to their own advantage, but because the confessional pluralism of the *asabiyyat*, henceforward the rule if not the Rule, could only exacerbate their rivalry. At the end of the civil war, no confession in fact seemed to be in a position to reproduce the privileged situation of the Maronites at the time of the foundation of the state in 1920. Contrary to some hypotheses, the Maronites could neither maintain their power nor hand it on to others. It is an inheritance to be shared, and any attempt to reconcentrate it to a single confession's advantage will bring about a new civil war.

Beyond these political considerations, there is the more theoretical question of the durability of a state power not founded on some kind of hegemony, even one that is incomplete. Once need not be an assiduous reader of Ibn Khaldun or a supporter of the theses of Gramsci to ask this question. And it is here that it becomes difficult to regulate the inherent tension between the necessity of having a stock of *asabiyyat* available in order to govern, and considerations of the equitable representation of various groups. Consociative democracy, as presented by Arendt Lijphard, is no doubt the best way of picturing a rational alliance between these two conflicting constraints. In this logic, the Taif Agreements, if we are optimistic, are the necessary corrective to the survival of a regime in which the hegemony of one group was not admitted and where, for various reasons both demographic and political, no other group is at present in a position to replace the failing power.

However, the initial contradiction between the domestic and the regional, which was the original raison d'être of Lebanon, disappears at the same time. If Lebanon was historically established as a sovereign country by means of an association between a local segment (the Maronites) and a foreign power (France), the consociative raison d'être at the heart of Taif must find another claim to legitimacy for the entity which has survived the attrition of its founding clan. Now Lebanon is not an island, and it is very tempting to reconsider the entire state unit, since its internal raison d'être (an essentially Maronite Christian political power) has gone. An attempt to ideologize, even mythologize, equitably organized community life among confessionally distinct groups thus becomes necessary, in order to give a Lebanon in the course of losing its original raison d'être a new reason to survive, since the risk is very serious that

Taif, instead of being a necessary adjusting measure, has been implemented in such a way that the delicate balance of constraints is being disrupted to a point where the survival of the state becomes almost impossible.

From 'small' to 'large': the potential for Arab democratization

Successful or not, these attempts to adjust to (local or regional) conditions are a central feature in the system. Larger units have not shown a similar ability to adjust, most probably because mission-oriented regimes, as implied by Rousseau, cannot handle politics by way of informal pacts. Recent successful democratic overtures in the Arab world have indeed been the result of pre-electoral informal agreements between those in power and significant representatives of the opposition. A national charter and, more importantly, an informal deal on the distribution of high positions in the state apparatus have been considered by Yemenis as a necessary prerequisite to the organization of elections. A national charter was also discussed in Jordan, and an informal deal was struck between the throne and representatives of the social society on the very limits of democratization before really competitive elections could take place. The Jeddah meeting has been the foundation upon which the Kuwaiti regime has been reconstructed, and Taif is the partly formal, largely informal foundation of Lebanon after the civil war. The ability to achieve this kind of *sui generis* pact before formal elections is thus an important feature of the system, probably much easier to attain in regimes which assume that survival is their first task than in those which give themselves some grandiose mission to accomplish.

What can the experiment of the 'small' Arab states tell us about the chances of democratization of their 'large' neighbours, that is to say the Arab world as a whole? First, that the democracy of the 'small' countries has quickly turned out to be a regional affair. For various reasons, the 'large' countries have begun to fear that overtures to democracy may end up taking root and become a standard of experience for other countries. Thus the 'large' countries of the region have developed a discourse openly hostile to such experiments, despite their character limited both geographically and in their effective significance. The Lebanese democratic experiment has frequently been criticized as a sign of westernization, general corruption and encouragement to extremism. King Fahd of Saudi Arabia openly criticized the elections in neighbouring Kuwait as an operation inimical to the traditions of the region. The same applies to Bahrain, where the Saudis have hardly troubled to disguise their part in the interruption of the constitutional experiment and where at the end of 1992 a consultative, nominated council was set up in the image of that announced by the Saudis for themselves. Iraq had also had little consideration for democratic forces in Kuwait. In all cases the 'large' countries, when they did not succeed in aborting democratic experiments, have systematically insisted on the allegedly 'singular' character of those 'small' countries where power-sharing has been introduced.

This is why, whenever a neighbouring power has the means to impose itself, its idea is to 'normalize' the situation by reproducing a (preferably) authoritarian power in these 'small countries': in the case of Syria, its own in Lebanon; in the case of the Saudis, that of the Sabahs in Kuwait. When it finally accepts that such normalization is harder to achieve than first appeared, the regional pole instead sets about manipulating the existing system. After reviling confessional groups in Lebanon, Syria has come to think of their political survival as necessary; the Saudis have accepted the Kuwaiti elections hoping they will prove ephemeral and lead nowhere. After showing their deep discomfort in the face of genuinely free legislative elections in Jordan in 1989, Damascus and Riyadh, Cairo and Baghdad have ended up resigning themselves to that event, saying it was the only possible solution – in Jordan, nowhere else. Many influential regimes in the Arab world were embarrassed by the Yemeni elections; if Yemen (reputedly the most backward country) could translate its social segmentation into a politically pluralistic country, 'why not us?'.

Secondly, in so far as the political culture of these societies was originally comparable if not similar, Lebanese, Kuwaiti and more recently Jordanian and Yemeni exceptionalism seems closely linked to the incapacity of incomplete hegemons in certain small countries to defend the states created for them without operating a power-sharing process, rather than to cultural features peculiar to the small countries concerned. This is why the 'risk of contagion' has finally been limited. For the 'small' states as well as the 'large' ones surrounding (or squeezing) them, both had an interest in insisting on the exceptional nature of this or that democratic experiment. The former, because this exceptionalism was to some extent a further raison d'être in a region permeated by calls for unification and by more or less open attempts at annexation; the latter to avoid attempts on the part of their own 'subjects' to repeat the democratic experience.

This does not mean that more democratic experiments of the type studied here may not yet occur. The case of Jordan shows us that overtures to democracy remain an instrument of legitimation for ruling clans feeling a threat to their survival, if not to that of the entity which they control. The violent demonstrations in south Jordan in the spring of 1989 were singular, in that opposition to the regime had gained a hold in sectors of the population on which Hashemite royal power had traditionally relied to defend itself against opposition in the (original) urban and Palestinian sectors. The troubles of 1989 broke out in a rural Transjordanian and to some extent Bedouin environment which had hitherto provided most of the troops for the semi-praetorian, semi-national army, and which had saved the throne several times in the past. The overtures to democracy, therefore, answered a wish among these sectors to be more equitably associated with the power structure, in the face of external dangers presented, above all, by Palestinian pressure.

The allegedly unitarian crusade of Iraq and Syria, as well as Saudi pressure, finally resulted in damage to the exceptionalism of Lebanon and Kuwait, as that of Bahrain in the past and perhaps Jordan in the future. Pressure from the 'large' countries has not spared the PLO, greatly perturbing those currents of thought aiming to democratize it.[4] Consequently the 'small' countries risk living more in tune with the 'large' countries of the area in future, and sharing the present reluctance of those countries to introduce democratic practices into their governments. However, it may be that while they lose their exceptionalism, which is now under permanent threat, the 'small' countries will end up showing their more powerful neighbours that liberal democratization and political pluralism come by way of recognition rather than the denial of the existence of various social segments, and even more important, that democratization is a useful tool for preventing civil wars.[5] To bring that about, the confessional, ethnic or dynastic rulers who govern most of the 'large' countries in the region will have to be seriously weakened. With their nationalist discourse suffering attrition as a result of the end of the Cold War and the introduction of the peace process, it does seem inevitable that they will be weakened. They could therefore learn from the example of the 'small' countries rather than trying yet again to normalize them, in order to avoid inevitable civil war such as broke out in Iraq immediately after the military success of the coalition.

The case of Iraq is interesting, in that according to the pattern currently accepted, the dictatorship in power, crushed by defeat, ought to have given way to another and potentially democratic regime. That did not happen because the Iraqi hegemon had two segments of fundamentally different kinds confronting it: the Kurds in the north induced by the weakness of the regime to make claims of a more or less openly separatist nature, and the Shi'ites in the south, who might have been tempted simply to replace the (Sunni Arab) hegemon which has held power ever since the creation of the state. The two claims could not easily be reconciled, and the key function of the Sunni Arab minority became apparent: it governed because it was as Sunni as the Kurds and as Arab as the Shi'ites. In calling for the country to be made a confederation, the Kurds alienated themselves from large sectors of the population both close to the regime and in the opposition. In raising fears of an alignment with Iran, the Shi'ite religious opposition alienated itself from Kurdish support. Calling for the democratization of so complex a society, one maintaining an artificially unified discourse, was much like squaring the circle, and gave extra years to the regime which itself maintained a missionary discourse showing that the territorial integrity of the country depended on its own survival. No consociation would be possible unless the various segments belonged to the same category. Thus after the defeat of Iraq, the Kurdish groups called principally for territory to be shared, while the Shi'ite groups were more anxious for power-sharing, or the devolution of power to their own advantage. Consociation presupposes a certain political uniformity between the claims of the various constituent segments and that was far from being the case in Iraq, at least immediately after the war.

However, a factor noted in the 'small' countries can be discerned in the 'large' countries too: the predominance of originally rural elements in the political system. This applies not only to Lebanon but also to Syria, not only to

Kuwait but also to Iraq and Saudi Arabia. This predominance is undoubtedly a partial explanation of the reproduction of authoritarianism in that the rural groups were previously only marginal in a pattern of imperial, centuries-old power handed on by the prominent figures of urban life (and so well described in Albert Hourani's numerous works). Groups which come to power thanks to the establishment of modern states, are more anxious for their immediate political survival than for the establishment of permanent powers. These rural *asabiyyat* which dominate urban life are strangers to it, which explains why Saddam's troops could destroy the Najaf mosques and Asad's the historic centre of Hama. Their urban policies in Damascus, Baghdad, Beirut and elsewhere cut deep into the urban tissue, for the city, still alien to them, was something to be controlled, combed through and dominated.

Rousseau's thesis of the feasibility of democratization in 'small' states may to some extent be confirmed, not so much because non-representative democracy needs to operate in small units where government is based on a referendary and quasi-permanent legitimacy as because, in the absence of influential democratic forces and a political culture generally favourable to the development of democracy, it may be easier to organize consociations in units of small dimensions. Power-sharing between segments of society, and attempts by one segment or another to rise to power, occur in a climate of relative familiarity where the stakes are obvious and limited. On the one hand, people know and recognize each other easily, while on the other the small size of the territory naturally eliminates tendencies to separatism as a permanent menace if the consensus should be broken. Hence the crucial importance of recognition of the organic segmentation of society as a pre-condition for its transformation into a democratic polity.

The permanent threat of absorption into a larger entity, even if it is sometimes brandished simply as a threat, is also a factor favouring internal entente and willingness to live together, conditions less easily brought together in entities of ten or twenty million inhabitants, where the permanent risk comes not so much from a more powerful neighbouring entity as from expansionist flight forward. More important, perhaps, the alienation from urban life which has been a feature of larger countries, can be circumvented in small statist structures. This is not, of course, because each citizen 'can easily be acquainted with all the others', as Rousseau wished, but because the splits between segments are not associated with large, autonomous, distant geographical zones, to which those segments may perhaps think of going, regarding them as an ever-present alternative to urban co-existence.

This is why the very rapid urbanization of the last three or four decades in the region as a whole is of a kind to change the split between town and country and make the city an increasingly exclusive scene of rivalry which is frankly segmentary or more openly political, and most often a mixture of the two. These are major cities of dimensions larger than those of Pericles' Athens or Rousseau's Geneva, and where urbanization is abrupt rather than cumulative.

The differences betwen 'small' and 'large' countries are thus becoming blurred, to the benefit of the sprawling cities and a hinterland which becomes an original, mythical fatherland for the various segments of society, rather than a usual place of residence for individuals. If the city ruralizes itself, it is greatly to the detriment of its former inhabitants, but social segments of rural origin are progressively urbanized, often without realizing it, by the state, the development of capitalism, and urban habits. The territorial dimensions of the state have come to lose their importance with all the 'large' ones in the region becoming 'small' ones, if not actual orphans, since the end of the Cold War, with an increased risk of western military intervention and the evident fatuity in the future of the 'missions' with which Syria, Iraq, Egypt and Algeria have credited themselves in the past. For the former 'large' countries as well as those which are still 'small', democratization appears a useful adjunct if not an indispensable mechanism in assuring the peaceful co-existence of *asabiyyat* which are still vigorous, and whose migration *en masse* to the city imposes the necessity of living together in forced as well as physical proximity to the other traditional or modern segments of society.

The small Arab countries have used domestic mobilization as a strategy for survival in a hostile regional environment. But such a strategy is probably unfit for this new era. Externally, democratization basically meant some form of identification with the West, and domestically a mechanism of power-sharing to cater for local centrifugal tendencies. The formula has therefore been closely related to nation-building on a small scale; while charismatic leaders elsewhere were mobilizing their 'masses', small polities were simply institutionalizing their segmentarity. Each was engaging in 'nation-building', but each on a different path.

Both paths may now have reached a dead end. Small countries have come to understand that their *sui generis* experimentation with democracy can hardly survive in an environment of conflicts and dictatorships. Mobilization regimes, in the larger units, are much less credible, having achieved few of their well-publicized objectives over the past 20 or 30 years. More importantly, the territorial status quo (and therefore the borders between 'small' and 'large' countries) is now threatened by reunification (Yemen), separatism (Iraq), satellization (Lebanon) or negotiation (Jordan/Palestine). A new 'Eastern Question' is thus emerging, where democratization as a device for self-preservation for smaller units of the Arab system becomes less efficient than in the past.

This chapter was translated from the French by Anthea Bell.

Notes

1   *The Social Contract*, Book 111, Chapter 4 'On Democracy'. Rousseau saw democracy as possible only in small political units. This idea prevailed in political thought

until Tocqueville in particular convincingly upheld the opposite view.

2 As I have tried to show in Salamé (1987b). See also al-Jabiri (1993).

3 On the connection between the appeal for external protection and an internal shift towards greater authoritarianism, see in particular the brilliant historical analysis presented by al-Naqeeb (1990).

4 The same might be said of the elections organized in Iraqi Kurdistan in 1992 which embarrassed not only the government of Iraq but also those of Iran, Turkey and Syria.

5 John Stuart Mill is among those who, on the contrary, thought that segmentarity could not go hand in hand with democracy, although examples such as Switzerland, The Netherlands, and Lebanon seem to contradict him. In his view, free institutions are next to impossible in a country made up of different nationalities. 'Among a people without fellow-feeling, especially if they read and speak different languages, the united public opinion necessary to the working of representative government cannot exist.' Mill probably failed to see that 'united public opinion' could become a favourite political legitimization for dictatorships.

4

Populism Contra Democracy: recent democratist discourse in the Arab world

AZIZ AL-AZMEH

The ubiquity of Arab discourse on democracy in recent years* requires little documentation or demonstration. The question of democracy, together with the allied concern with the notion of civil society, is addressed in the Arab world in a myriad of political, academic, journalistic and other writings, and is the subject of inveterate commentary in casual conversation, in politico-academic conventions and conferences, no less than in academic conferences convened by universities and political or para-political institutions in Europe and the United States. In the 1980s, a number of pan-Arab organizations were founded to promote, in many different ways, the political adoption and public propagation of democratic norms, and a number of existing institutions changed direction to promote the same cause. The Arab Human Rights Organization and the Union of Arab Lawyers are just two cases in point.

A prolific body of discourse on democracy has thus emerged, introducing the term 'democracy' into virtually all principal vehicles for the dissemination of contemporary Arab political discourse. With the exception of the radically primitivist islamist discourse, the question of democracy has become a major constituent in the political vocabulary prevalent in the Arab world today, and cuts across virtually the entire ideological and political spectrum; it is invading even the most archaic Arabian polities. Despite this, there has not yet emerged a specific canon of democratic writing to which reference is made by the various parties to democratic discourse, be they liberal, nationalist, islamist, or statist. This is unsurprising; the following pages will seek to demonstrate the central thesis that contemporary Arab democratic discourse is less the ground of a national political consensus than a term used in political contestation and the attempted long-term accumulation of ideological hegemony. Hence the terms of reference

* I should like to thank Tawfiq Shomar for invaluable research assistance in connection with this study.

of the various writings and inflections on democracy are highly partisan and sectional, which makes it crucial to investigate the ideological contexts in which democratist enunciations are made, and the political orientations which sustain them. One central feature of the contemporary currency of the notion of democracy in Arab political and cultural life is the assimilation of democratic vocabulary by political discourses which, in their preponderant presence and effect, are out of sympathy with the liberal notions of democracy and at best ambiguous and multivocal. Instrumentalism is thus a primary feature of democratic advocacy in the Arab present. Liberal democratic demands and liberal democratist criticisms of the status quo are made, as we shall see, by forces – specifically islamist ones – with profoundly anti-liberal ideological orientations; and these demands and criticisms are put forward in tandem with a populist, anti-liberal, inflection of democracy which renders it consonant with hegemonistic cultural and political aspirations carried by these forces.

Instrumentalism is thus a primary feature of democratic advocacy in the Arab present. It is manifest both in short-term arguments for democracy with immediate political grounds and purposes, such as the islamist protests against the termination of the electoral process in Algeria in December 1991. It is also manifest in medium-term political discourse, i.e. the body of writings diffused among a readership more restricted than that of newspaper readers (although some such writing is published in dailies), and aimed at forming the opinions of opinion formers who contribute to newspapers and other mass media. This body of writing targets the educators, and aims to educate them in the context of developing projects for cultural hegemony and of contestation over the control of civil institutions, like professional unions, by the various political and ideological currents at play.[1] Whether this discourse is capable of actually *instituting* democracy as a permanent feature in long-term Arab political language is uncertain, and will depend on whether political transformations in the Arab world during this decade will lead to the enracination of democratic institutions in public life, which in turn depends on whether or not a civil and political consensus emerges.

This last matter lies outside the scope of this essay, which is based on the medium-term theoretico-political discourse referred to. This is a discourse generated by and disseminated for the local-national as well as the pan-Arab intelligentsia along lines of communication which can be said to constitute the pan-Arab intelligentsia as such. These lines of communication consist of institutions and publications with intersecting memberships and readerships. such as the Centre for Arab Unity Studies (Beirut), the Arab Thought Forum (Amman), the monthly journal *al-Mustaqbal al-arabi,* various human rights organizations, professional societies (of lawyers, sociologists, and others), and various official and semi-official pan-Arab organizations, such as Arab league institutions, and informal networks of governmental and extra-governmental consultancy and of higher education.

The discourse in question is therefore one that weaves democracy into strategic ideological nodes of large-scale political and politico-cultural currents, and generates, through the instrumentalization of the democratic advocacy, specific ideological interpretations and consequent long-term political commitments, explicit or implicit. This entire process, it must be emphasized again, is one which involves almost exclusively that section of the Arab intelligentsia which reads a fairly uniform body of theoretico-political publications, and which interlocks through various organizational networks, and which is also connected by corporatist ties that arise from the close connection between academic careers and qualifications, and the service of state and inter-state Arab organizations – or the not inconsiderable tendency of large numbers of Arab intellectuals to construe their public role in terms of such service, not least in relation to an ideal Arab state governed by political rationality which some Arab intellectuals see represented in their own person. Needless to say, freedom of speech as a concomitant of democracy comes naturally to a group that owes its very corporate existence to the craft of speech, but it comes naturally only when the social and political advancement brought about by the freedom of speech is curtailed.

Democracy as propounded in much of current Arab political discourse is generally endowed with a virtually talismanic quality, as a protean force capable, when meaningfully put into practice, of solving all outstanding problems. It has become an ideological motif as ubiquitous today as Arab unity or Arab socialism once were in an Arab past which, though proximate, seems to have receded into the mists of time. It is presented as self-sustaining, almost self-generating. The imperative of democracy, according to one opinion, is sustained by no other than democracy itself; for, in this circle of the imagination, there can be no democracy, except with more democracy (al-Jabiri 1992, 12). It goes without saying that the polemical hyperbole of this type of democratic enunciation is not merely a self-sustaining matter, nor one that is simply generated by the relative closure, in varying degrees, of democratist politics upon the intelligentsia who produce it, circulate it, and consume it. The air of unreality which pervades this rather characteristic statement is not merely the result of the ritual declaration of loyalty to democracy which bespeaks a reputation for intellectual independence, regardless of how meaningless the gesture may be. It is also directed against a pervasive current of Arab scepticism, now hugely strengthened by the Algerian experience of 1990–91 concerning the very possibility of democracy in the Arab world. This sceptical trend among Arab intellectuals questions the desirability of a liberal democratic position divorced from considerations of social justice or of social democracy, on the grounds of being both irrelevant and meaningless in the absence of certain economic and social preconditions,[2] and is distinct from, albeit in political and ideological continuity with, notions of popular (Soviet-style) as opposed to liberal democracy favoured by Ba'thist and cognate political leanings. The allergy to notions of liberal democracy disembodied from social and economic justice is such, indeed, that a recent constitutionalist criticism of nasserism was countered by a robust defence of its popular-democratic nature, which was implicitly regarded as over-riding its constitutionalist shortcomings (Dirgham 1981).[3]

Yet hyperbolic and polemical statements are not arbitrary, but revelatory of assumptions that often remain unstated. The discourse under consideration yields a circular notion of democracy as a self-explanatory and self-sustaining form of historical and political miracle-making. For it is indeed a common feature of the discourse on democracy recently predominant in the Arab world that it is largely uninterested in the historical and politico-theoretical conditions of democratic discourse in any but the most cursory of senses. Just as the main currents of Arab political thought in modern times had treated the notion of liberty without taking into account its local and European emergences, thereby making it amenable to nominal valorization in a multitude of frequently discordant discourses (al-Arwi 1981, 52, 107), so contemporary Arab political discourse has tended to adopt democratic enunciations in a nominal fashion, thereby making it possible for the notion of political liberties to be interpreted in a variety of different ways that each valorize it for a particular ideological current, many of them anti-democratic.

There is no mystery in this. Contrary to a common prejudice prevalent in the Arab world and in the West, there is no pathological exceptionalism that governs the fortunes or misfortunes of Arab political thought, and renders them absolutely *sui generis,* and well without the bounds of the normal analytical tools of the humanities and social sciences, or beyond the remit of normal causalities that operate in history. For it is manifest – a manifestation bracketed by democratic enunciations of a talismanic nature such as those indicated – that the advocacy of democracy is primarily a fact of politics, and not a contribution towards the ultimate salvation of the Arabs and the definitive solution to all their political and social problems. Whereas there is in western Europe a spasmodic yet long-term socio-political concord, which has governed democratic systems on constitutional (France and Germany among others) or on institutional basis (Britain), the Arab world displays a condition of flux and a lack of social-structural crystallization in which such a civil, political, and ideological concord could exist in conditions of relative long-term stability. This accounts for the openness of the contestation which in turn overdetermines democratic discourse, lending it a conjunctural rather than historical orientation. Hence the correlative phenomenon noted by one observer, that constitutionalist discourse in the Arab world tends to be highly formalistic, not to say formulaic, for it was not, in the majority of cases, the result of an historical socio-political consensus. It could thus be formalistically invoked as a ground for the suspension and curtailment of constitutions and of constitutional procedures (Sa'if 1992, 236 & 236 n.22) – it was widely expected that if the FIS had had the chance to assume power and achieve a parliamentary majority in Algeria in 1991, it would have subverted the liberal constitution and overturned it by means of its parliamentary majority, and the comparison between such a possibility and the Nazi accession to power in the 1934 elections was constantly brought to mind by Arab commentators. Needless to say, this also applies to the conjunctural nature of constitutions that are often not based upon an active national consensus.

The same observations would be true of democratic enunciations in recent Arab political discourse. Let us now turn briefly to the conditions for the constancy and wide incidence of Arab democratic discourse in the past decade, before proceeding further with the analysis of the manner in which democratic enunciations are appropriated by the various ideological discourses at play in the Arab world today, and a description of the ideological genera of democratic discourse.

Primary among the conditions conducive to the rise of democratist discourse in the Arab world in recent years is the combined effect of internal social crises and the international pressures for pluralism brought about by the final stages of the Cold War and in the disintegration of the communist bloc. This had a double effect, generating a particular criticism of liberal democracy and a particular inflection of the democratic enunciation. The criticism of liberal democracy is based upon the contention that democratic reforms are being introduced by Arab states such as Egypt and Jordan as a response to the globalization of the democratist polemic directed at the communist bloc by the Cold War, and that these reforms propose a notion of political pluralism based upon a formal legal equality that occludes social and economic inequality, and indeed reinforces the consolidation of such inequalities as are generated and encouraged by IMF-led reorientations of the economy.[4] As for the democratic inflection implied by this, it is a democratist discourse yielded by state-inspired processes of political liberalization. This is, in general, grounded in arguments from political engineering of an evolutionist and gradualist nature, in which democracy is regarded as a gradual process consonant with the centrally directed evolution of the body politic to a state of maturity. Consequently, statist discourse on democracy tends to be technocratic and legalistic in its dirigism, and does not seem to have penetrated a wider Arab democratic discourse from which it faces a cautious implicit welcome but relentless criticism on grounds of insufficiency. But it is likely that such resistance will be reviewed once the recent Algerian experience (despite its pronounced historical specificity) has begun to be assimilated by circles of the Arab intelligentsia outside Algeria and Tunisia.

Correlative with the thesis that the ubiquity of democratic discourse is not entirely home-grown or the result of local Arab political processes that imply various degrees of mobilization, despite the presence and furtive and restricted activities of civil institutions like the Arab Human Rights Organization (Labib 1992a, 12–13), are other theses, similarly concerned with the statist and even dirigist origins of democratic discourse. Primary among these is the observation, stated in the spirit of criticism, that gradual political pluralism was being introduced by some Arab states as a mechanism for diffusing social tensions attendant upon IMF-led economic transformations. As one acerbic commentator stated, participants in bread riots (Egypt, Algeria, Tunisia, Morocco) 'demanded bread and were given freedom' (Baydun 1992).

Such scepticism towards the technocratic notion of democracy partakes to a large extent of the widespread argument against democracy from its imperfection both in the West and in the form of which it is introduced in the Arab world, which regards this imperfection as, in some sense, an indication of irrelevance or of the inevitability of failure. In terms of political analysis, this view tallies with a recent thesis which sought to explain the durability of the Arab state in the 1970s and 1980s by using forces of opposition to the state as the independent variable in the stability equation (Zartman 1990, 220-46),[5] and seeing manipulated (Egypt), controlled (Morocco) and emergent (Tunisia) pluralisms as the primary factor in stemming systemic dysfunction at the political level. For Arab democratic critics, such features of state-managed democracy simply underline the alienation of the state with respect to society, a matter which will be taken up in detail below, for this assertion of alienation is a major, perhaps *the* major, feature in democratist discourse, which has important consequences for the political and ideological direction of this discourse.

Yet this criticism of state instrumentalism and control in emergent Arab pluralist processes sometimes turns to melancholy and to a thoroughgoing historical pessimism. For this sceptical criticism of Cold War-related dirigist democracy, of what has been termed 'democratist subcontracting' (Labib 1992a, 188 & 1992b, 100), is sometimes allied to a scepticism concerning the very historical likelihood of democratic change in the Arab world in its present stage of development. This ultimately amounts to a discourse which ascribes to Arab societies changeless historical essences and, like a parallel discourse on Arab exceptionalism of much circulation in the western media and western academic statements, devolves to a discourse of congenital incapacities, to what has been recently described as a 'politological Renanism' (Farag & Roussillon 1992, 355)[6] – the reference, of course, is to an analogy with Ernest Renan's thesis concerning the congenital intellectual incapacities of the Semites. There is here a finalist notion of the past, as one whose changelessness was precipitated at its very beginning, and which thus pre-determines both present and future entirely. Be that as it may, the Arab world, and most particularly the 'crowd' (what right-wing nineteenth-century French polemic called *la foule*) is regarded from this perspective after a manner reminiscent of Gustave Le Bon, who regarded it as an irrational herd easily driven by demagogues, wreaking destruction upon civilized order. Le Bon remains very popular in the Arab world, where the notion of an irrational crowd has been inspired by the images of blind rioting and of the monstrous creature born of the Iranian revolution.[7] There is postulated in this contemporary Arab Renanism a 'basic personality' of the Arabs, one which is profoundly permeated by a medieval 'anthropo-cultural presence' which disallows the very notion of liberty (Labib 1992a, 81). This prescribes continuities in the basic feature of medieval Arab political tradition, that of the 'obedience paradigm', so that popular uprisings clamour, not for liberty or democracy, but obedience to God. Public opinion therefore clamours, as it did during the Gulf War, for a 'liberating dictatorship' rather than be content with a democracy that subjugates Arabs to outsiders (Labib 1992a, 99–100, 102).

To these considerations may be added other, less dramatic considerations. The incidence of illiteracy and state interference in the electoral process deform democratic expression.[8] The weight of tradition and of the 'medieval presence' in the Arab present is ambivalent, according to another author, as Arab-Muslim political culture combines certain ideals of egalitarianism with practices of despotism which are, however, accentuated by the political practices and predilections of modern Arab states (Abu Jabir 1992, 77-9). But this ambivalence is not left in a condition either of inertia or of balance, according to another critic, as even room for difference within the Arab-Islamic tradition was overdetermined by despotism and indeed served the purposes of despotism (Labib 1992a, 81, 82–4, 92–4).

It is at this point that the democratist criticism of Arab society itself joins forces with a scepticism towards pluralism as the combined effect of international politico-economic subcontracting and the sublimation of internal social torsions. For in this critique, the international discourse on pluralism is seen to have imposed upon the Arab world the proposal of a pluralism based not necessarily on political forces and currents representing *citizens*, as much as on representing a centrifugal plurality of sectarian and ethnic groups over and against common national citizenship (Sa'if 1992, 230). There is ample material for this in the Arab world. For instance, it is this type of pluralism which is manifestly in mind in the ethnic and sectarian composition, in London and Washington in 1991 and 1992, of an Iraqi opposition that is out of phase with the realities of the modern Iraqi polity. This other, anti-democratic type of pluralist *diktat,* is locally grounded in what some authors regard as a primeval and necessarily abiding tradition of sectarianism in the Arab world which is inimical to democracy (Abu Jabir 1992, 80). It goes without saying that this Balkanist view of the Arab world – less an eternal socio-political fact than a policy statement, as it indeed was in the nineteenth-century Eastern Question – has become increasingly prevalent as an instrument of US-inspired policies in the Arab world in the post-Cold War period.

It is noteworthy that the sectarian and ethnicist notion of democratic representation in terms of specific ascriptive constituencies rather than of an open citizenry was almost never theorized and is still unreflected in modern Arab political thought. The only significant reflection was the honest theorization of Lebanese political sectarianism by Michel Chiha, who regarded parliament as a kind of Senate for the sectarian notables and warned quite explicitly against 'excessive democratic tastes' as destructive of the Lebanese political fabric (Chiha 1957, 19, 35).[9] For the rest, and with the exception of Lebanese political theorists, neither the present American-backed Iraqi opposition nor indeed any other political group has sought to produce a political theory of communalist democracy, despite the communalist workings of certain political arrangements, including the allocation of parliamentary representation in Jordan along lines of

sect and ethnicity. Egyptian Copts, in contrast and with few marginal exceptions, had throughout this century consistently eschewed the idea that political
constituencies in Egypt be formed along sectarian lines, and it is only in very
recent times that such a tendency is being advanced by small sections of
Egyptian Copts in tandem with and with the backing of the Muslim Brothers.
Communalist democratism is beyond the confines of the present discussion, as it
is almost entirely confined to oral, unspoken, or entirely unreflected practical
actions, or to highly sectional journalism. It does not form part of formal political expression in the Arab world, and is used in a highly mitigated form even by
representatives of Kurdish autonomism in Iraq. For this, like other expressions
of democratism in the Arab world, is expressed as regional autonomism on the
basis of a uniformity of citizenship – the terms normally encountered in liberal
democratic discourse.

It is thus liberal democratic notions that abound, positively or as unattainable
desires, in the folds of contemporary Arab political discourse. But this abun-
dance carries particular inflections which betoken discursive appropriation by
ideological currents that will be taken up now. It is liberal considerations, particularly of representativeness, which drive Arab democratist discourse in its various tendencies, including the liberal which, in its pure form, is not often
encountered, as it has few political vehicles. When it does occur, it is most often
employed, in a naive or a disingenuous form in civil-libertarian criticism, often
by anti-libertarian forces, of state activities, perhaps most particularly with the
criticism of the Algerian state in 1991–92.[10]

Liberal democratism, as I have said, is only very infrequently unmitigated
when not being used polemically. Even a body as singularly motivated by a
civil-libertarian impulse as the Arab Human Rights Organization considered it
necessary to issue a statement, without being called upon to do so, regarding
Salman Rushdie stating that the freedom of expression should be subject to
respect for matters holy (Al-Azmeh 1989, 78). Implicit or explicit recourse is
made in this and similar cases to a notion much discussed in democratist discourse, that of the appropriateness of liberal democracy, of European origin, to
Arab conditions. The discussion is fruitless, for it rests on an ahistorical and
exclusivist notion of the Arab present as self-subsistent and in real continuity
with the past (Al-Azmeh 1992). It describes on the one hand what is perceived
as the conditions leading to the rise of democracy in western Europe, and on the
other hand despotic traditions and present conditions in the Arab world, finally
coming to the unsurprising conclusion that the one is not the other (Sabri Abd
Allah 1990, 6–13). This lack of correspondence accounts for judgments of scepticism towards democracy, as well as melancholy pessimism about the realism
of expecting it in the Arab world, which we have encountered above, the political and ideological implication of which will be taken up presently.

Before this, however, it is important to underline the fact that the debate on
this matter is one over the structural suitability of democracy for Arab conditions, which assumes that its introduction in the Arab world is a form of trans-

plantation, a rustic metaphor abounding in the Arab discourse on social and political institutions. Some authors find that the liberal democratic model, being transplanted from a foreign body-politic, is *ipso facto* a recipe for anarchy, proven, according to one, by the case of Sudan.[11] Another expresses scepticism in underlining the necessity of properly considering the connection between democracy and political stability, both of which should be conceived in terms of the social basis of such democratic arrangements as may arise.[12]

In a less immediately practical vein, some fruitfulness is injected into the discussion when historical considerations on the genesis of democracy are addressed. Foremost among these is the contention – most often ignored – that there are no means by which the orthodoxy of democracy can be measured, as the very notion of an orthodox democracy which is complete, immaculate, and utterly consummate, is absurd. It is also rightly asserted that it is highly to be doubted whether the matter of democracy in the contemporary Arab world can be considered or adjudged with reference to its origin. Such origin is most often, in Arab writing, attributed to the rise of the bourgeoisie in Europe, but it is a highly noteworthy fact of history that the self-same bourgeoisie was at the forefront of anti-democratic forces in nineteenth-century Europe (Sa'if 1988, 84, 86). Thus the argument from historical particularity is rejected in favour of an historical vision which seeks to regard the proper historicity, and the politics, of democratic contention in the Arab world, as part of a broader movement of Arab modernism (Sa'if 1988, 86). And, it is asserted, if the genesis of liberal democracy were indeed entwined with capitalism, the proper historicity of capitalism, its various complex relationships to democracy, are themselves matters that do not admit of definitive pronouncements, for capitalism as an international phenomenon does not congenitally favour democratic political forms. Indeed, democracy was a political form of varying historical fortunes in Europe, and is not born either whole or impeccable. The implication drawn is that arguments from Arab political immaturity or cultural and social unpreparedness, lack a political and historical focus and direction (Abd al-Majid 1990, 82–3, 92–3). No one would speak of France having a congenital incapacity for democracy, but would attribute to historical and social forces the fact that the relative institutional stability of the Fifth Republic was preceded, in the historically relatively short period of two centuries, by four republics, a commune, three revolutions, a restoration, and two empires.

It is manifest that the considerations outlined above are directed against a notion of democracy which can be described only as naturalistic and essentialist – in short, a notion which holds historical trajectories of Europe, as of the Arab world, to be entirely separate, each being self-identical, and essentially immutable, this subtending a romantic and organicist notion of history and of society – this is a notion of history as a path in which little changes beyond appearance, and of a society which is essentially homogeneous, both of which are standard in right-wing nationalist and populist movements world-wide, and implicit in all assumptions of the 'incommensurability' or 'incompatibility' of cultures, as in 'mosaic' models of society imposed upon the Arab world, and assumed to be the motor of Balkan history, but in fact ultimately derived from one central principle of modern European history – *cuius regio, eius religio.* Democracy is thus assumed to be either fully consummate, or open to criticism from imperfection. In both cases, it is assumed to be specific to a history entirely apart from that of the Arabs. This notion of history and of society, politically correlative with populism, is a profoundly metaphysical structure of large sections of irrationalist modern Arabic political and social thought, associated with classical Ba'thist ideology and its cognates – although it is alien to the other, positivist and historicist current of Arab nationalist thought, represented by Sati al-Husri. It rests on regarding the history of an historical mass such as 'the Arabs' or 'the Europeans' as being the natural history of a number of changeless essential features which can be subject to change only under the artificial and perforce superficial impact of external forces which, however, cannot have any substantial and durable effect. Thus changes can only take the form of subversion, corruption, accretion, rise, and fall. This natural history excludes real transformation and admits only those changes which can be attested as 'authentic' in relation to the essence of this nature.[13]

It is therein that are grounded the conceptual assonances between the democratist discourse and those of the islamist, the neo-nationalist, and the left-wing populist tendencies. It is these conceptual assonances that provide the major pathways for the passage of democratist discourse in recent Arab political thought, and that inflect this discourse with a naturalism that oversees its appropriation by populism. It is a populist discourse on democracy which is central to contemporary Arab democratic discourse, and it is to this that we now turn.

For populist discourse to proceed properly, the notion of democracy has to be brought into relation with the 'nature' of the people for whom it is claimed, and this claim has to be fulfilled by bringing the state into connection with the people, or rather the nature and essence of the people, through representation, which is conceived as some kind of 'correspondence' between society and state, so that the essence of a people and of their history is directly figured as the state. The trajectory of the populist discourse on democracy is one which has its initial terminus in an unintended but telling concordance between the main critiques of state despotism by left-wing authors and islamist ideologues, who both claim the state to be alien to society. This reaches its final terminus in the islamist discourse on how best to remedy this situation, by bringing representation into correspondence with the supposedly islamic essence of the people. This critical line which underlines, with much pathos, the state of estrangement, diremption, noncorrespondence between society and polity anchors its criticism on the romantic assumption of an original identity, whose restoration is to be sought by democracy. It should be clear that this arcadian vision of a self-identical utopia (a cognate of the notion of an 'acephalic' society attributed to simple societies which even anthropologists have, for all intents and purposes, abandoned), unflinch-

ingly oblivious of the elementary facts of political sociology, is a constant trope
of Romantic right-wing populism world-wide.

The actual constituency of the state is itself a matter of contestation, reflecting a political conflict between various ideological tendencies, one that is most
sharply polarized in Algeria and Tunisia. The constituency of the state is represented as people-tradition, and this has been the major 'sociological' support of
islamist democratism and, with a particular inflection, of old-style nationalism.
It is thought that 'the people' carry historical depth defined chiefly by Islam,
and that this culturalist over-determination of history is what in essence defines
society. On the other hand, the constituency of the state, its social material, is
represented by both the liberal and the left-wing opponents of the islamist project as 'civil society' – this representation is particularly accentuated in Tunisia
and Algeria, but has some occurrence in the East. Its incidence is such[15] that
some islamist ideologues, and the theoretical auxiliaries of islamist politics, are
tending to appropriate the term 'civil society' by infusing it with an islamic content and grafting it onto the populist notion of political constituency whose
'expression' should be the state.

This latter attempt is aided and abetted by a naive criticism of the Arab state
as being disconnected from society. It is almost invariably, and always implicitly, assumed that the state and the group that wields immediate power within it
are identical. This thoughtless rhetorical conflation – curiously identical, incidentally, with the decidedly unsociological medieval Arab notion of the state[16] –
is then transposed to the assertion that 'legitimacy' resides wholly outside the
space of the state, and remedying this dysfunctional manifestation of a presumably original correspondence is the task of democratic activity.[17] Within the
parameters of this mode of thought, it is therefore understandable that the call
should be made for dissolving the imposed 'identity' between state, society, and
rulers, and for the state to 'withdraw' from civil society (al-Jabiri 1992, 15).

Civil society is thus represented as a sort of protoplasm out of which political
equity and democracy can emerge naturally. The precise composition of civil
society can be, and is, the subject of contestation, with islamists claiming this to
be 'the people' defined by what they understand to be islamic heritage in direct
continuity with its Medinan beginning, whereas liberals and other modernists
find it in modernity. But the immediate political terms by means of which the
notion of 'civil society' is used are in any case related to the rise of islamism,
most particularly in the Maghreb. In the case of Tunisia, for instance, the notion
was used by the non-state intelligentsia to counter state activities and allocate an
independent space for independent party and other organizations, after the intervention of the army in politics in 1984. The space of exclusion designated by
this term was then widened in 1989 to comprehend political islamism represented by the aborted Nahda party of Rashid Ghannushi on the grounds that it is
at variance with national civil consensus (Zghal 1991c, 138, 141–2), and is now
freely used by the state. Prior to this, Tunisia (and this observation can be gener-
alized over the Arab world) had not seen serious use of the notion of civil soci-

ety, due to the connection between state and intelligentsia which promoted an etatist and developmentalist vision of social and cultural action (Zghal 1991c, 156);[18] this situation also seems to account for the lack of an Arab political sociology in any serious sense and the primacy, instead, of an apologetic sociology by and for bureaucrats, inspired by a vulgar marxism or by a discourse on authenticity.[19] This position of near-oblivion before the social is now in recession, due to the relative closure of the state apparatus and explosion of a seemingly irrational and incomprehensible crowd on the street which has to be accounted for. Indeed, it appears to be the case that this discourse on diremption, islamist and non-islamist alike, is propounded by groups within the intelligentsia whose education-driven social mobility is unmatched by access to the state, as well as by members of previous political elites (ex-'revolutionary' politicians) whose erstwhile social mobility that had accrued from the state has been shorn or immobilized. An aetiology therefore had to be invented, tracing the estrangement of state and civil society to the rejection by colonial societies of colonial states (Labib 1992a, 94–5).

Civil society, thus construed, is vulnerable to attack. It partakes of the same rigidity and presumption of tangibility and clarity of definition, indeed of full and pre-given presence, and unambiguous invariant, that characterizes the notions of democracy explored above. Both have finalist features, which opens democracy to rejection on grounds of imperfection, and civil society to judgment on grounds of existence or non-existence. This construal is clearly ahistorical, and has not in general incorporated some of the more productive and sophisticated sociologico-political considerations that float about the face of Arab democratic discourse,[20] but do not seem to strike political or ideological roots. The criticism levelled against the notion of civil society is in the first instance political. It insists that the primary purpose of the notion is political and that it is specifically geared to the exclusion of islamism and the revivification of the modernist tendency in Arab history which, according to this critique, is defunct and survives only as the instrument for the survival of military and bureaucratic oligarchies (Ghalyun 1992, 734, 752). To this directly political criticism are added glosses that show just how simplistic is this notion of civil society, and how unusable, sociologically speaking, is the notion of civil society, indeed how unthinkable it is without a notion of the state (see Ghalyun 1992, 736ff for indications).[21]

To this criticisim of 'civil society' as a notion geared towards excluding islamism from the bounds of legitimacy, is added the assertion of the necessity for including within the ambit of civility old family and religious forms of organization, without this implying that these subtend democratic tendencies, and despite the assertion that Arab civil society is incoherent and constitutes essentially an explosive mass (Ghalyun 1992, 743, 748–9). The matter therefore devolves to the necessity for resuscitating sub-political social networks to inject 'new blood' and reclaim 'the vital forces that will participate in the future'. The 'return to society' itself (Ghalyun 1992, 749)[22] therefore delivers this criticism back, after its sociological detour, to its initial parameter, that of state and society in estrangement contrary to a more properly natural correspondence, and the necessity of reconstituting the former from the protoplasm of the latter.

This protoplasm can only consist of essential continuity conceived in the manner outlined above. And it is herein that the discourse of identity on which is founded the islamism of the last quarter of this century is activated in such a way as to comprehend the identity of 'the people' and of historical experience, or heritage (*turath*). Both – people and historical experience – are simultaneously posited as identical and in correspondence of islamism, with the substance of islamism, namely the nominative 'Islam'. For it is essential that 'the logic of historical continuity' be fully acknowledged in state construction (Husayn 1984, 10), and this logic subtends the emphasis on a putative culturalist imperative – Islam, according to the islamist understanding of it – which is explicitly counterposed to modernism construed as Weberian purposive, pragmatic rationality as opposed to 'rationality' that is mindful of ultimate ends and purposes which is attributed to the politics of the parties of God.[23]

This counterposition in the process of return to the nature of society from its real history, and therefore to the fulfilment of authentic representativeness, the representativeness expressed in cultural identification, is said to be the true affirmation of autonomy as against heteronomy, the resuscitation 'of an historical state that is not extant' in place of 'an extant but unhistorical state' (Nuwayhid 1992, 203–4), the realization of justice and representativeness as it appears in terms of a politics of nostalgia. The general will and popular choice are further placed on a plane of identity and mentioned in the same breath as divine will,[24] for it is assumed that both wills are concordant by virtue of the fact that 'the people' and islamism are concordant, and that this concordance is manifest and self-evident.

The 'essence of democracy', therefore, aims by various means to 'unify the will of the nation' in order to restore the norms of historical nature, i.e. develop the historical mission of islamic-Arab civilization (Husayn 1984, 10); democracy therefore accomplishes no less, but no more, than to release the pre-existent unity, direction, and will of 'the people' (Baydun 1992). For, contrary to the presumed divisiveness of western democracy, a divisiveness disastrously manifest, according to the leading Arab islamist thinker and politician Hasan Turabi, in its supposedly misguided Sudanese application, authentic (islamic) democracy rests on 'the spirit of consensus', not on the consideration of majorities which are not consummately representative, as they fail to bring minorities into the ambit of their consensus (al-Turabi 1984, 16–17). This awesome elision of difference from the general will and totalitarian impulse towards political homogenization – a classical theme in right-wing ideologies east and west – is open to more ambiguous and apparently gentler formulations in terms of a pragmatics of political efficiency.[25] But it is supported by appeal to the prophetic tradition to the effect that the community cannot err, as it cannot concur on iniquity (*batil*) (al-Turabi 1984, 13). The political technique of this consensus is 'direct democracy' grounded in modern technology and which makes possible the immediate expression of popular will, an expression counterposed (in terms curiously similar to the populist arguments for teledemocracy put forward by Ross Perot in the 1992 American presidential campaign, which assume that the controller of the medium controls the foundations and articulation of opinion) to classical democracy, which produces, according to this view, a Leviathan to which the popular will is transferred by means of parliamentary representation severed from its fount and origin, the immediate life and essence of the people (al-Turabi 1984, 5, 13) – again, 'life', 'essence' and cognate notions are staples of right-wing vitalist notions of society and politics. Islamist democracy, whose notion of uniform and consummate sovereignty was supposedly taken over by western democracy and adulterated by a transposition of the source of sovereignty from God to man, is the only one in which popular representation is 'accurately and minutely' activated in a state whose fundamental principle is that the source of popular sovereignty is divine sovereignty. In this way the unadulterated origin of sovereignty is put back in charge (al-Turabi 1984, 15), and the blasphemy of attributing to man the primary divine function of sovereignty is arrested (al-Turabi 1984, 14).

Pluralist democracy is therefore judged inadequate, not only for being imperfect in contrast to its islamist alternative, but also because it allows for the hegemony of existing elites (of various histories, but in all cases 'inauthentic' and 'un-islamic'), and because electoral processes work by the manipulation of consent (for example, in al-Turabi 1984, 16). In contrast, islamist democracy is consummate and totally representative, for this democracy disallows what is unauthentic by decreeing the illegitimacy of 'loyalty for the enemies of society'; even communists, one islamic leader with some apparent reputation for modernism and toleration states, may organize legitimately if they make themselves subject to the overweening loyalty towards 'society'[26] – by which is undoubtedly meant social order as understood by political islamism; and party political life is indeed permissible, according to some, provided parties declare loyalty to Muslim values and rulings (al-Awwa 1991, 136). It is Islam, after all, which is the fount of human rights, centuries before the notion arrived in the West, and these rights in Islam are not only prior, but superior, for in Islam they figure as shar'ist imperatives and divinely ordained duties – but the declaration of atheism or of positions at variance with basic Muslim dogma cannot be considered to be a right, as it constitutes a form of sedition, and the social system based upon religious belief, like any other system, is entitled to protect itself against seditious activities (Amara 1988, 42, 51–3, 55).

Thus, unmediated transitions and full correspondences are posited between history, Islam, society, and the desired polity which should come to correspond to society, which is changeless history, in turn necessarily and sufficiently described by religion, all of them as interpreted by islamism – in this series of correspondence, incidentally, the notion of civil society is redundant, indeed unthinkable, for it is lost in the indistinctness of identity. It can therefore only be introduced as a rhetorical effect, in order for the term to be appropriated by a set of indications and interpellations which are entirely inapposite. All the terms of islamist discourse on democracy are variations on the theme of nature to which a return is proposed, of an ontological presence which is pre-given and regained, of authenticity affirmed in its entirety as the true element of democracy, by plurality which is not an internal but an external feature of society. Thus Hasan Turabi can state that pluralism is the pluralism of civilization, each impermeable, self-subsistent, *sui generis*. Within the islamic sphere of life, the search is for the one truth that unites and does not divine or allow the hegemony of part over part.[27]

The western conception of pluralism and of human rights, therefore, is merely a slogan aiming at producing fissures within islamic domains.[28] The notions of democracy and of human rights, according to the leading islamist Rashid Ghannushi, are 'a malign ideology', a 'new secular religion', propagated by contemporary colonialism headed by the United States (Ghannushi 1991, 84).

The accent on unicity and identity is thus primary and constitutive, and among the islamists only a small and marginalized minority position postulates a thorough-going pluralism of the liberal variety.[29] The pluralism that is entirely accepted by islamist discourse is not of a civil or political nature, but of a religious patrimonialism. There is an acceptance – indeed, and encouragement and positive valuation of sectarian communalism in the name both of the doctrine of *dhimma* and of appeal to reality which is supposed to have remained static since the time of Muhammad (Husayn 1984, 11–12). The 'nature' of society is such that a homogeneous civility yielding notions of national citizenship is shunned, and has been, according to one islamist theorist of sectarianism, constantly rejected by the 'nature' of Arab-islamic society ever since Ottoman reforms began reforming society and subverting the culture and civility of sectarian communalism (al-Sayyid 1992, 243). Thus, assuming the identity of history and society, of society and the state, and the monadic plurality of sectarian sections, facts of nature, all of them, constitute the *leitmotif* by means of which islamist discourse, of which islamist democratism is fully part, seeks to translate its ideal of societal corporatism into a state corporation.

As can be seen, the notion of a severance and mutual alienation between state and society has acted as a conceptual and ideological pathogen, yielding a populist notion of society, and in most instances a 'correspondence theory' of the state, articulated most succinctly by Hasan Turabi. This notion and its pathogenic consequences have led to an almost hegemonic role played by islamist discourse which, basing itself on the results of mass mobilization as much as on an international islamist revivalism (which, it must be stressed, has conditions and causes unrelated to the notion of a return to a prior nature – Al-Azmeh 1993, 6ff & Al-Azmeh 1992a, chs 1, 3, 6), is claiming Islam to be the nature of the people, and itself to be the tongue of this nature. In keeping with the populism of the notion of estrangement, large sections of the non-islamist Arab intelligentsia, pro-islamist, anti-islamist, and would-be *politicien*, are tending to succumb to the pathogenic consequences of the thesis of severance and non-correspondence between state and society, and to adopt finalist views on the 'nature' of their society defined in islamic terms (Al-Azmeh 1991d, 6ff).

This grid of misrecognition is the result of systematic stunting by Arab states of liberal and left-wing movements, of their flirtation with religious elements, and of the very convincing messages sent by terrorism, most particularly in Egypt and Algeria. It is equally derived from the conviction carried by western representations, both islamophile and islamophobe, of Arabs as Muslims in essence, this being a 'post-modern' form of racialist stereotyping which super-islamizes Muslims and things islamic, and forms an essential part of the rhetoric by means of which the North–South divide is consolidated after the Cold War in a manner that barricades the North from the effects of its international economic policies (migration, terrorism, civil wars), and places the South without the bounds where juridical rationality (including democracy) is relevant. This grid of misrecognition, of super-islamization, of ahistorism, is also, of course, fully laden with political consequence, primary among which is the readiness, now confined to Egypt and floating Mashriqi and some Maghrebi Arab nationalists, to promote the idea of an islamist-nationalist alliance with view to promoting democracy and a messianic notion of nationalism that one major strand of Arab nationalism has bequeathed upon islamism (Markaz dirasat al-wahda al-ara-biyya 1989). The instrumental notion of liberal politics that islamists have adopted where it has entered the pluralist process is regarded with an amplitude of generosity more alarming for its historical myopia than praiseworthy for its open-mindedness. When not decrying the very notion of parliamentary democracy, islamist writers have often emphasized the conjunctural nature of their adherence to pluralism as a means of curbing the despotic proclivities of the state so long as it does not support political islamism (Awwa 1991, 136).[30] As for nationalism, the true variety, according to Ghannushi, is no other than that based on 'the islamic repertoire'.[31] Islamism has come a long way from the point when, nearly ten years ago, one of its prominent representatives could complain that a large-scale conference on democracy ignored and neglected islamist tendencies.[32]

Rarely are historical and realist theses on democracy advanced in a manner to counter the spread and ubiquity of democratist populism. Rare are the discussions of the impossibility, indeed the entirely imaginary nature of notions of direct democracy, of the necessary imperfections of all democracies, and of the despotic nature of all plebiscitary and other notions of unmediated democracy (Zaynah 1992, 35–9, 57). Rare indeed are the positions that underline the necessity of secularism for any democratic order (Zaynah 1992, 13–14 & Amin 1988, 320). Rare also are the instances in which are expressed, in writing, the widespread realization, even by proponents of nationalist-islamist dialogue, that islamist movements in headlong democratic process, like the FIS, 'slaughter this stammering, maladroit democracy, which perhaps came much too soon'

(Boudjedra 1992, 76). And widespread are those positions which, while antithetical in intent to islamism and not succumbing to populism, yet describe democracy as a normative system based on reason and public-spiritedness, almost bereft of political contestation (for example Zaynah 1992; Munif 1992; Umlil 1991), for that at best speak in very general terms of the historicity and political nature of democracy (for example al-Khuli 1991, 137; Abd al-Majid 1990, 91; Labib 1992a, 103–4). In other words, Arab democratic pluralist theory, beyond the terms of the populism dominated by islamism, is still a marginal phenomenon, without an ideological or political centre. Its ahistorical perfectionism, its desire for full representativeness, causes it to veer, *volens nolens*, to populism which it cannot sustain politically. Thus adrift, contemporary Arab democratist discourse feeds the main political carrier of populism at present, which is the totalitarian plebiscitarianism of political Islam, for other forces had been almost eradicated by the Arab state as organized political forces – albeit not as very strong cultural, ideological, indeed, historical constants of modern Arab life.

Notes

1   For a detailed study of the practice of this hegemonic project in a particular case, see Roussillon (1990, 17–50).

2   See, for example, Isma'il al-Alawi's intervention in the proceedings of the conference *al-Tajarib al-dimuqratiyya fi'l-watan al-arabi* (1981) convened by Muntada al-fikr wa'l-hiwar, pp. 69–73 (henceforth *al-Tajarib al-dimuqratiyya*).

3   See also the responses to Tariq al-Bishri (1984) in the proceedings of the conference *Azmat al-dimuqratiyya fi'l-watan al-arabi* (Beirut, 1984) convened by Markaz dirasat al-wahda al-arabiyya (henceforth *Azmat al-dimuqratiyya*).

4   See, for example, the interventions of Husam Isa and Lakhdar Ibrahimi in the proceedings of the conference *al-Dimuqratiyya wa huquq al-insan fi'l watan al-arabi* convened by Markaz dirasat al-wahda al-arabiyya (Cairo, 1984). See also Labib (1992a, 99–100) and Labib (1992b, 22–3).

5   See also the excellent account of the emergence of recent Arab political pluralism by Ahmad Thabit (1992).

6   On the wider issue of Arab and orientalist and neo-orientalist concordances see Al-Azmeh (1986).

7   Two Arabic translations of Gustave Le Bon's *Psychologie des foules* (1895) were published in 1991. One is a new edition published in Algiers of the 1924 translation by Fathi Zaghlul; the other is a recent translation by Hashim Salih published in London. A recent account of Le Bon and his tradition can be found in Todorov (1993).

8   Salah Hafiz, intervention in the round-table discussion 'Mustaqbal al-dimuqratiyya fi'l alam al-arabi' published in *Mustaqbal al-arabi*, 138, 1990, pp. 115–16 (henceforth 'Mustaqbal al-dimuqratiyya').

9   I thank Fawwaz Traboulsi for drawing my attention to this point.

10 For instance, the liberal criticism of Ali Oumili in *al-Quds al-arabi* 5/10/1992 and the islamist criticism of, say, Ramadan al-Shami (1992, 16–28) and Hasan al-Zayn

(1992, 6 and *passim*).

11 Faruq Abu Isa, intervention in 'Mustaqbal al-dimuqratiyya', p. 109.

12 Al-Sayyid Yasin in 'Mustaqbal al-dimuqratiyya', pp. 100–101.

13 On this matter see Al-Azmeh (1991b, 468–86 and 1992b). See also Roussillon (1991).

14 See the remarks of Usama al-Ghazali Harb in 'Mustaqbal al-dimuqratiyya', p. 105.

15 This is well illustrated by the published proceedings of two major conferences on the notion of civil society: *al-Mujtama al-madani wa dawruhu fi tahqiq al-dimuqratiyya* convened by the Markaz dirasat al-wahda al-arabiyya (Beirut, 1993), and *Gramsci wa qadaya al-mujtama al-madani* held in Cairo in 1991 (published in Nicosia, 1991).

16 On this see Al-Azmeh (1983, 71ff and 1986, 41ff).

17 See, for instance, Muhammad Barrada's intervention in *Azmat al-dimuqratiyya*, p. 43.

18 On the etatist fixation of Arab intellectuals, see Sharara (1980, 217ff).

19 See the remarks on Algeria by Lahourari Addi (1991, 221–7).

20 For instance Sa'if (1992, 231) and the intervention of Kamal Abd al-Latif in *al-Mujtama al-madani*, pp. 734 and 748.

21 Agreement with all the terms of this account is not implied by its citation.

22 See also Ghalyun's intervention in *Azmat al-dimuqratiyya*, p. 343.

23 Ibid, p. 433.

24 Rashid Ghannushi, intervention in *al-Insan*, 1/5 1991, p. 18.

25 Tariq al-Bishri, intervention in *Azmat al-dimuqratiyya*, p. 640.

26 Rashid Ghannushi, interview in *al-Manabir*, 5, 8 (1990), p. 37.

27 Al-Turabi, intervention in *al-Insan*, 1/5 1991, p. 12.

28 Ibid, p. 13.

29 For instance, Khalid Muhammad Khalid (1985). See Abd al-Majid (1990, 92) and the overview by Krämer (1992).

30 On the political credibility of Tunisian islamism, see the positive statements of Rashid Ghannushi in Markaz dirasat al-wahda al-arabiyya, ed. (1989) *al-Hiwar al-qawmi al-dini, passim* and Ghannushi (1987, 300–308) and compare with Mouvement de la Tendance Islamique (1985, 179–200). See also the comments of Abd al-Qadir Zghal (1990).

31 Ghannushi, intervention in *al-Insan* , 1/5 1991, p. 18.

32 Abd Allah Nafisi, intervention in *Azmat al-dimuqratiyya*, p. 840.

5

The Oil Rent, the Fiscal Crisis of the State and Democratization

GIACOMO LUCIANI

In the 1960s and early 1970s numerous countries abandoned democratic government and came to be ruled by authoritarian regimes. Several attempts at theorizing
this tendency ensued, presenting it as a necessary feature of neo-
imperialism. Then, in the late 1980s and early 1990s, a good many countries abandoned authoritarian rule and reverted to some form of popular participation in political life, leading to a revival of theories which propose democracy as the necessary
outcome of modernity – however defined – or of economic and social progress.[1]

Many of the new democracies remain quite fragile, and a reversal of the trend
cannot be ruled out; yet a trend is there for all to see.

In an international context characterized by multiple democratization
processes, the Arab world stands out as an exception – possibly, together with
the rather more complex case of China, as *the* major exception. Although at different times one or other of the Arab countries appeared to be on the brink of
democratization, none has in fact engaged in this adventure.[2] In none of the
Arab countries has a popular movement in favour of democracy developed, that
might be compared to the one that was crushed in Tiananmen Square.[3]

The striking singularity of the Arab world in this respect has led to several
interpretations, frequently emphasizing the cultural and social peculiarities of
Arab societies.

While it may be difficult to dismiss such interpretations entirely (all countries
or regions differ, and there are ways in which the Arab world differs from the
rest), they implicitly tend to support the view according to which there is something unique about the Arab world – a view associated with the orientalist tradition. If we accept this view, we are inevitably left to conclude that the same
rules do not apply there as in the rest of the world.

The factor differentiating the Arab world, and impeding democratization, is
implicitly or explicitly identified as Islam. The fact that Islam is still widely perceived as a threat, thanks to unfortunate episodes such as the Rushdie affair,
seems sufficient for western democracies to condone authoritarian and illegiti-

mate government in the Arab world, such as would hardly be tolerated else-where (for a critique see Salamé 1993, 32). The case for asserting a fundamental incompatibility between Islam and democratic government is supported by the circumstance that a majority of the non-Arab islamic countries also are non-democratic.

Thus, western governments not only abstain from actively criticizing the gov-ernments of Saudi Arabia and other smaller Gulf emirates, and are contented with a very formal and restricted electoral exercise in Kuwait; they also have lit-tle objection even to a government that orchestrates a thinly disguised military coup for the sake of derailing an electoral process that it was in the process of losing out to the opposition, as in Algeria.

In the following pages I will review some of the most important develop-ments of the past decade and ask to what extent they can be explained by struc-tural rather than purely superstructural considerations. My interest lies specifically in the role of oil rent as a factor perpetuating authoritarian govern-ment, and in the fiscal crisis of the state as a factor encouraging greater demand for democracy.

In an earlier essay (Luciani 1987) I argued that a state whose government derives most or a substantial part of its revenue from rents accruing from the outside world[4] (the rentier states) will display a political dynamic different from that of states in which the government is sustained through taxation of domestic economic activity (which I dubbed 'production states'). The distinction between rentier and production states was used to explain why the former should not be expected to democratize, at least as long as they remain rentier.

Subsequently, I also proposed a related argument, according to which the fis-cal crisis of the state – linked to the decline or disappearance of the source of rent – may be an important stimulant to democratization processes (Luciani 1988).

Taken together, these two arguments contribute to explaining some of the peculiarities of political-institutional developments in the Arab countries.

In this chapter, I will highlight the fact that oil rent continues to play a central role in most Arab countries, notwithstanding the drop in oil prices. I will further argue that even in countries in which a fiscal crisis emerged long ago, govern-ment is pursuing a policy of adapting to a smaller rent rather than accepting the need to change the economic foundation of the state, precisely in order to avoid changing the institutional system. Finally, I will propose some considerations about why the latter strategy appears to favour the progressive growth of islamic – as opposed to other forms of – opposition.

The rent, democratization, and the fiscal crisis of the state

The argument linking the fiscal to the political foundation of the state has histor-ical roots in the process that led to revolution and democratization in Europe.[5]

Whenever the state is in a position to buy consensus by distributing goods, services and income in exchange for little or nothing, it does not need democratic legitimation.

A state that has access to a rent accruing from the rest of the world – such as oil rent – may experience power struggles and factionalism, but is unlikely to experience a popular demand for democracy. While individuals, groups and factions, both within and outside the ruling elite, will constantly fight to enlarge their share of the rent, they will seldom advocate the adoption of democratic norms or an enlargement in political participation. In such a state, there is always an opposition, but the opposition will not be any more democratic than the ruler. Democratic methods will not appear as the most promising means to achieving the desired goal, simply because all groups will have a particularistic agenda, which is not conducive to the organization of consensus and majority support. In rentier states, one must be wary of declarations of democratic intent as expressed both by the ruler and by its immediate critics: the occasional idealist notwithstanding, such utterances are merely tactical.

The roots of democratic institutions are in the state's need to tax in order to support its activities. Taxation, especially modern direct taxation of the individual, requires compliance, and is unlikely to develop under authoritarian rule. In the short term, authoritarian governments may impose greater fiscal discipline if they follow on the heels of populist governments; however, in the long run authoritarian governments are not effective in developing the state's fiscal capability.

The need to widen the fiscal basis of the state is therefore an inducement to democratize. A state confronted with a fiscal crisis is obliged to resort either to cutting expenditure or to raising taxes. A third alternative – deficit spending – has always been popular among both authoritarian and democratic governments, at least in the short term. However, the only form of deficit spending that entails strictly no form of outside control is when the deficit is financed by the creation of additional money. This soon leads to inflation, which may be repressed through administrative price fixing and controls (a widespread practice in the Arab countries), but sooner or later leads to loss of confidence in the national currency. In several Arab countries in which money creation has been a preferred solution for financing the deficit, an ever-larger part of the population has developed ways to gain access to foreign currency, and domestic transactions have come to be conducted in foreign currency (dollarization): the government has in this way progressively lost its monetary sovereignty and ability to finance the deficit through money-creation.

Sources for financing the deficit through debt may be sought in the domestic or the international market. Very few Arab countries have resorted to domestic borrowing, as the latter always entails a relationship of trust which in most cases is simply not there. The public would never willingly entrust its savings to a government that it has no control over, and whose past record is one of unpredictability and lack of concern for the rights of its citizens. Many Arab countries have ended up running large external debts simply because their governments do not dare to issue treasury paper denominated in their national currency. Resorting to domestic borrowing from a willing public (which of course is different from forcing domestic institutions to lend to the state) is akin to taxation in that it requires compliance and a degree of democratic control.

The alternative to deficit spending is increasing taxes. A state resorting to increased taxation, especially if direct taxation is involved, is bound to meet a demand for control through democratic institutions, as most forms of modern taxation require widespread compliance, which can be obtained only under conditions of democratic legitimation. Here we must distinguish between the different forms of taxation:

1. Taxes on international trade require no legitimation, nor even full control of the national territory; hence they have historically been resorted to by bandits and non-governmental actors as well as weak governments. Whenever they are used on a large scale, they encourage smuggling, and facilitate the development of systems of power parallel to and competing with the state.
2. Taxes on property – especially immovable property, such as land or buildings – are easy to assess and difficult to evade, and require minimum compliance; taxes on the income of companies, especially if levied on a few, preferably foreign companies, are also relatively easy to collect, and require little political legitimation; on the other hand, taxes on the income of individuals are complex to administer, imply a direct relationship between the individual and the state, are vulnerable to cheating, corruption, etc. They are feasible only under conditions of substantial democratic legitimation.
3. Taxes on domestic goods and services are easy to levy, if they are in the form of a simple excise on necessities: they are vulnerable to avoidance by contraband, but the latter is often effectively discouraged by the low unit price of the taxed good (e.g. salt, tea, petrol). Such taxes are not very common in Arab countries, in part because the islamic ethic is rather against them, in part because the Arab governments have traditionally subsidized, rather than taxed, a key set of consumer goods. Also, excises, especially on basic necessities, are not a very dynamic form of taxation, as consumption does not increase with income. Other, more modern forms of taxation, such as a sales tax, or VAT, require extensive administration and come close to a direct income taxation on individuals in establishing a direct relationship between the tax-payer and the state.

States do not resort to more complex and politically costly forms of taxation out of a sense of justice or enthusiasm for democratic participation, but because simpler forms of taxation such as customs duties and excises soon reach their limit, and do not grow as rapidly as national income. Except when the power of government is checked by the popular will as expressed through democratic institutions, a government will systematically tend to appropriate a growing share of national income, and cannot be satisfied with an economic base that guarantees only a decreasing share of the total pie.

This is also why no authoritarian state facing fiscal crisis seriously considers cutting expenditure – except for the very short term and under conditions of duress. Cutting expenditure inevitably entails the loss of instruments of control – be they the notorious subsidies on consumer items, direct control over industry, banks and a large number of other economic activities, or social services. The authoritarian state imposes its monopoly not just on the use of force, but on all key economic and societal activities as well; in so doing, it destroys the bases of its fiscal future (state industries will never pay taxes; government banks will never stimulate private savings; subsidized consumer goods cannot be taxed; guaranteed social services impose a burden that grows as a function of population numbers...). However, retreat from this widespread control is costly: 'privatization' is a declaration of weakness and sets the stage for the development of civil society, the multiplication of decision-making centres and eventually democratization.

A state perceiving the need to cut expenditure or resort to increased taxation, or both, may increase its legitimacy and strengthen its position by either carrying out or maybe for some time simply announcing a process of democratization. Actual movement towards democratic institutions may take a long time, but should be sustained and visible. The argument linking a fiscal crisis to democratization should not be understood in a mechanistic fashion. The state can go a long way simply on the basis of its monopoly of force; it may take years, indeed decades (e.g. Spain) for political reform to be carried out, once the state has lost legitimacy. Yet, the writing, so to speak, will be on the wall.

On the contrary, states that do not face a fiscal crisis and enjoy continuing access to exogenous rent will be able to postpone democratization indefinitely. If, for reasons other than those considered here (e.g. a war of national liberation, or an external threat), political participation comes to be enlarged, it is likely to generate unstable majorities and short-lived participatory institutions. The temptation to seize power and not be accountable for the sharing of the booty is simply too strong.

One may perhaps add that, while rule by repression can certainly last a long time, both technological and societal change are making the task of the naked bloody dictator increasingly difficult. We are witnessing growing international interference, which is only partly the result of decisions taken by foreign governments. The development of international communications, the ease with which controls can be circumvented, the intensification of international economic, scientific and cultural intercourse provide many occasions for protest or opposition. This tends to reduce durability of authoritarian regimes under conditions of fiscal crisis. However, regimes with access to external rent, in amounts that may be small in absolute terms but still quite substantial relative to the country's size, population, standard of living and economic opportunities, enjoy an important advantage in sustaining their rule.

The argument linking democratization to a fiscal crisis may be combined, but does not coincide, with similar arguments concerning the necessary coincidence of economic and political liberalization. It is stated that economic liberalization will, in due course, create an entrepreneurial and managerial class that will eventually demand a say in the administration of government. I believe that there is considerable merit in this line of reasoning, but intuitively remain of the opinion that whenever the state is fiscally independent of such a bourgeoisie, it may well avoid democratization, though the reverse is never the case. The concept of a dependent bourgeoisie has been proposed in this respect: the problem with it is that there is hardly any country in which at least a section of the bourgeoisie is not dependent of the state and political power. In most democratic countries the net balance of transfers between the corporate sector and the state is either in favour of the latter or uncertain; on the contrary, however, in rentier and fiscally undeveloped states the bourgeoisie enjoys extensive benefits and transfers from the state, while it hardly contributes anything to its finances.

Similarly, the argument runs parallel to what is sometimes posited about the importance of civil societies. Assuming that the latter can be defined in an operationally meaningful fashion (I am inclined to believe that one would inevitably fall back on economic concepts, such as trade unions, industrial associations and the like – more generally: civil society = private sector), I would propose that civil society becomes more important whenever the state is in crisis, be it fiscal or of another nature, and society takes up some of the roles that would otherwise pertain to the state.

Implicitly, I assume that the state will expand to the limit of its economic capabilities. If it has the means to do so, the state will do everything, and there will be nothing that civil society (the private sector) can do except in support of the state. If the state does not have the means, and must obtain them from society (the private sector), then there is a chance for the latter to limit the power of the state. The demand for democratic participation is the foremost tool to limit the power of the state.

Reality, of course, is much more complex. There are obviously many more factors that influence the demand for democracy: exposure to the experience of other countries, social stratification, income inequality, absolute poverty or illiteracy, religion and religious/ethnic segmentation. Furthermore, a demand for democracy is one thing, its feasibility something entirely different: democracies may be in demand and yet fail or be derailed. Sometimes some of the key players simply blunder. The Arab countries provide us with examples of each of the above.

The dynamics of Arab public finance

We shall now present an overview of Arab public finance to illustrate the key facts that are relevant in the light of the above discussion. A word of caution is necessary at the outset, as the comparability of public finance figures is always questionable. Arab governments are not generous of information regarding the details of their finances, And even the most widely used international sources simply do not cover several key Arab countries, and offer insufficient coverage of others. Hence, the data surveyed in the following pages comes from different sources and may not be strictly comparable. For this reason, we have focused on shares and ratios rather than absolute values, as the former are likely to be more reliable than the latter. Also, given the common tampering with national currencies' exchange rates, international comparisons in dollar terms are avoided.

Bearing all these caveats in mind, let us look at Table 5.1, which presents government expenditure as a percentage of GDP for a group of Arab countries. It shows that the state occupies a key role in the use of available resources in most Arab countries, including oil producers, such as the UAE, Kuwait and Oman, as well as non-oil producers such as Egypt and Morocco. The role of the state is somewhat more limited in Algeria, Jordan, Tunisia, Yemen; and in Iran it is considerably more limited than in any of the Arab states.

Table 5.1: Government Expenditure as a Percentage of Gross Domestic Product – Selected Companies

	1982	1983	1984	1985	1986	1987	1988	1989	1990	1991
Algeria	n.a.	n.a.	n.a.	34.5	36.8	34.0	37.8	33.3	28.1	26.5
Bahrain	38.1	41.7	37.2	37.9	42.7	45.0	27.6	41.3	26.6	n.a.
Egypt	63.6	54.1	56.0	53.3	57.0	59.3	55.3	55.5	63.5	51.0
Iran	30.8	28.8	24.3	22.7	21.2	19.9	20.7	17.7	19.9	n.a.
Jordan	41.0	38.6	33.7	38.8	35.8	39.2	37.5	38.1	36.9	n.a.
Kuwait	56.0	59.6	57.4	51.3	52.8	46.8	46.0	46.9	n.a.	n.a.
Morocco	37.7	32.5	29.8	30.6	28.9	27.9	n.a.	n.a.	n.a.	n.a.
Oman	46.8	49.9	51.2	51.0	57.0	44.8	47.0	44.7	39.7	n.a.
Saudi Arabia	46.5	46.1	47.6	46.9	48.5	49.0	42.6	39.5	n.a.	n.a.
Tunisia	39.6	42.1	41.6	38.9	41.5	36.2	35.5	36.1	36.2	33.0
UAE	n.a.	n.a.	n.a.	n.a.	n.a.	40.0	41.5	37.7	n.a.	n.a.
Yemen	45.6	41.8	36.0	30.0	26.6	32.8	n.a.	n.a.	n.a.	n.a.

Expenditure in oil-producing countries follows an anti-cyclical pattern, showing a tendency to increase relative to GDP when the latter decreases, because of declining oil exports. The same is not true for other countries. Generally, we may detect a tendency to a reduction of the expenditure/GDP ratio in the latter part of the 1980s, indicating some weakening of the state.

Table 5.2 measures the importance of government deficit as a percentage of GDP. As discussed above, deficit spending is the easiest way to confront a fiscal crisis. One should note that the Arab Gulf oil exporting countries do not run significant deficits (figures for expenditure in the UAE and Kuwait include transfers to investment funds abroad – which is a way for those governments to show less fiscal strength than they actually have). The notable exception is Oman. For all other countries, deficits are commonly very large, although a tendency to a decrease is visible in more recent years, when dollarization intensified and pressure from international lenders for them to put their houses in order became more stringent. Note that Algeria's deficits have been small, and the government had surpluses as recently as 1990 and 1991.

Table 5.2: Government Deficit as a Percentage of Gross Domestic Product – Selected Countries

	1982	1983	1984	1985	1986	1987	1988	1989	1990	1991
Algeria	n.a.	n.a.	n.a.	-3.3	4.5	3.5	8.3	2.2	-3.6	-1.7
Bahrain	-2.4	6.8	1.6	-1.0	4.4	10.2	-3.9	8.6	-7.1	n.a.
Egypt	17.0	9.5	11.7	10.6	12.9	23.9	21.1	22.1	25.1	8.5
Iran	5.8	6.5	4.1	3.9	8.8	7.3	9.5	3.9	1.8	n.a.
Jordan	7.8	6.1	7.4	7.9	6.3	11.6	9.4	5.7	3.5	n.a.
Kuwait	-8.5	-8.0	-12.5	-7.8	-29.2	n.a.	n.a.	8.6	n.a.	n.a.
Morocco	11.4	7.7	6.0	7.3	7.7	4.5	n.a.	9.0	n.a.	n.a.
Oman	8.5	8.9	11.4	10.6	25.0	4.9	11.9	9.0	0.8	n.a.
Tunisia	5.2	8.4	4.9	5.1	7.3	4.7	3.8	4.3	5.3	4.1
UAE	n.a.	n.a.	n.a.	n.a.	n.a.	13.4	17.7	11.3	n.a.	n.a.
Yemen	16.9	17.8	14.1	10.6	3.1	11.8	n.a.	n.a.	n.a.	n.a.

Note: a negative sign indicates a budget surplus

Figures for expenditure and deficit are the ones most commonly referred to. They are important, and already indicate a difference between the increasingly severe fiscal crisis affecting some Arab countries, and the flexibility of others in adjusting to the lower revenue levels. However, the essential differences do not surface until we consider the figures for the sources of government revenue, and the evolution of oil rent. The latter reached an extraordinary level in the early 1980s, and then declined in conjunction with the reduced demand for Arab oil, and later with the dramatic fall in oil prices. Yet oil rent, albeit diminished relative to the peak level of 1981, continues to play a dominant role in Arab politics.

Table 5.3 details the incidence of 'exogenous revenue' over total revenue and grants for a group of the Arab countries and Iran. Exogenous revenue includes oil revenue and other sources of finance directly accruing from abroad, such as:

• Grants for Jordan, Yemen and Egypt. In the case of the latter, military grants are not included as they are not considered part of the central government budget.

• Investment income for Kuwait for years up to 1986, for which reliable figures are available.

• Suez Canal revenue for Egypt.

As only financial flows which could be clearly identified as accruing from abroad were included, the table may present an underestimate, but certainly not an exaggerated view of the importance of exogenous sources.

Table 5.3: Oil Revenue as a Percentage of Total Revenue – Selected Countries

	1982	1983	1984	1985	1986	1987	1988	1989	1990	1991	1992
Algeria	n.a.	n.a.	n.a.	43.1	23.2	22.0	25.8	39.1	49.8	50.8	n.a.
Bahrain	73.4	67.4	68.4	70.2	62.7	61.0	56.8	58.9	65.0	61.8	63.1
Egypt	n.a.	n.a.	n.a.	n.a.	n.a.	20.8	20.4	18.0	39.5	33.5	n.a.
Iran	n.a.	59.4	45.9	40.1	20.7	30.5	26.9	20.1	16.9	16.4	48.0
Jordan	36.6	34.3	21.2	31.3	23.5	21.7	24.6	33.7	18.8	n.a.	n.a.
Kuwait	93.8	93.6	93.6	94.6	95.8	n.a.	n.a.	85.9	91.2	80.5	90.2
Libya	n.a.	n.a.	n.a.	n.a.	65.2	66.8	58.2	47.2	61.6	n.a.	n.a.
Oman	89.4	85.7	81.0	82.2	73.6	82.2	79.7	81.2	85.1	79.7	82.6
Saudi Arabia	n.a.	n.a.	69.4	66.2	55.5	64.9	57.2	66.2	76.1	n.a.	n.a.
Tunisia	n.a.	14.6.	14.8	n.a.	n.a.	n.a.	n.a.	n.a.	n.a.	n.a.	n.a.
UAE	n.a.	n.a.	n.a.	n.a.	79.1	82.3	74.2	86.1	86.4	82.4	n.a.
Yemen	n.a.	16.2	14.0	11.0	24.8	24.3	27.4	24.0	24.6	19.8	12.9

The figures clearly indicate a sharp difference between, on the one hand, the Gulf oil-producing countries and Libya, where oil revenue accounts for at least 50 per cent of total revenue, and commonly much more than that, and all the others. Not only is the dependence of these states on oil revenue overwhelming, but there is absolutely no tendency to a reduction of it. Notwithstanding the fall in the price of crude oil since the latter part of 1985, no attempt has been made to develop alternative domestic sources of income.

Two other countries, Iran and Algeria, were in the past very dependent on oil revenue, but their reliance on this source of revenue decreased with the fall in oil prices and their respective oil export volumes. This decline shows that the two countries developed some, albeit limited, domestic sources of revenue alternative to oil. However, in both cases dependence on oil income has increased in recent years, And they now appear to be in the process of going back to their previous status of rentier states.

All other countries in Table 5.3 are in an altogether different category. In the case of Jordan, which has no oil revenue, grants have progressively declined, more rapidly so since the Iraqi invasion of Kuwait. In the case of Yemen, grants have declined but oil revenue has increased rapidly since 1986, and compensated for them: hence Yemen enjoyed relatively more stable access to exogenous finance, at least until the early 1990s. In the case of Egypt, exogenous sources declined in importance until 1989, but the trend was sharply reversed thanks to its participation in the war to liberate Kuwait. Finally, Tunisia does not offer figures that separate oil income from other sources of revenue after 1984: but its limited incidence in that year and the declining importance of the small

Tunisian production clearly indicate that oil income is not an important factor in Tunisian finances. Morocco does not feature in the table, as it enjoys no oil revenue at all.

Table 5.4: Tax Revenue as a Percentage of Total Revenue – Selected Countries

	1982	1983	1984	1985	1986	1987	1988	1989	1990	1991	1992
Algeria	n.a.	n.a.	n.a.	45.6	59.0	62.0	62.2	55.5	46.9	45.9	n.a.
Bahrain	13.6	19.8	19.7	18.9	23.5	24.2	25.4	26.0	24.3	25.4	n.a.
Egypt	61.0	61.8	58.6	60.5	60.5	62.0	64.1	48.0	53.6	n.a.	n.a.
Iran	30.6	35.0	40.9	48.6	68.1	58.8	61.8	68.0	74.2	73.9	40.0
Jordan	46.0	47.8	57.3	50.8	47.6	49.5	51.1	47.0	58.2	48.1	n.a.
Kuwait	5.0	4.8	4.6	3.3	2.3	n.a.	n.a.	3.6	n.a.	n.a.	n.a.
Morocco	80.2	83.9	85.9	84.3	91.5	89.3	n.a.	n.a.	n.a.	n.a.	n.a.
Syria	n.a.	n.a.	n.a.	n.a.	n.a.	62.1	68.8	72.6	74.2	74.5	71.2
Tunisia	75.1	78.9	72.3	73.4	74.2	74.3	72.6	73.5	76.5	81.6	80.1
Yemen	53.2	69.5	69.2	72.5	62.5	59.0	56.1	55.9	57.4	34.1	46.4

Table 5.4 shows the incidence of tax revenue over total revenue and grants. Tax revenue is not necessarily the complement to oil revenue, as there are other sources of non-tax revenue beside oil which can play a role: in particular, property income or profit from economic activities geared to the domestic market. It is notable that tax revenue appears to account for more than 50 per cent of total revenue in only five countries, that is Morocco, Tunisia, Egypt, Syria and Iran. In the case of Syria, it seems that tax income includes taxes on foreign oil companies, and is therefore exaggerated. It is notable that taxes play such a limited role in Jordan,

In Tables 5.5, 5.6, 5.7 and 5.8, I analyse which taxes are most important in individual countries. Figures are presented as a percentage of total revenue and grants, and reference should be made to Table 5.4 to assess the relative importance of each tax with respect to total tax revenue. Table 5.5 details the importance of customs and other taxes on international trade. They indicate that this source of revenue remains very important for several governments, although its importance appears to be on the decline. The high figure for Tunisia, in contrast with the considerably lower figure for Morocco, is particularly noteworthy. Generally, import taxes are used as an instrument to tax migrant incomes, and part of the decline in Jordan or the Yemen may be attributed to a decline in migrant remittances. The figure for Jordan remains strikingly high in the light of the limited importance of its tax revenue over total revenue. It is easy to see why the decision to liberalize imports may be viewed with a degree of anxiety by many Arab countries, as a substantial decrease in import tariffs would have a potentially sizeable impact on their finances.

Table 5.6 details the relative importance of indirect taxes. The figures are generally low by international standards (in 1990, the comparable figures were 29 per cent in Italy and the UK, 28 per cent in France, 24 per cent in Germany), but only marginally so in the cases of Algeria, Morocco and Tunisia.

Table 5.5: Customs and Other Taxes on International Trade –
Selected Countries

	1982	1983	1984	1985	1986	1987	1988	1989	1990	1991
Algeria	n.a.	n.a.	n.a.	4.6	5.4	7.6	6.5	7.2	7.3	7.2
Bahrain	5.9	10.0	9.4	7.7	8.1	7.4	8.5	8.3	7.4	8.0
Egypt	19.2	15.8	16.5	15.2	13.3	11.5	12.7	13.2	11.6	12.0
Iran	8.0	11.4	11.4	9.0	11.2	7.9	5.8	9.1	7.5	6.3
Jordan	25.9	24.4	27.7	22.7	21.2	24.4	26.4	19.7	21.4	15.4
Morocco	20.3	18.2	17.7	16.0	14.2	12.7	14.4	14.0	14.8	14.6
Tunisia	27.2	31.3	28.3	28.1	25.2	24.6	26.5	26.6	27.4	28.0
Yemen	32.2	42.1	39.0	42.3	34.3	24.4	19.4	18.6	16.8	n.a.

Table 5.6: Indirect Taxes as a Share of Total Revenue –
Selected Countries

	1982	1983	1984	1985	1986	1987	1988	1989	1990	1991	1992
Algeria	n.a.	n.a.	n.a.	22.9	29.9	30.8	30.2	26.3	23.4	21.6	n.a.
Bahrain	1.5	1.9	2.4	2.6	3.5	3.6	3.7	3.9	3.4	3.3	n.a.
Egypt	8.5	12.0	11.6	11.3	10.5	16.3	16.8	17.2	11.8	17.7	n.a.
Iran	4.0	4.2	5.2	8.0	11.1	8.7	7.8	4.7	4.2	6.7	5.5
Jordan	5.5	7.3	8.8	8.8	10.3	11.7	12.2	13.6	16.6	12.3	n.a
Morocco	32.7	36.3	37.3	37.5	46.1	45.8	26.0	28.1	27.0	20.3	22.2
Tunisia	20.8	21.3	19.7	19.7	21.7	22.0	20.9	19.2	19.0	22.3	23.2
Yemen	4.7	5.4	6.4	7.0	9.2	11.0	9.6	8.9	10.2	n.a.	n.a.

Table 5.7: Income Taxes as a Share of Total Revenue –
Selected Countries

	1982	1983	1984	1985	1986	1987	1988	1989	1990	1991	1992
Algeria	n.a.	n.a.	n.a.	16.4	21.4	21.0	22.4	18.9	13.7	15.1	n.a.
Bahrain	2.2	2.8	3.6	3.7	4.2	4.6	3.8	3.8	5.0	5.0	n.a.
Egypt	16.5	17.7	13.2	14.5	15.7	17.9	18.8	21.3	16.0	14.0	n.a.
Iran	7.3	7.8	9.5	13.4	21.4	18.2	19.3	12.0	9.9	11.5	12.3
Jordan	7.9	8.0	9.8	9.0	7.8	7.6	6.8	6.6	13.1	11.6	n.a.
Morocco	15.6	17.5	18.6	18.5	18.9	18.9	n.a.	n.a.	n.a.	n.a.	n.a.
Tunisia	14.7	13.5	12.2	14.3	15.6	13.3	11.8	12.3	12.3	14.3	12.4
Yemen	7.6	9.4	10.3	11.4	9.7	11.1	18.4	19.3	20.1	n.a.	n.a.

Finally, Table 5.7 focuses on income taxes. The limited importance of these international standards is clear (in 1990 the equivalent figures were 52 per cent in the United States, 39 per cent in the UK, 36 per cent in Italy, 17 per cent in France and 16 per cent in Germany), with the notable exceptions of Algeria, Morocco, Tunisia and Egypt. However, in the case of the latter – as well as in the case of Yemen, whose high figure is a surprise – income taxes are almost entirely (90 and about 65 per cent respectively for Egypt and Yemen) paid by corporations. Morocco is the only Arab country in which taxes on individual incomes have exceeded taxes on corporate income (as is normal in the industrial countries) ever since 1982.

The case of the GCC members

The Arab oil producers in the Gulf have been able to adjust to a lower level of oil rent because of the nature of government expenditure, which involved waste that could be curbed, and infrastructure investment that could be cut back. Also, reserves had been accumulated in the early 1980s, which could be used to ensure a soft landing.

Saudi Arabia is the most interesting illustration of the continuing importance of oil rent. It is a more interesting case than any other Gulf emirate, primarily because of its size, both geographic and demographic, which implies that the country has much more complex 'needs' than the other emirates. Infrastructural development, security and social services are much simpler propositions in other GCC members, Oman being the only other country that faces a vaguely comparable challenge.

Government expenditure in Saudi Arabia has followed a path which is closely related to the personality of the king. In the Faisal years, expenditure on government services grew less rapidly than GDP, allowing for ever larger resources to be developed to investment both domestically and internationally. In the Khaled years, preceding the decline in oil revenues, expenditure on government services began to grow somewhat more rapidly than GDP, but only marginally so. Finally, in the Fahd years, from 1983 to 1990, expenditure on government services continued to grow, while GDP declined (Luciani 1990, 79).

Saudi budgets in the second half of the 1980s were characterized by persistent, albeit diminishing, deficits, as expenditure cuts lagged behind revenue declines.

The smallest total expenditure was recorded in 1989, a year in which the demand for Saudi oil began to look more promising. In 1990 the Iraqi invasion of Kuwait changed the terms of the equation, as it led to considerable increases in both revenue and expenditure. The increase in revenue was temporary to the extent that it was due to the short-lived price boom. It was however permanent to the extent that it was linked to an increase in exported oil quantities. Indeed, the experience of the late 1970s and early 1980s has convinced Saudi Arabia that quantity, rather than price, maximization is in its best interests. Accordingly, it is now pursuing a policy of relatively low prices and growing oil production capacity, which promises a smoothly increasing oil rent in future decades.

Ever since oil revenue proved to be unstable, there has been a good deal of discussion in Saudi Arabia about reducing subsidies and increasing non-oil revenue. In fact, subsidies were cut back, though mostly in areas that do not directly affect the Saudi national population. In some cases, e.g. housing loans, the rules have not been changed but delays have increased, effectively restricting access to benefits. Nevertheless, the fact remains that Saudi citizens do receive handouts from their government. Albeit less generous than in the past, these handouts are still a substantial, if not the sole, source of their effective income.

As for non-oil revenue, some users' fees were introduced, and rates on key utilities, including electricity and water, were increased (though in the aftermath of the Gulf War they were reduced again). A clumsy attempt at imposing an income tax on expatriates was made in January 1988, but had to be withdrawn in a matter of days. The net result of the above is that non-oil revenue went from 42 per cent of the total in 1988 to 24 per cent in 1990, mainly because of the increase in oil revenue.

The absence of taxation uncouples government revenue from economic development. It is normally the case that government revenue increases automatically whenever the economy grows, because of direct and indirect taxes. Hence, the government has a strong interest in promoting economic growth and supporting investment even in infrastructure that is not immediately profitable as this will enhance growth and hence government revenue. But in Saudi Arabia this is not the case, as the absence of taxation eliminates the essential link between growth and government revenue. The development effort of the government is dependent on the level of oil revenue and is therefore potentially unstable.

Nevertheless, the Saudi government has evidently reached the conclusion that it is easier to adopt an oil policy that will guarantee slow but steadily increasing access to oil rent rather than adopting policies to develop non-oil revenue.

The primary preoccupation of the Saudi government, alongside guaranteeing its territorial integrity and security against domestic subversion, as shown by the importance of allocations to the military and security apparatuses, is indeed that of strengthening the foundations of its rent by pursuing a policy of keeping prices down while increasing production and exports. This entails substantial investment in expanding oil-production capacity, some of which may be financed by debt: but the rates of return on oil sector investment in Saudi Arabia are such that debt financing is certainly not a problem.

In recent years, the share of Saudi expenditure officially accruing to defence and security (Table 5.8) has declined somewhat – from almost one half of total expenditure in 1989 to slightly less than one third in the 1993 budget – but remains by far the largest allocation. Only a fraction of it pertains to expenditure obligations that could not be postponed or rescheduled. Similarly, allocation for education and health and social development include substantial expenditure for new projects in a contest in which unused physical capacity is not uncommon. Allocations for scholarships (part of education), subsidies and the specialized development funds could all be scaled down, if it became necessary to do so. This is not to say that the Saudi government is wasting money – it appears, on the contrary, to have obtained relatively good value for its money. Rather it is just to point out how confident the government seems of continuing access to its rent sources.

Table 5.8: Saudi Arabia: Budgetary Allocations 1989–93 (SR million)

	1989	1990	1991	1992	1993
Defence and Security	73,855	51,898	51,898	54,270	34,093
Education	24,000	26,191	26,191	31,118	14,087
Health and Social Development	10,550	11,791	11,791	12,247	6,980
Transport and Communications	8,280	9,228	9,228	8,250	9,078
Economic Resources	5,000	n.a.	n.a.	7,990	2,095
Subsidies	5,325	7,183	7,183	7,967	8,928
Municipal Services and Water	n.a.	n.a.	n.a.	6,296	61,636
Specialized Development Funds	6,000	n.a.	n.a.	4,636	9,167
Infrastructural Development	2,570	n.a.	n.a.	2,090	8,000

Why then does the Saudi government run a deficit? It is, I suspect, mainly because it feels the need to offer to the domestic financial sector an asset which banks and individual investors alike may consider attractive, in order to encourage domestic investment and the repatriation of funds.

The extent to which the government still has access to oil rent (as a continuing flow or as an accumulated stock) is shown by the relative ease with which the extraordinary financial burden of the Gulf War was borne. One can hardly think of any other country that could have done this without seriously affecting the standard of living of its citizens (indeed, ever since the war the Saudi economy has been in a boom, and one does not hear about the unemployment problem any more). Iraq, it may be interesting to note, managed the same in the early years of the war against Iran, again thanks to its oil rent.

What is true for Saudi Arabia is even more so for the other GCC countries. The fiscal difficulties of the Arab Gulf producers are frequently misinterpreted as being much larger than they in fact are. There are abundant private savings in these countries which investors frequently find difficult to employ in forms other than holding large cash balances and hoarding gold. So much so that the issuing of government bonds would be a wise policy, even if not a fiscal necessity.

Notwithstanding massive, if highly unequal, rent redistribution, dissatisfaction does emerge in Saudi Arabia and may even be said to be widespread. The existence of criticism and occasional revolt is well documented, but these manifestations fail to constitute a political movement. They are inevitable and existed even when oil rent was at its peak. Protest is likely to focus on the terrain of corruption or morality yet the regime commands overwhelming means of control/ co-option, which it uses actively to compete on the terrain of islamic legitimation.

The fact that protest is voiced in islamic terms may give the impression that it adds up to a coherent political opposition movement. However, the common islamic language is not sufficient to transform generic dissatisfaction and revolt into a political movement, all the more so since Islam is a divisive as much as a uniting factor, and the Saudi government itself legitimizes its deeds in islamic terms.

The situation is no different in the other members of the GCC, including Kuwait – notwithstanding the limited electoral exercise that took place there. The Kuwaiti elections followed a process of mass expulsion of expatriate workers, in an instance of economic self-mutilation which only a body that is exogenously supported could possibly tolerate, let alone actively provoke. The fact that Kuwait was able to dispose of the most productive component of its population is striking confirmation of the rentier nature of the state. The return to independence was accompanied by the promulgation of an extremely narrow definition of citizenship, with the clear intent of reducing the number of possible claimants to redistribution of the rent. Within this narrow body of citizens, only a small percentage had the right to vote, as a majority were excluded by multiple requirements. Even so, the election's results were interpreted as a defeat of the ruling al-Sabah family, as many 'opposition' figures were elected. Nonetheless, the same ruling family proceeded to form a cabinet which did not in any real sense limit its control of power, but simply included a few token members of the opposition: so much for democratization!

The case of Algeria

In contrast to the GCC members, which may be expected to enjoy continuing access to oil rent and maintain political institutions that are remote from democratic practices, other Arab countries have enjoyed faltering or uneven access to outside sources of revenue. The case of Jordan was recently analysed, and the close correlation between the decline in exogenous revenue and democratization highlighted (Brynen 1982). Here, I shall discuss two other contrasting cases, Algeria and Egypt.

Both Algeria and Egypt owe their difficulties to the fact that they spent in excess of their oil rent even in the heyday of the early 1980s, accumulating a level of debt which absorbed a large share of the rent in subsequent years, further compounding the effect of declining oil prices. In the case of both countries conditions of fiscal crisis have been reached. However, while Algeria retains a substantial rent base, and may aim at restoring itself as a rentier state, Egypt can entertain no such hope. The peculiar aspect is that, while Algeria has embarked on a process of democratization which aborted at an advanced stage, Egypt has made no significant progress towards either democratization or the solution of its fiscal problem for a decade or more. Recent economic policy reform in Egypt was not accompanied by parallel political evolution.

The case of Algeria is in many ways especially interesting. Algeria is a country in which the state enjoys extraordinary historical legitimation, because of the war of independence. No other Arab country can claim the same. Algeria has a past and a present of very close intermingling with Europe – more than some like to admit – and nobody can seriously think of taking off the *paradiaboliques* through which key European media are readily accessible. Algeria has a more egalitarian society than possibly any other Arab country, and a high incidence of literate, urban population. Ethnic segmentation exists and is a problem, but it is one that, at least until now, has not led to either separatism or violence. In short, Algeria is in many ways a perfect candidate for democratization.

Algeria well illustrates the argument linking the fiscal crisis of the state to democratization. The legitimation of the FLN began to falter when the oil rent decreased. In the early years of his tenure, President Chadli never thought of democratizing: he could afford to show a less stern face than Boumedienne because the regime had much larger funds available than before. He could afford to be 'generous', including with former political opponents of Boumedienne's. He also presided over a regime that made a succession of grievous mistakes, concentrating investments on expensive, capital intensive industrial projects; and insisting on excessively high prices for the country's major hydrocarbon resource, natural gas.[6] Little employment was created, and much of the gas liquefaction capacity remained idle because the gas was priced out of the market. Large-scale debt was incurred and when the oil bubble burst in the mid-1980s Algeria was left with costly idle industrial capacity, widespread unemployment and not enough hard currency to pay for essential food imports. The food riots of 1988 forced a rethinking.

The fiscal crisis of the state had to be fully exposed before the regime took notice, but then Chadli moved more decisively than most of his Arab counterparts. While the process of democratization was advancing – notwithstanding the fact that it repeatedly yielded surprises: the legislation of the FIS, its victory in municipal elections, and so on – economic reform was also taking place.

1988 is the key watershed year: government expenditure as a share of GDP peaked, and so did the deficit – although the latter remained well below what it had been in Egypt. The recurrent deficits were almost entirely monetized, leading to inflation and excess liquidity in the system. The parallel rate for the dinar (on the free currency market which is largely domiciled in France) worsened rapidly, and the ratio of the unofficial to the official rate of exchange went from slightly above 3:1 in 1987 to almost 6:1 in 1988. Furthermore, unemployment was acute and growing, and the country faced a balance of payments crisis.[7]

In 1989 the dinar was officially devalued; since then a policy of progressive changes in the exchange rate has reduced, but not eliminated, the gap between the parallel and the official rate. The progressive devaluation of the dinar is the key to the increase in oil and gas revenues in 1990–91, together with the improvement in the price of crude oil contingent upon the Iraqi invasion of Kuwait.

In 1988 a new petroleum code was enacted, which inaugurated the process of opening up the hydrocarbon sector to foreign activity. This was continued in 1991, when new rules were introduced to allow foreign partners not just in the exploration for new, undiscovered reserves, but also in the exploitation of known fields.[8]

The pace of reform did not accelerate until 1991. Municipal and provincial elections which saw a massive victory for the FIS had been held in 1990. Key reforms introduced in 1991 were:

• Fiscal reform: the tax administration was significantly reinforced, and a tax reform framework was adopted under the 1991 budget law. The new system was expected to rely on three major income taxes: value-added tax (VAT); a revised profit tax; and a general income tax. The latter was to substitute the previous schedular taxes on various types of income.
• Subsidies reform: in order to rein in the deficit of the compensation fund (created in 1990 to administer consumer and producer subsidies) a number of items were removed from the list of subsidized goods, while the price of others was brought closer to actual cost. The compensation fund is financed through special earmarked taxes on imports and domestic production (*taxe compensatoire*), and a surcharge on this was also imposed.
• Trade reform: imports were liberalized, through the removal of import licence restrictions and granting of full access to foreign exchange at the official rate.
• State industry reform: state enterprises were reorganized into a certain number of holding companies, in order to make them responsible for their economic results, and eliminate the practice of automatically financing the deficits out of the government budget.

It may be argued that these reforms were not bold enough and did not suffice to stimulate private investment and overturn the tendency towards growing unemployment. Yet the Algerian government accomplished in two years things that it has taken the Egyptian government close to 20 years to do. As political elections approached at the end of 1991, the country was very much at the bottom of the J-curve of economic reform: the population clearly felt the burden of the fiscal crisis of the state, while the benefits, in terms of accelerated development of the private sector, were still to be seen. Democratization was intended to confirm the legitimacy of reform and consolidate its path: the experience of other countries proves that painful reforms can obtain the support of a majority of the voters, if they are credibly and equitably enacted and explained.

However, the process of containing expenditure implied that the government fell short of meeting the social needs of the people. The door was thus opened to the progressive formation of various support groups inspired to islamic solidarity. It is out of these groups that the FIS was born. It is the experience of offering an alternative to government that marks the difference between islamic protest in Saudi Arabia and Islam as a political movement in Algeria. The organization of social services implies the ability to raise voluntary funds, while the government does not feel legitimate enough to raise taxes. Yet, reality is in fact even more complex, as the islamic solidarity initiatives were at least in part funded by Gulf money, hence part of the complex web of regional redistribution of the oil rent. Also, there may have been contacts between rising islamic groups and the parallel economy – *trabendo* – as it is commonly the case between realities that – though with differing long-term aims – they have a tactical common interest in escaping the control of the state.

The rise of the FIS in previous years is thus not difficult to explain: as the state was obliged progressively to abandon some of the ground it had occupied in society, it opened the door to competing forces performing some key social tasks. It is not difficult to prove that newcomers moved by a sense of mission can do better at limited tasks than an entrenched and demoralized bureaucracy. Hence the electoral victory of the FIS in the municipal and provincial election was in a sense no surprise.

However, its victory in the political elections which followed was, at least in part, the result of multiple mistakes: in the choice of the electoral system, which exaggerated the FIS electoral result and opened the door to a two-thirds majority; in the conduct of elections, in which many potential supporters of the government ended up by not voting; in the electoral campaign, in which the pro-democracy forces spent more time quarrelling with each other than taking the FIS seriously. In any case, the victory of the FIS is by no means a disproval of the main thesis of this essay – that a fiscal crisis may lead to democratization in order to provide a new source of legitimation for the state: this is exactly what happened, except that the process was derailed. Notwithstanding the clear will on the part of the government to engage in democratization, and the existence of so many conditions favouring it, the process aborted. But the question of democratization was not, and could not be, wiped off the political agenda.

It is, I believe, noteworthy that the first political leader to emerge following the disguised coup, President Boudiaf, appeared to be still pursuing the goal of democratization in the context of economic liberalization. He seemed to be prone to redefining the terms of the democratization process, in a way that would have kept it sufficiently democratic while excluding the FIS from access to power. At the same time, further moves were made in the direction of liberalizing the economy and reducing the overwhelming state control of all aspects of it.

Both policies were reversed following the rather mysterious assassination of the president. The new Prime Minister, Belaid Abdessalam, had been one of the key protagonists of Algerian industrialization policy in the 1960s and 1970s, but had been excluded from government in the early 1980s, when the wrong decisions were made, with respect to gas pricing in particular. He quickly moved to reintroduce import controls, and steered away from the crucially important policy of selling oil reserves, which had been expected to improve the government's financial position and encourage foreign oil companies to invest in Algeria with even greater determination.[9]

With respect to international debt, a policy of biting the bullet was inaugurated:[10] Algeria would not accept any diktats from international organizations or private banks, it would tighten its belt and pay back what it owed. Such an appeal to pride (arrogance?) and patriotism, however, holds very little promise for the masses of unemployed youth. It simply opens the door to increased '*trabendo*' activity: as usual, prohibition stimulates contraband.

The fiscal position of the state deteriorated rapidly. The budget for 1992 had been expected to close with a small surplus, but by the end of the year it was largely estimated to have recorded a deficit of about 10 per cent of GDP,[11] larger than in any previous year. This was in part due to the fact that the government fought inflation by, among other things, reducing the rates of the VAT and customs tariffs (thus undermining government revenue).[12] With inflation estimated at 40 per cent at the beginning of 1993, a budget for 1993 was announced in which the deficit was expected to double, and reach the unprecedented level of 40 per cent of government receipts.[13] In short, the Abdessalam government was counting on hydrocarbon revenues in the medium term and on the printing press in the short term. The association between renewed reliance on monetary inflation and exogenous revenue with return to authoritarianism and repression is striking.

When we look at these policies, in conjunction with the certainty that gas exports will increase in the coming years – the energy minister expected gas exports to increase from 34 million cubic metres in 1991 to 70–75 million by the end of the decade[14] – it is evident that the government primarily aimed at reestablishing its rentier foundations. A relatively short period (two or three years) of stern discipline and repression was expected to considerably reduce the debt service burden. If so, the available rent would increase thanks to both the decline in debt service and the increase in hydrocarbon exports. Abdessalam appeared to believe that what was needed was simply to redress the mistakes that were made in the early 1980s, when insistence on excessively high prices ruined Algeria's gas-export drive, leaving huge liquefaction investment unutilized; and debt-financed investment was undertaken in the misplaced expectation that prices would continue to rise.

The Algerian government, having rejected in all but words the option of democratization, resorted to repression in the hope of succeeding in re-establishing the rentier foundations of the state. Yet this strategy is doomed; even if the hydrocarbon rent increased in the rest of this decade, this will not allow for enough public investment – and of the right kind – to reabsorb a pool of unemployed which is constantly fed by population dynamics. Stimulating agriculture and labour-intensive industrial projects is a must, and a result which can be obtained only by encouraging private investment, from within the country as well as from abroad. The path of economic liberalization will therefore need to be resumed, immediately positing the question of a redefinition of the respective roles of the state and the private sector, and of taxation. The return to authoritarian rule can thus be a parenthesis in Algerian history, and the question of democratization will continue to figure prominently on the political agenda.

The case of Egypt

Egypt proves that it is quite possible for a government to muddle through and indefinitely postpone democratization even while its fiscal position is clearly and irreversibly out of balance.

Egypt may be said to have faced a fiscal crisis throughout its modern existence. The need for reducing subsidies with all its implications (that go well beyond government finance) was already evident in the 1970s. The policy of *infitah*, which Sadat inaugurated in 1974, was little more than a limited foreign trade liberalization and acceptance of direct foreign investment in a limited number of sectors. It was immediately clear that the policy could not possibly succeed unless subsidies on key food items and controls on agricultural prices were removed, interest rates and the foreign exchange rate liberalized, private investment freed from multiple restrictions, state industry run commercially and progressively privatized. Indeed, what is striking about Egypt is that a list of necessary measures was clearly identified as early as the mid-1970s, one on which, albeit with important nuances about implementation details, all professional commentators agreed. The first steps in the direction of abolishing food subsidies were taken in such an inept manner that they led to the riots of 1977 – since transformed into a textbook case in the literature on structural readjustment. The regime promptly backed down and decided that economic reform is too dangerous to be seriously pursued. The possibility of capturing several sources of rent simultaneously (oil, the Suez Canal, grants and soft loans in connection with the Arab–Israeli conflict) was offered to the country in the late 1970s and early 1980s, allowing the regime to postpone all unpleasant decisions.

When Mubarak came to power, an expectation was created that he would again undertake economic reform and couple it with democratization. Timid steps in that direction were greeted with great hope. However, the mood soon changed: in the mid-1980s rent faded away and the regime appeared simply to sit on its problems. The conflict with international credit institutions and foreign donors became increasingly bitter, but the Mubarak government made massive use of its geopolitical role, in essence, to impose its own terms.

This policy of 'passive resistance' to international pressure certainly did not lead to brilliant economic results. Notwithstanding partial deregulation in agriculture and limited price adjustments for basic foodstuffs and energy prices, large fiscal deficits were accumulated year after year. Inflationary pressure intensified, and artificially low interest rates encouraged a rapid increase in the dollarization of money balances. Economic growth declined to 2 per cent in 1989–90, well below the rate of population growth.[15]

Notwithstanding such dismal results, it was only after the Gulf War, at a time when the Egyptian government hoped again to be able to extract some monetary benefit from its favourable strategic position, that a deal was struck with the IMF and the World Bank, leading to economic reform, including a decrease in government expenditure and increased taxation. Measures that were taken in 1991 include:

• Unification and liberalization of the exchange rate.
• The freeing of commercial bank interest rates.
• The beginning of an auction system for treasury bills, to put an end to monetization of government deficits.
• The reduction of government expenditure and deficit.
• The introduction of a general sales tax.
• New, more forthcoming regulations to encourage direct foreign investment.
• A renewed programme of privatization of state economic holdings.

If the reform process continues to be vigorously pursued, it will inevitably change the nature of the relationship between state and society in Egypt. However, it is extremely significant that this programme was only undertaken in conjunction with a steep increase in outside foreign assistance. In the latter 1980s Egypt received official transfers of between US$700 million and 1 billion per year. But in 1990–91 official transfers from countries belonging to the coalition opposing Iraq reached $4.8 billion, or 15 per cent of GDP. In the following year, the figure was expected to decline to $1.5 billion, still well above previous levels. At the time when it launched its economic reform programme, the Egyptian government probably hoped for more sustained official transfers, in conjunction with the security arrangements that were to be inaugurated by the Damascus declaration. That this came to naught was a disillusionment for the government in Cairo, but its only hope was to forge ahead with economic reform.

Given that official transfers are unlikely to continue at a high level for long, the tax reform announced to date still appears insufficient. Certainly more will need to be done with respect to personal income taxes – an area on which government had promised action at the time of writing.

Economic reform has thus taken place without any significant shift towards democratization. The inflow of exogenous finance may have contributed to this, but it is only part of the explanation. Two key elements appear to be: the role of the military; and the preference of the bourgeoisie for controlled rather than genuine democracy. The military is still the most important political structure in the country, as it produces the president, who in turn controls all power. The military enjoys a separate budget: military loans and grants from abroad, as well as profits from military enterprises accrue directly to the military budget, and are not recorded in the central government budget (hence they do not feature in the figures in Tables 5.1–5.7). Only transfers from the central government budget are recorded as defence expenditure: the latter has progressively declined from about 21 per cent in 1987–88 to about 15 per cent in 1990–91. Clearly, this trend will need to be sustained in the context of fiscal reform: how far will this be acceptable to the military?

The lack of enthusiasm in the bourgeoisie for real popular participation in political life can also be understood in the light of both historical and contemporary realities. Historically, it was through the use of socialist slogans and manipulation of the masses that Nasser destroyed the power of the old bourgeoisie, and the danger of a return to populism must be very clear to today's private entrepreneurs. Furthermore, all holders of economic wealth have become accustomed to investing in financial assets abroad, and they will be extremely cautious before committing themselves to productive investment at home – in other words, the bourgeoisie has effectively become de-nationalized. At the same time, the Egyptian masses are so impoverished that they certainly cannot contribute to the fiscal needs of the state, and on this basis lay a claim to democratic participation. Hence what we see is a kind of collusion between the military and the new private entrepreneurs (representing just a fraction of Egypt's financial investment potential) with a view to keeping the lid on the impoverished majority. The latter, together with the marginalized fringes of the technical and commercial strata, increasingly react by resorting to violent opposition based on the islamic rallying cry.

Yet the coalition supporting the regime is fragile and vulnerable to islamic terrorism. It is fragile because it is inconceivable that all new entrepreneurs feel well represented and served by the regime in power: if economic reform succeeds, the private sector expands and becomes the main economic support of the state, and government will need to be more accountable. And it is vulnerable because continuing – albeit low-level – islamic violence can effectively destroy the tourist trade and discourage private investment, both foreign and domestic.

Hence, at some point, indeed sooner rather than later, the Mubarak regime will feel the need to increase its democratic legitimation and hold elections in which opposition forces stand a better chance of gaining some influence on the conduct of public policy. In this context, diffusion of power and rehabilitation of the role of the national assembly is also extremely important. However, islamic opposition may, as in Algeria, lead to exactly the opposite result: an intensification of repression, and slippages in the implementation of economic reform.

An optimistic view of Egypt's future would point to the experience of Morocco, which has long recognized and come to terms with its fiscal difficulties. As our statistical analysis has shown, Morocco is the one Arab country that has succeeded in developing a reasonably modern fiscal system. It is also the Arab country that has run a system of constitutional government with multiple parties and coalitions for the longest period of time. Morocco remains a controlled democracy – the king is above the law and manipulates his country's democratic institutions with considerable cynicism. Morocco cannot be called a democratic state, but the path to further democratization is quite clear, as the king is mortal and the crown prince may inaugurate a new era (the Spanish precedent is bound to be significant here).

Conclusion

The nature of the economic foundation of the state is more useful in predicting what may not happen rather than what will happen. The rentier nature of the state is a strong factor in discouraging democratization in all countries that have access to a significant oil rent, and I would be surprised if any of the rentier states were to democratize. On the other hand, the presence of a fiscal crisis creates the expectation that a country may embark on a process of democratization, though certainly does not guarantee the outcome. Many other factors come to play in determining the prospects for democratization, and even cases that *a priori* appear promising, such as Algeria's, may turn sour.

Yet in the absence of democratization the fiscal crisis is unlikely to be overcome. Private investors, both domestic and foreign, will not feel confident about investing in a country where persistent repression and fiscal imbalance inevitably project a threat of instability. Economic stagnation is likely to ensue, and is in fact the record in many Arab countries.

A combination of weak, repressive governments and economic stagnation may continue for a long time, and there is no assurance that it will at some point evolve towards democratization. Yet logically it is impossible to believe that illegitimate government may be perpetuated indefinitely simply by resorting to repression.

Notes

1   The swing from authoritarian to democratic rule began in southern Europe: Portugal, Spain, Greece and Turkey. It has been almost universal in Latin America – where only smaller countries such as Haiti and Cuba stand in contrast, while Peru has had a, presumably temporary, relapse. In Asia, popular movements for democracy gained considerable successes in South Korea, Hong Kong, the Philippines, Thailand and Pakistan. They emerged but were crushed in China and Myanmar (Burma). In sub-Saharan Africa mass movements for democracy emerged in practically all countries in which there is no active civil war, including Kenya, Zaire and Nigeria. Plus, we have had the collapse of communist regimes in eastern and central Europe. All of which amounts to an overwhelming trend indeed.

2   Judgment about a factual degree of democratization is inevitably subjective. A relatively free press exists in a few Arab countries, but this is not synonymous with democratization, especially in view of the fact that circulation is very limited. Contested elections are held more or less regularly in some countries, but they appear to be either constrained by the imposition of limitations on either all or key opposition parties, or extensively rigged. Movement towards or away from democratization is just as important to my argument as the attained degree of democratization. Judgment about dynamics is easier in the light of analysis of the run-up to elections and election results. There appears to be widespread consensus in the press and among academic analysts with respect to which country is moving in which direction, and it is to such consensus that I will refer.

3   The Arab countries have witnessed several cases of mass participation in political events. Some of these were sustained for many years – such as the independence movements in Egypt, the war of liberation in Algeria, and nowadays the *intifada*, to name but a few. Shorter eruptions of mass political activism – sometimes manipulated from above – have been common. Hence one cannot maintain that mass participation is unknown or even unusual in the Arab countries. The striking fact is that practically no sustained political movement nor mass protest has yet been recorded primarily in favour of democratic rule – just a few groups of intellectuals or merchant families.

4   It is essential that the rent should accrue from the outside world directly to the government. If the rent is generated domestically, it is purely a factor of income redistribution within the country: the task of the government in covering expenses may be facilitated, but the strength of the state remains directly related to the strength of the domestic economy. If the rent is generated exogenously, the strength of the state is related to economic conditions in the rest of the world. Furthermore, the rent must accrue directly to the government. If the rent is captured by private citizens or firms, the state must still resort to taxation to capture it in turn. Taxation of a limited number of large companies, especially foreign ones, such as oil companies, is tantamount to direct access to the rent. However, taxation of a large number of individuals, e.g. migrants, has entirely different political implications.

5   Goldstone (1991). Goldstone's key theoretical hypothesis is as follows: 'large agrar-

ian states of this period were not equipped to deal with the impact of steady growth of population. Pressure on resources led to persistent price inflation. Because the tax systems of most early modern states were based on fixed rates of taxation on people or land, tax revenues lagged behind prices. States thus had no choice but to seek to expand taxation. This was all the more true as population increases led to the expansion of armies and hence to rising real costs. Yet attempts to increase state revenues met resistance from the elites and the populace and thus rarely succeeded in offsetting spiralling expenses. As a result, most major states in the seventeenth century were rapidly raising taxes, but were still headed for fiscal crisis' (p. 24). The same is true for today's Arab states.

6 This judgment follows, among others, the authoritative opinion of Nordine Ait-Laoussine, paper submitted to the Third Annual conference of the Centre for Global Energy Studies, London, 5–6 April 1993.

7 Unless a different source is mentioned, the discussion of the Algerian economy is based on: IMF, *Algeria – Recent Economic Developments*, May 1991, mimeo.

8 *Petroleum Intelligence Weekly*, December 23, 1991, p. 3; *Le Petrole et le gaz Arabes*, 16 December 1991, p. 23.

9 'Algérie: la tentation dirigiste', *Le Monde*, 5 November 1992.

10 'Le premier ministre algérian réaffirme son opposition au rééchelonnement de la dette de son pays', *Le Monde*, 24 November 1992.

11 'Le labyrinthe algérien', *Le Monde Diplomatique*, February 1993.

12 'Le gouvernement algérien bloque les salaires', *Le Monde*, 10 March 1993.

13 *Financial Times*, 5 February 1993; *Middle East Economic Digest* 5 February 1993.

14 *Middle East Economic Survey*, 7 December 1992 and 8 February 1993.

15 Unless a different source is indicated, the discussion of Egypt's economic situation is based on: IMF, *Arab Republic of Egypt – Recent Economic Developments*, August 1992, mimeo; and United States Embassy in Cairo, *Foreign Economic Trends and Their Implications for the United States – Report for the Arab Republic of Egypt*, June 1992, mimeo.

Note on sources to the Tables

Algeria	IMF, 'Algeria – Recent Economic Developments', Table 25-26-27 p. 59–61
Bahrain	IMF, GFS Yearbook 1992, pp. 199–20, for 1982–91; for 1992 EIU, Country Profile, Bahrain, 1992–93
Egypt	IMF, 'Egypt – Recent Economic Developments', pp. vi, 118
Iran	IMF, GFS Yearbook 1992, pp. 297–8
Jordan	For 1982–90 IMF, GFS Yearbook 1992, pp. 438–9; for 1991, EIU Country Profile, Jordan, 1992–93
Kuwait	For 1982–89 the primary source is IMF, GFS Yearbook, 1992, pp. 331–2; investment income data (hence also total revenue data) are only available until 1986. For 1989–92 EIU Country Profile, Kuwait, 1992–93
Morocco	For 1982–87: IMF, GFS Yearbook 1992, p. 384; for successive years EIU Country Profile, Morocco, 1992–93
Oman	IMF, GFS Yearbook 1992, pp. 424–5
Saudi Arabia	Middle East Economic Survey 36:15 11 January 1993 B3

Tunisia   IMF, GFS Yearbook 1992, pp. 532–3

Yemen   For 1983–91 IMF, GFS Yearbook 1992 p. 569; until 1989 total revenue figures include grants; for 1991–92 EIU Country Profile, Yemen, 1992–93

UAE   EIU, Country Profile, UAE 1992–93

6

Demographic Explosion or Social Upheaval?

PHILIPPE FARGUES

Academics and politicians share a common view – a rare occurrence – of Arab demography. They see it as a dynamic force, a mass travelling under its own momentum, which is bound to exert ever greater pressure for some time to come. Both accept that rapid population growth creates problems first for the economy and thereafter for the social and political situation. Population growth increases all kinds of economic demands, starting with essential goods and services, and quickly overwhelms the capacity of the productive apparatus to respond. Among the rival claims of consumption, savings and investment, demography puts excessive strain on the first: in other words, it restricts development.

The state is responsible for the misfortunes of its citizens. When the population cannot itself meet the needs of its own growth, it is to the state that it turns. If internal savings or external aid cannot be mobilized, then the state can meet such needs only with refusal. The people's growing demands then become violent – from 'bread riots' to all kinds of protests against unemployment or lack of housing – to which the state responds with repression. There is thus a sort of automatic mechanism by which demographic growth hinders the quest for democracy. This feeling of powerlessness is echoed by the novelist Rachid Mimouni in a recent essay: 'Mad demography has hastened the destruction of the world and its values. One even wonders whether it is at the root of all Algeria's problems. The 4,000 classrooms built every year can no longer accommodate the children entering school for the first time. The ranks of the unemployed swell inexorably. Agricultural land shrinks like the proverbial wild ass's skin' (Mimouni 1992). Paradoxically, it is at a time when signs of an opposing trend among the population become apparent that this fatalistic vision is almost unanimously expressed.

I shall first demonstrate that the present structures of Arab populations now hold within themselves the end of the demographic 'explosion' and that the decline promises to be more rapid than is widely accepted.[1] Within demographic trends which are still rising, there are beginning to be dips which are more or less pronounced depending on the country or population group. This does not however mean that their demands will follow the same pattern, since social progress should take the place of demography in raising global demand. Thus in the Maghreb, it is surely no longer so much the number of children reaching school age – which has already begun to decline from one year to the next – but rather the increased demand for schooling, and only that, which has led to the overcrowding lamented by Mimouni.

I shall go on to show how the destabilizing effects of demography go beyond the economy. The increase and subsequent slowing of demographic rates has come about against the backdrop of a revolution in knowledge and the means of its transmission, of a new state of awareness contradicting the old values. Previously, the importation of technical knowledge by an elite opened the way to demographic growth: in response to advances in medicine, production and communications, the death rate had fallen since the beginning of the twentieth century (Fargues 1986). The next phase of the demographic transition, and particularly the fall in the birth rate, was instead a result of widening access to education.[2] Today, the slowing of the birth rate is due to mass access to knowledge which is no longer technical but general, and to the way it is transmitted: no longer privately, within the family, but publicly, through schooling. The effect of schooling has gone further than taking the education role away from the elders of the family, since, being aimed solely at the young, it spreads from the bottom up, and has in fact turned the ancestral order on its head. Knowledge has brought its own influence to bear on the hierarchies of generation and sex that still form the power structure, in the family at least, and perhaps also in society as a whole, with the result that the young hold more qualifications than the old, and women catch up with men. In this way, as it runs its final course, the demographic explosion is giving way to social upheaval.

The demographic fall

Only two or three decades ago in the Maghreb, and less than one in Mashreq,[3] large families were the norm except for a very small highly educated urban minority for whom it would have been difficult to combine a public existence, where women are on an equal footing with men, with producing a large family.[4] Except in cases where there was a fecundity problem, the average couple produced between seven and nine children.[5] Less than a generation later, at the start of the 1990s, the old pattern seems to have disappeared for ever: the young adult now has a family which is half the size of the one in which he grew up. The total fertility rate is now only 3.0 children per woman in Tunisia, 3.5 in Morocco, 4.6 in Algeria, 4.7 in Egypt, but still 6.0 in Syria (Figure 6.1).[6] The fall in the Maghreb is almost an exception. It is reminiscent of two experiences 25 years earlier: in its sharp fall, it is like that of southern Catholic Europe, and in its widespread extent, like that of the Far East. But both these events took place against a completely different backdrop: the rapid secularization in Mediterranean Europe and the industrial take-off in south-east Asia. There was no such similar trend in the Arab world where the resurgence of Islam and persistent under-development seem to create the opposite conditions.

Figure 6.1 Total Fertility Rate 1960–2025

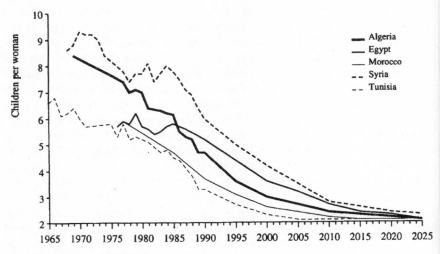

Source: 1995–2025 revised Plan Bleu projections

From demographic to social pressure

Such a change in family size should calm demographic fears. In all Arab countries the rate of population growth has now started to fall (Figure 6.2). At a remarkably similar time throughout the Mediterranean Arab world, around 1985 –1990, the absolute number of births itself stabilized and even fell.[7] In Egypt, the curve peaked in 1986, with nearly 2,000,000 births (1,928,000): five years later, the figure had already dropped by 10 per cent, with 1,754,000 births in 1991.[8] The same phenomenon occurred at the same time in Tunisia (235,000 births in 1986, 205,000 in 1990) and in Algeria (845,000 births in 1985, and 739,000 in 1989).[9]

The quantitative effects of the stabilization of the birth rate are spread over time, following the advancing age of the generation in question. The health care infrastructure, the only area where newborns have any effect, is the first to experience the results of a slackening of demographic pressure. Six years on – the start of the 1990s in Egypt and the Maghreb – and the primary schools feel the effect. But it will not be until 20 to 25 years later, that is, around the year 2010, that the numbers entering the labour market or needing housing will cease to grow.

Yet in none of these areas has the stabilization of the figures led to a levelling of demand. Not in the neo-natal or infant care: the reduction of the number of children in the family is accompanied, as often happens, by a wish to improve health status, and we are only too aware of how far there is to go before health care is delivered equally throughout the population. Nor, as long as there are groups of people without access to school, will it reduce demand for education. In Morocco, for example, there were 4 million children of primary school age, i.e. between 6 and 11, in 1990. This figure will be the same in the year 2000. If the participation rate in education remains at its present level, which is only 53 per cent because of the low figures for the countryside against the town and among girls against boys, the numbers in school will cease to rise, and will remain at the present level of 2.1 million. But if access to schooling is extended to a figure of 100 per cent,[10] in the year 2000 there will be as many pupils as there are children, i.e. 4 million. The 1.9 million extra children to be catered for (90 per cent more) will be the result not of demography, but of the extension of schooling, that is, of social progress. On the other hand, in all the countries where access to basic education is already universal, or nearly so – Iraq, Jordan, Lebanon, Syria and the countries of the Gulf in the Mashreq, Algeria and Tunisia in the Maghreb – provision of schooling has now reached a ceiling.

Figure 6.2 Natural Growth Rate of National Populations 1950–2025

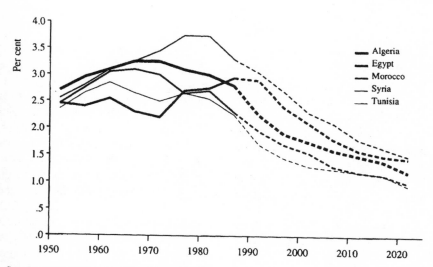

Source: 1990–2025 revised Plan Bleu projections

A similar pattern will emerge a few years later when it comes to creating jobs or building homes, in other words the specific needs of young adults: future

additional costs will be due less and less to the rise in their numbers and more
and more to their rising aspirations. Of the various phenomena that have contributed to the current overload in the urban labour market in the Arab world,
demography – meaning numerical growth of the generations and rural to urban
exoduses – will certainly have been the most visible, if not the most potent. The
mass rural exoduses of the 1960s and 1970s are now a thing of the past throughout the Arab world, with the possible exception of the Sudan, where civil war
and recurrent droughts recently drove thousands of peasants onto the roads to
Khartoum. Everywhere else, spatial mobility has largely taken the form of
exchanges between towns (Escallier & Signoles 1992), a straightforward redistribution between towns of the active population, with no effect on overall urban
employment. Natural demography on the other hand, will continue to exert
growing pressure until the generations that have stabilized reach an 'active' age,
which ranges from the year 2005 in Tunisia to 2020 in Syria. In the meantime,
the situation will vary greatly from one country to another, with the varying
birthrate of the 1970s and 1980s making their effects fully felt.

**Figure 6.3 Growth in Potential Demand for First Employment
1990–2025**

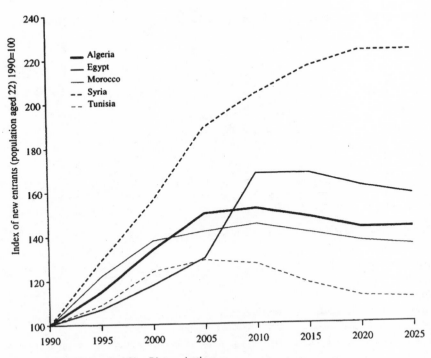

Source: 1990–2025 revised Plan Bleu projections

The potential numbers of those seeking a first employment are largely contained within the 20–24 age group.[11] The projection for this group (see Figure 6.3) gives the demographic component for the change in numbers of those entering the labour market. In Tunisia, a rise in this figure of only 30 per cent is expected, whereas Syria will pay for its delay in controlling the birthrate with a four- or five-fold rise. Between these two extremes, Algeria, Egypt and Morocco will have to respond to a rise of about 50 per cent in potential demand during the next thirty years.

Figure 6.4 Growth in Potential Creation of Jobs 1990–2025

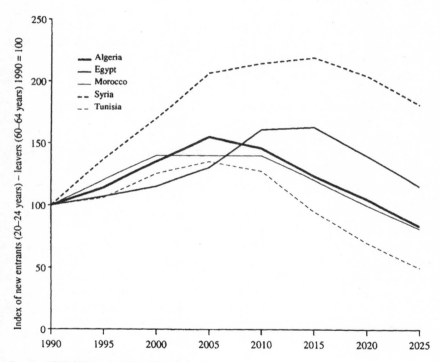

Source: 1990–2025 revised Plan Bleu projections

But the population of working age includes not only new arrivals on the labour market, but also all those who have joined it during the previous 40 years (see Figure 6.4). So the total numbers will continue to grow for much longer than the previous figure, in fact, until the number of those leaving the group (60–65 year olds) exceeds those entering (20–24 year olds). This point is not too far off in Tunisia (the year 2015), Morocco or Algeria (both 2020), but it is off the projected map in Egypt (2025) – where the effects of the resurgence of the birth rate between 1973 and 1985 will be felt for some time – and most of all in Syria. In the meantime the jobs to be created each year will peak at figures ranging from 40 per cent above their 1990 level, in the case of Tunisia, to 125 per cent above in Syria. The future pressures on the Arab countries vary widely and are in inverse relation to how long ago their demographic rates began to fall.

Demography determines the growth of the potentially active population – the 20–65 age group – but not the growth of the population that is in fact active, in other words those employed or searching for employment. The latter depends equally on two social factors, each with opposite effects. A significant rise in the age of entry into the labour market, chiefly due to the rise in the numbers in education and increases in academic qualifications, tends to slow down the growth of the active population. Conversely, the arrival of women on the urban labour market – or the increase in their numbers in the Lebanon, Tunisia or Egypt, where they have been present already for some time – tends to accelerate it. The real unknown factor lies in the potential for growth in the female sector, as these figures started from such a low base.[12] Whereas demographic projection can give us some idea of the scale of future male employment it is of no help with female employment, that is, with half of the total potential active labour force. In the unlikely event of women catching up with men's level of activity by the year 2025, the total demand for employment will have increased by 70 per cent above its present level in Tunisia and by 300 per cent in Syria (see Figure 6.5). In this scenario, the growth of the population would play a relatively minor role (with an increase ranging from 15 per cent in Tunisia to 125 per cent in Syria), compared to the social evolution that will result in employment being open to women.

The simple fact that there are on average 60 years between a person's birth and his retirement from employment makes some forecasting possible. One can say with certainty that the labour market will be under demographic pressure while the numbers entering it are greater than those leaving; this will be the case for between the next 25 and 50 years, depending on the country. But during this period, the social factors of demographic deceleration, education and the change in the status of women, will take the place of demography itself in determining the volume and variety of the demand for employment.

The erosion of an old order and internal disparities

In family matters, as in other things, innovation began with a subtle change: as with so many other social changes, the shift from the large to the smaller family has taken place gradually. Starting with an elite, a very small minority of the population – meaning one with no perceptible influence on average demographic indicators – the shift towards a smaller family has begun to spread within some sub-groups of society without really affecting others. Half-way through this process of diffusion, Arab populations today are more heterogen-

Figure 6.5 Growth in the Total Demand for Employment 1990–2025

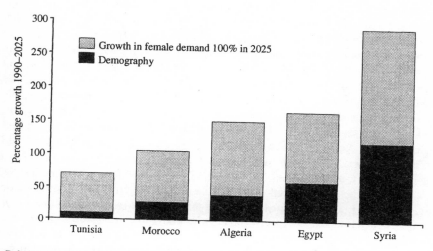

Relative variation in the numbers of potential new entrants onto the job market (author's calculation, based on revised Plan Bleu projections)

eous than they were in the past and probably more than they will be in the future. The statistically average Arab couple, producing four children in all, is no more common in the ordinary way of things than the extremes that still coexist with it: the large family of seven children or more and the one which is increasingly replacing it, with only two or three children. During this transitional phase, almost all the criteria which create perceptible differences within the population also map out the levels of fertility.

Geography provides the most visible of the dividing lines and perhaps the most instructive of the processes at work. Whereas at one time population growth was uniformly malthusian throughout the Arab world – apart from in the Arabian peninsula,[13] for reasons mentioned below – the town now stands out from the countryside, where the birth rate remains virtually unchanged. The contrasts brought about by place of residence are nowhere as pronounced as in the central Maghreb. In Morocco, the average rural family size is five children, in Algeria it is seven – to the point where whole sectors of the rural areas seem to be cut off from this modernization of the family – whereas the city dwellers have, in just one generation, come to the stage it took a century to reach in Europe. With average family sizes hardly any larger than in Europe – 2.3 children per woman in Morocco and Tunisia, 3.0 in Algeria (1992) – the new urban generations have nearly completed a demographic transition that their mothers had not even started.

Partially masking the contrast between town and country, regional differences have also deepened in the past 20 years. Contact with the modern life and the outside world has brought about the introduction of the smaller family in cities and in areas bordering the Mediterranean. The figures for 1988, for example, show that women were still producing more than six children in southern Algeria (6.7 in Quargla, 6.5 in El-Oued) or in the Aurès (6.2 in Batna) but already less than 4 in the north (3.6 in Algiers, 3.8 in Ain Temouchent, 4.0 in Oran or Tipaza). Despite its small size, the Lebanon itself displays strong regional contrasts: from Beirut (2.3 children per woman) to northern Lebanon (4.3 children per woman), there co-exist two different stages of the demographic transition.[14] In all cases the figure rises from the coast towards the interior, whether in Morocco, Tunisia or even in Egypt, where the average family in Port Said has 3.6 children, but in Fayoum 8.2. The cultural models encountered through international migration to some extent reinforce the geography of demographic transition: the Maghreb, which has a foothold in Europe through its émigrés, has experienced a marked decline in its birth rate[15] whereas the Egypt of the *infitah*, strengthening its Arab exchanges by a million and a half expatriates in the Gulf, saw it rise again temporarily from 1974 to 1985.

Cleavages within the population caused by the economy can also be observed in demography. For a long time, a smaller number of children was the prerogative of the rich. Poor people, for whom children represented the highest wealth, resisted strongly.[16] In the towns, in the Maghreb at least, the situation seems now to be the reverse, with material hardships forming a new barrier to high birth rates and poverty and high population growth no longer proceeding hand in hand. As in a number of industrial countries, the variations in family size relative to family income in Morocco are now beginning to form a U-shaped curve (Cered 1989), with large families being found at the two extremes, particularly among the very wealthy.

History itself has an effect on the demographic disparities of the time. The fact that religious affiliation is the factor producing the greatest disparity between the different birth rates within the populations of the Middle East cannot be imputed simply to geography, or even economics.[17] The total contrasts – rather than mere demographic disparities – seen until recently between the communities of the Lebanon, tightly enmeshed in the fabric of the country and its economy, even though they do not make a coherent whole, is striking. With a total fertility rate of about 2.4 children per woman in the mid-1980s,[18] the Christians of Lebanon seemed to have already completed their transition, whereas in southern Lebanon and the Bekaa, the Shi'ites, with six children per woman, had hardly begun (Lebanese Family Planning Association 1984). Because of their centuries-old plurisecular contact with European Mediterranean Christianity, the former had at the same time experienced some of the family changes of the twentieth century, whereas the latter had gone through this crucial period in demographic history in relative isolation. Nowhere is the religious basis for the birth rate so strong as among the Palestine population. The Christians in Israel stabilized their birth rate at the beginning of the 1980s at 2.4

children per woman, a few years ahead of their fellow believers in the Lebanon. Under different political and economic conditions, the inhabitants of Gaza, very largely Muslim, have never experienced the slightest drop in the birth rate; far from it – at exactly the same time as the *intifada* (1987–90) it reached its highest ever peak, at 9.5 children per woman.

Population and income

The size in the drop of the birth rate, its timing, and the extent of its spread throughout society, whether general or restricted to certain groups, depends on a variety of causes. The policy of the state is one: in the Arab world, the lowest birth rate is to be found in countries where public action in favour of limiting the birth rate is the most vigorous or well-established.[19] But, it seems that state intervention has fuelled a trend which had already begun rather than initiating it: campaigns to encourage contraception were effective where certain sectors of the population were already beginning to practise it,[20] often against the odds. Egypt and Tunisia (1964) and Morocco (1966) were the first to adopt official programmes for limiting births. To get around the problem of the still largely conservative attitudes on family matters, the state emphasized the *fatwas* that recognized that some contraceptive practices conformed to divine precepts.[21] In fact, Egypt, Tunisia and Morocco saw their birth rates fall ten years before Algeria, and 15 years before Syria, Jordan or Iraq. In Algeria at the beginning of the 1970s, President Boumedienne launched a counter-campaign – 'our pill is development'– to stress the importance of the economy, and the precedence of the development of the production infrastructure over the modernization of family structure: the demographic question could only be resolved by economic solutions. At the first world population conference in Bucharest in 1974, Algeria, in perfect harmony with China,[22] labelled birth control as one of the vices of 'imperialism'. Limiting the population of the Third World was a way of clearing the ranks of 'anti-imperialism'. President Chadli Bendjedid then brought about a complete reversal of this when he introduced, from 1982, the most thoroughgoing neo-malthusian campaign in the Maghreb. But the birth rate had already begun its decline three or four years earlier.

Demography could have reacted as much to political economy as to population policy in the strict sense of the word. The classic theory established a strong link between economic development and limiting the birth rate, by stressing the effect by which the second follows the first. As the family's standard of living rises, we are told, the children progressively lose their role as producers, that is their economic usefulness, and acquire an emotional value, in other words they represent a cost: and this is why fewer are produced. Recent experience in various parts of the world, particularly the Arab world, seems to contradict this: in spite of the model, we now see demographic changes accelerated by economic crisis and non-development and others, conversely, halted by prosperity.

Between Arab countries the greatest differences in wealth depend on whether or not they produce oil. On the one hand there are under-developed economies that have, nonetheless, a relatively diverse productive sector, and on the other, economies organized totally around oil income and its redistribution. Non-oil-producing countries, where, without much help from the state, families have to face the costs of the modern child and the necessity of using their labour – female included – to ensure their income, have seen their birth rate fall. On the other hand, in the oil-producing states where, thanks to wealth derived from exports which grew constantly during years 1974–84, allowing the prince to continue to keep his subjects, birth rates have remained high. The lack of household taxes, the meeting of the costs of childhood from public funds and keeping women at home thanks to imported female domestic staff, have prevented any change in the birth rate. The welfare state has offered large families a stay of execution by short-circuiting the factors of demographic transition – particularly in female education – just at the time when they were beginning to appear.

Tunisia and Morocco illustrate the first type of experience; Saudi Arabia and the Gulf states, and perhaps also Libya,[23] the second. Between the two groups, the majority of Arab populations have only some of the features of income-dependent demography. Algeria and Iraq, despite their oil wealth, are too well-populated for the state to help families substantially. In Algeria, the collapse of oil and gas income in the mid-1980s coincided with a fall in birth rate (Fargues 1990), attesting to an income-dependent reaction. The total fertility rate had not changed at all between 1981 (6.39 children per woman) and 1985 (6.24), all years of high revenue. During the five years following, it diminished by 1.5 children per woman falling to 4.71 in 1990. Egypt also had a period of income-related reproduction at the beginning of the *infitah*. After a decade when it constantly fell (1964–73), the birth rate rose again during the next (1974–85). It was probably less to do with military demobilization – something that often leads to a brief rise in births – than with the input and redistribution of various external resources: the Suez Canal and oil again, American and Saudi aid, tourism and the savings of émigré workers were all sources of income which increased the circulation of goods and services beyond what Egypt was producing. Migration itself contributed to the renewed rise in the birth rate, because of the Egyptians' contact with the large family standard common in the Gulf.[24] One can probably apply 'income' explanation to the record birth rates in occupied territories: in divorcing reproduction from its costs, both Palestine and international solidarity movements (for example, UNRWA) enabled families to raise numerous children without having to rely on their own resources,[25] which went hand in hand with a political desire to wield the demographic weapon.

Increasing equality between the sexes

It is changes in society and a woman's place in it, rather than state policy and economic systems,[26] which have brought about the gradual extension of the smaller family pattern. The steady progress in the introduction of schooling for girls during the past 25 years is the most significant change. In all Arab countries, female education is now the most important factor in differing birth rates.[27] Whether average family size is still large (Syria) or already small (Tunisia), there is the same stratification, ranging from illiterate women, who still bear many children, to women with secondary or higher education who have completely rejected the norm of the large family (see Figure 6.6). In Tunisia and Morocco, as for some time already in the Lebanon, women who have attended secondary school or university produce barely any more children than their European counterparts: with a total birth rate of 2.5 children the demographic transition in this group is almost complete. The fact that schools, which were for a long time strictly reserved for boys, are now open to girls, will have been a powerful force for demographic change.

Figure 6.6   Variation in Childbirth Rates, According to the Education of the Woman 1990

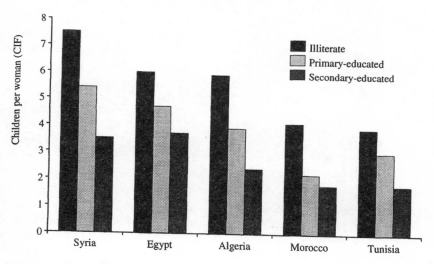

Source: extrapolation dating from 1990 of the most recent figures available

Because of the relationship between fertility and education, the latter becomes a very accurate predictor of the future pattern of the former. It is at about the age of seven that literacy is achieved, at 11 that secondary school begins and at 15 it is decided that for the rest of one's life one will belong to one of the following classes: illiterate, primary educated, secondary or higher educated. It is not until 15 years later that a woman produces her children: the average age of fertility is around 30. The schoolchildren of 1992 will become, on an average, the mothers of the year 2008. An examination of the present figures shows that in 15 years'

Philippe Fargues

time the level of education of these women will be much higher than that of today's mothers. Imagine what a census shows if one defines a generation not by the year of its birth but by the year of its thirtieth birthday (see Figure 6.7). In Algeria, for example, the birth rate for 1990 (4.7 children per woman) was the product of a still largely illiterate majority (60 per cent of women at age 30). But the speed at which the division of women by level of education is changing can clearly be seen: in the next 15 years, illiteracy will have all but disappeared from among the population of childbearing age. So the present population structures – in this case the classification of girls by level of schooling – are predictive of the future decline in fertility.

Figure 6.7 The Rise of the Educational Level of Women in Algeria

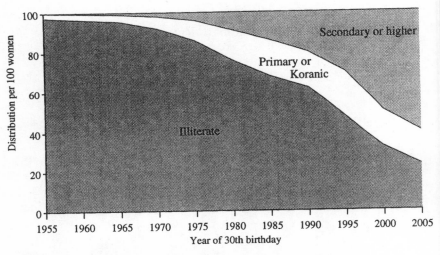

Source: 1987 Census (year of 30th birthday = 1987 – age + 30)

The second indicator of differential rates of fertility is women's exclusion from or acceptance in the professional sphere, i.e. economic activity in the public sphere.[29] The Arab countries, as with most of the Muslim world, have a remarkably low figure for female participation in urban economic activity: it ranges from less than 5 per cent in the Arabian peninsula to hardly more than 25 per cent in Tunisia, against a world average of around 50 per cent. Does this mean that women are absent from work itself, or simply from the picture the statistics provide? Men create the statistics as they, not their wives, generally fill in the census forms: the figures indicate that, in men's minds at least, women should not work. Their activity rate is in exactly inverse relation to their average fertility (see Figure 6.8).

At first sight, there is nothing exceptional about this relationship. In all societies, domestic responsibilities increase along with the size of the family and, beyond a certain level, militate against the mother's participation in employment outside the home. But there seems to be another reason, more specific to Arab societies, behind the mutual incompatibility of work and childbearing. In various Arab countries is seems that a large number, or even the majority, of women who work before marriage, leave their job on marriage or just before, that is before they even have a child.[30] It is the husband and not the children who keeps the woman out of the labour market. Because of this, the link between activity and fertility is not the result of the direct effect of large families on the absence of women from urban work; rather, both these circumstances depend on yet a third: the prevalence of the patriarchal family. The erosion of it, which is very uneven between both countries and sectors of society, may have brought about a diversification in women's roles, that is, a simultaneous lessening of her domestic role (leading to the drop in the birth rate) and an increase in her external activities. Demographic transition has accompanied the disappearance of the male monopoly in public life, not only in school but also in employment. What is happening here is clearly a convergence between the status of men and women.

Figure 6.8 Female Activity and Fertility

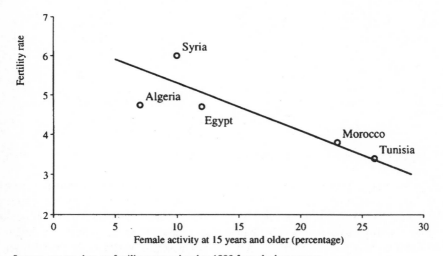

Source: census data on fertility extrapolated to 1990 from the last survey

Increased equality of the sexes is not confined to greater integration in public life. Marriage itself and family life have been affected, a change which is revealed by civil registration data. Until recently, marriage patterns followed certain rules which formed a coherent system. A man married a woman on average ten years his junior, who therefore came from a more populous age group

than his own. The surplus of available women was absorbed through remar-
riages, which were more common for men than for women: either through
polygamy (marriage by a man already married at the time), or more often
through a second marriage after repudiation of the previous wife (marriage of a
previously married man). The inequality in age was to some extent the basis of
the inequality of rights. Polygamy, which seems never to have been very common in the Arab world, is decreasing everywhere: it happens only in between 2
and 10 per cent of marriages (it is prohibited in Tunisia). Divorce, which
according to Egyptian or Algerian figures was very prevalent in the first half of
the century (affecting more than a third of marriages), has also greatly declined
(see Figure 6.9). Almost as a chain reaction, the age gap between spouses, a
source of male domination over women, is decreasing as its two regulators,
polygamy and repudiation, themselves disappear: in most Arab countries, the
gap is now less than five years.

**Figure 6.9 Decline in Polygamy and Repudiation in Algeria and
Egypt 1900–1990**

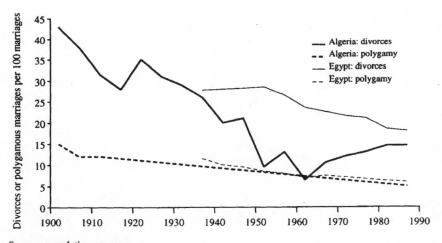

Source: population censuses

Access to education reveals another aspect of the growing equality of the sexes.
Allowing for different time scales and significantly different low and high
points, the same phenomenon has been repeated throughout most Arab countries
(see Figure 6.10). The generation born at the beginning of the century remained
largely illiterate. For this reason, schools did not at that time introduce inequality between the sexes. Open only to the children of the elite, they certainly
accepted more boys than girls.[31] But as for the masses, neither boys nor girls
ever attended. Then when mass schooling began to be introduced it benefited
only the boys: the generations of girls born before 1920 in Egypt or Syria, or

Figure 6.10 Average Level of Education by Sex and by Generation

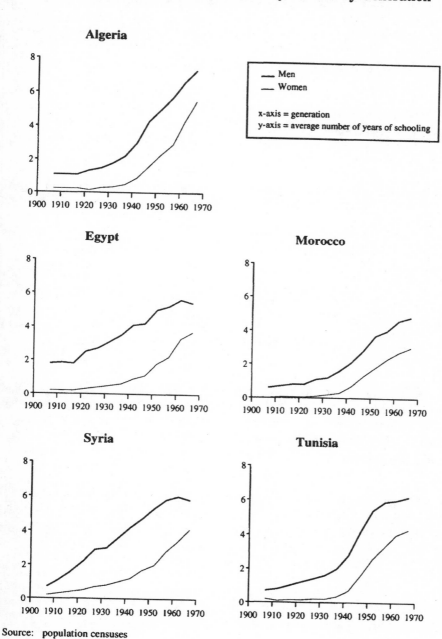

Source: population censuses

before 1940 in the Maghreb, had no access to such education. Schooling had introduced another type of inequality between the sexes. In the middle of the century the expansion of schooling for girls at first progressed more slowly than the extension of the length of schooling for boys. So the gap between the sexes got even wider, until the generations born between 1950 and 1960, which were the most unequal of all (Figure 6.11). It was not until after the 1960s that the

Figure 6.11   Average Gap in Education between Men and Women

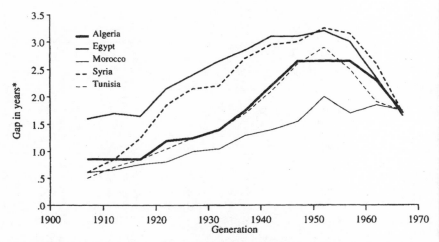

*Average number of years of school of men (ANYS) minus ANYS of women (author's calculation based on population censuses)

inequality of opportunity began to be eroded. The striking simultaneity of the change, from the east to the west of the Arab world, is a reminder that the advancement of girls was part of the spirit of the age. The modernizing trends by which girls were no longer deprived of schooling were in fact world wide and were mainly promoted through the efforts of international organizations, most notably Unesco. Girls then caught up with boys very quickly.[32] In Algeria, for example, thanks to the advances of primary education following independence, young girls reaching marriageable age are hardly less literate than the men they are to marry (see Figure 6.12). The sexual inequality caused by schooling will, in its extreme form, have affected relatively few generations. These generations will now be aged 40 to 60: the age of power

The double hierarchy of the generations

At the same time as the hierarchy of the sexes is slowly losing its legacy of

Figure 6.12 Reduction of Gender Inequality in Relation to Literacy in Algeria

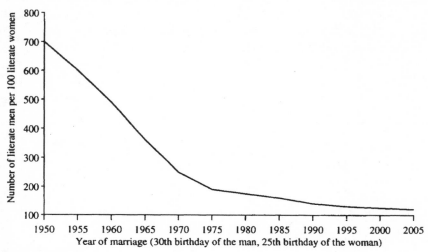

Year of marriage (30th birthday of the man, 25th birthday of the woman)

Source: 1987 census

men's three advantages – age, education and economic activity – the hierarchy of generations has been reversed by the expansion of education. The contradiction is particularly marked in the Arab world because of a particular feature in the history of its demographic transition: the phase in which mortality alone declines lasted a little longer than elsewhere, almost a century in Egypt, for example. It overturned family structures.[33] The first effect of the decline in mortality while the birth rate itself remained constant (if not higher),[34] was that the number of children surviving increased. There was a time when a third of young children did not survive, in some areas half the children in any one family. In the years preceding the fall in the birth rate, around 1960, infant and child mortality struck only one in ten. This is why people born around 1960 come from the largest families: greater than the ones before, which had been decimated by high mortality, and greater than those to come, which were to be reduced by birth control. It is this generation who, on reaching adulthood, will be in the greatest competition with their peers, in various areas where there will be relative shortages: employment, housing and even marriage. The pressure of numbers of young adults, i.e. those aged 20–29, is as high as it has ever been or will ever be (see Figure 6.13). The second effect of a decline in mortality is that the generations are forced to coexist for longer. As is the case with children, adults have also benefited from progress in health care: where once death overtook them young, now they survive to old age. Today, a young man will live alongside his father beyond the time when once he would have already succeeded him. In a still strongly patriarchal society, the father holds on for longer and longer to a source of power to which the son has to wait longer and longer for

access. In Algeria, for example, married men with families living in the same
house and under the authority of the father (thereby depriving them of effective
authority over their own family) form a group whose size has increased consid-

**Figure 6.13 Proportion of 20- to 29-year-olds in the Population
Aged 20 and Over**

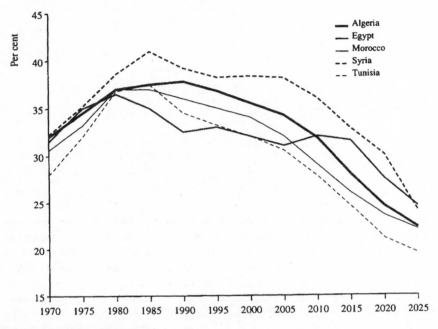

Source: revised Plan Bleu projections

erably and whose age profile also changed during the 1970s (see Figure 6.14).
In the recent past, a very early marriage used to hold the son of the family home
for a while, but these days even those marrying later are prevented from leaving
through lack of jobs and housing. In this way, demography has set the scenario
for horizontal competition between peers and vertical conflict between generations.

This conflict is occurring in the wake of a period of rapid and widespread
expansion in schooling, which has given the current generation of sons a sort of
monopoly on knowledge. This generation has not only emerged from illiteracy,
but has also in growing numbers entered secondary and higher education,
whereas among the fathers there are many who are either illiterate or who did
not progress beyond primary school. A comparison between the levels of literacy of sons and fathers[35] reveals this generational gap in knowledge (see Figure
6.15). In all countries it follows the same 'inverted-U' curve. Before 1950,

Figure 6.14 Proportion of Married Men not Heads of Household in Algeria

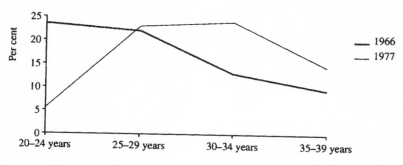

Source: population censuses

young men of 25 were scarcely distinguishable from their fathers, since neither group had ever attended school. Equality between the generations will be re-established when the fathers themselves become literate. This will be around 2030, when the schoolboys of today – who for the first time in history will make up the whole of that age-group – will become the 'fathers'.[36] Between the two points, a century of inequality has passed, during which the up-and-coming generation of 25-year-olds will have been much better educated than the 60-year-olds holding power. Because in Algeria and Tunisia schooling has expanded particularly quickly and from a base of widespread illiteracy, it is there that there is the greatest scope for conflict. In Algeria this scope for conflict is further reinforced by the legitimacy conferred upon the youth by its monopoly over written Arabic. The divide is least marked in Egypt, where schooling has been established a long time but is expanding slowly. But everywhere, even in Egypt, the generational dissociation between knowledge and power is too strong not to put a strain on political systems.

Conclusion

Men no longer dominate women. Fathers no longer dominate sons, but the sons themselves have entered a new sort of competition which sets them against one another. The patriarchal nature of the family has been seriously upset and, mirroring it on a giant scale, so has the 'neopatriarchal' order of the whole of society (Sharabi 1988). Against this background there has grown up a counterblast which in the name of religion calls for the restoration of differences between the sexes, codified by the *shari'a* but thwarted by the strong pull of social change, which challenges the validity of hierarchy of generations, inherited from the tribal order of *jahiliya* (the pre-islamic age). This challenge accords with the deep structures which, from the 'rattling of autocratic power' would shape the

Figure 6.15 Changes in Educational Inequalities between Father and Son

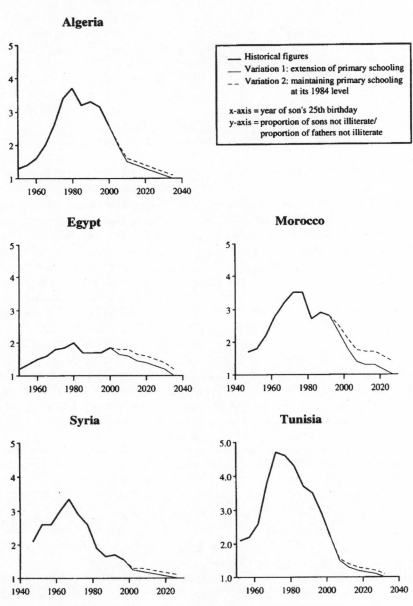

Source: most recent population censuses (Algeria 1987, Egypt 1986, Morocco 1982, Syria 1981, Tunisia 1984)

Arab mental universe: in the image of the encampment of tents rather than the pyramid, the ideal of equal men organized around a chief who is supposed to derive his power not from the status accorded to his position, the 'generation', but from his skill in manipulating custom (Khuri 1990). It could be thought that the rivalry between peers and the general conflict which accompanies the transition from one egalitarian state (the widespread illiteracy of the past) towards another (universal schooling of the future) all support this challenge. The examination of the structures of age and education of the population shows that we are looking at a very brief interlude in demographic history. We know already that when they reach adulthood, the younger generation will no longer be under the same pressure from siblings within the family, as the birth rate has fallen. We also know that when today's schoolchildren themselves become fathers, the dissociation between power and knowledge will have become blurred. In its extreme form, the imbalance will have lasted only a generation. But however short-lived it may have been in the history of demography, the transformation of present population structures is yet strong enough to lead to political disorder.

This chapter was translated from the French by Elizabeth C. Harrison.

Notes

1 Several organizations, whether international (e.g. the United Nations) or not (American Bureau of the Census), create and promote this image of the future of world demography. They overestimate the future growth of most of the Arab countries, for reasons whose technical aspect cannot be examined here and which have chiefly to do with the particular impact of women's education on the birth rate. Their results – for example, as published in 'World Population Prospects as assessed in 1990', *Population Studies no. 126* (New York, United Nations, 1991) – can be compared to those drawn by Plan Bleu (as in 'L'Avenir démographique de la rive sud de la Méditerranée. Projections de la population et de l'emploi et réflexions sur la migration', working paper of the *Plan Bleu,* 1992).

2 The various effects of education, whether dispensed within the family or at school, have been studied in another context – that of black Africa – in the following: Caldwell (1982) and Caldwell & Caldwell (1990).

3 With the exception of the Lebanon, which was the first of the Arab countries to show a drop in the birth rate in the 1960s. See *al 'Usra fi Lubnan* (2 Vols), (Beirut National Office of Family Planning, 1974); Courbage & Fargues 1974; Chamie 1981.

4 There are still no studies in historical demography which date the appearance of malthusian behaviour in Arab societies. It was apparently not as soon to appear as in Turkey, where it was common in Muslim families in Istanbul at the beginning of the century (Duben & Behar 1991).

5 Final number of children per woman according to the birth rate of the time.

6 Although it draws on a comparative analysis of all the Arab countries, this chapter is routinely illustrated by data from the five countries presenting the clearest figures

(with the exception of Kuwait): Algeria, Egypt, Morocco, Syria and Tunisia. Unless otherwise stated, the demographic indicators cited come from adjustments made by the author with Youssef Courbage, which have appeared in various publications of INED and the Plan Bleu.

7   While there was a steady fall in fertility, the total numbers of births continued to grow, due to the simple fact of the increase in the number of women of childbearing age.

8   These are the most recent figures available to the author.

9   This pattern probably repeats itself in other countries too, most especially Morocco, where the records do not allow an annual analysis of births.

10   Obviously an unrealistic supposition.

11   If everyone entered the active population at age 22, the potential demand in a given year would equal one fifth of the 20–24 age group.

12   Figures for female economic activity have hardly any meaning in rural Arab areas, see Zurayk (1985).

13   In Saudi Arabia, the rate for urban females is as high as in the country: 8.56 children per woman aged 45–49 in towns, and 8.73 in the countryside (al-Mazrou & Farid 1991). In the United Arab Emirates, which are more than 80 per cent urbanized, the total fertility rate for native women was still as high as 8.0 children in 1988. See ESCWA (1989) *Demographic and Related Socio-Economic Data Sheets for the Countries of ESCWA*, no. 6 (Baghdad, United Nations, 1989).

14   The author's calculations, from the age pyramids drawn up from the first nationwide demographic survey since the civil war: Kasparian (1991).

15   Courbage has demonstrated the close 'buckling' relationship between fertility and emigration in the Maghreb: one of the causes of emigration was the long period of high fertility, yet emigration in itself has led to a drop in fertility which has led to a drop in emigration itself (Courbage & Fargues 1974).

16   The micro-economic theory of fertility – examining the decision to reproduce in terms of cost-benefit analysis – has been so extensively covered in the literature as not to need mentioning here. There are two key articles: Becker (1960) and Caldwell (1976).

17   The situation in the 1970s was such that any analysis of the different influences on fertility revealed the dominance of economic factors. See Chamie (1981).

18   The only representative study of the Christian population in the Lebanon does not allow a direct calculation of the fertility of the time, but provides data (age pyramids) which allow for an indirect estimate (Kasparian 1990).

19   This effect, which is much to the credit of the countries concerned, is not observed in all parts of the world.

20   The figures for Egypt show the beginnings of malthusian behaviour among the younger generations: but at the same time, the birth rate was rising in the generation above, whereas global fertility remained constant (Fargues 1986).

21   Various *fatwas* dating from the 1950s, all supporting birth control, are quoted in *Attitudes de l'Islam face à la régulation des naissances* (New York, The Population Council, 1967).

22   China was at that time preparing, in some secrecy, a strict policy of one-child families in complete contradiction to its position at the conference.

23   Libya has no source of reliable demographic data whatsoever: the figures provided by international organizations on this country have been obtained by analogy with

countries with a comparable economy, and thus have no informative value.

24 For the same reason, one could assume that migration to Europe has accelerated the decline of the birth rate in the Maghreb.

25 In a somewhat similar way, in England in the nineteenth century, the birth rate reacted to benefit allowances for children, income and housing (Boyer 1989).

26 C. Makhlouf Obermeyer (1992) makes a direct link between the status of women and the political system in their impact on fertility.

27 Including in Saudi Arabia, which has however remained almost outside the drop in fertility: for the 45–49 age group, the number of children per school-educated woman is 7.1, against a figure of 8.7 children for illiterate women (al-Mazrou & Farid 1991).

28 This is why the classic projections – particularly those of the UN – overestimate future fertility, which they obtain by simple extrapolation of past fertility. If the components of average fertility are extrapolated – breaking down women of child-bearing age according to level of education (data available 15 years in advance and only fluctuating slightly in the longer term), and studying the fertility of each level of education – much lower figures are obtained. See *Plan Bleu* (1992).

29 This really refers to urban activity: rural female activity (which is anyway difficult to measure) does not introduce the woman into a 'public role'.

30 Result obtained in various studies by the author.

31 Data from the end of the nineteenth century in the Arab provinces of the Ottoman empire show that this dual characteristic of schooling – limited provision and imbalance in favour of boys – were themselves variable, depending on the regions and religions. See Cuinet (1896).

32 Schooling for girls is not developing everywhere: in rural Morocco, it remains limited.

33 For a theoretical approach, see Ryder (1983).

34 Jean-Noel Biraben's work on Algeria (1969) has revealed an almost continuous rise in the Muslim population between 1891 and 1956. The author attributes this to an almost uninterrupted rise in the health of the population. I have put forward another explanation elsewhere, which is the progressive stabilization of marriage partners and the decline in divorce.

35 Comparing the rate at age 60 to the rate at 25.

36 Unless there was a resurgence in illiteracy, in which case the ratio shown in Figure 6.15 would drop below 1.

PART II

CASES

7

Socio-economic Change and Political Mobilization: the case of Egypt

ROGER OWEN

Introduction

Most political analysts still operate within a very restricted set of assumptions when it comes to an attempt to understand processes of democratization. Put at its most simple, the vast majority continue to rely on some variation of the formula that capitalism produces a bourgeoisie, which in turn promotes liberalism and, eventually, democracy.

Nevertheless, in recent years, this simplistic notion has been subject to a variety of criticisms in both its European and its Middle Eastern forms.[1] Such criticisms have proceeded along the following lines:

• It draws on an idealized, ahistorical picture of what democracy ought to consist of.
• It is forced to view the bourgeoisie, wrongly, as a unified and coherent class-political agent of progress.
• It tends to ignore the role of other classes or social groups in the promotion, or widening, of democratic practice.
• It also tends to ignore the impact of wars, crises and other conjunctural factors in either putting an end to a democratic experiment or in re-starting it after a period of dictatorship, for example, in the case of Germany and Japan after the Second World War.

In opposition to such a notion, some historians have begun to call for a subtle, less deterministic approach: one that pays proper attention to the historical possibilities of the context and of the times, one that focuses more narrowly on the actual practice of democracy and on the constitutional and other frameworks which define both its limitations and the possibilities for further expansion.[2]

It is with this in mind that I come to consider the case of Egypt since 1970. My main argument is that the revival of multi-party politics was largely introduced from the top, though as part of a policy of finding partners for the regime in a 'liberal' project in which those individuals and groups who might be supposed to benefit from the new economic policy of *infitah* – and the subsequent debt-led attempts to reduce public spending and re-structure the economy. Thus they were offered limited participation in a system of elections and interest representation designed to exclude the lower classes from the political process while at the same time paving the way for a gradual whittling away at the policies of universalism, as well as the examples of positive discrimination in favour of workers and peasants, introduced under President Nasser. It is also important to note that, as far as the accompanying electoral structures were concerned, it was necessary to find means to counteract reliance on the now obligatory principle of one person/one vote with measures to ensure that a majority of the electorate was, nevertheless, effectively disenfranchised.

I will further argue that such projects were quite common in parts of the Third World in the 1970s as one-party, statist, regimes were forced to reform their economies in response to growing international debt. This also involved political arrangements very similar to the type of limited multi-partyism described by many contributors to the influential study *Elections Without Choices* (Hermet, Rose & Rouquié 1978).

It follows that, if such projects are introduced from the top, and if they are also designed to exclude large sections of the population, the analysis of their relationship to class formation, socio-economic change or large-scale political mobilization is unlikely to be simple or uni-directional and will require much more subtle delineation. I begin by providing my own reading of the process as begun by Sadat, before going on to concentrate more fully on the re-activation and consolidation of the system under Mubarak.

Sadat's introduction of infitah *in its economic and political forms*

Sadat's efforts to consolidate the weak position in which he found himself immediately after his succession took a number of forms, most obviously the proclamation of a new economic policy *infitah* to overcome what he defined as a severe economic crisis as well as an accompanying relaxation of some of the most repressive features of the late Nasser period. Both initiatives had much in common: they involved a loosening of administrative control over the legal system, greater respect for private property and a willingness to tolerate a wider degree of public criticism. Moreover, both were calculated to appeal to well-defined popular constituencies which had clearly identified themselves as supporters of the somewhat half-hearted openings announced by the Nasser regime following the 1967 military defeat, for example, during the 'open society' debates of 1968. Finally, the principles that were supposed to underpin this initiative were enshrined in the 1971 constitution with its emphasis on personal liberty, freedom of opinion and the sovereignty of the law.

The economic component of *infitah* was widened and more precisely delineated in the aftermath of the limited military victory of 1973, in particular in Sadat's 'October speech' of May 1974. This at once served to divide those social groups who might hope to benefit from it from those much larger groups who began to see its aims of encouraging privatization, foreign investment and reform of the public sector as a major threat to their interests. The same speech also made reference to the need to complement economic with political reform, ushering in a long process of public discussion on the future of the Arab Socialist Union, which finally culminated in the decision to allow three of its platforms to contest the November 1976 general election as distinct ideological tendencies.

It seems unlikely that President Sadat himself had any particular blueprint for a reformed political system at this time. From his point of view the major imperative was to ensure that the single party could no longer be used as a base for the still-powerful nasserite opposition. For the rest, there seems to have been a genuinely popular input into the debates, with politicians, journalists and intellectuals often pushing the process towards pluralism much faster than the regime itself wanted to go. However, Sadat was quick to see the advantages of the new proposals, moving to limit the number of licensed political groupings to three, one rightish, one leftish (but excluding the mainstream nasserites) and a government-controlled centre. He then institutionalized this formula with the Parties Law of 1977 which laid down strict conditions for the formation of new parties, in effect banning the establishment of any that could possibly appeal to a widespread regional, religious or working-class constituency.

As it began to take shape before the major political storms of the late 1970s, the new political structure consisted of the following elements:

• the government's National Democratic Party dominating the People's Assembly and providing the preferred, and privileged, base for the supporters and beneficiaries of economic *infitah*.

• limited, largely token, representation of other social interests in the Assembly or, after 1980, in the new Shura Council (including that of westernized women attracted by Mrs Sadat's divorce law reform).

• a continued reliance on a combination of subsidies and a re-formed police force to maintain working-class and peasant acquiescence.

The multiple vicissitudes of this system between 1977 and 1981 need not detain us. Suffice it to say that its representative and managerial function was much reduced as a result of the 1977 'food' riots, the regime's fear of opposition to the Camp David peace agreement and the mutation of many islamic groups from instruments of grass-roots social action to centres of increasingly active opposition. Some might even argue that it was only the oil boom of 1979 onwards and the export of discontent through mass labour migration which kept it going as long as it did.

The practice of Egyptian democracy under Mubarak

When the new Mubarak regime decided to call elections in early 1984, as required by the constitution, it relied on a legal framework consisting of three main elements. The first was the constitution of 1971 itself, which contained various references to electoral procedures, although embedded in a document hastily drafted for quite a different purpose, namely the legitimation of the new Sadat regime.[3] It also contained provisions for the creation of a supreme constitutional court, eventually established in 1979, with some rather indefinite powers of interpreting the constitution itself. This court soon came to play a significant role in the constitutional politics of the 1980s in ways that I will describe below.

The second part of the legal framework was the Parties Law of 1977; and the third the Mubarak regime's own Electoral Law of 1984 which consciously tried to create a system by which the government party, the NDP, would receive every possible advantage while limiting opposition representation to an acceptable minimum. For example, parties were required to obtain 8 per cent of the national vote before receiving any seats in the People's Assembly, with the votes of those parties that did not manage to meet this threshold being transferred to the majority party. Moreover, coalitions of parties which might have allowed them, jointly, to obtain the necessary minimum were expressly disallowed. Another measure designed to limit access to the assembly by potentially dangerous opponents was the clause outlawing independent candidates, on the grounds that, as the main architect of the law, the then Prime Minister Fuad Mohieddin freely admitted, such persons might not be 'known' to the regime.[4] This law was later amended, in 1990, to allow a return to the Sadat-period system of two-candidate electoral constituencies for which any individual or the candidate of a recognized party could stand.

Three other aspects of Mubarak's policy at this time are important. First, his regime decided to go along with the current practice by which electoral registers were maintained by the police, who were also responsible for the designation of polling stations (Shukrallah 1991). It also used the continued state of emergency to limit the right of parties to hold rallies or leaflet supporters. Second, in order to convince the public that opposition parties were to be given some opportunities to obtain representation in the assembly, the regime did not obstruct the New Wafd's appeal to the state council to be allowed to organize itself as a party, even though, strictly speaking, it fell within the category of inadmissable organizations as defined by the 1977 law. In the same way it also permitted the Wafd's two main leaders – Fuad Serag Eddin and Ibrahim Farag – to win their legal case for the reinstatement of their political rights taken from them in 1978. Third, the regime used the election as an essential ingredient in its strategy towards the islamic political movements by allowing the New Wafd to enter a tacit alliance with the banned Muslim Brothers so as to ensure mainstream – and moderate – religious representation in the assembly, while continuing to pursue its harsh campaign against those it identified as religious extremists.

An examination of regime policy initiated during the 1984 elections, and then developed through the subsequent elections of 1987 and 1990, suggests the stabilization of a system with a number of basic characteristics.

1.   Elections were marked by a considerable degree of irregularity and malpractice. In some cases these were the inevitable result of the teething troubles attendant on re-establishing a system of up-to-date registers and properly supervised polling stations after a considerable lapse of time since the last freely contested national election in 1950. But there is also much evidence of interference by the bureaucracy and agents of the government party, the NDP (see for example Hendricks 1985; Farag 1980 and 1991; Abd-Allah 1992, section II). Given that it is impossible to estimate the extent of such interference on a national basis it is also impossible to know whether it was more intense than that in any other Third World country where elections are dominated by the regime's own party, for example, Mexico or India (Cornelius et al. 1989, 30–37). Furthermore, as in most similar situations elsewhere, it proved impossible for the opposition to generate widespread protest in support for its allegations of unfair electoral intervention (Cornelius et al. 1989, 36).

2.   The government party has won every election with an over two-thirds majority. Given the fact that the president remains at its head, this has given the regime the ability not only to dominate the People's Assembly but also to hand-pick its own parliamentary supporters by selecting those who could appear on the party's electoral list. This has also allowed the president to drop supporters who have lost his favour, although some of them were then able to return to the assembly as independents after the 1990 election. Nevertheless, its many advantages notwithstanding, the party itself has not developed its own organizational identity in terms of the holding of regular congresses, the establishment of branches or the recruitment of local activists. It follows that, in spite of the repeated calls by the president for its invigoration, the suspicion must remain that he and his advisers are at best ambivalent about whether the NDP should be allowed to develop a distinctive ideology or an independent existence of its own.

3.   A considerable degree of orchestration of elections was required to persuade both Egyptians and outsiders that they constituted a genuine exercise of free choice. In part this involved a willingness to bend the regime's own rules, either by allowing organizations that were technically illegal to participate (the New Wafd and Muslim Brothers in 1984) or by turning a blind eye to the formation of coalitions (the Socialist Labour/Liberal/Muslim Brother alliance in 1987). In part it also involved making the best of the opposition's successful appeal to the unconstitutionality of the Party Law's ban on independent candidates. This it did by allowing one independent to stand per constituency in 1987 and then opening up the whole system to independent candidates in 1990.

4.   Opposition parties have had only limited success in their efforts to ensure that elections were conducted in a way that they regarded as fair. In addition to the legal campaign against the ban on independents conducted by lawyers associated with the Wafd, there was also the attempt by a number of parties to use the opportunities provided by the fact that the 1990 election campaign coincided with Egypt's participation in the international coalition against the Iraqi occupation of Kuwait to try to ensure that it was supervised by the judiciary (not the ministry of the interior) as stated in the 1971 constitution. Here the regime responded to the challenge by arranging for the secondment of several hundred judges and prosecutors from the Ministry of Justice to the Ministry of the Interior. But this was not enough to satisfy the leaders of most of the opposition parties who continued to argue that such a small number of persons could not ensure the proper conduct of the ballot in over 15,000 polling stations established and controlled by the police. The result was a wholescale boycott by all major parties except the NDP (Progressives). Meanwhile, the question of how to interpret the constitutional requirement for the supervision of elections by a 'judicial organization' remained unresolved (Farag 1990; Shukrallah 1991; Hill 1990).

5.   While the government party has been given essential support by state bodies at all levels, the opposition parties remain surrounded by restrictions preventing them from making contact with any important interest group in the wider society. This strategy involved the continued ban on groups that had a natural, and historical, link with significant social forces, for example, the nasserites and the Muslim Brothers, until such time as their leadership might split into factions and so reduce their popular appeal. It also involved the maintenance of the rules preventing parties from meeting potential constituencies except in a very limited way during the election campaigns themselves (Shukrallah 1991). The result was that parties remained very largely the self-defined representatives of ideological or historical trends with no way of testing whether they had any widespread popular following except through the unsatisfactory process of the occasional national ballot. Just how much the leaders of such parties were willing to go along with these restrictions is unclear. As a rule they seem to have been willing to criticize them without going so far as to do anything that might cause their organizations to be banned. It is also significant that the leadership of the New Wafd quickly abandoned plans to build on its status as the official opposition after the 1984 election by nominating shadow ministers and introducing other mechanisms designed to underline its role as a viable alternative to the NDP government.[5]

6.   In spite of the weakness of the opposition, the regime developed a system of managing the People's Assembly designed to reduce still further the possibility of challenge to its rule. Debates on important bills of great public interest, for example, those concerning the reorganization of the public sector or the intro-

duction of amendments to the state of emergency, were rushed through in no more than a couple of days at most. Meanwhile, the speaker made it as difficult as possible for opposition members to obtain a hearing. And yet when the regime's own supporters wanted to get legislation through the assembly at great speed – for example, the recent (July 1992) law cancelling a Court of Appeal verdict justifying the continued temporary leadership of the Lawyers Syndicate by a group of its opponents – it was passed at a hastily convened sitting, with only 30 members present, in a single day (Saad 1992, 2). Finally, as Hani Shukrallah (1991) has noted, the assembly has been encouraged to surrender certain of its constitutional rights to the president, such as its power to ratify arms deals with foreign countries. In these circumstances some basic constitutional issues concerning the relationship between the executive and the legislature, for instance the notion of cabinet responsibility, have never been properly tested.

The controlled multi-party system: a regime perspective

To judge from the words of his advisers, one of the reasons why President Mubarak was persuaded to return to a system of contested elections in 1984 is that his personal identification with democracy would give his regime a legitimacy different from that of his two predecessors, Nasser and Sadat. Nevertheless, there is plenty of evidence that his approach to the experiment was one of great caution. To begin with, his speeches have consistently made the point that Egypt's pre-1952 exercise in pluralism was a total failure, with the parties of those days occupied with their own disputes and incapable of uniting their efforts to confront the demands of national independence.[6] He has been equally insistent that the introduction of democracy is a difficult business and can only be properly achieved over a long period of time. As he put it in an interview in November 1983:

> Do not ask me to follow the same democracy as the UK, France, the US or Germany. We want to reach that standard of democracy, but we cannot do so overnight.[7]

And he repeated the same argument in February 1987.

> We are providing doses of democracy in proportion to our ability to absorb them. We are forging ahead but we need time for our democracy to fully develop.[8]

Lastly, the president has always made clear that, in his mind, there is a very close relationship between economic progress and democracy. On the one hand, democracy 'ensures prosperity' (Makram-Ebeid 1989, 423). On the other, democracy requires economic advance and, if there has to be a choice between them, it is the needs of the economy that must come first.[9] While all such remarks clearly contain an element of special pleading, we must also allow that they provide a significant pointer to President Mubarak's own views.

Beyond such published statements, we can only infer how the regime views its own experiment and, in particular, what it sees as the balance of advantage and disadvantage. This has not stopped analysts from offering suggestions as to what such advantages might be. But in almost every case their arguments are based on inference rather than direct evidence.

However, comparison with similar situations in other non-European states can provide us with a series of educated guesses as to how the regime might evaluate the practice of supervised democracy so far. I will mention five here (Springborg 1989, particularly Chapter 2 and Bianchi 1989, particularly Chapter 1):

1.   The appeal to democracy (however limited in practice) bolsters the legitimacy of the regime both internationally and domestically. As far as the former is concerned, it has made it easier for the president and the US congress to provide aid, while very much reducing the possibility that Egypt will be criticized for human rights abuses.[10] Meanwhile, on the domestic front, elections became an important asset by encouraging people to obey the regime of their own volition and so reducing the costs of coercion and of reliance on the police and army to maintain order.

2.   As Springborg seems to suggest, the appeal to democracy and the ability to utilize the services of a relatively free party press proved to be an important factor in the regime's efforts to bolster civilian control over the army. This was particularly important in the struggle to contain the military's expansionist tendencies under Marshall Abu Ghazala (Springborg 1989, Ch.2).

3.   As already stated, the re-introduction of competitive party politics proved to be an essential ingredient in the strategy of encouraging the mainstream religious movement to work within the system at least until 1990 when the Muslim Brothers joined in the boycott of the elections.

4.   The regime's provision of an arena for regulated opposition provided it with a number of mechanisms for dividing its critics while using them as a link to certain influential groups within Egyptian society.

5.   Elections provide a safety valve for critics of the regime while offering it an opportunity to gauge the strength of opposition to its policies.

Above and beyond this, I would wish to argue that the system of controlled pluralism has proved of inestimable advantage to the regime in its efforts to manage a complex process of economic liberalization. I will deal with this point more extensively in the following section.

Egypt's liberal project

There is little doubt that the basic stimulus to the policies of liberalization pursued by both Sadat and Mubarak was the need to confront certain fundamental problems within the Egyptian economy. Looked at from this perspective political reforms were seen largely in terms of their role in building up support while, at the same time, helping to defuse some of the tensions that more liberal economic policies were sure to engender. All this is well captured in some of the important speeches given by President Mubarak to mark the 40th anniversary of the revolution in July 1992. As he asserted forcefully in his speech at Alexandria University:

> When I took office in October 1981 the economic situation was truly frightening. But when I shouldered the responsibility before citizens, I was forced to delve deeply into every issue to find out how we are progressing and how to help the citizens overcome the crisis. It is not at all possible to remain silent about and give in to the situation we are in. If we do surrender, we become worse off than the Soviet Union, Russia and many other countries: I do not need to mention what is happening in those countries: they are completely broke and begging other countries for help.... Thank God, we adopted measures 15 years before them and salvaged ourselves.[11]

And as he reported to the NDP congress a few days later:

> The people have learned that the first elements of progress are stability and true democracy. Without these things our national effort is wasted on secondary issues that neither fulfil our goals nor ward off danger.

And he went on: 'True democracy does not rest on slogans that are empty of any significant content when the situation requires a responsible stand. The issue now is not one of opposition and government, it is an issue of the homeland. The homeland is undergoing a crucial test which has been forced upon it at a time when it is exerting all its efforts to escape the bottleneck, overcome its economic difficulties and realize its goal of providing a good life for future generations.[12]

Here there is no hiding some of the worries which the president so obviously felt about the threat that would be posed by overt popular hostility to his economic programme. Nevertheless, it would seem fair to assert that, looked at purely in its own terms, his liberal project has been relatively successful so far. On the one hand, the regime has managed to maintain support for its policies while holding potential opposition largely in check. On the other, there has been significantly little pressure on it to push faster towards either a completely free market or a completely open political system. I will now deal with each of these points in turn.

The positive interaction between the regime and its supporters is most clearly shown in the case of the rural landowners. This stratum, usually identified with persons owning ten *feddans* or more of land, is generally regarded as an essential prop for any Egyptian administration and, as Binder and others have demonstrated, has consistently managed to obtain significant representation in any twentieth-century parliament or popular assembly (Binder 1978, section II). Nevertheless, the attack on so-called rural 'feudalism' following the famous Khamshish affair of 1965 did great harm to the alliance and it was one of the first things that Sadat set himself to repair after becoming president (Ansari 1986, Ch.7). This he did in a series of highly symbolic gestures, first by allowing a court to decide in favour of those owners who were petitioning for the return of their sequestered land, then by insisting that the official definition of a 'peasant' for electoral and representative purposes should be someone who owned up to 50 *feddans*, rather than the 25 *feddans* ceiling that had obtained during the Nasser era (Sadowski 1991, 81). Various measures designed to reverse essential features of the nasserite land reforms followed, particularly where they related to restrictions on the relationship between landlord and tenant.

The alliance between the regime and the rural landowners became even closer as a result of the first Mubarak-period election in 1984. Then, fear that such people might defect from the NDP to the opposition Wafd, as well as the need for their co-operation in getting out the peasant vote, led the government to allow its supporters in parliament to prepare a comprehensive reform of the existing land law (Springborg 1990, 446). And even when this proved too controversial and had to be laid to rest, the administration was certainly complicit in allowing these same landowners to take matters into their own hands by raising rents and evicting tenants. Meanwhile, strong pressure from NDP members for further amendments to the Nasser land reform has continued to be taken seriously by the regime even if, in the end, it has always shied away from endorsing its demands too strongly.

Similar instances of concerted pressure from businessmen and entrepreneurs are more difficult to find. Perhaps the most obvious examples are those demanding the extension of the economic privileges granted to foreign capital under Law 43 of 1974 to native Egyptian concerns as well. For the rest, the supposition must be that members of these groups are more concerned to use their government contacts to protect themselves individually against bureaucratic interference or inertia rather than as a way of lobbying for major innovations in the *infitah* regime.[13]

Much the same point can be made in support of the argument that the Mubarak government has faced remarkably little pressure for wholesale privatization of the public sector, with the handful of exponents of such a view, like Dr Said Naggar, giving the impression of being lone voices crying in the wilderness. The usual explanation for this situation is that Egyptian entrepreneurs remain largely dependent on the state for vital favours. But as I will suggest later, the fact that Egypt has not yet passed through its import substitution phase, provides the larger context for this argument, ensuring that local business is still too weak to cope either with foreign competition or joint ventures, while policies of liberalization, capped in the late 1970s by the oil boom, have reduced the importance attached to manufacturing industry as the driving force of the economy, thus obviating much of the need for employees to press for the creation of the institutional structure necessary for independent bargaining between capital and labour.

Pressure for a move towards a more open democracy has been somewhat greater. But even here it has been confined largely to a small circle of politicians, intellectuals and journalists without, it would appear, gaining the attention of a larger popular audience. This is partly the work of the regime itself whose practices have done so much to reinforce the sense of great cynicism about party and electoral politics in the population at large. But it can also be explained in terms of the nature of islamic politics in Egypt: with the Muslim Brothers apparently content to accept only minimal representation in the People's Assembly in exchange for its use as a platform for demands for the further implementation of parts of the *shari'a* and much of the bourgeoisie united in support of the regime's ban on religious parties – encouraged by what is taken to be the dreadful warning provided by the electoral victory of the FIS in Algeria.

Prospects and possibilities

The Egyptian political system is dominated by the president who has either been granted, or has accumulated, vast powers. At present he is elected for seven years by a two-thirds majority in the People's Assembly. President Mubarak has now been nominated for a third term, 1994–2001, which most observers believe must be his last. It is in the nature of such systems that the choice of his successor will begin to become important sometime in the later 1990s. Questions for the future concern the possibility of a challenge by an opposition candidate and the correctness of the present conventional wisdom that Egypt requires a military man as president if the army is to keep out of the political arena, confident that its interests are being properly taken care of. In these circumstances, it seems likely that the regime will want to change the present system of electing the president in the People's Assembly to one of popular election.

As has already been argued, the regime is supported by most sections of the Egyptian bourgeoisie dependent upon it for jobs, protection and support. They share an interest in the slow-paced economic reform as well as in preserving a system in which the workers and peasants are virtually disenfranchised and unrepresented at the political level.[14] In spite of the development of private sector activity it seems unlikely that an independent fraction of entrepreneurs and merchants will emerge to mount a political challenge to NDP dominance. We can hypothesize that this could happen only if the legal system protecting private property and private economic activity were enormously improved.

The system of controlled pluralism extends far beyond that of the parties and parliamentary elections to embrace all of Egypt's associational life. This is well illustrated by the rules limiting trade union activity or by the regime's interpretation of the now infamous 1964 Law of Association in such a way as to refuse a licence to any organization which, in the words of the director-general of the societies' department of the Ministry of Social Affairs, might 'imply any political trend'.[15]

The most immediate challenges to the present system come from two directions: the economic and the religious. The policies of stabilization and structural adjustment are bringing great hardship and uncertainty to many and will generate popular support only if they produce greater, and better distributed, wealth within a relatively short time. Economic discontent also provides an important encouragement for the more militant approach of many of the islamic associations. This has two dangerous implications for the regime. First, it threatens the strategy of dividing the militants from the islamic mainstream by blurring the boundary between the two. Second, it makes it more difficult for the regime to maintain its tacit alliance with islamic groups by which they obtain official toleration for a role in the management of the lives of large sections of the urban poor (see for example Ben Néfissa 1992).

Turning to possible mutations of the present political system I will try to indicate the major directions it might take by employing aspects of the three scenarios that Cornelius and Craig have suggested for Mexico in the 1990s (Cornelius & Craig 1991, 115–19; Cornelius et al. 1989, 15–37). These are what they style 'immobilism', 'political closure' and the 'modernization of authoritarianism'. Justification for their use comes from the fact that Egypt and Mexico share a number of important similarities, notably the institutionalization of one-party rule within a framework of multi-party politics.

Immobilism

In Egyptian terms, immobilism means a continuation of the present situation in which socio-economic and religious tensions are managed by a combination of controlled multi-partyism and the use of an expanded Emergency Law. This obviously depends on continued economic growth and an ability to manage the process of structural reform without too much disruption.

As far as electoral politics are concerned the maintenance of the existing system requires a continued ability to orchestrate elections, providing the urban electorate with just enough apparent choice to tempt them to the polls without allowing them the opportunity to vote the NDP out of power. It could also involve an alliance with some or all of the opposition parties to drop their threats of boycott in exchange for constitutional or legal reforms designed to make the electoral process more open and fair. In such an atmosphere, the continued fragmentation of the opposition due to new parties being formed or old ones splitting can probably be taken for granted.[16] It is also axiomatic that the one group with power to mobilize electoral support in the poorer quarters of the towns and the suburbs (the Muslim Brothers) is forever excluded from full participation.

Political closure

Political closure would be an obvious, and perhaps necessary, response to increasing civil unrest encouraged by both economic hardship and religious revivalism. It would involve a recognition of the failure of party politics to canalize discontent or even, as President Mubarak currently seems to hope, to provide active help in the maintenance of social peace.[17] The result would be a clamp-down on public criticism of the regime, particularly of those organizations and parties that tried to make an issue of the accompanying increase in human rights abuses.

Whether or not such a policy could be sustained permanently is another matter. It would seriously compromise the legitimacy of the regime both at home and abroad. It would also encourage tensions within the elite itself, between liberals and reactionaries, between supporters of the islamic associations and others and, as happened in the mid-1980s, between the army and the police over responsibility for domestic security. For all these reasons the regime would certainly wish to present such a closure as only a temporary measure.

The modernization of authoritarianism

An attempt to re-invigorate Egypt's corporatist structures might be a consequence of the breakdown of either of the situations just described. It would be an obvious option for any leader who takes over the presidency from Mubarak at a time of economic and political crisis. But it might also come to seem a necessity for the present regime faced with a loss of control over large sections of an increasingly urban society.[18] According to Amir Salem, the director of Cairo's Legal and Research Centre for Human Rights, only 7 per cent of Egyptians now belong to a party, a syndicate or a union.[19] The regime might well conclude that the only way to reach a significant proportion of the rest would be to reorganize the NDP as a more aggressive, mobilizing force in association with a variety of dependent popular organizations. One possibility could be to hand over to the NDP the administration of the social fund set up under World Bank auspices to target the really poor, in imitation of Mexico's Program Nacional de Solidaridad, a key element in the attempt to rebuild the government party's working-class constituency.[20] A new ideology and a more ambitious set of economic and social goals might also be required. This would be in marked contrast to President Mubarak's present emphasis on reducing expectations and requiring little of Egypt's citizens other than that they help to keep the peace lest they make economic reform more difficult.[21]

Finally, the one scenario which is most clearly excluded is the development of the present political system in a direction in which the opposition obtains greater and greater popular support until it is able either to form a government or even to capture the presidency. For one thing, in a system like the Egyptian, the opposition cannot be viewed as an autonomous entity, independent of either the divisive tendencies within the political structure or the policies of the regime. For another, the development of the institutional expressions of the variegated economic and social interests on which a pluralist system depends clearly takes much longer than most optimists have supposed.

In these difficult circumstances leading members of the Egyptian opposition have been right to concentrate their efforts on constitutional politics and, in particular, on exposing the many contradictions and anomalies in the 1971 constitution. Normally, as in Algeria in 1989, the attempt to create a new political order would have been accompanied by the drawing up of a new constitution. But, in Egypt, political, as well as associational, life is still dependent on interpretations of a document hastily put together as part of Sadat's assault on the nasserite system of social supervision which he sought only partially to amend. It has yet to be shown that it provides a sound basis for either the independence of the judiciary or the protection of the rights of assembly, association and individual freedom upon which a fully functioning democracy must depend.

Beyond that, as these same leaders well understand, they must find a way to break through the barriers with which the regime has sought to surround them and which make it impossible for them to recruit widespread support from any of the potential popular constituencies. Up to now, they must accept some of the blame for their continued impotence as a result of their own authoritarian practices, their divisions and their inability to formulate clear-cut alternatives to present government policy. But the rewards for being able to overcome these tendencies is clear: if just one or two parties managed to make such a breakthrough, they would soon be able to establish a substantial electoral dominance over their smaller rivals.

Lastly, opposition politics would be further strengthened by the process of elite fragmentation which, in the longer run, is likely to accompany the development of a mixed and much more market-orientated economy. This will inevitably create conflicts of interest which the regime will find increasingly difficult to manage. It will also create demands for greater freedom and regularity which, in turn, will open up new spaces for political activity. Finally, the development of private-sector industry will produce conflicts between workers and employers which the old techniques of labour management will no longer be able to contain. Much will depend on which political forces are best able to anticipate such future trends and to put them to their own advantage.

Conclusion

My major argument has been that the Egyptian regime's construction of a controlled multi-party regime has been primarily a response to a series of urgent economic necessities, most obviously a growing international debt. I have also argued that this policy has to be viewed as part of the larger project of the creation of a domestic coalition in support of a gradual liberalization and restructuring of the economy. Political mobilization in this context then becomes the management of a predominantly bourgeois constituency combined with a strenuous attempt to de-mobilize workers, the urban under-class and the peasants. Meanwhile, elections have their role to play as a significant mechanism for reducing the cost of repression while creating opportunities for regime supporters to gain access to those with power as well as, on occasions, being able to participate in the policy-making process itself.

It has also been part of my argument that it is quite wrong to employ comparisons that, in any way, suggest that there are similarities between the introduction of multi-party democracy in Egypt and the establishment of democratic procedures in western Europe, however they are to be understood. Like can only be compared with like: and if we want a better understanding of what has been going on in Egypt over the past 20 years we can only look to other parts of the non-European world for assistance. It is the context of post-colonialism development which defines both the problems and the possibilities open to Egypt's contemporary political actors.

Just as important, the comparison with western Europe is wrong for another reason and that is that it involves the juxtaposition of events and processes that took place over centuries with those that have taken place in Egypt over a couple of decades at most. In the former case, and given such a long time horizon, a significant input from this or that class or this or that process (for example the development of private property) can sometimes be discerned. But everything is necessarily much more conjunctional in the latter: as yet there has been no possibility for contemporary practices to harden into structures with predictable procedures, and there is always the chance that the whole experiment will suddenly be abandoned as it was in 1952.

As for the longer run we can only speculate. However, within such a time-frame it is probably reasonable to assume that the future of Egyptian democracy will be heavily influenced by the system of economic management and whether or not this leads to the development of a more capitalist economy complete with the rules, the legal framework for the defence of private and corporate activity which history suggests as providing the best encouragement for pluralist political activity. I would hazard a guess that such a development will only begin to take place in earnest when Egypt's industrialization has intensified sufficiently to allow the emphasis to shift from import substitution to export promotion, with all the extra institutional support which that entails. This is the Turkish example, which also suggests that a similar form of association with the European Community would give Egypt a tremendous push in the same direction.

Epilogue (May 1993)

Since the completion of this essay Egypt has seen a development with serious implications for its political future: the attacks on tourists and police by Muslim militants beginning in the autumn of 1992. Although this was accompanied by relatively little loss of life it was interpreted by President Mubarak as a dangerous form of economic warfare to be defeated by the use of all the force at the government's disposal. Even so, according to the minister of tourism, losses to the industry, which is said to employ one out of every ten Egyptians, were estimated to total $1 billion for the 1992–93 winter season.[22]

The political consequences have been just as significant. Efforts to contain the Muslim militants have lead to mass arrests up and down the country, bringing the total number of persons detained without trial to some 30–40,000 by April 1993. A substantial number of suspects have also been killed outright by the security forces. The resulting abuses of power, including torture and the use of military courts to try suspects, have been criticized in strong terms by the Egyptian Organization for Human Rights as well as international agencies such as Middle East Watch.

Just as important, the campaign against the terrorists has led to a considerable blurring of the distinction that the Mubarak regime had attempted to maintain between Muslim moderates and extremists. The minister of education's clumsy attacks on teachers who are alleged to have encouraged their female pupils to wear the *higab* has been interpreted by many as an attack on religion itself. So too has the regime's policy of sending the security forces into dissident mosques and its sustained effort to make it more difficult for the Muslim Brothers and their adherents to win control over the leadership of a number of professional associations including those of lawyers, doctors and engineers.

The campaign against the militants, and the restrictions on freedom which it has so obviously involved, has served further to undermine what little public confidence there was in the role of the legal opposition. It has also placed a great strain on the alliance between the Muslim Brothers and their parliamentary allies, the Socialist Liberal and Socialist Labour parties, thus virtually putting an end to President Mubarak's strategy of encouraging moderate religious elements to find a place for themselves in his controlled, multi-party system.

The ability of the regime to mobilize its forces against the militants shows that the old authoritarian structures are still in place, at least as far as issues of security are concerned. Nevertheless, the importance still attached to structural adjustment shows that economic considerations, including the opinion of Egypt's creditors, can act to restrain government policy. Meanwhile, the multi-party system, however weak, remains in place and is likely to continue to do so. In these circumstances, while there has certainly been a move in the direction of the option I have called 'political closure', this is not yet irreversible, leaving other options still open, whether the 'immobilism' represented by a further series of highly managed elections or the turn towards a 'modernization of authoritarianism' to be attempted by either Mubarak or a successor.

Notes

1   For Europe, see for example, Blackbourn & Eley (1984). For the Middle East, see Waterbury (1991).
2   For example, Eley (1992),
3   To use Arjomand's apt definition, the 1971 Egyptian constitution is basically an 'ideological' document (Arjomand 1992).
4   A story related to me by Ahmad Baheddin.
5   Information from Mona Makram-Ebeid.
6   For example, 'President Mubarak's Address Marking the 40th Anniversary of 23rd July Revolution', *BBC Summary of World Broadcasts*, ME/1441, A/4 (24 July 1992).
7   Interview on Cairo Radio, 6 November 1983, quoted in Ami Ayalon (1986); 'Egypt', in Haim Shaked and Daniel Dishon (eds), Middle East Contemporary Survey, No. VIII, 1983–84, Tel Aviv, The Dayan Center, The Shiloah Institute, Tel Aviv University p. 362.
8   Quoted in Makram-Ebeid (1989, 423n.).
9   For example, 'Egyptian President's Speech at Alexandria University', 18 July 1992, *BBC Summary of World Broadcasts*, ME/1438, A/2–3 (21 July 1992).
10 For example, the criticisms of the US Congress made by Middle East Watch, New York, in its report, 'Behind Closed Doors: Torture and Detention in Egypt' as reported by Tony Walker, *The Financial Times* (28 July 1992).
11 'Egyptian President's Speech at Alexandria University', *BBC Summary of World Broadcasts*, ME/1438, A/2–3 (24 July 1992).
12 'President Mubarak's Address Marking the 40th Anniversary of 23rd July Revolution'.
13 For a similar argument, see Waterbury (1991).
14 This argument can also be found in Springborg (1989, 173–4).
15 Quoted in 'Interview with Amir Salem', *Al-Ahram Weekly* (30 July–5 August 1992) p. 21.
16 For example, no sooner was the new Young Egypt Party formed than it split into four separate splinter organizations under four different leaders. See *Al-Ahram Weekly* (30 July–5 August 1992) p. 2.
17 'President Mubarak's Address Marking the 40th Anniversary of 23rd July Revolution', A/6.
18 Over three-quarters of the Egyptian population now live in towns of over 10,000 people and more than half in Cairo, Giza and Alexandria. See El Kadi Orstrom (1990, 30).
19 'Interview with Amir Salem.'
20 For Mexico see Laurell (1992, 52).
21 'President Mubarak's Address Marking the 40th Anniversary of 23rd July Revolution', A/6–7.
22 'Tide of tourism flowing again' *Middle East Times/Egypt* (25–31 May 1993).

8

The Integration of the Integrists: a comparative study of Egypt, Jordan and Tunisia

GUDRUN KRÄMER

The transition from authoritarian rule to a more open, plural(ist) and liberal order of government and society poses tremendous problems, particularly when attempted under difficult socio-economic conditions. In the Middle East, the issue is rendered especially complex by a combination of structural problems of socio-economic and political organization, exacerbated by demographic pressures as well as ethnic and religious cleavages, and of cultural and religious factors that, in the search for authenticity variously defined, have acquired major significance for actual politics as well as for political debate.[1] Both dimensions, the structural and the political cultural, have to be considered in the issue dealt with here, namely the integration of the islamic movement into the existing political framework and its inclusion in the process of liberalization. Its very strength, and attempted inclusion, marginalization or exclusion will effectively shape the process of political opening, liberalization and democratization. The outcome, the Algerian experience notwithstanding, is still open. In spite of rapidly growing interest in the subject, it will, therefore, be a matter of defining questions and fields of further research rather than giving any conclusive answers to the questions raised here.

Liberalization as crisis management

All over the Arab Middle East, and in particular in the three countries considered here, the last decade has witnessed a new wave of popular unrest to which governments have responded with a strategy of repression plus controlled political liberalization which was usually termed democratization (*al-taharruki ila'l-dimuqratiyya, al-tahawwul al-dimuqrati,* etc). Social and economic tension accumulated over a period of time, sharpened by a critical reduction of government finances forcing regimes to cut back on social services, erupted in urban riots that threatened to put the regime's legitimacy, if not its very survival, into question. In the present context it may be noted that the so-called bread riots that shook Egypt in January 1977, Tunisia in January 1984 and Jordan in April 1989, were neither directed nor dominated by the islamic opposition. The remarkable sensitivity (not to say outright fear) of the regimes concerned to unrest among what is commonly called 'the street'[2] may help to explain why their reaction was not confined to repression, but included important concessions in both the socio-economic and the political spheres. In order to restore calm ('social peace' and 'national union') the governments announced modifications of the pro-gramme of structural adaptation recommended by the IMF and the World Bank. At the same time, they decided to expand the process of political liberalization which had been initiated before (in Egypt since 1975–76, in Tunisia since 1981, and in Jordan since 1984). In the following months civil liberties were extended, the freedom of expression and of association distinctly enlarged, opposition papers licensed, human rights groups registered and political parties legalized.

Yet liberalization left the underlying power structure virtually intact. The size and role of the army and security services, the state monopoly over TV and the radio, the concentration of power in the hands of the ruler and the networks of informal personal ties ('power centres') remained basically unaffected. The areas of legitimate political expression and activity remained circumscribed, and old taboos still in force (the existence of God, the person of the king or presi-dent, the competence of the army). Formal measures included a party law restricting the bases of party formation (issued in Egypt in 1977 and revised in 1979; issued in Tunisia in May 1988, and in Jordan in August 1992) and a national charter *(mithaq watani)* – Tunisia 1988 and Jordan 1991, with obvious parallels to the Egyptian National Charter of 1962 – defining a set of values, aims and principles ('national consensus') binding on all, and delegitimizing all those refusing to subscribe to them. The national charter was drawn up with the participation of wide sections of society, including representatives of all major political movements and associations from the left to the 'moderate' islamists. The party law, by contrast, was prepared by the government alone. Demanding adherence to certain principles that the regime claimed to represent (the 'values' of religion, national unity and sovereignty, the Arab-islamic character of state, culture and society, or, in the Egyptian case, the 'inevitability' of the socialist solution), it ruled out all truly alternative candidates. It also banned parties based on religion, ethnicity, class, sex or region, leading to the apparent paradox that while all parties had to adhere to the values of religion, religious parties were expressedly barred.[3] Religion in general, it was argued, and Islam in partic-ular constituted the common ground shared by all and therefore no monopoly, guardianship or tutelage *(wisaya)* over them by any individual or particular group could be tolerated. In fact, the competition over who represents 'real' and 'true' Islam *(al-islam al-sahih),* and who is the better protector of both faith and (civil) society provides one of the core issues of the political contest.

Reality is, of course, more complex and government policy less clear-cut than the legal framework would suggest. What is to be observed in Egypt and Jordan, and to a lesser extent in Tunisia, is in fact a much more flexible and ambivalent approach combining seemingly contradictory policies. One of the characteristics of the current stage of liberalization is the fact that political organizations which by the letter of the (party) law should be excluded from legal political activity are actually tolerated by the government. This refers notably, albeit not exclusively, to the islamic 'moderates'. The major exception to the rule of intended ambiguity, putting overt islamist activity at the government's mercy, was Algeria where between the riots of October 1988 and the 'constitutional coup' of January 1992, the full cycle of legalization and electoral success to growing fear, confrontation, repression and eventual banning of the islamic opposition was completed.

Still, the purpose of liberalization from above is clear: it is to stabilize the system in a situation of acute crisis, to broaden its base of support, to enhance its legitimacy at home and abroad and to prepare the ground for a wider distribution of responsibility for structural reform involving stringent austerity measures. It is to contain discontent and to marginalize, and if possible delegitimize, all those that refuse to be co-opted into the system or are regarded as too great a threat to the regime to be recognized as legitimate political actors. Since the critical weakening of the left, the islamic movement has come to be the prime target of government strategies of co-optation and exclusion.

The challenge of political Islam

Wherever, over the past two decades, Arab regimes have embarked on a course of controlled political liberalization, loosening the restrictions on political articulation and association, islamist activists have emerged as the strongest force of opposition. The strength and attraction of islamic political movements are related, but cannot be reduced, to the socio-economic crisis faced by the societies considered here. Generally linked to the phenomena of societal malaise and crisis, of relative deprivation resulting in alienation and the disaffection with the status quo of wide sections of the population, their rise is widely seen as an expression of protest (Waltz 1986).[4] Islamic movements express some of the grievances and aspirations of civil society, widely considered to be an indispensable prerequisite of democratic life, but to be largely absent in Arab (Muslim) societies. It is assumed here that nuclei of civil society are indeed (re)emerging in the Arab world – charitable and professional associations, pressure groups of various kinds from business associations to human rights groups – and that on an as it were formal level, i.e. irrespective of their political aims and convictions, islamist activists form part of that civil society.[5] Whether they can be regarded as such in terms of their commitment to the pluralist, liberal and democratic values commonly associated with the concept of civil society, hinges entirely on an assessment of their ideological position, more particularly their views on state-society relations in the ideal 'islamic order', and not just the particular states or regimes faced by them, whose intervention in society and culture they so strongly denounce as harmful and illegitimate.[6]

In spite of intensive research and coverage, the social base of major islamic movements such as the Egyptian Muslim Brotherhood (as distinct from militant underground organizations uncovered by the security services) remains ill-defined. Whenever they are allowed to compete in not too repressive electoral campaigns, they obtain important shares in municipal councils and national parliaments. And yet, because of manipulation ranging from the definition of constituencies to outright government intervention, election results do not provide reliable data on the sources of their strength. By and large, islamic activism continues to be a predominantly urban phenomenon. Its appeal to (semi-) educated youth and the intelligentsia, whether classified as socially peripheral or not, is amply documented by a strong presence on university campuses, particularly at the faculties of science, engineering and technology. But its appeal reaches far beyond the disaffected youth of high ambition and rural origins so frequently described, and deep into the urban middle classes with considerable commercial and financial power and interests, who cannot be regarded as marginal, nor do they see themselves as such. The islamic current is strongly represented in professional associations of the educated middle class, especially those segments operating independently of the bureaucracy and public sector (lawyers, engineers, medical doctors, pharmacists). 'Islamic' banks, investment firms, co-operatives, self-help and charitable associations are active in both formal and informal sectors of society and the economy (albeit not necessarily linked to political islamic groups).[7] Arguably related to this class bias, support among industrial workers seems to be restricted; nor has political Islam succeeded in gaining a stronghold over the peasantry.

While the relation of the islamic movement to civil society is controversial, it is almost universally seen and described as the only, or at least the most serious, challenge, threat and alternative to the existing order of state and society. The view of islamic activism as a threat is easy enough to understand with regard to the regimes in power, but it is also widely reflected in the critical literature of both Middle Easterners and outsiders. It needs, however, to be reconsidered. For while it is undeniable that various islamic groups from the Islamic Liberation Party *(hizb al-tahrir al-islami)* to the Algerian Front Islamique du Salut *(jabhat al-inqadh al-islamiyya)* do effectively pose a threat, or at least a challenge, to the existing order, others such as the Jordanian Muslim Brotherhood and arguably large and representative parts of the islamic movements of Egypt and Tunisia do not. One might go even further. For while it is clear that the islamists put themselves forward as an alternative, if not the only alternative, to the existing political, social and moral order ('Islam is the Solution', 'The *Qur'an* is Our Constitution'), it may well be asked how exactly this alternative is to be defined, particularly in the domain of economics.

Widely used terms such as threat, menace, challenge, infiltration, subversion, betray not just the sense of fear and suspicion pervading the discussion, but also the tacit assumption (or deep conviction) that islamic politics and political movements are essentially illegitimate. The unease with which the issue is treated shows how difficult it is to distinguish between on the one hand (legitimate) dissent even if based on religious foundations and expressed in religious language, and on the other (ambivalent) challenge and (illegitimate) threat. It demonstrates the difficulty of defining under what conditions religious language and symbols may legitimately be used, and not just 'exploited', for political purposes (foreign relations, the death sentence, abortion?). It points to the need to explain adequately why the Italian and German Christian Democratic Parties are to be recognized as legitimate actors, and why the Tunisian Renaissance (Nahda) Party, which had gone as far as to renounce violence and drop any reference to Islam in its name, is not.

Focusing on their role as protest movement, as a challenge and a threat to the existing order, tends to bias an assessment of islamist strategies. Public as well as scholarly attention has been held by militant fringe groups propagating a strategy of revolutionary armed struggle against the regimes or society as a whole which are classified, and delegitimized, as infidel. Egypt, Syria, Tunisia and Algeria have illustrated the wide range of islamic militancy. Yet revolutionary violence and clandestine underground work found wider acceptance only after previous attempts at non-violent struggle and integration had been suppressed by the government in power. The islamic mainstream, represented by the Muslim Brotherhood(s) and affiliated organizations such as the Tunisian Mouvement de la Tendance Islamique (MTI) turned Hizb al-Nahda, advocates a reformist strategy of gradual transformation of individual behaviour, state and society (*tadarruj*) via integration into the existing legal-political framework. The political system is recognised as legitimate (with a distinction sometimes being made between political and religious legitimacy), and legal recognition as a religious or social association actively sought. The main aim is to see islamic ethics, norms and legal codes (the *shari'a*) applied. All opportunities to exert influence and to bring pressure to bear on government and society are used. The mission (*da'wa*) concentrates on education, the media and, if possible, the associational and political sphere proper, including participation in municipal, parliamentary and presidential elections (see also Esposito & Piscatori 1991). This does not imply any deliberate restriction of activities to political work in a narrow sense. Only in rare cases have islamic groups sought legalization as a political party which, by necessity, would involve such a limitation.

The strategy of integration can be seen as the rule, and not the exception, of islamic activism. But it has always been the object of internal debate and criticism. The islamists share the dilemma of all protest movements that pose as a radical alternative to the existing order and value system, attempting to set up a counter-society of moral incorruptness, be they religious fundamentalists, left-wing revolutionaries or certain groups among the conservationist greens. Differing from most other political groups in that they developed independently of, and indeed in direct opposition to, the state apparatus, and that they are able to project a sense of purpose, community and identity, they owe their appeal of purity and autonomy to their distance from established (party) politics (*al-hizbiyya*), reflecting a widespread view that politics in general and party politics in particular are dirty business. Integration into the given political framework cannot but cost them some of this appeal. It cannot but compromise the uncorrupted. In addition, it is not just a question of accepting the 'political' or 'electoral game' as such (and the general use of the metaphor is revealing enough),[8] but also of weighing the costs and benefits of participation. What can they gain in joining a political process on terms that are essentially defined by the government – with the deliberate aim of securing its hold on power and keeping out any serious contenders? But again, what are the choices when one attempt at confrontation after the other has been crushed by a state apparatus vastly stronger than the militant vanguard of the righteous? A critical assessment of present realities and past experiences seems to have convinced important sections of the movement that in spite of all limitations to liberalization from above, which are there for all to see, there is no alternative to the gradualist strategy, including political participation (see for example the contributions to al-Nafisi 1989). And yet, given the extent of internal hesitation and outside suspicion, the outcome can hardly be more than what Abdelbaki Hermassi (1991, 203) has described as 'conflictual participation'.

Government response

Given the strong appeal of islamist discourse and activism, government response to the islamists' search for recognition and political participation can rightly be regarded as the real test of its intentions, and of the chances and limitations of the liberalization process in general.[9] The question whether, considering their programme and behaviour, democratization (or economic restructuring on IMF lines) is possible with the islamists has often been asked. And yet it cannot really be answered until it is seriously tried. If democratization is seen as an effort to bridge the gap between state and society and to facilitate co-operation and negotiation required to implement painful economic restructuring, can the islamists be excluded without jeopardizing the entire operation? Could their emphasis on self-assertion ('authenticity'), self-reliance and distributive justice allow for the 'cultural packaging' of economic reform qua austerity that some analysts think is needed in order to make it effective? (Camau 1991, 43). Does their rejection of foreign intervention allow for co-operation with western partners or the IMF?

The external factor must not be underestimated in this context, for there has always been an important link between the attitude of regional and global powers and the freedom of manoeuvre granted to domestic political actors, particularly the islamic movement. To question the nationalist credentials of one's rivals and opponents is very much part of the political game, not only in the Arab Middle East, and the islamists have not been excepted from the rule. Like everybody else, they have periodically been charged with being the agents of the enemy of the day, be it the British, the Americans or even the zionists, Iran, Libya or Saudi Arabia. Yet judged by their actual commitment to the sacred causes of national sovereignty, the liberation of Palestine, or mobilization against foreign military deployment in the area (see the Gulf War), their record is impeccable. If consistent denunciation of foreign intervention gained them support and admiration at home, it also created foreign pressure to control and possibly restrain islamic 'xenophobia'. Jordan provides a telling illustration of the conflicting demands of external powers and domestic constituencies. In Egypt, negotiations with the British over full evacuation in the late 1940s and the 1950s and with Israel over peace and self-determination in the late 1970s and early 1980s contributed towards the suppression of the islamic movement. In Tunisia the link with Algeria is vital for any understanding of policies vis-à-vis the islamic movement.

And yet the logic of liberalization has to be understood primarily in the context of domestic politics, or to be more precise, the constellation of domestic political actors. In a simplified manner, it can be seen as a triangle (or, if the islamic militants are classified as a separate category, a quadrangle) made up of the regime, non-religious political actors including opposition parties, human rights groups, professional associations, trade unions, etc. and the islamic movement, somewhat crudely divided into 'moderates' advocating non-violent strategies of gradualism and integration and radicals propagating the violent overthrow of the system. The call for human rights protection, guaranteed political participation and government accountability, whether called *shura* or democracy, provides a common platform to all opposition movements irrespective of their views on socio-economic organization and foreign policy, uniting them against government intervention and repression. At the same time, the issue of Islam, if seen not so much as a set of moral values, principles and aspirations, but as a system of legal, social and political organization, tends to act as a divisive rather than a unifying force. It does not appear that intensified efforts to establish a dialogue between the islamic, the Arab nationalist and the liberal currents have as yet achieved much progress.[10] In a long-term perspective, the values and objectives of the islamists calling for an application of the *shari'a* on one hand, and the notions of state and society advocated by leftists and liberals on the other, may be irreconcilable. This is particularly true with regard to the issue of women. Under the conditions of restricted political contest, however, there are many possibilities of conflict and co-operation. Relations are not fixed, but largely determined by considerations of convenience and mutual advantage. Moderate islamists can be used by the government against its opponents on the left and in the militant islamic camp; the government can also try to rally the left and the liberals against the fundamentalist threat; or it can be pressured by the secular opposition to suppress their most powerful rival.

What then is the logic of liberalization granting the islamists a certain measure of recognised political expression and participation? Is it, as the Egyptian case seems to suggest, primarily an attempt to 'defuse the threat of fundamentalism', to separate the moderates from the militants and to contain, marginalize and delegitimize the latter? Are the islamic moderates allowed to operate openly in the political arena (with or without formal licence as a political party) primarily so as to expose their basic weakness in ideological as well as practical terms, that is to discredit them and thus reduce their appeal as a viable protest movement? And would genuine liberalization involving free elections after a period of free competition result in the weakening of the islamists, whose strength has been widely attributed to long-term repression of the non-religious liberal and leftist opposition? Would the legalization of various opposition parties therefore not damage their interest in countries like Jordan where they used to enjoy a virtual monopoly over political activity? Is liberalization mainly used by the regime to rally secular critics to its cause by holding up the threat of islamic fundamentalism as the Tunisian case seems to suggest?

Islamic approaches to democracy

In secular circles, the democratic credentials of the islamists are seriously questioned. Doubts regarding their commitment to the intrinsic value of pluralism, tolerance and democracy are widespread. They can only partly be reduced to government propaganda (especially marked in Tunisia, but also pursued in Egypt and to a lesser extent in Jordan) presenting political Islam as public enemy number one, unacceptable because of its message (obscurantist, reactionary, irresponsible, utopian), its character (extremist, *khariji*), its methods (violent, terrorist) and its real or alleged links to hostile external powers (Iran, Saudi Arabia, Libya, Great Britain, the USA and even Israel). It is clearly an attempt to turn the islamists' favourite weapon against them and to declare the champions of authenticity to be themselves unauthentic – *takfir* (excommunication) reversed as it were.

Mainstream islamic positions on pluralist, democratic and liberal values and principles are indeed ambiguous.[11] Considering the stakes involved in this highly politicized debate it could perhaps not be other. Because of their concern for authenticity, islamic authors have shifted the emphasis from a discussion of the required socio-political foundations of pluralist democracy to its cultural and religious dimensions, debating the cultural acceptability of the model rather than its feasibility and efficiency in solving the problems of contemporary Arab society. Islam, they claim, is the only valid expression of authenticity, and the solution to all problems of private life, state and society. Islam is the yardstick by which to measure values, goods and institutions. Hence the necessity either to prove that liberal and democratic notions, structures and procedures can in fact be traced back to islamic tradition provided it is freed from obscurantist interpretation and repressive practice, or else to show that Arab-islamic tradition is both radically different from, and at the same time superior to, western style liberal democracy, on a moral as well as a practical level. Attention has so far focused on authors of the second category ranging from Sayyid Qutb, Abu'l-A'la al-Mawdudi and Imam Khomeini to lesser lights such as the Egyptian Abd al-Salam Faraj with his famous treatise on 'The Forgotten Duty (of *jihad*)'. Radically denying the legitimacy of the existing order of state and society and advocating the sole sovereignty of God *(hakimiyyat allah)* symbolized by a strict and exclusive application of the *shari'a,* they can see liberal democracy only as part and parcel of the West's intellectual onslaught *(al-ghazw al-fikri)* designed to undermine and corrupt Arab-islamic culture and identity.

Once the mainstream is looked at, a different, more blurred picture emerges. In spite of much ambivalence and hesitation, attitudes to pluralist democracy are generally speaking not as antagonistic as is commonly assumed. In accordance with the widely accepted formula that techniques and institutions of non-islamic origin may be adopted as long as islamic values are preserved intact, their views are remarkably flexible with respect to modes of political organization, but highly restrictive with regard to the freedom of political, religious and artistic expression. They are more advanced than is commonly acknowledged concerning the recognition of human rights and the notion of citizenship, but strictly conservative when dealing with the role of women in politics and society. The touchstone of the 'islamicness' of any given order is the application of the *shari'a,* not any specific political system, the caliphate included. What distinguishes them from the radical fundamentalists is the degree to which they are able to conceive of a certain autonomy of the political sphere and of human freedom in interpreting God's law. Political organization is seen as belonging to a sort of neutral zone (neutral in the moral, legal and religious sense of being *mubah*) to be regulated according to the changing requirements of place and time. Under the conditions of modern mass society, representative government restricting the personal power of the ruler is seen as the most appropriate form of political organization. Even multi-party democracy can be accepted, provided it remains within the 'framework of Islam', i.e. provided its laws as well as individual and collective behaviour conform to the provisions of the *shari'a* (what they usually do not explain in detail, however, is who defines them and how). The principle of consultation *(shura)* is presented as the functional equivalent of western parliamentary democracy, doubly authenticated by its roots in Islam and pre-modern tribal custom. The principles of egalitarianism, justice and freedom (from government intervention and foreign interference) are strongly emphasized.

This leaves sensitive issues such as full equality between men and women as well as between Muslims and non-Muslims, of unrestricted freedom of faith and conscience, including the right of Muslims to change their faith or abandon it altogether, and of the precise relationship between divine and popular sovereignty, controversial and basically unresolved. Put briefly, 'moderate', modernist islamic political thought might be said to have evolved in the direction of pluralism, but not of liberalism. And yet, as Esposito and Piscatori have remarked in a stimulating article, the notion of democracy may well have become 'accepted as a marker, a kind of signpost of public life, a powerful symbol of legitimacy seen to be a universal good', and it may be true that 'almost all Muslims today react to it as one of the universal conditions of the modern world. To this extent, it has become part of Muslim political thought and discourse' (Esposito & Piscatori 1991, 438 & 440).

Still, doubts persist whether today's advocates of democracy among the large and heterogeneous islamic camp would still respect the principles of pluralist democracy, accept criticism and grant others the right to participate if they were ever to gain power. Critics point to their internal organization which is characterized by authoritarian leadership, a virtual absence of *shura* (consultation) and excessive group solidarity (ironically equated with *hizbiyya*). Not that those features were restricted to islamic organizations. They are in fact equally characteristic of nationalist and leftist groups, which, however, are not usually exposed to the same level of criticism. Critics also point to a lack of tolerance when it comes to dealing with political rivals and opponents.[12] The experience so far gained from various broad-based opposition alliances formed in Egypt, Syria, Iraq and elsewhere, indicates that while islamist activists practise co-operation with all political actors claiming adherence to the values of religion in general and Islam in particular (nationalists, liberals, royalists, dissenting Ba'thists, nasserists), they usually exclude the advocates of 'atheist' leftist ideologies, first and foremost marxists and communists. Co-operation in periods of heightened tension such as the Nasser and Asad eras, or of acute external threat such as during the Suez Canal War in the 1950s or the Gulf crisis in 1990–91, is seen as the exception rather than the rule.

In spite of extended co-existence and occasional co-operation, relations between islamic and secular currents remain marked by suspicion and haunted by the spectre of violence (Hermassi 1991, 198). There are deep misgivings regarding the long-term objectives of the islamists. There are serious doubts whether their commitment to the democratic approach is a 'strategic option' or merely the tactical choice of a less costly means than armed struggle to come to power, and then to establish an un-democratic islamic system with the *Qur'an* as its constitution and the *shari'a* as its source of law (Zghal 1991a, 205). Doubts are nourished by speculation on possible links between the 'moderate' organizations advocating a legalistic strategy of reform qua integration, and a militant underground preparing for revolution if the long-term objectives are not fulfilled quickly enough and as fully as expected. Sayyid Qutb's justification of revolutionary counter-force *(radd al-i'tida)* in the face of overpowering might (or structural violence as Johan Galtung might have said) provided the theoretical reference to those speculations. The links between the Egyptian Muslim Brotherhood and its Secret Apparatus *(al-jihaz al-khass)* in the 1940s and 1950s, and between the moderate and militant branches of the Tunisian MTI in the 1980s and early 1990s, serve to reinforce the image of one integrated and co-ordinated islamic movement only tactically split into legalistic moderates and militant radicals.

It is part of the problem that precise information on 'real' objectives, cross-links and double talk can hardly be obtained by a researcher, no matter whether local or foreign. What matters in actual politics though is the fact that not only the regimes but also sizeable parts of the public ask those questions and that their misgivings influence their behaviour vis-à-vis the islamic movement and the latter's search for legalization. Fear of the islamists creates sympathy and understanding for the government line, even if this implies a general restriction of political rights. Fear of the islamists allows the state to posture as the protector of genuine authenticity, expressing both national identity and real Islam, and at the same time of civil society, and indeed of civilization, against the threat of obscurantist fundamentalism. The old argument that it is a matter of either state authority forcefully asserted or anarchy and chaos, well known from classical treatises on islamic politics, is still put to good use.

Case studies: Egypt, Jordan and Tunisia

Egypt

In many ways, Egypt has acted as a trend-setter, both with regard to its islamic movement and to government policy vis-à-vis political Islam. The islamic current in Egypt is probably the largest and most heterogeneous in the entire Arab Middle East, ranging from self-avowed modernists searching for new ways of reconciling faith and modern society to the most intransigent militants opting for a complete break with society, radical retreat and armed *jihad*, from islamic charitable and self-help associations to islamic banks, investment and computer companies, from islamic associations *(jama'at islamiyya)* active among students, artisans and professionals to the Muslim Brotherhood, attracting men and women from diverse social backgrounds. Among the few groups and strata not noticeably involved are industrial workers, peasants, and of course the Copts.[13] Not only is the Egyptian Muslim Brotherhood the oldest islamic political movement of broad impact in the Arab world, it also has accumulated the widest experience in strategies of integration, conflict and confrontation. The government approach of accommodation, co-operation and exclusion has been followed elsewhere, notably in Tunisia. In Egypt, the characteristic interplay of domestic factors (the triangle of regime, secular opposition and the islamic movement(s), both 'moderate' and 'radical') and the impact of foreign affairs on the room of manoeuvre granted to the islamists can be studied in detail and in their subtle, or often not so subtle, interaction. A few sketches will suffice here.

From the beginning, Hasan al-Banna (1906–49) had held high ambitions for the Society of the Muslim Brothers (Jama'at al-Ikhwan al-Muslimin) founded by him in 1928. They were to represent not just the Muslim community of Egypt, let alone parts of that community, but Islam as it should be properly understood, lived and implemented, and to use Egypt as a springboard from which to reform and unite the entire Muslim *umma*. By the late 1930s the Muslim Brothers had succeeded in establishing a strong and diversified organization for which politics was but one field out of a broad range of activities. Their well-known rejection of multi-partyism *à l'égyptienne* and their refusal to be in any way considered an ordinary political organization lobbying for particular ('selfish') interests did not, however, imply any rejection of the existing constitutional order. The established order was recognized as legitimate, though in need of reform to make it fully islamic, in both the moral and the social sense.[14] Nor did it imply abstention from politics. All attempts, however, that were made from the early 1940s to join the political process and openly participate in parliamentary elections either failed or were foiled. While the Brotherhood as such was not involved in the political contest, some of its prominent members, including al-Banna himself, stood as independent candidates. They were all defeated – be it because of government manipulation or British intervention, as they themselves claimed (see for example Abd al-Halim 1979, vol. 1, 294–8 and 324–9; Abu'l-Nasr 1988, 34–44).

Their consistent defence of the national cause (Palestine, Suez, British evacuation and later Camp David and the Gulf War) gained them respect and legitimacy on purely secular terms and beyond their own circle of sympathizers. At the same time, relations with the regime as well as the non-religious political forces from the Wafd to the left were poisoned not only by the Brothers' claim to righteousness and exclusive representation of the nation's and indeed humankind's highest values and aspirations. There was also persistent doubt about the 'real intentions' of the Ikhwan and their suspected double strategy, a doubt that incidentally was also voiced inside the organization. The Special Apparatus (*al-jihaz al-khass*, generally known as Secret Apparatus) set up by Hasan al-Banna in the early 1940s to train fighters against the British on the Suez Canal and the zionists in Palestine (and it was widely supposed the political enemy at home) epitomized the issue.[15] The relative weight of the Society of the Muslim Brothers registered as a charitable association active in social, educational and religious work on the one hand, and of a militant, if not openly terrorist, clandestine apparatus on the other, was at issue then and to a certain extent still is.

After the military coup of the Free Officers in July 1952, internal debate over appropriate forms of political action and participation intensified.[16] Whereas a number of prominent Ikhwan advocated co-operation with the regime and its political institutions, including the newly created Liberation Rally *(hai'at al-tahrir)*, Hasan al-Hudaybi (1891–1973), the new supreme guide elected in October 1951, adamantly refused to see the Brotherhood drawn into, and of necessity be reduced to, the political sphere proper, let alone to register it as a political party as had been suggested by its highest decision-making body, the Guidance Office *(maktab al-irshad)*, in September 1952. The role he and his supporters were seeking for the Brotherhood, that of moral arbiter and political adviser to the regime, providing guidance without sharing responsibility, was rejected by a military group unwilling to share power. Mounting tension came to a head when in the crisis of March 1954 the Brothers sided with General Naguib, calling for a restoration of the constitution and parliamentary life ('purified' though of its 'corrupting' elements, i.e. the old party system). Their call for political freedom was combined with trenchant criticism of government policies in the most sensitive foreign policy issue of the day, British evacuation from the Suez Canal. The signing of the Evacuation Treaty in October 1954 coincided with the beginning of government repression, to be followed by another wave of arrests in the summer of 1965.

The great trial or persecution (*al-mihna*) of the Nasser era (to be echoed in Syria and Iraq in the late 1970s and early 1980s), served as an experience from which different lessons were drawn by different victims and observers. Best known are the young activists who, even under the less repressive rule of Sadat and Mubarak, followed the analysis of Sayyid Qutb (1906–66), literary critic, teacher and late convert to political Islam, first arrested in 1954 and hanged in 1966. In his commentary on the *Qur'an (fi zilal al-qur'an)* from which the famous treatise, 'Signposts', was taken (*ma'alim fi'l-tariq*, circulated in 1964), Qutb declared the established regime to be un- or pre-islamic (*jahili*) and revolutionary counter-force against its violent suppression of the *da'wa* to be not only legitimate but imperative.[17] Vulgarized Qutb supplemented by Mawdudi, studded with quotations from the Holy *Qur'an* and excerpts from the works of Ibn Taymiyya (d. 1328) and Ibn Qayyim al-Jawziyya (d. 1350) served to justify indiscriminate violence against a system and a society that were denied any legitimacy whatsoever. Studies on the militant camp from al-Jihad to al-Najun min al-Nar and from Shaykh Abd al-Hamid Kishk to Shaykh Umar Abd al-Rahman propagating the duty of *jihad* against infidels and apostates abound.[18] What has been less well studied is the path of those who from the shock of the Nasser years drew the conclusion that a head-on confrontation with a regime as powerful and well entrenched as Egypt's was impossible, self-destructive and irresponsible, and that only a return to the old strategy of integration into society and participation in the formal political process held any hope of ultimate success. It was essentially a return to the long-term strategy of education and persuasion, combined with material services offered by a wide network of mosques, schools, clinics, banks and companies (see al-Nafisi 1989, especially 26f, 177–201, 238–49). The lessons were partly put into practice by the survivors of the old Muslim Brotherhood organization who, by 1974, had been released from prison or allowed to return from exile. It was also practised by some of the Jama'at Islamiyya which, from the early 1970s, had succeeded in establishing themselves (initially with active government support) in urban neighbourhoods, at university campuses and among middle-class professionals.

To the extent that, from 1975–76, the nasserist single-party system was modified to allow for a process of controlled liberalization, the Brotherhood gradually revised its stand on democracy and multi-partyism, cautiously distancing itself from some of the positions of the master, Hasan al-Banna.[19] Still, its status remained ambiguous. While the Brotherhood was permitted to reorganize and to engage in overt activity in all spheres of public life including elections and parliamentary politics, it was denied any kind of legal recognition, even as a religious and charitable organization. When, in a remarkable step taken after long and controversial debate, in 1990 it requested registration as a political party the demand was rejected.[20] And yet, the Muslim Brotherhood and Jama'at Islamiyya were very much part of the official political game. The struggle for human rights, political participation and government accountability, against Israel and overwhelming American influence in the area, provided opportunities to cooperate with other political groups and currents. Parliament was by no means inaccessible. There were ways to cope with the legal restrictions by nominating independent candidates and by entering into coalitions with the legalized parties.[21] The Brothers' record of successful political mobilization, broad social base and involvement in the expanding islamic business and banking sector[22] created envy and suspicion among their critics and rivals, but at the same time made them attractive as coalition partners. If in the alliance with the Wafd (1984–87) the Brotherhood was still a junior partner, the balance changed in its favour when, in 1987, Muslim Brothers and prominent members of the Jama'at joined with the Labour and the Liberal Parties (both still called socialist at the time) to form an islamic alliance *(al-tahaluf al-islami)*. In a process of what was described by Iman Farag as 'party squatting', the weaker parties were more or less taken over by their islamist partners (Farag 1991, 24). Conflicting views on economic policy or foreign relations were no deterrent to co-operation. All groups and parties were considered potential partners except for the marxist and neo-nasserist left, grouped in and around the Tajammu Party, which in spite of quite remarkable overtures aimed at establishing some religious credibility for itself was rejected as atheist and even anti-islamic (Krämer 1986, 62–8; *al-Musawwar* 27 March 1987).

Government response to the phenomenon of islamic 're-awakening' *(al-sahwa* or *al-yaqza al-islamiyya)* and the broad and heterogeneous movement supporting it has been as mixed and variegated, as flexible and full of ambiguity, as the entire process of economic and political liberalization initiated in the mid-1970s (Bianchi 1989, 3–34). With characteristic modifications in key and style, Mubarak continued Sadat's approach of absorbing at least part of the message, making concessions in areas that are sensitive from a broader moral and religious perspective, but of applying tactics of delay at best and repression at worst in areas that are regarded as politically relevant in a stricter sense.[23] Significant concessions have been made in the fields of information and education. Religious instruction at school has been intensified and 'anti-religious' doctrines from darwinism to frivolous poetry banned. Religious (i.e. predominantly islamic) programmes on TV and radio have been greatly expanded, religious papers licensed or religious pages added to the dailies and weeklies of the so-called national press. Alcohol has been banned in individual provinces and on the flights of Egypt Air. On several occasions, 'anti-islamic' books have been confiscated and their authors prosecuted. Here, however, the government is treading on delicate ground for although atheism and blasphemy are anathema and not openly discussed in Egyptian society, the restrictions on freedom of expression are not universally popular with a population that is overwhelmingly religious, but as a rule shuns bigotry. Resistance, sometimes open, often tacit, but always persistent, has been offered in the area of law and order. The call for the application of the *shari'a* or at least of its spirit and guiding principles *(maqasid)* has been universally acclaimed. But all attempts made by islamist deputies to see the *shari'a* codified as the law of the land and to have 'un-islamic' laws of European origin repealed have been effectively blocked by the government party (see for example Abd al-Fattah 1984; Peters 1988).

Whether the game can be continued indefinitely is of course an open question. It appears that at the price of considerable concessions on issues considered not to be of primary political relevance, at least not in the sense of challenging government control over economic and political decision-making, the Mubarak regime has succeeded in integrating the advocates of a non-violent ('moderate') strategy of islamic reform in and outside of the Muslim Brotherhood, and in marginalizing the militants. In spite of ruthless persecution, however, they have not been eliminated; nor do their sources of support seem to have been critically reduced (providing the justification for a continuation and even extension of wide-ranging emergency legislation first imposed by Sadat in September 1981). The government's position is strengthened by the fact that the militants' propagation of uncompromising confrontation involving the break with society and the family *(takfir wa-hijra* – excommunication and withdrawal), and the stirring up of what is commonly called 'sectarian conflict' *(fitna ta'ifiyya)* menacing the 'national union' of Muslims and Copts, which is seen with pride as a characteristic of Egyptian history and national character, are generally condemned as a violation of genuine (Egyptian) authenticity. The state's claim to be the only, or at any rate the most potent, protector against *fitna,* anarchy and terrorism, is thus gaining in credibility (Ajami 1983).

The position of those in the Muslim Brotherhood and the Jama'at who advocate the traditional path of the *da'wa* is more difficult. They are under pressure from the militant and the impatient who view all efforts at integration with utmost suspicion and who at least ask for some tokens of success. The Brotherhood's self-assumed role as the voice of 'real Islam', of reason and moderation, counselling restraint and patience to well-meaning but ill-guided youth, renders them useful to the government, more useful probably than the *shaykhs* of al-Azhar who are widely seen as mere tools in the hands of the powerful. Yet it cannot but fuel this suspicion. It is a delicate balance that has to be maintained by the major actors in the government and the islamic camp. But given Egypt's reputation for successful bargaining, compromise and ambiguity, known to less charitable observers as muddling through, it may prove to be more viable than the confrontational line tried before – and elsewhere.

Tunisia

The Tunisian case offers close and striking parallels to the Egyptian one as far as government strategies are concerned, and interesting distinctions once the islamic movement is looked at. Compared to the Egyptian Muslim Brotherhood, the Tunisian islamic movement is relatively young and only emerged as an organized actor of wider impact during and after the Iranian Revolution of 1979.[24] It had not been involved in the strikes of 1978, and nor does it seem to have played a prominent part in the riots of January 1984.[25] Being denounced as mere partisans of the Egyptian Muslim Brotherhood by their critics, and as Iranian agents by the regime, lacking solid roots in either the national or the trade union movement, the islamic current nevertheless succeeded in firmly establishing itself in the Tunisian arena. With its consistent criticism of cultural alienation and moral degradation, corruption and personal rule, it came to be viewed as a symbol of change, and an alternative to the existing order of politics and society. As in Egypt, its appeal was particularly strong among the urban middle class, high school and university students, and more specifically among what Elbaki Hermassi has called the 'proletarian intelligentsia' (*lumpenintelligenz* to vary a well-known marxist category), and Abdelkader Zghal the 'new social periphery' (Hermassi 1984, 39–44; 1987a, 286–99; 1991, 192, 195f; Zghal 1991b, 211f, 216f). Support among industrial workers, by contrast, seems to be weak. In the summer of 1987, its numerical strength was estimated at some 5–6,000 activists (Hermassi 1991, 195f). Again unlike Egypt, links to islamic banks, which were first registered in Tunisia in 1985, seem to be feeble if existent at all (Moore 1990, 236, 243–6).

The largest local islamic movement, which out of diffuse roots officially constituted itself in May 1981 as the Mouvement de la Tendance Islamique (MTI, *harakat al-ittijah al-islami)*, distinguishes itself from the Muslim Brotherhood by the degree to which its leaders, Rashid al-Ghannushi and Abdelfattah Mourou in particular, have been prepared critically to review past experiences and to revise previous positions, not only on questions of strategy, but also on core concerns of islamic activism such as the application of the *shari'a* and the status of women. The MTI's founding manifesto of June 1981 showed an effort to learn from previous setbacks and to pursue a course specially adapted to the historical, social and cultural conditions of Tunisian society. In numerous statements, interviews and articles, Rashid al-Ghannushi and other spokesmen of the organization made a point of emphasizing the issues outlined there:[26] the need for interaction *(tafa'ul)* and for integration into Tunisian society, the need to take up the demands and grievances of the popular masses rather than repeating to them the pious formulas of the past – so dear to other islamist activists (such as the Egyptian Ikhwan), but sterile and quite irrelevant to present realities (see for example Ghannushi 1989b, 25ff). Interaction with Tunisian society rather than Islam writ large implied specificity. It implied an adaptation to local political culture, deeply marked by French culture (though possibly less traumatically so than in Algeria), and the recognition of the values of pluralism and tolerance, liberty and democracy as part not only of European civilization but also of a universal heritage. It implied the option for a specifically Tunisian path to Islam and modernity. Little concerned for the niceties of *shari'a* and Islamic jurisprudence *(fiqh)*, the MTI developed into an openly political organization operating on an islamic platform. In the face of widespread suspicion, al-Ghannushi in particular did not tire of declaring that a democratic approach, based on the total renunciation of any kind of monopoly over Islam and truth, or of any tutelage *(wisaya)* over the will of the people, was the MTI's 'strategic option', and not merely a tactical choice to be abandoned at the earliest convenience.[27]

While Tunisia's islamic movement made remarkable efforts to distance itself from the Egyptian model and to establish its credentials as part and parcel of Tunisia's political landscape and heritage, government strategies appeared at least initially to be closely modelled on the Egyptian example.[28] Almost from the beginning, the MTI's declarations of good faith were ignored. On 18 July 1981, six weeks after its founding, the MTI leadership was arrested. During the short periods of relaxation, invariably followed by contraction and repression, the islamists had little chance to build confidence and prove their democratic convictions. Government repression of one of the more sophisticated islamic movements alienated a growing number of adherents. By the summer of 1984, when al-Ghannushi and other leaders were released from prison, a radical wing had formed that opted for armed struggle rather than political persuasion.

The surge of islamic militancy in turn alienated the secular opposition, predominantly urban middle class, professional and academic, partly organized in professional associations, human rights groups and political parties. Relations between the islamists and the non-religious opposition were deeply ambivalent. The opposition's dilemma was compounded by the fact that opposing the MTI could not but be seen as support of the government. The early phase of repression in 1981–84 had created a certain amount of solidarity with the victims, irrespective of political differences, conflict and competition. But solidarity did not outweigh the doubts regarding the islamists' real intentions. These were reinforced by a secret strategy paper of the interim MTI leadership circulated in late 1983, which outlined the need to establish personal links with key figures in government and opposition and to strengthen contacts with islamic movements abroad.[29] After a short reprieve, the sequence of the events of 1981–84 was repeated in 1984–87. Following on a series of confrontations at university campuses and popular suburban quarters of the capital and several other towns in the country, the MTI leadership was arrested in March 1987 on charges of high treason and sedition. In early September, al-Ghannushi was sentenced to life imprisonment. By that time, Bourguiba was where Sadat had been exactly six years earlier. Conflict between the state and the islamic movement had escalated to open confrontation, and the clandestine branch of the MTI prepared for a coup in order to liberate their leaders (Hermassi 1991, 197–9, 201; Burgat 1988, 253, 255; Köhler 1992, 14f).

Here the parallel ends. Bourguiba's removal from power on 7 November 1987 seemed to offer hope for a new beginning in the relations between government and opposition. Like Husni Mubarak in Egypt, the new president, Zayn al-Abidin Ben Ali, lacked revolutionary legitimacy and personal charisma and was therefore in greater need of co-operation with domestic political actors than his predecessor had been or had thought himself to be (Moore 1988; Vandewalle 1988; Ware 1988; Leveau 1989).[30] The MTI reacted positively to Ben Ali's conciliatory gestures (Hermassi 1991; Zghal 1991b; Köhler 1992, 15–24). After being amnestied in May 1988, al-Ghannushi confirmed the previous strategy of democratic competition, non-violence and the commitment not to organize within the armed forces and the security apparatus. But, and equally important in the Tunisian context, he also declared the MTI's readiness to recognize the Code of Personal Status of 1956, the touchstone of Tunisian modernism, granting equal rights to women in marriage and divorce as one possible result of *ijtihad* (i.e. not necessarily the ideal or permanently acceptable one). Having made this crucial concession, the MTI was invited to participate in the formulation of the national charter, which was signed on 7 November 1988 by one of its representatives – although only in a personal capacity. But the demand of the Renaissance Party *(hizb al-nahda)* – formed by the MTI in late January 1989 on a strictly political platform – to be legally recognized was rejected in June (Hermassi 1991, 199; Leveau 1989, 7–9). As a consequence, the movement was not directly involved in the parliamentary elections of April 1989. Majority vote effectively reduced the chances of the opposition to win a credible amount of seats. Unlike in Egypt, no electoral alliances were concluded between islamic organizations and secular parties. However, islamist activists campaigning on 'independent lists' received about 13 per cent of the vote, with a reported rate of up to 30 per cent in the suburban quarters of Tunis and in the cities of the southern littoral (Hermassi 1991, 200–202; Leveau 1989, 9–11). The pattern was repeated in the local elections of June 1990. Al-Nahda, which in April 1990 had obtained a licence to publish its paper, *al-Fajr* (seized in June, banned for three months and finally 'frozen' in December of the same year), but was still denied official status, did not openly participate. Out of a total of 3,734 independent candidates, 34 islamists were elected (Esposito & Piscatori 1991, 432f; Tessler 1991, 24).

Shortly after, tension rose considerably, partly linked to the confrontation in the Gulf in which, after some hesitation, al-Ghannushi and other spokesmen of al-Nahda openly took sides with Iraq (for example al-Ahnaf 1990, 99–114). In a third repeat of the cycles of 1981–84 and 1984–87, the government stepped up its campaign against the threat of 'terrorist fundamentalism'. In the early summer of 1991, revelations about new armed conspiracies and attempts to infiltrate the state and security services ushered in a new wave of arrests among islamist activists. The previous policy of keeping repression within certain limits in order to prevent solidarity between the islamic movement and the general political public, most notably the non-religious parties and the human rights organizations, was abandoned. The government was clearly out to break al-Nahda's back. Al-Ghannushi himself had left the country in May 1989. Abdelfattah Mourou, one of the MTI's founding members and a leading advocate of the legalistic strategy, announced his intention of forming a new, moderate and democratic islamic party (Maghreb-Machrek 1991, 74).

By 1992, the situation in Tunisia had reached a deadlock. In spite of all moves and concessions made over the previous decade, and more specifically since Ben Ali's coming to power in November 1987 (the recognition of Tunisia's specific identity, of democracy, pluralism, the Personal Status Law), the islamic movement was denied legal recognition. Caught between a government bent on destroying its most powerful critic and opponent, and a radicalized membership despairing of gradualist strategies of integration into a system that seemed determined to reject them, the moderates had been effectively marginalized. The islamic movement was systematically construed as the most dangerous enemy not only of the regime and the established order, but of civil and indeed of civilized society (Larif-Beatrix 1987, 39–41; Leveau 1989, 7–11; Waltz 1986, 653). Largely independently of its declared policies, it was presented as a threat to domestic peace, economic development and to Tunisian cultural identity. Against widespread suspicion of cross-links and double strategy, less so between the MTI/al-Nahda and rival underground organizations such as the Islamic Liberation Party than with a militant underground wing of the movement itself, the government pursued its policy of co-opting liberal and critical intellectuals. The well-known argument that no group of Muslims, let alone the MTI, the Nahda Party or any of its heirs and affiliates, could claim a monopoly over Islam was again brought into play. And if it was a question of who protected the highest values of the faith best, the argument continued, it was the government and not the semi-educated advocates of intellectual closure (Ware 1988, 598f; Vandewalle 1988, 618).[31] Political elite culture at home, largely opposed to islamic formulas of cultural identity and socio-political organization, and the looming shadow of neighbouring Algeria abroad, seem to account for much of the hostility the islamists met with in their effort to transform Tunisia into an islamic society. As a thoughtful observer remarked, the islamic current had thus 'become socialized into, but not included in, the Tunisian system' (Vandewalle 1988, 612).

Jordan

Several distinctive features mark the Jordanian experience when compared to Egypt and Tunisia. They include the impact of ethnicity and tribalism on social organization and political behaviour, the sources of regime legitimacy, the weight of the foreign policy factor and, last but not least, the pattern of relations between the king and the local islamic movement. Against great odds and many hopes and expectations, the Jordanian entity, widely seen as the very epitome of artificiality in the region, has been successfully consolidated. A concomitant sense of Jordanian national identity, however, has not yet fully evolved. Analyses of internal cohesion, conflict and stability have focused on the ethnic (or, to be more precise, the ethnico-political) divide between 'native' (Trans-)Jordanians (largely of bedouin origin) and Palestinian citizens on the one hand, and the family, tribal and communal factor on the other. Political or ideological preferences not pre-determined by communal or tribal loyalties, by contrast, have been treated as secondary.[32] The king's claim to religious legitimacy based on his descent from the Prophet, distinguishing his rule from that of his Tunisian and Egyptian counterparts, may still have a role to play with regard to the tribes and the small religious establishment in the country. Generally speaking, however, relations between the king or state and society developed on the basis of function and services (Sayigh 1991, 174). Compared to Egypt and Tunisia, Jordan offers a more complex set-up, in which islamic activism and communal loyalties (referring to the Palestinians in particular) are to a certain extent connected or interrelated.

Government policy has been described by one well-disposed observer as combining 'firmness with disruptive forces and tolerance towards all citizens who identify with the state' (Wilson 1991, 1). The islamic movement has so far not acted as a disruptive force posing a threat to the regime. On the contrary. Jordan, therefore, provides one of the few cases of an Arab government and islamic movement pursuing a non-confrontational political strategy over an extended period.[33] Traditionally, the Muslim Brotherhood has played not so much the role of opposition, but of virtual ally, and at times of client to the king. In parallel to the Egyptian mother organization, the Jordanian branch of the Brotherhood was registered under the law of charitable clubs and associations and was therefore not affected by the dissolution of political parties in 1957. Unlike in Egypt, however, this status was preserved over several decades, during which the Brotherhood was in fact the only politically orientated organization tolerated in the country. Again unlike in Egypt, it established no underground organization or military wing for which there was after all no need. Shorter periods of tension excepted, for example, when in 1955 the head of the Jordanian Brotherhood (*al-muraqib al-amm*), Abd al-Rahman al-Khalifa, was arrested and its publications suspended for four years, the Brotherhood acted in support of the king against his critics and opponents at home and abroad (Arab nationalists, nasserists, Ba'thists and the PLO). As in Egypt and Tunisia, relations between mainstream moderates and militant anti-regime groups such as the Islamic Liberation party (*hizb al-tahrir al-islami*) founded in 1952 by Shaykh Taqi al-Din al-Nabhani, or islamic *Jihad bi-Bayt al-Maqdis* established in 1980 by Shaykh As'ad al-Tamimi, were marked by tension and competition.[34] The Brotherhood's two main objectives were, and still are, the application of the *shari'a* and the liberation of Islamic Palestine. The focus of activity has been on education and publications, and gradualism (*tadarruj*), co-operation and participation in the official political framework, its strategic option.[35] Long before the recent stage of liberalization, leading Muslim Brothers had joined parliament and the cabinet as deputies and ministers.

The islamic current in general and the Muslim Brothers in particular were also the first to benefit from the process of political opening or 'democratization' initiated in the mid-1980s (al-Sha'ir 1984; Gubser 1988; Robins 1991; Brand 1991).[36] By then, they had attracted a following among virtually all groups and strata of Jordanian society. Their growth among Palestinian youth and university students, notably at the universities of Amman and Yarmuk, as well as among professional associations, has been generally registered.[37] The by-elections of March 1984, which it was widely assumed were left relatively free in order to allow the regime to take the pulse of public opinion, provided a shock to the ruling circles, notably the tribal leadership which had grown used to seeing certain constituencies as virtual fiefs. Three of the six seats reserved for Muslim candidates were won by islamist activists, among them Laith Shubailat, a well-known engineer from Amman (not a member of the Ikhwan) and two other independents in Irbid, Jordan's second largest town and a traditional stronghold of islamist activism (Darwish 1990, 165–8; Robins 1991, 190–94).[38] In the immediate aftermath of the *intifada* the march towards democratization was halted. At that stage, government response to increasing tension was repression, not liberalization.

The riots of April 1989 ushered in a new phase in the cycle of relaxation and restriction characteristic of state response to domestic unrest in all three cases considered here. The riots were certainly inspired by the *intifada*. But, as it is widely noted, they were not initiated by the Palestinians; and, this is less well documented, nor were they spearheaded by the islamic opposition (Hudson 1991, 418; Brand 1991, 15–18; Abu Jaber & Fathi 1990, 69f). The parliamentary elections of November 1989, which like their forerunner in 1984, were seen as a test of the public mood, were remarkable for two reasons:[39] first the strong showing of islamist candidates who won 32 out of 80 seats, among them 22 Muslim Brothers as well as 10 independents, some of them with links to the militant islamic resistance groups in the West Bank and Gaza; second, and closely related to it, the declining weight of ascriptive ties of family, tribe and community in determining electoral behaviour even in a society generally described as highly traditional and solidly patriarchal. In their analysis of the elections Abu Jaber and Fathi noted, however, a trend towards individualism and fragmentation reflecting the deep confusion of a public that selected their candidates mostly on the basis of personal acquaintance rather than ideological choice (Abu Jaber & Fathi 1990, 72ff). Concern about the impressive results of the islamic current, which were continued in May and June 1990 in local council elections in Zarqa (predominantly Palestinian, where the Muslim Brothers won nine out of ten seats) and Rusaifa (four out of nine seats), however, did not lead to a slowing down in the process of political liberalization. The Ikhwan in particular were closely involved in the new stage of 'democratization'. The commission named in April 1990 to formulate a national charter included several prominent Muslim Brothers as well as independent islamists (Darwish 1990, 256).[40] In October 1990, at the height of the Gulf crisis, Abd al-Latif Arabiyyat, a lawyer and leading Muslim Brother, was elected speaker of the parliament, and on 1 January 1991, after lengthy bargaining and hesitation, five Muslim Brothers joined the cabinet as ministers of education, religious affairs, justice, social development and health (but left barely six months later in July, when a new cabinet was formed under Tahir al-Masri (Esposito & Piscatori 1991, 430f; Maghreb-Machrek, No. 131, January–March 1991, 75).[41] Possibly in order to contain the islamic movement by creating counter-weights among the non-religious opposition, restrictions on individual liberties were further eased and the ban on political parties lifted (Abu Jaber & Fathi 1990, 84; Amawi 1992, 27ff). At the turn of 1989–90 some of the core demands of the opposition, the Muslim Brothers included, were met when martial law was 'frozen', the 'Anti-Communist' Law of 1953 repealed, the power of the intelligence services restricted and press control relaxed. The national charter, which was ratified in June 1991 by a national congress of some 2,000 participants, finally sanctioned a multi-party system which was confirmed by parliament in August 1992 (Amnesty International 1990; Mus'ad 1991, 64; Brand 1991, 20f).

As far as domestic affairs are concerned, accommodation and co-operation between the islamic movement, the government and the non-religious opposition seem quite possible. Muslim Brotherhood demands centre around the application of the *shari'a* (with equal rights guaranteed to non-Muslims and women – within the framework of Islam), the fight against corruption and unrestrained powers of the intelligence services and for the granting of political freedom. They fully endorse the principles of political diversity and pluralism (*al-haqq fi'l-ikhtilaf*), including the (powerless and hence innocuous) communist party with which they co-operated during the campaign against American military intervention in the Gulf.[42] Whether the Muslim Brothers and islamist independents really stand to benefit from continued political liberalization which would inevitably give more room of manoeuvre to their political rivals who had been suppressed in the past is another question.[43] Islamist and non-religious activists are basically united in their demand for political freedom at home and the defence of the Arab national cause abroad. It does not appear that controversial issues such as the application of the *shari'a* or structural adjustment on IMF lines could block the liberalization process to the same extent that they have done in Tunisia.

It is foreign policy that could weaken, and possibly break, the traditional link between the king and the Muslim Brothers. In spite of their unswerving commitment to the liberation of Palestine conflicting with the king's policy of de facto co-existence with Israel, mutual interest in continued co-operation had always been strong enough to overcome latent tension. In the long and bitter conflict with Syria which was only settled in 1985, the Muslim Brothers had served as useful allies of the king by supporting their Syrian counterparts. There had been considerable tension when, during the Iraq–Iran War, they criticized the king's backing of Iraq against the Islamic Republic of Iran which, especially in its early years, had found a positive echo in Jordan and the Israeli-occupied territories (Satloff 1986, especially 55–8; Rekhess 1990). The Gulf War, ironically enough, provided a positive atmosphere for democratization as it created solidarity and close co-operation among virtually all political actors in the country, and unprecedented support for the king. The preparations for American-sponsored negotiations with Israel in the summer and autumn of 1991 changed the situation entirely, affecting the crucial area where conflict between the king and the islamic movement is almost impossible to avoid (Brand 1991, especially 34–7; Mus'ad 1991, 56; Gubser 1988, 104).[44] During and after the elections of 1989, the Muslim Brothers had again declared their refusal to recognize Israel, their rejection of all UN resolutions on Palestine and unconditional support for Hamas and the *intifada*. They had repeated their call for *jihad* to liberate all of Palestine and condemned negotiations with the zionist enemy as illicit (*munkar shar'an*) (al-Kaylani 1990; Darwish 1990).[48] In a situation similar to that faced by government and opposition in Egypt during the Camp David peace process, the king may be tempted, or even forced, to halt liberalization in order to continue his policy of *rapprochement* with the US and his conservative neighbours in the Gulf. He may opt to trade accommodation with supporters at home for reconciliation with his donors abroad, and in the worst of cases, he may have to sacrifice peace at home for peace with (or, as less well-meaning observers might even say, appeasement of) his neighbours. Countervailing pressures are immense, and the prospects of liberalization in Jordan will be closely linked to the evolution of Arab–Israeli relations.

Ambivalences and ambiguities

After decades of islamist activism, and a somewhat shorter period of political liberalization, the dilemma of both regimes and islamic movements still appears to be unresolved. Relaxation and repression have both been tried. Accommodation has alternated or been combined with relentless persecution of the opponent. The strategy to absorb the message and pre-empt the issues liable to galvanize a wider protest movement (social inequality, moral laxity, blatant favouritism, excessive corruption, lack of political freedom), to co-opt its original bearers – preferably on an individual basis and at any rate within a framework defined by the regime and its supporters – and to marginalize and delegitimize those who refuse to co-operate, has been widely applied.[45] Yet the situation is still marked by a pervading sense of uncertainty, of suspicion and distrust, complicated by multiple cross-cutting and contradictory pressures from within society and from abroad.

Two factors have so far facilitated the government tactic of accommodation-cum-exclusion. At home, misgivings concerning the democratic credentials of the islamic movement have tended to rally leftist and liberal actors to the government which, compared to the advocates of *hakimiyya*, *jihad* and a radical break with all things foreign, still promises to be the more credible champion of national unity, social peace and even cultural identity. The pattern of alliance between the government and various segments of the secular opposition is continued, and co-optation of liberal and critical minds against the threat of medieval obscurantism widely practised. Abroad, the islamists' criticism of foreign intervention (including the structural adjustment programmes of the IMF and World Bank), of co-operation with the West and negotiation with Israel accounts for international acquiescence in repressive government action.

In a number of cases, including Egypt, Jordan and unified Yemen, the government strategy of accommodation and repression, of flexibility in matters of culture, education and morality, but not of power and security, has been relatively successful. In all of them the political elite is more receptive to the idea of islamic political activism provided it is 'moderate', rooted in local society and endowed with nationalist legitimacy. The situation is different in Algeria and Tunisia, where the role of Islam in politics and society is more controversial, and the local islamic movement of much more recent origin. In Algeria and Tunisia, the experiment in co-operation has been abandoned in favour of outright repression, following the example set by nasserist Egypt in the 1950s and 1960s, with its known and rather mixed results. For if it convinced a majority of activists of the 'inevitability of the gradualist solution', it persuaded a determined minority that there was nothing left but armed rebellion to destroy the power of those who spread corruption on earth, and stand in the way of the *da'wa*. The resort to repression cannot but radicalize growing sections of the islamic movement, particularly among mobilized youth impatient for quick results, who never put much hope in the incrementalist strategy of the 'moderates'. To them, co-optation is an attempt to tame the only truly alternative (and legitimate) force in society. In Algeria and Tunisia, the governments seem intent on excluding the islamists irrespective of their declared programmes and policies. Under these circumstances, oportunities to prove good faith are limited, chances to engage in confidence building virtually nil, and the prospects for liberalization bleak.

Notes

1   To a certain extent, the debate about democracy has replaced the one about (Arab) socialism of the 1950s and 1960s, with similar questions being asked, patterns of argument being set forth and conclusions drawn. What we hear and read about democracy in the Arab world, therefore, often looks like a *déjà vu* (or rather a *déjà lu*), offering some rather revealing insights into the persistence of basic notions and assumptions regarding Arab (islamic/Muslim) politics and society. See for example, Markaz dirasat al-wahda al-arabiyya (1984); Ibrahim (1988); Hudson (1991); Salamé (1991); Camau (1991); Krämer (1992); Faath & Mattes (1992).

2   Registered, for example, by Bianchi (1989, 6).

3   Perhaps a parallel could be drawn with the Palestine issue where a similar constellation – centrality of the cause combined with the effort to control or marginalize its

original and most 'authentic' champions, here the Palestinian national movement represented by the PLO – can be observed.

4   Waltz (1986) defines islamism as being overdetermined. See also Sivan (1985), Dekmejian (1985) and Ayubi (1991).

5   The situation is best documented with regard to Egypt and the Maghreb countries: see for example, Bianchi (1989), Baker (1990), Dwyer (1991), Faath & Mattes (1992). See also Ghabra (1991).

6   See Camau (1991), introduction pp. 9–12. With specific reference to Tunisia, see Zghal (1991) and Baker (1991).

7   For an overview, see Moore (1990) and Sid Ahmed (1990).

8   Iman Farag (1991, 23) has rightly emphasized the prevalent use of the 'game' metaphor.

9   The question has been put with particular clarity with regard to Tunisia, see for example, Leveau (1989, 7f) and Lamchichi (1989).

10 For an important document of one such approach, see Markaz dirasat al-wahda al-arabiyya (1989).

11 For a fuller treatment, see Krämer (1992a) and (1993). Included are representatives of the Muslim Brotherhoods of Egypt and Jordan, the islamic movement of Tunisia as well as individual authors close to the 'moderate' islamic current, such as Muhammad Salim al-Awwa, Fahmi Huwaidi, Muhammad Ammara, Munir Shafiq, Muhammad Fathi Uthman or Kamil al-Sharif. For some recent discussions of the issue, see Binder (1988), Jedaane (1990) and, published after this paper had been drafted, Huwaidi (1992) and Zartman (1992).

12 If Lebanon serves as a reminder of what sectarianism and intercommunal strife can do to a 'fragmented' Arab society, Sudan is frequently referred to when the dangers of political islam, the application of the *shari'a* by an ageing dictator, and the 'democratic' convictions of an islamic leader (Hasan al-Turabi) are being discussed. Turabi, together with Rashid al-Ghannushi, has always stood out as a champion of integrative strategies. For differing perspectives, see El-Affendi (1991) and Ibrahim Ali (1992).

13 Among the large body of literature on political islam in Egypt, see Carré & Michaud (1983), Kepel (1984), Bianchi (1989), Springborg (1989), Roussillon (1990), Baker (1991), Ben Néfissa (1992).

14 For Banna's political concepts, see notably his circulars 'Mushkilatuna fi daw al-nizam al-islami'; 'Risalat al-mu'tamar al-khamis' and 'Ila l-shabab' in *Majmu'at rasa'il al-imam al-shahid Hasan al-Banna* (n.d., n.p.); also Rizq (1985) and Ghanim (1992).

15 For a sharply critical approach, see the Wafdist historian Abd al-Azim Ramadan (1982). For Muslim Brother perspectives, see Shadi (1981) who is critical and Kamal (1987) who is apologetic.

16 On the following, see notably the memoirs of Muslim Brother activists Abu'l-Nasr (1988); Shadi (1981, 116ff) and Abd al-Halim (1979, vol iii, 117ff).

17 For critical analyses, see Carré (1984); Diyab (1987) and al-Khalidi (1991).

18 For different perspectives see notably Sivan (1985); Jansen (1986); Sayyid Ahmad (1989) and Khouri (1990).

19 On the re-orientation of the Muslim Brotherhood, see Krämer (1986, 90–128); Krämer (1992a, 346–9); Forstner (1988); Farschid (1989).

20 For the debate within the Brotherhood and among Egyptian parties on the creation

of an islamic party, see *Liwa al-Islam* (Cairo) 26 February and 28 March 1990.

21 The process of liberalization in general and of parliamentary elections in particular has been too well studied and documented to be analysed here. See Hinnebusch (1985) and Krämer (1986). For elections see Cooper (1982); Krämer (1984); Krämer (1987); Hilal (1984); Makram Ebeid (1989); Farag (1991).

22 On islamic banks see Roussillon (1988 & 1990). According to Moore (1990) who speaks of 'synergies' between islamic revivalist politics and islamic economics, islamic banks held 17 per cent of all deposits in the commercial banking system in the late 1980s (pp. 237 and 249–54). The prominent role of wealthy Muslim Brothers in the *infitah* sector is documented by Imam (1986) especially 205–19. See also Springborg (1989, 23–40).

23 For a comparison with the nasserist era, see Sayyid Ahmad (1989).

24 The history, ideology and politics of the islamic movement in Tunisia have been studied relatively well; see notably the contributions by Elbaki Hermassi (Muhammad Abd al-Baqi al-Harmasi) 1984 and 1987a. See also Ghannushi's comments on Hermassi's essay in Markaz al-dirasat al-wahda al-arabiyya (1987a, 300–308). Also Abd al-Latif al-Harmasi (1985), Puppé (1985–86); Waltz (1986); Burgat (1988); al-Hamidi (1989); Lamchichi (1989) and Magnuson (1991).

25 See Middle East Report no. 127 (October 1984), issue on 'Insurrection in North Africa'; also Tessler (1991).

26 Text of the founding manifesto (*al-bayan al-ta'sisi*) in Ghannushi (1989, 157–60). For Ghannushi's collected lectures and articles see Ghannushi (1984) and (1989). On the ideological evolution of the MTI see also al-Harmasi (1985) and Hermassi (1987a).

27 For example Ghannushi's lecture *al-Haraka al-islamiyya wa'l-tahdith* delivered at Khartoum University in 1979–80, his articles *Fi'l-mabadi al-asasiyya lil-dimuqratiyya wa usul al-hukm fi'l-islam* and *al-Islam wa'l-unf* and his interview with *al-Mujtama* (Kuwait) July 1981. All these are reprinted in Ghannushi (1989) 31–44, 49–69, 71–6 and 141–7. For a more recent statement see Ghannushi (1990) 8–16. Internal debates about the legalistic strategy are reported by Abd al-Hayy Bul'aras & Hisham al-Haji (1984).

28 For the Bourguiba era, which will not be dealt with here, see Hermassi (1987b); Hermassi (1991, 193f, 204); Larif-Beatrix (1987); Leveau (1989, 4f, 9–11).

29 Puppe (1985–6, 109–13, 133–43); Waltz (1986, 653f, 658f) quoting an interview with Mourou in *Jeune Afrique*, 7 August 1985. French translation of the strategy paper in *Sou'al*, 5 (April 1985) pp. 179–200.

30 First measures of political relaxation are listed in Ministère de l'Information, *Consolider le processus démocratique* (Tunis, March 1989).

31 For a sharp left-wing attack on the MTI turned Nahda see for example al-Hammami (1989).

32 For new approaches, see for example McLaurin and Jureidini (1984); Layne (1988); Brand (1991).

33 The islamic movement in Jordan, closely related to the one in Palestine or the West Bank, Gaza and Israel, is among the less well known in the Middle East. See Cohen (1982, 144–229); Satloff (1986, 34–58) stressing the impact of the Iranian revolution in raising the 'spectre of islamic activism'; Ubaydat (1989); al-Kaylani (1990); Mus'ad (1991).

34 See for example Cohen (1982) 209–29; interview with Tamimi in the newspaper of

the Jordanian Muslim Brothers *al-Raya al-Islamiyya*, 23 March 1990, 4f.
35 See for example the collection of essays by Kamil al-Sharif, prominent sympathizer and former minister of *awqaf* (1984) and al-Sharif in Ibrahim ed. (1989).
36 Full documentation is to be found in Darwish (1990).
37 For example Gubser (1988, 98); Satloff (1986, 45f). For associational life and the private sector in Jordan see al-Sha'ir (1991). Rodney Wilson's contribution on islamic banking (1991) and Moore (1990) provide excellent documentation, but unfortunately no discussion of its links to the islamic political movement.
38 Robins also discusses (1990, 200f) the link between the size of constituencies and the dominance of the traditional family or tribal networks at the expense of ideological groupings such as the islamists or communists,
39 For analyses see Darwish (1990, 169–71, 242–9, 257–67); Robins (1990, 55–9); Duclos (1990, 47–75); Amawi (1992, 26–29); Abu Jaber & Fathi (1990, 74–81); Brand (1991, 18–22). For a Muslim Brother perspective see *Liwa al-Islam* (Cairo) 30 December 1989, pp. 42–5.
40 A complete list with status and political affiliation can be found in the English translation of the national charter prepared by the Dar al-Orouba, Amman (n.d.).
41 See also the interview with Abd al-Rahman al-Khalifa in *al-I'tisam* (Cairo), December 1989, p. 3.
42 See their election programme and the statements of islamist deputies during the vote of confidence on prime minister Mudar Badran's policy programme in November–December 1990, in al-Kaylani (1990, 142–68, 197–200); also Darwish (1990, 559–61, and for the debate 344ff). See also the series on the political strategy of the Jordanian islamic movement in *al-Raya al-Islamiyya* (Amman), March 1990.
43 Asked by Mus'ad (1991, 74).
44 On the newly intensified relations between the Jordanian Muslim Brothers and Iran, see Legrain (1991, 124–7).
45 Rémy Leveau's cautious speculation (1989, 17) on parallels between the 'old' equilibrium of military men and *ulama* and the modern equilibrium between the military and the islamic opposition is not entirely convincing. The Sunni *ulama*, after all, did not seek power or even direct and recognized political participation, whereas most contemporary islamic movements do.

9

Socio-economic Change and Political Implications: the Maghreb

ABDELBAKI HERMASSI

One of the important features of late development since the 1960s is the break-down of the early nationalist social contract. By this contract the poor forfeited their political rights in exchange for material benefits insured by the govern-ment. Its breakdown, which amounts to a genuine crisis in legitimacy, means that political authorities now have to contend with an increasing level of dis-content; to cope with this discontent political authorities are pressured to achieve both a growing accumulation of benefits and a higher level of legiti-macy.

An indication and by-product of the new situation is the politics of *infitah* which encourages market forces and state disengagement and which pushes people, unions, students and even welfare beneficiaries to fend for themselves.

But what must be stressed – because it is less obvious and often less well per-ceived – is people's disengagement from the state. Indeed, it is now possible to find groups, communities and individuals who manage to make a living entirely outside the official arena of administration, business, banks and various institu-tional channels. This phenomenon finds part of its expression in what is known as the informal sector which is growing and has drawn the attention of many economists.

One should also mention the phenomenon of ethno-entrepreneurship. For north Africa, this concept applies to Sfaxi-s, Jerbians, M'zabi-s, Kabils and Soussi-s; all of which form entrepreneurial communities bound by common val-ues, inner solidarity and control of inside information. These communities gen-erate entrepreneurial talent and offer opportunities that are drawing 'the smartest and the best' away from government service. The few monographs written on his topic provide useful insights into the ways in which ethno-entrepreneurship is affecting society and politics.

Mention should also be made of *trabendo* activities which have increased dramatically in the past few years and which provide an illustration of how it is possible for a growing number of people to succeed outside the official power structure.

All these developments have one enduring and crucial consequence: the relativization of the role of government in comparison to the early days of the post-colonial state.

Let us look at how government has perceived this new configuration and attempted to cope with it.

Tunisia's president, Ben Ali, recently encapsulated the challenges Tunisia now faces as it attempts to reconstruct its political community in the 'post Bourguiba' era, which started on 7 November 1987:

> What we need is a reconciliation at one and the same time of our society, our cultural identity and the geographical and political culture of our country. One of the conditions of that national reconciliation remains democracy which appears as the passage necessary for the emergence of new elites dedicated to the cause of progress and capable of assuming their duties selflessly and with competence. This project also necessitates the reconstruction of (a system of) values without which we cannot assure our survival and our evolution as a national community in the world today...nationalism, citizenship and work. [1]

Despite their differing responses, no government from Rabat to Tripoli has been able to ignore the powerful forces that Ben Ali hinted at in his speech: a need for greater economic efficiency, the challenge of inter-generational political renewal, the need for a new consensus and for the creation of greater public liberties. This represents the sort of compromise that neither Habib Bourguiba nor Houari Boumedienne would have entertained a generation ago, guided as they were by the notion that the state, through its institutions and centralized organization, could control society.

Perhaps nothing has better symbolized the disarray and the retreat of the state during the last decade than the adoption in all countries of the Maghreb of policies of economic liberalization designed to overcome the bottlenecks of earlier economic management, the emergence and gathering strength of political contestation and the limited liberalization that most rulers in the region now pay at least lip service to. A generation after independence the north African countries have had to recognize that the political configurations and economic strategies that have sustained their development until the present can no longer meet current challenges in a dramatically changed world economy and amidst state-society relations that have fundamentally altered during the last three decades.

A few recent events highlight this change. Normally immune from economic or internal political pressures, the Qadhafi government was obliged in 1987 and 1988 to relax its injunctions on private trade – one of the cornerstones of the regime's 'revolution' – and set in motion steps towards political liberalization, which ultimately resulted in the publication of a document that, in the Libyan context, can only be termed highly unusual: *The Green Charter of "Human Rights"*.[2] If in Algeria, Tunisia and Libya some of the old rhetoric with its hackneyed references to the struggle for independence and the need to preserve state economic control persists, in the past few years a number of new words have crept into public discourse. References to 'austerity', 'efficiency' and 'productivity' linked to 'personal responsibility' and 'human rights' now punctuate the political vocabulary of all of the north African leaders.[3] In Algeria, after almost three decades of one-party rule, the government suddenly called upon 'civil society' to behave responsibly during the June 1990 local municipal elections. A few months earlier, Algeria's new constitution had pointedly dropped any reference to socialism and, after years of castigating multinational companies, allowed direct foreign investment. In November 1988 Tunisia's new president, Ben Ali, proposed a 'National Pact' that would give all organized groups in the country a chance to help elaborate its future; this was in marked contrast to the personal rule of Habib Bourguiba, which had seen the virtual evisceration of any form of opposition. In Morocco, a certain degree of political pluralism, a more market-oriented economy and the extraordinary religious and charismatic link between ruler and ruled had seemingly muted the growing bifurcation between state and society found in other Maghrebi countries. In Morocco, political difficulties have been less the result of friction between the population and its ruler than a result of the conflict between monarchy and political elites over how the state should be managed. Even so, the 1981 and 1984 upheavals in the kingdom's major cities showed how fragile this carefully calibrated system remains. The king's answer to the lingering difficulties has been to introduce a number of economic measures – including fiscal reform; higher taxes, particularly for the middle class; reform and privatization of public enterprises and greater attention to exports – but no meaningful political concessions.

The legitimacy of the state during the first period of state-building in Morocco, Tunisia and Algeria originated and was sustained by the dual roles it assumed after independence: as guardian of a strong and carefully nurtured bond between the state and its subjects, and as arbiter and broker of economic patronage. This symbolic link was particularly important in Algeria and Tunisia – and after 1969 in Libya – where the state emerged as the embodiment of the nationalist struggle and as the only force capable of creating an internal *thawra* (revolution) that would modernize the political community. In Algeria and Tunisia this fusion of symbolic and real economic power was institutionalized in a one-party system: the Front de Libération Nationale (FLN) and the Destour Party dispensed patronage and were the symbols of independence – even if in the latter case the confusion between charismatic ruler and party was part and parcel of the political game.[4] Unlike Morocco, where the constitution expressly forbids a one-party system, all other political parties in Algeria, Tunisia and Libya were outlawed or simply eviscerated. The state controlled most forms of social and political expression. In Algeria and Tunisia – and Libya after 1969 – leaders talked of the creation of an irreversible social order that would transform even the attitudes and identity of individuals. So convinced of the success of their mission was the first generation in Tunisia that one close observer called

President Bourguiba's creation 'the New State'.[5] And so thorough was the state's seeming political and ideological hegemony that at least one observer writing on the country's labour movement – completely erroneous in hindsight but certainly believable at the time – wondered whether it could ever re-emerge as an autonomous social force.[6] By 1980 the claim that the state could create – or recreate – a national society was heard less often, and its role as a catalyst in transforming society no longer taken as self-evident.

By that time, both aspects of the earlier state-society relationship had been substantially altered throughout the Maghreb with the exception of Libya: rapid population growth and overall economic stagnation had made it virtually impossible to keep the social contract intact. The initial rationale for extending or maintaining state power in order to survive challenges posed by the former colonial power had dissipated; the nationalist myth and the perception of the role of the state as modernizer in Algeria and Tunisia lost its former coherence as the party and its leaders lost their appeal. The continued existence of what Ahmed Ben Salah once called an 'inevitable tutelage' was questioned (cited in Camau 1987, 31). Indeed, the islamist movements that emerged full-blown in the 1980s in all north African countries after a little-noticed – or even ignored – gestation period, which dates back to the 1960s, brought to the fore a number of groups that challenged the lingering symbolic pretensions of the government and denigrated its performance as 'economic allocation agent' (Burgat 1988). The rapid emergence of private voluntary associations and parallel markets in each country – Algeria's *trabendo*, Tunisia's *marché noir*, Libya's *suk tunisi* – were but one expression of the shortcomings of the state in economic matters.

The politics of economic stagnation and adjustment

The *infitah* strategies in Morocco, Tunisia and Algeria emerged at approximately the same time in the early 1980s, even though in the Tunisian case it is perhaps more accurate to speak of a restructuring or re-privatization after the lacklustre attempt at market economics that followed Ben Salah's dismissal. In Libya the reversal was postponed until 1987, partly because the enormous revenues the government continued to enjoy allowed it to ignore economic imperatives. By the end of 1986 Morocco and Tunisia had changed their investment codes to allow for greater private-sector participation. Each government had either rescheduled part of its debt or accepted stand-by arrangements for restructuring plans suggested by the World Bank or the International Monetary Fund. Despite the self-imposed austerity plan of 1983, Algeria finally entered into an agreement with the IMF in July 1989. By that time its investment code (1986) had dramatically extended facilities for the private sector in the country. In Libya, the 26 March 1987 introduction of *tasharukiya* now allowed private trading and enterprises in which individuals could contribute capital, thus rescinding one of the cornerstones of the previous 'partners, not wage-earners' policy encoded in the *Green Book*. And although in Libya this limited form of *infitah* was imposed from above – and not the result of pressures from below as in other countries – the unexpected change hinted at the economic hardships that the Republic was labouring under.

In each case the redefinition of the role of the state in economic development has been fostered not only by an emerging reconceptualization of that role (see below), but also by a rapidly changing international economic environment and a global logic that has progressively narrowed the scope of intervention left to local governments. Unlike Latin America or sub-Saharan Africa, where the inquiry into the relationship between international capital, local capital and weak or strong state structures has led to the formulation of a number of competing explanations, there has been no equivalent development in north Africa. In lieu of a systematic review, I shall here confine myself to a few introductory remarks on the interaction between changing local and international economic conditions.

First, it is important to put the *infitah* – here defined as the permanent transfer of the production of goods and services from public bureaucracies and enterprises to private companies and other non-public organizations – that each north African country has adopted to a wider context. As in many other areas of the world, the new economic sensibility in north Africa is both part of a global phenomenon and a reflection of objective conditions inside each country and within the region. The rethinking of what is now considered the development orthodoxy of the 1950s and 1960s has been a powerful reality since the 1970s, stimulated in part by international financial institutions such as the World Bank and the International Monetary Fund. There is little doubt that, as John Lewis has recently remarked in a broader setting, in the Maghreb 'attitudes about the centrality and the capacities of governments as promoters of development have changed dramatically' (Lewis 1964). The ambitious efforts made at independence to prove that the state could be the initiator, regulator and enforcer of irreversible social and economic reforms – the state as Leviathan – were scaled back.

It is in this context that President Benjedid noted in 1981: 'the kind of management which regulated (national enterprises) during the 1960s and the beginning of the 1970s no longer fits with the present exigencies of national development nor with the necessities of management for the decade of the 1980s.' And it was this same realization that prompted the then director of Tunisia's central bank, Isma'il Khalil, to call for a renewed commitment to private-sector initiative.[7]

In all Maghrebi countries – but particularly in Algeria and Tunisia – the story of development since independence had been one of active state intervention in all sectors of the economy. With the exception of Libya until the 1969 coup, each country's legal system, its fiscal and monetary policy instruments and a tangle of regulatory mechanisms were meant to protect internal markets from undue interference. Particularly in Tunisia until 1969 and Algeria until 1980, the adoption of a command system was seen as the most promising road towards impressive economic growth and social restructuring – a strategy that demanded the creation of a complex structure of multiple layers of bureaucracy and control mechanisms, either derived from the Soviet model or as a result of the economic controls and extensive central planning left by the French. Thus the state not only occupied the traditional commanding heights of the economy but had penetrated the lowest levels of economic interaction as well. The most extreme form of state intrusion in the economic lives of its citizens, however, was to be found in Libya when, after 1975, a private sector was not only discouraged but became outright illegal – a phenomenon that sparked the growth of a burgeoning black market, which eventually contributed to the revival of some of the regime's earlier economic measures.

If in Libya this evisceration of the private sector was undertaken on ideological grounds, in the other countries of the Maghreb strong state intervention was seen as a pragmatic necessity. It would allow planners to circumvent a number of potentially troublesome realities that could offset economic progress: the persistence of factions and regional differences; the existence of institutions for implementing economic policy that were weak; the presence of underdeveloped markets or trade structures orientated towards the former colonial power, and finally, the fact that doubts remained about the ability or willingness of the private sector to shoulder part of the burden of development. Running through much of Algeria's and Tunisia's economic literature of that early period is the strong conviction that markets could bring about only incremental change, and not the wholesale restructuring that was deemed necessary. Furthermore, economic planners believed that markets were incapable of fine-tuning the economy – and that firm and resolute policies were needed if the chaos of the market economy were to be avoided.

The state in Morocco, Tunisia and Algeria, in varying degrees, had been called upon at independence to take charge of the transfer of resources and authority in the wake of France's withdrawal. In Morocco this takeover resembled more an extension after independence of colonial economic policy in the country's agricultural sector (Swearingen 1987). The same continuity marked other sectors of Morocco's economy and was not seriously altered by the so-called 'Moroccanization' campaign of March 1973, which was largely nullified by the 1983 investment code.[8] Neither Muhammad V nor Hasan II has shown a determination dramatically to alter the benign laissez-faire approach that traditionally marked economic relations between ruler and ruled. From the end of the 1950s, Moroccan laws continued to favour private local and foreign investment and the *zahirs* published at the time of the Moroccanization measure carefully skirted around the question of outright expropriation. The government's economic role was largely restricted to large-scale projects that the private sector remained uninterested in. Unlike its neighbours, Morocco did not try to create or recreate a new class to guide its development strategy. On the contrary, the king attempted to preserve the power of the urban bourgeoisie and the old rural elites:

because of its current social role and particular history, the Moroccan bourgeoisie in part legitimates both the political and the economic system

Until it began to market oil in 1961, Libya had been highly dependent on the rents paid by Great Britain and the United States for military bases in the country. As in many rentier economies, and faced with a population marked by a weak sense of national identity, King Idris felt little inclination to attempt the creation of a political community or to create state institutions. A relatively few trusted advisers were all that were needed in an economic system that, until the deposition of the king in 1969, showed more interest in simple disbursement of funds than in actual economic planning or policy. Despite its claims to a radically different political vision – mobilizational rather than passive; popular rather than exclusionary – the Qadhafi government after 1969 intensified even further the *dirigiste* nature of the country's economy, excluding at one point all private economic actors entirely. But, in contrast to Algeria or Tunisia, it was unclear whether this added to the capabilities of the state. Indeed, one of Qadhafi's assertions was that the country's political and economic system was run by 'people's power' and not by the institutions of a state. Since the extraction of resources from the population has never been a necessity, because of the country's oil riches, the claims of Libya's leader have until now not been put to the test – although they may be at some future point, when they may be found to be severely lacking.

In Tunisia and Algeria the transfer of authority at independence led to an important rupture with the political and economic legacy of the colonial past. Both opted for one-party systems and some form of socialism – rescinded in Tunisia in 1969 – which replaced a large part of the old economic and cultural elite and produced a consensus for reform and for an extension of the state's administrative capacities throughout each country.[9] Although both countries managed to achieve impressive economic growth during most of the two decades following independence, by the end of the 1970s much of the earlier optimism about the ability of the state to manage and direct economic development had dissipated. The questioning of economic paradigms was fuelled and accelerated by the realization that, despite the record of economic growth, a number of severe structural problems marked their economies – difficulties further exacerbated by a decade of uncertainty and crisis that started in the mid-1970s and by growing political contestation.[10]

The dismal performance of the local economies had an important, though unintended, political side-effect. In all countries of the Maghreb part of the earlier rhetoric – outspoken in Algeria and Libya; somewhat muted in Tunisia and Morocco – had been the achievement of equality and economic justice for its citizens. As economic performance faltered, so did the state representatives' claim to be the sole actors capable of promoting development – a claim further tarnished by charges of mismanagement and corruption among public-sector managers, party apparatchiks and the economic elites. In all cases – although muted somewhat in Morocco and controlled in Libya – this close identification of the state or party with economic progress and subsequent stagnation inevitably produced a spill-over effect that led to a number of sustained political crises in systems where contestation was closely circumscribed or impossible. The contestation or urge to reform has come in essence from two groups: those who argue the institutions of the state can be reformed and act as a new catalyst for development, and those who insist that they have lost their ability and their credibility to do so.

The politics of institutional decline and renewal

Irrespective of the type of regime found in the Maghreb in the late 1970s – monarchist, military, semi-democratic – the questioning of the role of the state in economic development was matched – and sometimes partly caused – by the emergence of increasingly vocal and diverse groups in each country. The crisis of the state, of the institutions that represented it, and the debates about possible alternatives emerged first among an opposition that was often deliberately left atomized, and in underground publications and speeches. These themes were later taken up, often willy-nilly and with the help of subterfuge by representatives of the state from where they filtered into official debate.

Sometimes this shift toward official recognition of a fundamental realignment of forces between state and society took years to accomplish – often only as a result of impending political or economic chaos. Morocco's first stage of state-building had been characterized by conflictual relations between the monarchy and the political parties. It pitted the monarchy, with its insistence on preserving the structures of the colonial system, against the modernizing vision of the country's political parties who wanted to construct a modern state with its own economic, political and social institutions. It resulted in the creation of a mixed authoritarian/populist system in which the king carefully distanced himself from those who claimed to represent popular opinion. The outcome, as in Tunisia, was a personalized system in which political power was highly concentrated, corruption became endemic, and there was an almost complete absence of any institutional possibility for criticism. Indeed, such was the hegemonic nature of power in both countries that whatever tolerated opposition did appear in the 1970s played safely within the consensual rules of the game. In Morocco, the consensual framework was reinforced by the dual role of the king as secular ruler and commander of the faithful: the secular opposition may contest the decisions of the head of the state, but it has overwhelmingly refused to attack those that carry a religious imprimatur. Similarly, the Moroccan military may attack the king as the head of the *makhzen* but – as happened at Skhirat – nonetheless lay down their arms to pray alongside him when he recites the *fatiha*. Despite the monarchy's extraordinary power to circumscribe contestation, the 1970s clearly showed that it was not immune from extra-legal or extra-institutional dissent: Morocco witnessed two military coup attempts, in July

1971 and August 1972, and an army uprising in March 1973. Although all were contained, they led to the realization that closer attention should be given to the nurturing of political institutions and to limitation of the king's virtually absolute power.

In Tunisia the political system never recovered from the 1969 crisis – the demise of the socialist experiment – and from the falsified parliamentary elections of 1981. The entire population, but in particular the peasantry, carries the bitter memory from the years of socialism of the dispossessions and abuses that were committed in the name of a co-operative system that was at one time beyond criticism and then suddenly recognized as a fraud. It is as a result of that defeat that the implicit social contract between the state and civil society was ruptured. Nothing, not even the period of rapid economic growth under Hedi Nouira, could put an end to the disappointment and the suspicion.[11] And it would take the removal of Bourguiba before the country's political parties reluctantly returned to the political arena.

It is from 1969 onwards that the Destour Party started to lose support and a number of its leading members began to form opposition parties: the Mouvement Démocratique Socialiste (MDS) and the Mouvement d'Unité Populaire (MUP). In reality the retreat was from the regime as a whole. As in Algeria, part of the elite as well as the new generation took up their grievances in a number of long-suppressed organizations – particularly the trade unions – or at places that traditionally fell outside the institutional control of the neo-Destour or the FLN: the universities and the mosques. In all Maghrebi countries, including Libya, it was these new (or renewed) forms of opposition that became the arena for political substitutions throughout the 1970s and the 1980s. All opposition – political, syndicalist and islamist – thus finds its origin in the failure of the political system that is indicative of a broader deconstruction of the state. In Tunisia and Algeria, meaningful political discourse was suspended for almost three decades while this gradual deconstruction took place. Under Bourguiba, the discourse was sidetracked by the succession issue. It took almost 20 years for it to emerge. During that time the growing bifurcation of the paternalistic pretensions of the party-state and a growing social and economic malaise not only led to the demoralization of the state's cadres but brought the country to the brink of civil war.

In Algeria also the dramatic reversal of economic policy – after Benjedid's assumption of power – led to a lingering crisis that was even more profound than in neighbouring Tunisia. The commitment to socialism under Houari Boumedienne had been an indelible part of the country's political discourse. Unable to isolate the opponents to the new economic strategy, as Bourguiba had quickly and effectively done with the public supporters of Ben Salah, Benjedid was faced with a crisis that festered into a barely concealed struggle inside the FLN – infighting that slowed down the *infitah* perceptibly and fanned the flames of the struggle between the party and the growing outside opposition. The pro- and anti-*infitah* factions within the central committee, the politburo and the national assembly remained unified on only one issue: to prevent the dispersal of power beyond the party. For that purpose intimidation, or outright violence during the 1988 riots, had become acceptable. But for a long time the FLN's fortunes had mirrored those of the neo-Destour: it had slowly become valued for what it could deliver rather than what it stood for. The symbolic value it once shared with the Armée de Libération Nationale (ALN) as the guarantor of national independence and egalitarianism had become severely tarnished. Then the adverse economic conditions of the early 1980s and the government's subsequent austerity policies proved that the party could no longer provide such patronage. Suddenly what once looked like a strong state collapsed almost overnight, when riots broke out. The symbolic role of the FLN and the ALN was irrevocably shattered when the 'People's Army' started shooting at young protestors who had systematically singled out FLN offices and state organizations in Algiers and other major cities. A regime that had remained in power for so long in reality had nothing more than a shared perception of its invincibility with its citizens, and quickly lost its power once the perception changed: President Benjedid's panic speeches in the weeks leading up to the riots, his vacillation during the first few days on what strategy to adopt, and deepening divisions among the top leadership, produced a momentary sense of impotence that was quickly seized on by the young demonstrators and then by the islamists.[12]

Algerian leaders were later to refer to the riots as the catalyst of the country's 'second revolution' that will lead to democracy and greater personal freedom. But the historical analogy is perhaps wrong. What the few days in October 1988 resembled more than anything in the country's recent history is 11 December 1961, when Algerians for the first time took to the streets en masse, pouring from the housing projects of Diar al-Mahsoul and Diar-el Saada into a united demonstration against the French. It was a demonstration that most French historians now agree provoked the psychological realization in the European mind that things could never be as they had been before. Those were precisely the words Chadli Benjedid repeated in his first public speech after the disturbance.

Faced with growing and sustained opposition, and with acute crises of legitimacy, rulers in the Maghreb have attempted partly to reconstruct some of the institutions and agencies that represent the state. Perhaps not surprising in the light of each country's political history, the initial effort in both Algeria and Tunisia has focused on reforming the FLN and the Rassemblement Constitutionnel Démocratique (RCD, formerly the Destour) and on creating some form of political pluralism. Although the rejuvenation of the party in each country had been announced and timidly attempted on several occasions since the later 1970s, it took the removal of Bourguiba and the October 1988 riots in Algeria to make real reform possible. How far this reform or rejuvenation will go remains uncertain. In each country the party has been the victim of personal power and the object of infighting. Indeed, one of the reasons why Qadhafi decided to suppress political parties is based on his notion that 'parties abort democracy'. The party had stopped being a force of progress and produced among its members a feeling of detachment, indifference and cynicism; such was the sclerotic nature of the FLN, for example, that on the eve of the first free local and municipal elections in June 1990, a sizeable minority of the party's apparatchiks defected when its fortunes were clearly declining. In attempting party reform Ben Ali and Benjedid had three choices: to institute a radical restructuring so as to make the party more compatible with the new challenges it now faces; to move towards a multi-party system; to disengage the party from the state. To some extent all three alternatives have been attempted, with varying degrees of success. Much has been done in each country to restructure the party in terms of new people, new ideas and new organization. Both the FLN and the RCD structures, from the local cells up, have been renewed. At the national congress of each party, new delegates have replaced old stalwarts and a certain amount of generational change has taken place.

But clearly internal reform of the kind that both Benjedid and Ben Ali wish to see will take a long time to accomplish; even now the central committee in Tunisia remains filled with designated members, and Algeria's national assembly retains its party apparatchiks – appointed, not elected, before the 1988 riots – who continue to boycott any further political and economic reforms. In addition, each country now has four distinct groups that influence possible reform: mainstream party members, reformers within the party, a (largely powerless) secular opposition, and the islamists. For tactical reasons the first two must engage occasionally in an unstable but almost unavoidable alliance against the islamists.

In both countries the political leadership had hoped that the national pact in 1988 or the preliminary reforms that were made in the wake of the Algerian riots would inaugurate an interim period that could be used to settle remaining inter-party disputes; but this has not happened. Progress in each country towards separating the party from the state has been halting. At the top level both Benjedid and Ben Ali remain head of state, and are in charge of the FLN and the RCD respectively. Both have attempted, however, to foster the separation by creating a stronger and more independent executive: in Algeria several senior ministers no longer belong to the politburo; in Tunisia a presidential council limits its member ministers to governmental functions.

The search for political pluralism and a greater measure of public liberty in each country continues to show the deep scars left by the one-party system, and by the systematic evisceration of all opposition during the 1960s and 1970s. On the surface at least, all Maghrebi countries have made remarkable progress in setting the parameters for a renewed debate on the role of the state: each now has a myriad of political parties and associations that until a few months ago would not have been tolerated; human rights organizations are flourishing and new press codes have been announced. Special institutions that once served exclusively to judge dissenters – the state security court in Algeria and Tunisia, the revolutionary courts in Libya – have been abolished. Libya, with its commitment to people's committees and people's congresses rather than parties, remains the only Maghrebi country where multi-party politics does not exist; but even here some sort of perestroika has been announced by Qadhafi, highlighted by the publication of the *Green Charter of Human Rights* and the release of hundreds of political prisoners (Vandewalle 1990–91 and 1990).

There are, however, a number of important caveats to be noted. The merging multi-party systems in Tunisia and Algeria have so far shown little promise for actual political contestation. Tunisia until now, and Algeria before the June 1990 local municipal elections, could be described as 'hegemonic party systems' where some opposition parties are legal, though in reality they have little or no chance of competing for power against the party that dominates politics. The April 1989 legislative elections in Tunisia, in which no opposition party managed to win a single seat in parliament, provided the first clear indication of the difficulties involved in moving away from a single-party system. In this regard Morocco presents a slight variation. The local and municipal reform of 1976 did delegate real authority over local administration, backed by budgetary power, to elected officials and elections – although certainly not free from inter-ference – are periodically contested at the local and national levels. The June 1990 elections in Algeria have been a significant exception to the trend noted above; but the disastrous result of the elections for the FLN and the threat they constitute for early national elections will undoubtedly not be lost on either Hasan II or Ben Ali!

Furthermore, the proliferation of parties in Algeria or Tunisia has so far had no substantial impact. Indeed, the governments here are reaping the fruits of their own recent labour, and hint at the lingering self-preservation instincts among the top leaders of the RCD and the FLN. The TCD has systematically pre-empted politics in Tunisia by incorporating opposition programmes (and leaders!) into governmental platforms, in effect virtually reducing the political arena to one that pits the dominant party against a still unrecognized islamic party. The hoped-for unity among political contenders after the signing of the national pact in November 1988 did not materialize. It represented Ben Ali's attempt to reach on a more formal basis – but through limited consultation – some form of national consensus: to define a common denominator and a mini-mum of principles on which all Tunisians can agree and that can be adopted as a basis for political actions and development.[13] As one former trade union leader who has led several battles against the government said: 'no one would have signed a few months ago, and no one will sign a few months from now.'[14]

Both the fortune of the national pact and the April 1989 legislative elections in Tunisia, as well as the outcome of the June 1990 local and municipal elec-tions in Algeria, provide evidence that each country's attempt at perestroika remains fragile and unco-ordinated. The most worrisome development is clearly that virtually all secular opposition has been destroyed, leaving Benjedid and Ben Ali in a precarious struggle against an islamist movement imbued with a symbolic value both the FLN and the RCD have lost – and growing fast. It also leaves both leaders dependent on a political party whose elites have often perceived security as more important than any real reform – a development that has sparked considerable speculation about the retention or potential for military influence in the politics of each country.[15] Only in Morocco has the social and economic elite shown a sustained ability successfully to merge both security and reform concerns.

Throughout the Maghreb, recentralization of power has paradoxically been linked in part to greater reliance on international capital needed for local development. Relatively small groups of decision makers have become allocative agents, using the 'power of the purse' to pursue specific economic and political goals. As a rentier economy, the Libyan Jamahiriyya represents the most extreme example of this recentralization – or perhaps more accurately, continued centralization – of power. In Morocco, the impact of foreign capital has been more subtle, but perhaps as far reaching. Particularly after the 1981 and 1984 riots, the maintenance of political order had become more dependent on international capital – which can make it possible for the people to buy food – than on the traditional power of rural notables. In all cases this new power has been justified by the wish to reconstruct a state to confront the socio-economic challenges ahead – a barely veiled restating of an earlier strategy which has been shown to be severely flawed.

Clearly, however, neither the *infitah* strategy, nor institutional restructuring or the timid attempt at political pluralism will suffice to allow the state to recapture its lost energy and confidence. Political reforms, at least initially and often for long periods of time, remain the occupation of an elite; economic reforms, however, are popular preoccupations. And here, each state in the Maghreb faces a paradox; it is able – if perhaps not always willing – to move forward much more rapidly with political reforms than with the improvement in the living conditions of most of its people. It is at this precise point that the time lag between the implementation and tangible results of economic policy becomes the politicians' nightmare. For no state in north Africa seems likely to succeed in successfully reconstructing itself without recapturing one of the two pillars that once sustained its fortunes; that of providing patronage, and that of maintaining, at least partly, its social contract.

In the Maghreb, this will undoubtedly be very difficult, partly for the reasons discussed above. Furthermore, in the past, tensions over the maintenance of the social contract were tempered by the implicit consensus provided by the second pillar: the strong symbolic bond between the state and its subjects. The latter has at least in Tunisia and Algeria – and to a lesser extent in Morocco and Libya – been irrevocably altered. The state in the years ahead will have less room to manoeuvre, fewer resources at its disposal, and a greater degree of cynicism or outright contestation to cope with than it has encountered since independence.

The problems of revitalizing the FLN in the wake of the June 1990 elections and the RCD in Tunisia have reopened the question of their usefulness in helping to reconstruct the state. In each country suggestions have been made to create an alternative 'presidential party' that would limit further polarization between the FLN and the Front Islamique du Salut or the RCD and the Mouvement de Tendance Islamique. In Tunisia, Serge Adda had suggested this new party could fall 'within the dynamics of the presidential programme and...in alliance with the Destour but independent of it, will be the guarantor of the values held by civil society and by the defenders of public liberties and human rights'. The same suggestion has been made in Algeria where some observers agree that having failed to reform the FLN, Benjedid may now be tempted to revitalize it. Only in Morocco where the king has managed skilfully to stay this kind of fray has this extreme polarization not taken place.

In stepping back from its traditional etatism the state in the Maghreb has been offered two choices: to hand down authority to lower levels, or to hand decision-making over to non-official actors. It is clear that in all countries some form of subterfuge has taken place: each government in its own way has tried the former and ignored the latter, except for economic purposes. It is hard to avoid the conclusion that in the Maghreb an attempt has been made to reshape economic policies that would allow each country to meet some of the expectations of the new international economic context without upsetting local political arrangements. There has been a growing concern with economic rationality, stimulated by international economic considerations, and a simultaneous attempt to disconnect the two. It is this machiavellian strategy of fusing authoritarian liberalism and the attempt to reap the rewards of a new wave of development without any of its unpleasant side effects that Clifford Geertz has called 'the rise of a combination of a smithean idea of how to get rich with a hobbesian idea of how to govern'.

It is not surprising then that a heavy dose of state centralized economic planning remains and that every move towards economic and political liberalization has been difficult to adopt and more often than not matched by a retrenchment of liberties in other areas or by an increase in bureaucratic control. Indeed, during the phase of Algeria's *infitah* that lasted until the October 1988 riots, it remained unclear whether its slow pace and restrictive scope concerning reform of the public sector was not simply an attempt by the state to postpone such reform, but rather represented an attempt instead to impose a new division of economic tasks that shifted the burden of efficiency toward non-state actors while leaving the state ultimately in charge. To that extent it resembled what C.H. Moore has noted for another case:

> Changing patterns of allocations rather than ownership may produce the kind of political economies that will give an exhaustive statist regime a new lease of life. Instead of managing economic exchanges directly, such a regime may manage them indirectly, while still continuing in principle to own the means of production. Supporting client groups then becomes less expensive because some of the costs are farmed out... (Moore 1986).

To conclude, let us say that judging from Tunisia's legislative elections in 1989, and Algeria's first municipal elections in June 1990, followed by the interruption of the electoral process in December 1991, north African governments are willing to proceed to some extent with economic liberalization, but they are much slower and more hesitant when it comes to proceeding with a genuine 'democratic transition'. The opening up of the political system remains controlled, and political parties are allowed only when they do not enjoy a broad social base; those with wide support are simply forbidden. To liberalize the economy but to keep control of the political process resembles very much Clifford Geertz's notion of 'authoritarian liberalism'.

What sustains this option of 'authoritarian liberalism' is a kind of collusion between political elites on one hand and entrepreneurs on the other. As long as this collusion persists, it is difficult to see how government accountability can develop knowing that, without it, democracy can hardly make any sense.

Equally important is the incoherent class structure which evolved out of the great bifurcation between those groups and classes that are incorporated into the world economy and those groups and classes that are excluded from it. To the extent that the islamists managed to appeal to the deprived and to the excluded, that is, all groups that are victims of state disengagement, most of the middle classes have lent their support to the status quo, thereby reinforcing the authoritarian-liberal formula. These are the lessons of Tunisia and Algeria where the future of north Africa is being written.

Notes

1   Speech by President Ben Ali at the closing of the special Congrès du Salut reported in *Al-Sabah*, 2 August 1988.

2   *al-Wathiqa al-khadra al-kubra al-huquq al-insan di asr al-jamahir* (Tripoli; The Green Book Centre, n.d.)....The charter was adopted by the general people's congress at al-Bayda on 12 June 1988.

3   See for example the interview by Mouloud Hamrouche, current prime minister of Algeria, in *L'Express* of 13 October 1989, in which he states that: 'reform in Algeria necessitates austerity. There will be no more blood, I hope (referring to the 1988 riots), but tears, yes.'

4   The 'Destour' has been renamed the 'Néo-Destour' the 'Parti Socialiste Destourien' and under the reforms by Ben Ali, 'The Rassemblement Démocratique Socialiste'.

5   *The New State* was the title of a book written by Muhammad Sayah, one of Bourguiba's closest advisers for most of his years in power.

6   See the conclusion to Eqbal Ahmed's doctoral dissertation, 'Politics and Labor in Tunisia', (Princeton University 1987). The answer to Ahmed's question was provided in 1978 and December 1985 when the Bourguiba government felt compelled to once again clamp down on the union.

7   See the letter from Khalil to president Ben Ali, 'Lettre de Ismaïl Khélil au Président de la république', reproduced in *Réalités,* 16 September 1988, pp. 12–14. Khalil reiterated his demand for economic liberalization and privatization in *Le Renouveau*, 5

August 1988.

8 The investment code was adopted in January 1983.

9 Both systems' notion of socialism, however, excluded the idea of class struggle. A good summary of Algeria's concept of socialism can be found in Etienne (1977). See in particular page 32: '...Algeria rejects marxism-leninism as being an ideology foreign to Africa; if it is inspired (by socialism) it is to blend with other legacies such as Islam, arabism and nationalism....' For Tunisia consult Moore (1965) and the appropriate chapters in Anderson (1986).

10 A good synopsis of these gradual reassessments can be found in Chatleus (1984).

11 Consult Djaït 'La deuxième heure', *Réalités,* 11–17 September 1988.

12 A more detailed account of the October 1988 riots and the challenges of opportunities they provided can be found in Vandewalle (1988–89).

13 Letter of Ben Ali addressed to all Tunisian national organizations and personalities, published in *Le Renouveau,* 5 August 1988.

14 Comment by Habib Achour to Vandewalle at the Carthage Palace, 7 November 1988. M. Achour is the former leader of the Union Générale des Travailleurs Tunisiens who confronted the Bourguiba regime on several occasions. He resigned from all UGTT activities a few weeks before the signing of the National Pact, at the request of Ben Ali.

15 For Algeria, consult Zartman (1987); for Tunisia see Ware (1985).

10

The Private Sector, Economic Liberalization, and the Prospects of Democratization: the case of Syria and some other Arab countries[1]

VOLKER PERTHES

Regarding their economic conditions, the Arab countries are passing through a period of historical change. There is a general tendency in all Arab countries to give the private sector more chances to participate in, and contribute to, economic life and economic developments.

Union of Arab Chambers 1991, 9

At many places, the world witnesses an expansion of democracy...while our Arab nation, in many of its countries, witnesses a persistent absence of all appearances of democracy.

Union of Arab Lawyers 1991, 148

Syria, like other countries in the region, has embarked on a course of economic liberalization in response to the severe economic crisis it faced in the 1980s. Though limited in comparison to what orthodox economists might dream of, Syria's economic reform programme was wide-ranging. Most importantly, the role of the private sector increased. The Syrian government also implemented some changes of formal regime structures, thereby, partly at least, responding to the dissipation into Syria of a regionwide discourse stressing the need for the Arab world to join in with a perceived international trend toward democracy, pluralism, and participation.

Carried away by wishful thinking which sometimes comes true, students of the ongoing changes in economic policies and political structures in the Arab world and other 'adjusting' developing countries may be tempted to assume a natural sequence of different features of change. This chapter asks for a more cautious approach. Neither are economic liberalization and democratization simply two sides of one coin – and it is far from clear whether the one necessarily demands the second – nor can elections be equated with democracy; and 'pluralism', a term which has become common currency in the official political language of the Arab world, and 'representation' do not necessarily mean participation in decision making, or democracy. To arrive at more general propositions about the relation of economic liberalization, private-sector growth, and the prospects of democratization in Syria or any of the other states under consideration, we should try to analyse: the impact of economic liberalization on the private sector and the role the private sector seems to play in decision making on economic policies; the scope and social content of political 'pluralization'; and the stakes that the ruling elite, the private sector and other forces of 'civil society' have in both economic and political restructuring.

Patterns of infitah

Syria's development path is by no means unique. There are not only general trends common to almost all developing countries, such as the exchange of development approaches focusing on import-substitution for others favouring export-led growth at some point in the 1970s or 1980s. Parallels are more striking, and differences more meaningful, when Syria is compared to some of her fellow Arab states with similar socio-economic conditions. The Arab states in general, despite their conflicts and discrepancies, not only show a high level of political and social interaction, and common political, economic, and socio-cultural features; they share also largely common, or at least mutually influenced, official and public discourses about, among other things, politics and development. All this makes it feasible to use the Arab regional system as a frame of comparative reference for each of its member states. In this chapter comparisons will be drawn between Syria and, to a varying extent, Egypt, Iraq, Tunisia and Jordan. All of them are middle-income countries, and they also range in the midfield of the Arab system as regards per capita purchasing power (al-Milaff al-ihsa'i 1992, 187, 190). Syria, Egypt, and Tunisia are minor oil producers. Iraq is a major oil state but is not a capital-surplus economy. Iraq's oil income could be absorbed locally, and the country has followed an oil-backed import substitution strategy which compares more easily to Syria or Tunisia than to the oil monarchies in the Gulf. Syria, Egypt, Iraq and Tunisia are republican systems which, for some time at least during the 1950s and 1960s, followed a supposedly socialist development path. In Egypt, Syria and Iraq, this socialist orientation involved land reforms and sweeping nationalizations of bigger commercial and industrial enterprises; and in all four countries it entailed far-reaching state control over foreign and, to a lesser extent, wholesale trade. The Kingdom of Jordan has always claimed a liberal economic system. Tunisia and Egypt officially buried their socialist orientations in the early 1970s; Syria and Iraq implemented a limited economic *infitah* (opening) towards the West and towards their domestic private sectors at the same time. In all five countries, still, economic development and growth remained state-led throughout the 1970s at least (Richards & Waterbury 1990, 239ff). Public expenditure increased tremendously by virtue of oil rents, Arab assistance, or easily available foreign credit. As foreign exchange accruing directly to the treasury seemed to be plentiful, government spending was lavish, and import policies relatively liberal. Private-sector activities increased in general, largely as a direct or indirect effect of increased government spending, and mainly in commerce, services and construction. The state, however, remained the main investor, and the public sector of each of the countries grew as fast as, and sometimes faster than, the private. In Jordan, for example, despite its constitutional private economy orientation, only a third of the national economy could be regarded as actually subject to free-market conditions, the rest being part of a more or less protected public or joint private-public sector (Sha'ir 1990, 645). In Tunisia, the *infitah* of the 1970s was accompanied by the establishment of more than 100 new state enterprises and a rise of total government expenditure relative to GNP from less than 30 to more than 40 per cent (Grissa 1991, 112). Development policies aimed at rapid modernization and quick growth, centring on import-substituting industrialization. At some point between the mid-1970s and mid-1980s these experiments ran into crisis: the public-sector industrial base was largely dependent on foreign inputs while it contributed little to exports; agriculture had been neglected and imports soared; expanded civil services and generally overstaffed, underproductive public sectors became a heavy burden on state budgets and contributed to the accumulation of foreign debt. When oil rents and foreign aid began to decrease from around 1983 onwards, and in several cases even prior to that, the structural deficits resulting from this development strategy became obvious (Humsi 1984, 223ff; Richards & Waterbury 1990, 219ff).

Syria's economic problems became conspicuous in the early 1980s when the government first tried to limit 'luxury' imports and then gradually began to stop the provision by the state-run bank system of foreign exchange to private importers. As of 1984 private importers had to provide their own foreign exchange and even public-sector enterprises could hardly obtain their foreign currency needs. This scarcity of foreign exchange was self-exacerbating since it led to shortages of imported industrial and agricultural supplies and even of basic consumer goods, and thereby to substantial decreases in industrial production and, subsequently, to increased black-market imports, rising inflation, and a rapid decrease in the value of the Syrian pound. In 1986, Syria almost went into foreign-exchange bankruptcy and began to delay its payments on World Bank debts (Kanovsky 1986; Perthes 1992b).

To cope with its economic problems, the Syrian government began to implement a programme of austerity and gradual economic restructuring, or adjustment. Since 1985, the features of a second *infitah* have become increasingly apparent. This new *infitah* was qualitatively different from that of the 1970s. In that earlier period public resources seemed almost unlimited and the state, by means of its expenditures, led economic development, opening or expanding existing fields for profitable private-sector activities. In the 1980s, however, with diminishing public resources and austerity budgets, the government tried to mobilize private capital and skim off some of its profits, thus hoping to uphold the state's sphere of operation and to save both the public sector and national and local government agencies from bankruptcy. Thus, foreign exchange regulations were liberalized step by step, allowing exporters eventually either to keep most of their foreign-currency earnings for their own imports, to sell their foreign exchange to the banks for what in all but name was a free-market rate for the pound, or to assign it to other importers through the banks. By the early 1990s, the banks, instead of being a state-owned means of control over private exports and imports, were thus reduced to the role of an intermediary – at best. Several government monopolies over the import of, and trade in, certain foodstuffs were lifted, as were some – not all – government monopolies over the trade in those domestic agricultural products that were regarded as strategic. Where such monopolies persisted, as was the case for wheat, cotton and sugar beet, government procurement prices were raised substantially. In 1986, a law was passed which legalized and assigned considerable privileges to foreign, Syrian-expatriate, and domestic Syrian investments in agricultural 'mixed-sector' projects. 'Mixed' refers to private-sector/state-sector joint ventures which actually are run as private shareholding companies since the government, holding a minority share, does not interfere with the conduct of business. Private industrial investments were also warmly welcomed. It took, however, several years, until the legal frame was remodelled so as to serve this goal. After most restrictions on private industrial investments had been gradually removed, an investment law was passed in 1991 which contained substantial measures of encouragement for domestic and foreign investments in industry or other fields. At the same time, the tax law was reformed (Perthes 1992b, Heydemann 1992).

Like Syria, Tunisia, Egypt, Jordan and Iraq all responded to their economic crises with a tangible drive towards a second, or deeper, *infitah* at some point during the second half of the 1980s. Tunisia started to implement an IMF-negotiated structural adjustment programme in 1986 which included a general liberalization of the economy from central government surveillance towards a stronger orientation toward the world market, and clear intent to privatize parts of the public sector (Ayari 1990; Moore 1991). In Egypt, several important measures to readjust the Egyptian economy towards a free-market system were implemented in 1987, including the creation of a free currency market through private banks (Union of Arab Chambers 1991, 509). Iraq also began a major move toward liberalization and privatization in 1987 (Lawson 1990; Chaudry 1991). Jordan increasingly tried to revitalize its private sector from 1985 and in 1989 signed an agreement with the IMF the prime concern of which was to liberalize foreign trade policies (Sha'ir 1990; Union of Arab Chambers 1991, 177ff).

There are considerable similarities to the sequence of measures adopted in each of these countries to encourage private economic activities. Parallels, in particular, lie in the initial emphasis of *infitah* policies, in Egypt, Iraq, or Tunisia, as in Syria, on increased freedom for private trade, and the gradual deregulation – where such a regulation existed in the first place – of the foreign-exchange market. Agricultural liberalization seems mostly to start with measures to encourage large-scale, domestic and foreign, investments, before allowing, in a second stage, individual peasants more freedom of decision on production and marketing. The former purpose required, in Egypt, Syria and Iraq, that the land-reform laws of the 1950s and 1960s be circumvented by new legislation that allowed the privatization of state land and reassured private investors. An outright abolition of the land-reform laws which still set upper limits to land-ownership was out of the question since such a move would offend a substantial part of the peasantry and probably open the way for excessive disputes between former landowners and beneficiaries of the land-reform. Thus, in Egypt, the establishment of joint-venture agricultural companies that would own large areas of land was allowed in 1981. In Iraq, long-term leases of vast estates of government land to private investors were made legal in 1983, as was the purchase of government land by the private sector in 1987. In Syria, as mentioned above, a 1986 law permitted the establishment of mixed sector agricultural companies. The government's share in each of these companies is paid in the form of reclaimed or virgin state land (Springborg 1990, 458 and 1986, 37; Hopfinger 1990).

Measures to effectively encourage domestic industrial activities came relatively late. In Syria, as mentioned, an investment law that provided equal encouragements and privileges to private and mixed sector industrial ventures, as had been allowed to 'mixed' hotel and tourism companies in 1977 and to agro-capitalist ventures in 1986, did not come into being until 1991. In Egypt, foreign investments in industry and Egyptian/foreign joint ventures were encouraged and privileged as early as 1974; Egyptian capital, however, was put on an equal footing with Arab and other foreign capital only in 1989 (Hill 1989). In Iraq, substantial measures to encourage domestic industry were put into effect in 1988, while import and wholesale trade, construction and agrobusiness had been the prime beneficiaries of preceding liberalization measures (*al-Nashra al-iqtisadiyya* [Baghdad], July 1990, 7ff; Lawson 1990, 40ff). Tunisia, whose leadership since the early 1970s explicitly aimed at creating a new class of private industrialists, seems to be a notable exception (Bellin 1991, 50ff). In the other cases, the initial commercial bias of economic reform became even more apparent since measures to encourage industrial ventures need far more time to show results than those to encourage commercial and service activities.

Privatization certainly was a feature of each of these economic restructuring programmes. Its scope, however, was limited and has nowhere meant anything like the dissolution of these countries' large public sectors. In Syria, actual privatization of public assets was limited to the transfer of agricultural land from government or co-operative property – by means of mixed-sector agrocompanies and by the dissolution and sale of unproductive state farms and 'production co-operatives,[2] – and the privatization of a limited number of touristic establishments, including a vocational school for tourism and hotel management. Besides that, however, there was a substantial de facto privatization of productive capacities and of public monopolies over foreign and internal trade. Since 1989, for example, the private sector has been allowed to import certain raw materials provided they pay public-sector companies such as the Hama iron and steel plant in foreign currency or in kind for the service of having them processed, i.e. by providing the public sector with some of the inputs the latter could not afford because of its foreign-exchange shortage. In 1990, the monopoly of public-sector trade agencies to import several basic foodstuffs and trade them domestically was lifted (Dalila 1990, 425ff; Perthes 1992b, 46ff). However, in such countries as Tunisia and also Egypt, the actual privatization of assets remained more limited than expected. Privatization measures mainly consisted of the transfer of government land, and a limited number of touristic and light industry establishments to the private sector, and of privatization by liberalization, i.e. the lifting of public-sector trade or service monopolies (Bouaouaja 1989; Grissa 1991; Springborg 1989, 259f). In Jordan, the partial or complete privatization of several state-sector companies, including the national airline, has been envisaged since 1986. So far (mid-1992), however, the process has remained in its initial, preparatory stage. Only Iraq actually sold a considerable part of government assets, including some larger factories for construction material and agro-industrial complexes, to the private sector (Lawson 1990, 32ff; Chaudry 1991; *al-Nashra al-iqtisadiyya*, July 1990, 7ff).

In contrast to Tunisia, Egypt or Jordan, Syria's adjustment programme, like that of Iraq, was home-made and not dictated in some form or another by the IMF or other foreign agencies. There are still differences regarding the extent of the openness to the world economy of the Iraqi and Syrian economies on the one hand, and the Egyptian, Jordanian, or Tunisian on the other. Direct foreign investment, in particular, is comparatively limited in both Syria and Iraq outside the oil sector. Iraq had not until 1991, and Syria has yet not allowed the establishment of private banks or opened an official stock exchange. Discussions about permitting private banking and a stock-exchange are under way in Syria (Ammash 1992, 99f, 120; Interview Ihsan Sanqar, Tishrin 9 December 1991; *al-Sharq al-Awsat*, 5 March 1993), and both countries – Iraq with its law on Arab investment of 1989, Syria with its investment law of 1991 – expressed their intent to allow foreign capital in on a larger scale than before. It seems, thus, that in terms of the economy and liberalization and privatization measures, it makes little difference whether or not the IMF imposes economic adjustment programmes.

Private sector developments

The most notable result of the second *infitah* Syria experienced in the second half of the 1980s was a remarkable growth of the private sector. In 1990, for the first time since 1963, private-sector capital investments outgrew those of the public sector. The private sector's share of foreign trade, which had decreased to some 10 per cent of the total in the early 1980s, rose to more than 20 per cent in 1986 and to 45 per cent in 1990. The private-sector contribution to Syria's manufacturing industry's net domestic product increased, according to official data, from 30–35 per cent in the mid-1980s to 43–44 per cent at the end of the decade (SAR 1988, 1991).[3] According to the Damascus Chamber of Commerce (1991, 9), the private sector now contributed 55 per cent of Syria's domestic product, covering 98.6 per cent of agriculture, 72 per cent of transport, 62 per cent of trade, 59 per cent of finance and rents, 50 per cent of building and construction, 37 per cent of manufacturing industries, and 13 per cent of services. Throughout the 1970s and 1980s, the private sector had employed some 60 per cent or more of Syria's industrial labour force, including construction; in 1991 the private sector's share crossed the 75 per cent mark (SAR 1992, 77).

The improvement of the private sector's position in the national economy as it is reflected in all available statistics was in the first place the result of the public sector's deteriorating performance.[4] Nevertheless, there was overall real growth in the private sector, accompanied by a partial restructuring within the private economy. Branches that grew exceptionally were those that had always been regarded as the most profitable and were now, as was the case during the first *infitah* in the 1970s, the prime beneficiaries of the reform package: import-export trade and commissioneering, land and property, services, internal trade with imported or locally manufactured consumer goods for mainly upper and upper middle-class use. Industry was, and still is, regarded as the more difficult way to profit. Income from trade is, on average, almost three times that of industry. Throughout the 1970s and the mid-1980s, therefore, big business, in Syrian terms, was limited to commercial enterprise.

The economic crisis of the 1980s affected both public and private manufacturing, whereas it generally did not harm private commerce and trade. Workshops and private industrial establishments that had been obtaining imported inputs via public sector channels were particularly hard hit by the crisis. Many small artisans and industrial workshops had increasingly to depend on merchants and middlemen to supply their raw materials or spare parts. Industries with export options and their own access to foreign exchange withstood the crisis better and were the first to benefit from the gradual deregulation of the foreign-exchange market and the lifting of import restrictions for those who could convincingly lay claim to legal access to foreign exchange. Since 1985, a considerable number of larger industrial establishments, employing a workforce of 50, 100 or even more, have been set up, many of them with Syrian expatriate, i.e. in all but name foreign, capital.

Both crisis and economic reform have thus contributed to the reinforcement, throughout the private sector, of an initial trend towards concentration within the private economy: the emergence of a remarkable group of larger-scale private establishments, in terms of capital, turnover, profits, and – as far as industry is concerned – employment, and an increasing gap between this upper stratum and the vast petty-bourgeois majority of Syria's private sector. Out of Syria's 85,000 industrial establishments registered at the Ministry of Industry in 1987, only an estimated 1,500 to 1,800 employed a workforce of 10 or more (Perthes 1992c). In 1990, the average capital of newly established private industrial projects did not exceed US$30,000, whereas the average capital invested in new industrial and service companies established according to the investment law of 1991 exceeded US$4 million (SAR 1991, 168; Damascus Chamber of Commerce 1992, 15).[5] Most larger commercial and even industrial establishments owed their position to some sort of deal struck, and to continuous business, with the public sector, or to specific privileges and even monopolies farmed out by the state to 'mixed-sector' companies in particular. Business with the state could, but did not necessarily, involve illegal practices. It did include the mediating of public-sector imports, the use of public-sector productive capacities, subsidized access to intermediary products from public-sector production, or the lucrative participation in Syria's exports-for-debt swaps with the former Soviet Union (Perthes 1992c).

Comparable developments could be witnessed in other countries under consideration. Private-sector activities generally started to increase considerably, both relative to the public sector and absolutely, as austerity and reform measures began to take effect. In Iraq, for example, with its dominant (public) oil sector, the private economy has always been of lesser importance – relative to the whole – than was the case in Syria. Development trends were nevertheless very similar. According to the Baghdad Chamber of Commerce, the Iraqi private sector's share of the domestic product increased from 18.6 per cent in 1980 to 33.6 per cent in 1988; its investment share rose from 21.5 to 27.8 per cent of the total, and its share of the industrial labour force from 31.9 to 45 per cent (*al-Nashra al-iqtisadiyya*, July 1990, pp. 6–10). In all countries, the private sector remained overwhelmingly small-scale while a new stratum of comparatively big business – and a new bourgeoisie – emerged in the 1970s and 1980s. This new bourgeoisie was mainly engaged in commerce, often in agriculture, to a lesser extent in industry, and sometimes in construction. Its common feature was that, for the most part, it was virtually created or at least nourished by the state. Prominent examples of this pattern are Egypt's famous Uthman Ahmad Uthman with his half-public, half-private construction empire (Baker 1990, 15ff; Springborg 1980, 38ff) or Iraq's contractor bourgeoisie, which is closely tied in to the regime. In Syria, no similar layer of influential building contractors has emerged, since the government established several large public-sector construction companies with the first *infitah* and the construction boom of the 1970s, the two biggest under the control of the Ministry of Defence. Some Syrian businessmen who had been working with remunerative government building contracts before, like A'idi or Yaqubian, were driven out of the construction business and had to engage in different fields, A'idi thereby becoming a privileged quasi-monopolist for luxury hotels and an effective privatizer of government establishments in this sector. Most of the illustrious, and a great number of less illustrious, Syrian state-fed businessmen worked in trade and related sectors. True capitalist entrepreneurs who, as Springborg defines them, 'perceive a market for goods and services and attempt more or less without assistance from the state to fill that market' did emerge in all the countries considered. Generally, however, they form the lower stratum of the bourgeoisie (Springborg 1989, 63ff; Khafaji 1986; Chaudry 1991; Sha'ir 1990, 645; Bellin 1991; Perthes 1991).

Increasing differentiation within the private sector has also led to a differentiation of economic interests and expectations regarding government policies. It has been noticed, with regard to Syria and other countries, that a certain part of the bourgeoisie, particularly its newer segments with close connections to the state and the public sector, sometimes referred to as the 'parasitic bourgeoisie' (Imam 1986; Khafaji 1986; Springborg 1989), has no interest in anything beyond limited liberalization (Richards & Waterbury 1990, 223f). They could not have gained anything like their current prominent positions in a free-market system; fully-fledged liberalization would put them at risk (Springborg 1989, 87; Perthes 1992c). Also, many industrialists are in favour of continued protection of national industries against foreign competition (Sadowski 1991, 95ff). Such a limited, or 'selective' liberalization (Heydemann 1992), as applied in all the countries under consideration, remains short of what should happen according to orthodox economic theory. It fails to abolish all subsidies, to expose public and private economic units to full-scale competition, and to privatize more than parts of the public sector which, so it seems, is there to stay in all Arab countries, albeit on a limited scale and forced to adopt more business-like behaviour. This may dissatisfy international monetary and aid agencies (Springborg 1989, 255ff; Sadowski 1991, 261ff) but it does not necessarily mean that the respective regimes are disregarding or counteracting the dominant interest of the private sector.

The limitations of political reform and 'pluralism'

The process of economic liberalization has brought about changes which, though limited in extent, are clearly more than just superficial and will not, it seems, be easily revocable. This is because of both the enhanced position of the private sector and the low probability that any of the states under consideration will once again have access to as substantial a rent income – in relation to the size of its economy – as in the mid-1970s.

Political reforms, in contrast, have been of a much more limited scope. Syria has, in 1990, seen the abolition of parts of the Emergency Law. 'Economic crimes', in particular, have been transferred from state security courts to the civil jurisdiction. The measure was thus part of economic rather than political liberalization. In 1991 and 1992, thousands of political prisoners were set free. The release of a substantial number of Syria's political prisoners was more than a pure propaganda move vis-à-vis the domestic and foreign, especially the US, public, where interest in human rights abuses in Syria had been increasing in the context of intensified US–Syrian interaction. Primarily, the act expressed a certain relaxation of domestic political strain, but it remained very much embedded in the form of an authoritarian presidential monarchy granting private amnesties on occasion – end of Ramadan or the beginning of a new presidential term of office – and it can hardly be seen as a sign of political change.

The system, nevertheless, has not remained entirely unchanged. In May 1990, Syrians were called to the polls to elect an enlarged parliament or *majlis al-sha'b* in which about one-third of the seats were reserved for 'independent' candidates, i.e. for deputies elected as individuals outside the common list of the Ba'th party and its smaller allies in the National Progressive Front. There was considerable competition among independent candidates and apparently only limited fraud – most candidates anyhow praised in some form or another the wise leadership of President Asad who had granted this democratic venture. Regarding the display of loyalty to the country's leader, the new parliament was not distinguishable from its predecessors. In 1991, the *majlis* unanimously nominated Hafiz al-Asad for a fourth term of office as president to which he was duly elected with what was claimed to be a 99.8 per cent majority of all Syrians eligible to vote. The powers of the president remain, constitutionally and as a matter of fact, almost absolute. The president, who at the same time is the general secretary of the regional (Syrian) and national (pan-Arab) command of the Ba'th Party and of the Syrian National Progressive Front as well as the supreme leader of the armed forces, appoints the prime minister and the cabinet and it is to him that the government is responsible. According to the constitution, the president can legislate by decree and without parliamentary participation, and, if circumstances so demand, he can veto parliamentary laws and dissolve parliament. Constitutional changes require his approval.

The duties – or rights – of parliament remain limited. There are certain red lines, well known to all, which must not be transgressed in parliamentary or public discussion: essentially, any critique of the president and the policy fields regarded as his own prerogative – security, defence and foreign policy (Seale 1991, 109) – would be a step over the red line. Parliamentary discussion and parliament's role in decision making shall, according to the regime's own idea which so far has not been challenged, be confined to 'non-political' issues. In an address to parliament in December 1991, Prime Minister Zu'abi explained that the 'democratic system in Syria' was embodied in the co-operation of government and parliament through which 'the people participate in the making of all decisions that relate to their economy and their daily affairs' (*al-Thawra*, 1 January 1992). The Syrian parliament thus functions as a consultative, quasi-corporatist forum, resembling to some extent the *shura*–councils of more traditional regimes (Cantori 1991, 6; Perthes 1992). For the regime, it is a place for consultation on request, that is, the discussion of bills. For more than a decade, all laws that have been passed by parliament have been introduced by the executive. Government performance in the fields of economy and services can be discussed, as can the legitimate local and group interests of acknowledged groups. The council as a whole is supposed to support the supreme authority, personified in the president, who will decide all matters of national concern. For individual deputies, parliament is a place to build up and cultivate connections, to supply *wasta* (mediation) to their clientele or constituency, to raise issues generally related to economy and services, and to draw attention to forgotten local problems. Oppositional tendencies would not be helpful; a deputy who is close to the regime will most probably be a more effective mediator than anyone with an anti-government stance.

Although the Syrian parliament is not, and is not intended to be, a democratic counterweight to the government, Syria's parliamentary reform of 1990, when the number of parliamentary seats was increased to include a larger number of independents, is not without significance. The parliament still has an absolute majority of Ba'thists securing the representation of all those forces that formed the traditional basis of the regime. Most Ba'thist deputies, representing the party itself, the trade unions, peasant union and other mass organizations, represent at the same time bureaucracy and the public sector, which are by no means negligible forces despite being at the losing end of the economic restructuring process.

The independent element, on the other hand, consists mainly of professionals and other elements of the educated middle class, of businessmen, especially of the new commercial bourgeoisie, and of a score of tribal leaders and men of religion, several of whom had served as independent deputies in previous councils. The increase in the number of independents thus demonstrates the relative decline in importance of the bureaucracy and the public sector as they reflect the regime's attempts to broaden its base by incorporating into formal regime structures an additional number of traditional elements, and, for the first time, private-sector representatives. It is also a sign that the Ba'th Party itself, though still needed for the control of some sectors of the population and as a patronage-generating network, has lost its ideological leadership and its once central role in policy-making. The Ba'thi majority in parliament is still useful in guarding the regime against too ambitious a role which representatives of the new economic forces might, at some point in the future, try to play. For the 'liberalizing' president, however, it seems, his own party with its 'pre-modern' functionaries and their socialist-radical discourse had become somewhat annoying. During the presidential campaign of 1991, the party was forced to keep a low profile, and it was publicly humiliated on the day of the referendum. While the party regional command waited for Asad in a Damascus military school turned polling station to cast his vote in their midst, the president showed up in the affluent Malki area, close to his office, accompanied not by party or government officials but by Badr al-Din Shallah, the veteran president of the Damascus Chamber of Commerce. The symbolism of the photo distributed by Syria's SANA news agency, showing Shallah's *tarbush* – headgear worn today by only a small group of traditional-minded businessmen – beside the president was well understood by the Syrian public.

Compared to Syria, or to Iraq whose parliament (*al-majlis al-watani*) sufficiently proved its rubberstamp character during the second Gulf War, both electoral and parliamentary participation in Egypt, Tunisia and Jordan are certainly wider in extent. Egypt can be said to have experienced two successive experiments in democratization. Sadat aborted his own attempt to establish a limited party pluralism from above when his experiment, creating democratic expectations that the regime was not prepared to fulfil, got out of hand and opposition parties started to oppose even Sadat's foreign policy (Nafi 1988; Hinnebusch 1985, 220ff; Zartman 1990). Mubarak opened out the system once again. Egypt's present political scene gives room for real opposition parties which to some extent represent different socio-economic projects, although the regime restricts their freedom of action and is extremely rigid in withholding permission for new parties to be established. There is real competition for voters although electoral laws and even electoral fraud limit the opposition's chances of ever winning a parliamentary majority. The parliamentary opposition can, as Springborg puts it, 'embarrass the government' but it cannot make any serious inroads at its expense; both elections and parliament 'are sites of unequal contest' (Springborg 1989, 192, 197) between a weak opposition and a government that tries to use limited democratization essentially as a safety-valve with which to control popular discontent (Springborg 1989; Dessouki 1990; Makram-Ebeid 1989; Nafi 1988). In Tunisia, the takeover of Ben Ali in November 1987 brought in a regime which explicitly committed itself to democratization. The space for oppositional activities was opened, parties were legalized, and multi-party elections held in 1989. Still, the regime refused to allow the establishment as a political party of the most powerful opposition force, the islamists, and the electoral laws were so tailored that the president's party took all the seats – leaving the parliament without even an embarrassing opposition. The most far-reaching democratization has been taking place in Jordan. Popular unrest in spring 1989 revealed the depth of the political and economic crisis the country had run into. Responding to this precarious situation, the regime decided to pluralize and democratize the system. In November that year elections were held which, although some gerrymandering did occur and parties were not allowed, probably were the freest ever held in an Arab state. These elections brought in a substantial opposition, both from the left and from the islamist right (Abu Jaber & Fathi 1990; Amawi 1992). Observers noted that this opposition proved weaker in parliament than it had seemed on the streets (Duclos 1990, 68ff), and the subsequent steps of the democratization process – the abolition of the emergency law and the passing of a party law – actually seemed to follow the regime's agenda rather than being pushed forward by parliament. Parliamentary discussion is still limited insofar as any critique of the monarch and his decisions is taboo. Apart from this, however, many parliamentarians show little restraint in their attempts to embarrass the government and demand change.[6] Furthermore, the Jordanian case represents a remarkable contrast to that of Egypt or Tunisia as well as to that of Syria or Iraq insofar as, since the elections of 1989, Jordanian governments have had to find themselves a parliamentary majority and have been able to do so only by compromising on cabinet posts and policies.

Three features regarding electoral and parliamentary participation, which are common to a greater or lesser extent to all countries under consideration, as to most other Arab states, are worth pointing out. The first is that their respective heads of state remain practically unaccountable. They enjoy wide prerogatives in, at least, security and foreign affairs. Since real elections have hitherto been limited, at best, to the legislative, the strongest decision-makers remain outside the field of competition (Salih 1991, 101). Secondly, all incumbent regimes, even if they allow elections to run freely, have still maintained at least some restrictions on the establishment of parties. Jordan's new party law, however, is exceptional; it rules that parties must not be financed from abroad, but it does not in principle prevent any ideological current from establishing a party (*Jordan Times*, 22 August 1992). Tunisia and Egypt do not allow the formation of islamist parties. In Syria, as well as Iraq, apart from the Ba'th, only such parties as have agreed to subordinate themselves to a de facto single-party system have been allowed. In 1992, Syria's president hinted that new parties may be established. He made it clear, however, that this could only mean the addition of new 'patriotic' groups to the Ba'th-dominated National Progressive Front (*al-Ba'th*, 13 March 1992). In all cases, including Jordan, the establishment of parties is subject to some sort of official approval (Thabit 1992, 12ff; Salih 1991, 100). The Algerian case whose shortlived democratization led not only to the emergence of a virtually unrestricted multi-party system (Hudson 1991a, 414) but also to the clear victory in the elections of December 1991 of the only real alternative to the incumbent power, has almost certainly determined even the 'democratizing' leaders of Egypt and Tunisia to maintain their restrictive policy regarding the establishment of political parties.

The third common feature is that wherever a privileged president's or regime party exists, this party itself has hardly undergone any internal democratization. Jordan alone of the countries under consideration has no regime party, and this might have contributed to the remarkable free competition in its 1989 elections. The decision of both Mubarak and Ben Ali after their respective successions to power to take over, formally or de facto, the leadership of the regime party with the presidency, indicated their intention to avoid a headlong plunge into pluralism (Zartman 1991, 17; Springborg 1989, 157). In several cases, most obviously in Egypt and Tunisia, regime parties have been transformed ideologically and in terms of membership according to the shifting orientations of the regime.

Important policy decision have, more often than not, been taken without any consultation with the wider party leadership. Not only the Syrian but more astonishingly also the Egyptian president has over the years failed to convene a single general party congress. Tunisia's Ben Ali continues just as his predecessor did or as Syria's Asad does to appoint instead of having elected more than half of the members of the RCD's central committee. Regime parties are used as power instruments by their countries' political leadership, but they are certainly not intended to develop into an independent centre of power (Abu Amud 1988, 119; Leveau 1989, 9; Springborg 1989, 155ff; Perthes 1990, 250ff; Zartman 1991, 17f). Popular participation through the regime party, which could theoretically be a democratic alternative to open multi-party competition, is therefore in practice extremely limited.

In its own propaganda, the Syrian regime may call itself democratic. More cautious, and frequently used in the recent official discourse about the development of political structures not only in Syria, is the term 'pluralism' (*ta'addudiyya*); even the Iraqi leadership, both before and after the second Gulf war, has been speaking about democracy and *ta'addudiyya* (Hudson 1991; Salih 1991). For decades, the term 'democracy' has been used by many regimes of the region, frequently in connection with 'popular', to back their claim that they were actually expressing the people's wish. This claim of 'revolutionary', 'national', or 'socialist' authoritarian regimes, between the 1950s and the 1970s, found some popular and a great deal of intellectual support (Jabiri 1992, 9f; Kanz 992, 72f). This is no longer so. In the recent intellectual discourse of the Arab world 'democracy' is more and more operationalized according to the concept of liberal democracy, i.e. as a form of government whose attributes are human rights, free political organization, government accountability and the principle of change of government through periodic elections (Abd al-Majid 1990, 81ff; Salih 1991). The recent self-characterization of the Syrian regime or others as pluralistic expresses, however euphemistic it is, some conceptual change. While it does not imply an acknowledgement of the need for democracy as it is currently understood, it contains an implicit acknowledgement of the existence of different legitimate interests in an increasingly complex society. The pluralistic project of the Syrian regime, and to different extents those of the others, demands a selective incorporation into regime structures of certain economic and social interests, notably those which are indispensable to secure resources needed to maintain the state and preserve the economic and political interests of the regime. The private sector with its different groups can come up with most of the economic and social functions demanded: it is generating surplus and foreign exchange, it might even be able to attract foreign credit more easily than the state,[7] and it provides opportunities for parts of the regime elite to transform some of its wealth into capital. An opening to other social forces, such as urban intellectuals, rural notables, or men of religion, may also be advisable for political reasons – as a substitute for the loss of allegiance on the part of the losers from economic adjustment. No deeper structural change of the system is intended. Asad has rejected outright demands for a more far-reaching democratization. Syria, he said in a speech to parliament in 1992, had developed its own appropriate form of democracy and party pluralism and would therefore not import any other country's form of democracy (*al-Ba'th*, 13 March 1992).

Syria's Asad may be more outspoken in this respect than some of his colleagues. 'Pluralism', however, in all liberalizing Arab states is but a selective adaption of democratic principles. Democracy comes, if at all, controlled and – as the Egyptian president put it – 'in doses' (Makram-Ebeid 1989, 423). Pluralization, as a regime project, is certainly not intended to lead to a gradual loss of power, but rather to consolidate, re-invigorate and, probably, rationalize the power and legitimacy of politically, economically and ideologically weakened regimes (Salih 1991, 90ff; Thabit 1992, 12ff; Krämer 1992). The question arises whether the private sector, or rather the bourgeoisie, or any other part of 'civil society' has an alternative, more ambitious project, and whether they are able and willing to push it forward.

Assessing the political power of the private sector

It is difficult to assess the political power, the power to influence concrete decisions, of the heterogeneous mass known as the private sector. This is particularly so in a country where the political structures do not allow much insight into political decision-making processes. Both the structure of the private sector, however, and sequences of economic policy decisions suggest that, as a whole, the private sector in Syria is still politically weak. Since the state is in bitter need of the private sector to contribute to the generation of foreign exchange, surplus and employment, one could guess that the bourgeoisie has acquired substantial power. The public image of private-sector businessmen has been considerably enhanced in the context of Syria's second *infitah*. Previously, mass media had frequently attacked the 'parasitic bourgeoisie' and blamed it, although without mentioning names, for the country's economic problems. Since the end of the 1980s, top-ranking Syrian businessmen such as Sa'ib Nahhas, the owner-manager of a series of 'mixed-sector' companies in tourism, transport and, recently, industry, have come to be interviewed in state-run newspapers or mentioned by name, positively, among other prominent figures attending public events. Image, however, should not be confused with strength. The private sector, as mentioned above, is extremely fragmented. The number of establishments with large capital investments and a considerable workforce is limited; an estimated half or more of all industrial establishments employs only family labour. There is no single private industrial or trading establishment so large that its collapse or closure would cause considerable damage to the national economy or create insoluble social problems. The bankruptcy of the largest private industrial company group in Syria would cause the loss of jobs for some 1,000 textile workers, most of whom would be able to find alternative jobs. This is not

much of a threat compared to the scenario of one of the biggest public enterprises like, for instance, Milihouse, the Ministry of Defence's construction company employing tens of thousands, or any of the public-sector textile companies
employing several thousand, going officially bankrupt. The only sector of the
economy in which the – rather unlikely – sudden shutdown of a private-sector
company or the rapid deterioration of its performance could actually create an
economic problem for the government is tourism where two companies have
quasi-monopolistic positions over first-class services. A similar, though less
strong example is provided by the export-orientated modern agricultural sector
which may come to be dominated, though not monopolized, by a handful of
'mixed' agrocapitalist companies. Both tourist and agricultural companies
undoubtedly have considerable bargaining power regarding their own business,
such as to enable them to put through exemptions from certain rules and preferential access to public resources. Since, however, they are not representative of
the entire private sector, and their importance remains sectoral, such individual
bargaining power is unlikely to translate into any substantial pressure on behalf
of the private sector as a whole. In other countries under consideration, the private sector is just as fragmented, with small-scale, family-run enterprises making up the bulk of industry as well as trade and services (Bellin 1991, 57;
Springborg 1986, 47; Khafaji 1991, 182; Sha'ir 1990, 660f). This fragmentation
may even be increased, as Bellin points out for the case of Tunis, by the individualism of small-scale entrepreneurs which does not work in favour of any collective action. Different parts of the bourgeoisie may choose group advantages
rather than gamble for collective gains. In such a dangerous situation for the
Syrian regime as the violent confrontation with the islamist opposition throughout 1979 to 1982, the government proved itself capable of splitting the conservative business community in two, gaining the allegiance of the merchants of
Damascus while those in Aleppo and Hama supported the opposition (Hinnebusch
1990, 288ff).

The private sector is not only fragmented, structurally and politically, it is
also to a large extent dependent on the state. This applies not only to that stratum of the bourgeoisie which has achieved its position and almost all of its
wealth by striking preferential deals with the public sector. Even though liberalization measures have been reducing the general dependency of the private sector on the state, the need to obtain official licences for imports, exports,
production and, in some cases, pricing, as well as the dependence of a large part
of private manufacturing on intermediary products from the industrial public
sector – such as, in the Syrian case, nylon thread, cotton yarn, gases, re-inforce-
ment bars, or cement – provides for a continuous 'petitionary quality' (Bellin
1991, 58) in the relationship of – in particular – industrialists with the state.

Individually, private-sector businessmen, in Syria as in other countries, have
for the last few decades been subject to the constant threat of prosecution for the
various economic offences and crimes that are part and parcel of their business
lives: offences against price-regulations, evasion of licensing, and, first and

foremost, currency-law offences and tax evasion. The state tolerated such offences, and sometimes openly 'expected' them to be committed. The transfer in Syria of such economic crimes from special security to civil courts lightened the threat. It did not, however, legalize such action. Doing what is legally still an offence weakens the position of private entrepreneurs in relation to the authorities and is likely to make them refrain from pressing political demands (Bellin 1991, 57, 62; Perthes 1992c).

As a whole, the private sector has little organizational power. Syrian entrepreneurs and self-employed may be organized in artisans' co-operatives, or in the chamber of commerce or chamber of industry of their province. The Union of Artisans' Co-operatives is a party-dominated mass organization that has now lost much of its significance; its main importance was to provide certain production inputs to its members. Since markets for these inputs, such as iron or wood, are becoming more and more privatized, the co-operatives have lost their importance as a service organization for their membership and remain mainly one of the lesser control mechanisms of party and state. The chambers of industry and commerce are much more independent and more important organizations. Chamber membership is advantageous for entrepreneurs who need certain licences for import and export, certificates of origin, and other services. Petty merchants and the owners of smaller workshops are usually not found in the chambers. Since no special organization of the business elite, such as the Egyptian Businessmen's Association or similar organizations in Tunis or Jordan (Azmi 1991; Bellin 1991, 60f; Sha'ir 1990, 661), exists in Syria – and the same applies to Iraq – the chambers, especially the chambers of Damascus which often speak for the rest and dominate the respective all-Syrian unions of chambers, have to serve as interest organizations both for the petty and medium, and for the *infitah* or 'parasitic' bourgeoisie. The latter is particularly represented in the Damascus Chamber of Commerce, and dominates its executive.

The chambers are financially independent, and they choose their executives relatively freely – the public sector has at least one representative in the executive of each chamber, and limited state interference occurs. The role of the chambers has been enhanced gradually. Licences for industrial investments, for example, have been distributed through the chambers of industry since 1990. Far more important, the chambers are, since 1980, incorporated into decision-making bodies, especially the Committee for the Guidance of Import, Export, and Consumption (Lajnat tarshid al-istirad wa'l-tasdir wa'l-istihlak), which is headed by the prime minister and has developed into the main governmental body for the discussion of and decisions about economic policies. The Damascus chambers or the all-Syrian unions of the chambers of industry and trade organize meetings with high officials regularly, and their boards are occasionally invited to an audience with the prime minister or president. Additionally, individual representatives of the business class have access to the highest representatives of the state and may be consulted. It can be assumed that such access is used to secure individual gains rather than to push forward collective demands.

Syria's ruling party has no significant membership among the business community. The same seems to apply to Iraq, but it contrasts with the Tunisian and the Egyptian case. In Tunisia, for example, the respective head of the 'Tunisian Union for Industry and Trade', the equivalent of other countries' chambers, has always been a member of the politbureau of the ruling party, both under Bourguiba and under Ben Ali (Ayari 1990, 715). Egypt's ruling NDP has become an instrument for the *munfatihum* under Sadat; under Mubarak their interests are said to compete with those of the bureaucracy and traditional business interests (Springborg 1989; 164ff). This is not to say that party officials in Syria or Iraq may not be involved in business or sponsor groups of profit-seekers. Both the 'Takriti' contractors (Khafaji 1991, 198ff) and Rif'at al-Asad's patronage network (Reed 1980) prove the case. But no member of the Syrian party's regional command or central committee has come to office as a businessman. Abd al-Ra'uf al-Kasm, Syria's prime minister from 1980 to 1987, had a business background; he was a university dean, however, before taking over his government post, and he has always been regarded as a leftist of the pre-1963 Ba'thist old guard. Some individual businessmen may join the party to seek patronage; evidence from interviews in Syria, however, suggests that a majority of business people, even those who are on intimate terms with the regime, try to avoid unnecessary interaction with the party. It is almost inconceivable that the Ba'th, which in Syria as well as Iraq is maintaining its socialist rhetoric and has a clear anti-bourgeois tradition, would follow the example of Ben Ali's RCD and try to solicit financial or electoral support from businessmen (Moore 1991, 91; Bellin 1991, 62f). In contrast to the NDP or the RCD, the Ba'th in its present form remains an obstacle to private-sector political demands rather than their vehicle, not because of its dominant position but because of its social composition and tradition.

Also, in Syria, there are no Uthman Ahmad Uthmans yet, illustrious members of the bourgeoisie emerging as presidential advisers who, for some time at least, may speak for both the government and the private sector. There are some government ministers whose political outlook is close to that of the private sector – such as Muhammad al-Imadi, Syria's outspokenly liberal minister of economy. Entrepreneurs, however, are not expected to become government officials. The opposite happens – some former junior ministers have become managers of 'mixed-sector' companies – though still on a smaller scale than in Egypt where the inclusion of former junior or senior government ministers on the boards of big-business or private-sector interest groups has become a regular feature (Imam 1986, 107ff; Azmi 1989, 172ff; Springborg 1989, 43f). The difference might simply be due to the fact that as yet there are still only a few big businesses in Syria.

The government does consult the private sector, and it is doing so formally, as mentioned above, through the Committee for the Guidance of Import, Export and Consumption, and through other bodies. But the government is certainly not an instrument of business interests. If we look into what has happened to certain demands of the business community we should bear in mind that a succession of political demands and government acts meeting them does not necessarily prove the strength of those who brought forward the demands. The government could equally well have acted in its own interest. The inverse relation makes more sense. We can say, with some certainty, that an interest group is politically weak whose demands do not find responses, or are met only late.

The sequence of certain private-sector demands and economic policy decisions in Syria suggests, accordingly, the political weakness of the private industrial sector at least. In general, the Chamber of Commerce seems to have been more successful than the industrialists. 'Mixed-sector' companies in tourism and agriculture which became a field of action for members of the chambers of commerce rather than industry were permitted – as mentioned above – in 1987 and 1986 respectively. An equivalent law for industrial ventures was not passed until 1991. A tax reform had been at the top of the demand list of both industrialists and merchants for more than a decade, but was not implemented until 1991. Actually, this demand was more important for the industrial bourgeoisie and petty bourgeoisie than for its commercial counterparts who, by the nature of their business, could more easily evade taxation. Regulations on imports and import currency, which are a concern of merchants in particular, were gradually softened, more rapidly than was the case with regulations on exports and foreign-currency export earnings which are a specific concern of industrialists. It is difficult to compare certain measures responding to the demands of industrialists with those responding to merchant demands. But it is striking that the importation by private merchants of certain products whose importation and production had been restricted to the public sector – such as sugar, paper, iron and tractors – has been allowed from the late 1980s, while their production by private manufacturers was still not permitted. It has been mentioned above that the *infitah* policies of most countries considered showed at least an initial commercial bias. And a specific weakness of private industrial – as opposed to commercial – interests in economic policy decision making has been noticed with regard to other countries under consideration too.[8] Egypt's state-independent productive bourgeoisie, for example, has been described as 'marginal political actors removed...from the state apparatus' (Springborg 1989, 262); they have, according to Enid Hill (1989, 21), not even been consulted over the 1989 investment law.

It appears in general that decision making on economic policies in Syria and comparable countries incorporates businessmen only in part, and that decisions connected with recent liberalization were very much a regime affair, insofar as their scope and timing were set by the respective regimes. The economic liberalization process was certainly in the interest of, but not dictated by, the (private) bourgeoisie or its organizations (Waterbury 1991, 8; Yashir 1992, 95, 98). Rather, economic needs enforced economic restructuring. The regimes attempted both to rid themselves of financial burdens and to mobilize private resources. The concrete aim of skimming off private-sector profits to foster the state's foreign-exchange budget involved the necessity of encouraging private-sector activities and reassuring private capital. Indemnification from economic failures by making the private sector responsible for a larger part of the economy may be an incentive for liberalization too (Leca 1990, 186). At the same time, privatization and liberalization measures could serve the private interests of the regime elite or a state-bourgeoisie. The decline of the state's economic resources and the declining attractiveness of employment in the public sector, as a result of austerity policies reducing wages and opportunities for gain, force state bourgeoisies to search for an alternative future for themselves and their offspring. Many from this stratum seek to achieve an individual move into the private sector. Since any attempt of the state bourgeoisie to preserve or reproduce itself as a class is virtually impossible (Waterbury 1991, 13f), the exchange of public for private inheritable power of disposal over means of production may be the most rational way for this stratum to secure the preservation of an elevated position in the social pyramid. The investment in legal private or mixed ventures of some of the wealth the state-bourgeoisie has amassed during the past decades is a feasible way to secure such a social transformation, and a further incentive for the political elite to embark on a course of economic liberalization.[9] Examples of this specific form of social mobility are found in all of the countries under consideration here. Look at the business activities of the brothers of the Syrian president, of the sons of his deputy or of his minister of defence as well as the widespread acquisition of farms by officers and party functionaries in Syria (Perthes 1991); at the integration of former government ministers into Egypt's private business elite, or consider the case of the former manager of Jordan's national airline who after his resignation from office bought the airline's fleet and then leased it to the same company. Historically, the transformation of Middle Eastern military bureaucratic elites into private owners of means of production is not without precedent; the big landowners of Syria and Iraq, for instance, were, as a rule, the descendants of Ottoman, or Sharifian, officers and administrators. Social alliances, such as the military-mercantile complex in Syria (Picard 1979) could, partly at least, be succeeded by amalgamation.

If the bourgeoisie are too weak to push through their economic policy objectives according to their own schedule, it is hardly imaginable that they could enforce on the regime a timetable for democratic change. Moreover, it does not seem that the bourgeoisie as a whole even has any such timetable or list of democratic demands. 'Why should a private sector that owes much of its position to the state and the public sector have to undertake open political action when it can try to obtain ... [its aims] at less cost to itself by remaining entrenched in bureaucratic and palace politics?' (Leca 1990, 183). Certainly, for a private sector obtaining monopolies and other privileges from the state, striking deals with state officials and living off public resources, neither democratization, transparency of political affairs, nor government accountability is an objective. No one, therefore, would expect to see the executive of the Damascus Chamber of Commerce, for instance, or the founders of any 'mixed' company for tourism or agriculture, at the head of a Syrian democracy movement. Things look different from the perspective of a majority of entrepreneurial industrialists and artisans. As a rule, industrial investments tie down more capital, and are less remunerative in the short and medium term than commercial ventures. Manufacturers, therefore, even though they may benefit from certain inputs or services provided by the state and the public sector, are negatively affected by the absence of government accountability, of transparency of decisions and deals, and, even more, of the rule of law. It is obvious, if we look at the Syrian case as an example, that not only individual industrialists but even the Damascus Chamber of Industry display far less support towards the regime than do the Chamber of Commerce or the cream of Syria's merchants. For example, the 1989 elections for the executive of the Damascus Chamber of Industry were won by a list of industrialists whose political and personal connections to the regime were less dense than those of their competitors.[10] This part of the bourgeoisie is doubtless interested in some democratization; however, it is not pressing for change, and could only do so to a limited extent. Thus, with one part of the bourgeoisie and petty bourgeoisie being in favour of more democracy but lacking any bargaining power, and the other part, having more bargaining power and closer relations to the regime but not being interested in democratic change, private-sector pressure for democratization remains extremely limited.

The forces of civil society

Any hope that authoritarian regimes will themselves, out of understanding of long-term necessities, sudden conviction, or under external pressure, implement political reforms of more than a defensive or limited nature, seems to be void of substance. If none of the political leadership and state-bourgeoisie, the ruling party or the private sector are pushing for democratization, the prospects for change toward political liberalization and democracy must depend on other social forces. It is notable that there are forces in civil society that actually show themselves to have a stronger interest in democratization than the bourgeoisie. Still, civil society is hardly a counterweight to the state, its ruling party and its security apparatuses, in most Arab countries. There is some reason to expect that ongoing socio-economic changes will increase the effectiveness of civil society all over the Arab world (Hudson 1991); however, there might be countervailing tendencies too.[11] What can be stated at present is that notable differences regarding the strength of civil society have been emerging between different states. Syria, and even more so Iraq, show a particularly unequal relation of power between state and civil society, as becomes clear through a comparison with Egypt, Tunisia, or Jordan.

There is, in Syria, no independent judiciary that could be expected to become an effective instrument for oppositional forces and thus virtually an institution of civil society. In Egypt where the regime has twice been forced by court order to revise its electoral law this is certainly the case (Hudson 1991, 412), and Tunisia's judiciary, too, has occasionally proven its relative independence of the regime (Zartman 1991, 24). Press freedom has been considerably increased in Egypt, Tunisia and Jordan. The electronic media of each of these states are still an instrument of the regime, oppositional media are discriminated against and sometimes repressed; the picture is, however, strikingly different from Syria, where even the Ba'th Party's allies are not allowed to run their own public papers. In Syria, as mentioned above, there is no effective legal opposition party which, as is the case in Egypt, Tunisia, and probably Jordan, could become the organizational backbone of certain bourgeois or even non-bourgeois interests. In Egypt, the Wafd and Liberal Parties represent certain business interests which do not find themselves sufficiently represented by the NDP; a similar development can be expected in Tunisia. Islamist political networks in Egypt, Tunisia and Jordan can even rely on their own economic networks thus gaining considerable autonomy (Makram-Ebeid 1989; Moore 1988b, 54; 1991, 91). Furthermore, in Syria, there are not even independent political personalities who could become a focus for loose oppositional circles. Respectable independents with some influence are either outspokenly non-political – in terms of party and government politics – like some leading industrial figures, for instance, or representatives of an outdated past, like the veteran nasserist leader Jamal al-Atasi, or integrated into the power structure like the economy minister, Muhammad al-Imadi.

State-independent associations may be the most important element of civil society. Almost all Arab states have severely restricted the freedom of their citizens to form, and organize in, voluntary associations, be they charitable, cultural, social, or political, by generally demanding that any association obtain a government licence and thereafter monitoring them through the ministries of social affairs or the interior. Both in Tunisia and Egypt, independent associations began to increase in number in the late 1970s. Lawyers' or journalists' organizations, the Tunisian League for the Defence of Human Rights, or political and social clubs were set up for the first time or started to prove their independence from the regime and, since oppositional parties were marginalized or repressed, became the effective spokespersons for the opposition (Nafi 1988, 82f; Karru 1987, 56f; Baker 1990, 46ff). In Egypt, civil associations proliferated further under Mubarak's liberalized rule. A restrictive law of association remained, however (Springborg 1989, 170ff), which enabled the government to ban, among others, the Arab Women's Solidarity Association in 1991. Tunisia's law of association was reformed after Ben Ali's takeover and allowed, for some time at least, the emergence of the most liberal associational life in the Arab world – with the exception of Lebanon (Zartman 1991, 16; Thabit 1992, 18). The ban on Tunisia's Human Rights League in summer 1992, however, indicates, that there too, the freedom of civil society ends where independent organizations come into conflict with the security apparatus. Syria is most restrictive against the establishment of non-state, non-party, or non-governmental associations: in 1990, the total number of legal social, cultural, scientific, educational, religious and charity associations in Syria did not exceed 504 – 150 less than ten years before (SAR 1981, 476; 1991, 413). Several elements of Syria's civil society whose counterparts in other Arab countries have been, and are, playing an important role in political liberalization and democratization were crushed and have not yet recovered. When, in 1980, the lawyers' union refused to announce its allegiance to the president and called for a one-day strike to protest against the continued application of martial law, its executive was impeached, imprisoned and replaced by loyalists. The same happened to the heads of the physicians' and engineers' unions. Civil society is deeply penetrated by the state, and previously more or less state-independent organizations as, for example, the students' union or the union of agricultural co-operatives, have been transformed to state-led corporations.

Trade unions can, in countries with a certain level of industrialization, become one of the most threatening forces to authoritarian regimes, and have in the Arab context done so, as for instance in Sudan. (Ali 1992). Tunisia might serve as an example of limited but still considerable trade union independence (Larif-Beatrix 1987, 38ff; Karru 1987, 56ff; Ferchiou 1991). In Iraq, all public-sector trade unions were dissolved in the late 1980s (Lawson 1990, 50). In Syria, although unions are numerically strong, their sting has been removed, and their leadership is widely incorporated into the leadership of party and state and is largely corrupted. Syrian and Egyptian regimes have been using similar patterns to transform their countries' respective unions from independent social movements into corporations under state control. Essentially, both countries have the same labour law, dating back to the Syrian-Egyptian union of 1958–1961. In contrast to their Egyptian counterparts (Bianchi 1986, 434ff), however, Syria's trade unions have not managed to use their incorporation into the system to gain an effective influence or at least veto power over economic policy decisions (Suwaydan 1980; Longuenesse 1988; Perthes 1990, 179ff). Based mainly in the public sector which is threatened by austerity measures, the unions are very much on the defensive.

Astonishingly enough, some relatively strong demands for political liberalization and increased government accountability arose from trade-union and public sector intellectual circles in Syria. A conference on 'National Creativity and Self-Reliance', held in 1987 under the auspices of the General Federation of Trade Unions and designed to support a government campaign to stimulate initiative, turned into a forum for university professors, public-sector economists and planners, and trade unionists to criticize not only government economic policies but also corruption, the interference of the security apparatus in economic affairs, and the general lack of responsibility and democracy (General Federation of Trade Unions 1987). This criticism obviously exceeded what the regime expected these circles to discuss. When the event was over, the president of the trade unions' federation reportedly accused some of the participating intellectuals of having spoiled the conference. One year before, the annual series of lectures organized by Syria's Economic Science Association, a group made up mainly of public-sector economists, including professors, had turned into a highly critical assessment of regime policies and their social effects (Economic Science Association 1986). As a result, the association was not permitted to hold its lecture series for three years. These events, however limited their effects, show that some drive for change may be expected from the medium, and probably lower, level of those employed in the state and the public sector. With the public sector, not only in Syria, being the major employer of intellectuals and the rest of the salaried middle class, a stratum which generally is well educated and shares, to some extent, the value orientations of its counterparts in the West, it is conceivable that a large part of the struggle between civil society and state actually takes place within the state apparatus.[12] In general there is wide discontent among the losers from austerity and adjustment of whom the salaried middle class are only a relatively small part. In Syria this discontent is still unorganized; in other countries islamist movements have been able to organize it partially. It is far from clear whether these more or less organized forces actually want democracy, or rather jobs and a decent income (Zghal 1992, 21).

Conclusion

A comparative assessment suggests that the difference between systems with a certain degree of democratic competition and political participation, as for instance, Egypt, and those with strong political control and even a high level of repression, such as Iraq or Syria, does not necessarily become translated into different levels of private-sector activities. Isam Khafaji (1991) contends that, at the end of the 1980s, Egypt's private sector was not more active than that of Iraq. The same could be said of Egypt and Syria. For the total of private-sector activities, thus, the question of representation and democratic participation does not seem to make too much of a difference.

The wave of economic liberalization passing through the Arab world since the mid-1980s results, in the first place, from the diminishing capacity to maintain the state-led growth strategies of the 1970s, and in some cases even to maintain the public sector and administration. At the same time, this liberalization furthers the social interests of the regime elite and the private bourgeoisie. Liberalization has not been enforced by the bourgeoisie, which would still be too weak for that, but the state has actually lost its grip on some economic levers (Richards & Waterbury 1990, 351f). Political power, in contrast, is not yet shared. Economic liberalization certainly demands some institutional arrangements for the consultation of private-sector interests whose co-operation is needed for the success of the experiment. Austerity policies accompanying liberalization are likely to involve the demobilization of certain rural and urban strata that had been highly mobilized in the early years of Ba'thist, nasserist or similar forms of authoritarian-populist rule. Liberalization, however, does not demand one particular political structure. Democratization, or more precisely, the gradual or sudden emergence in an increasing number of Arab states of political systems securing political plurality, human rights and the principle of change of government through periodic elections, is possible but not guaranteed. Limited pluralism as granted by several regimes in the region is defensive and a matter of 'system maintenance' rather than of actual democratization (Krämer 1992, 24); it secures the incorporation of indispensable groups into regime structures and aims at regaining some legitimacy. Authoritarian regimes may thus introduce a measure of superficial and selective democratization, or pluralization, without giving up their effective monopoly of political power – providing institutionally against an oppositional majority in parliament and setting red lines that must not be crossed (Naqib 1991, 342f). It is possible, however, and both the Egyptian and Jordanian examples might bear this out, for such limited democratization to get out of hand, and create not only demands but also momentum for a deepening of the process.

In all the countries under consideration, demands for democratization were not brought by the private sector or a bourgeoisie growing in strength but, in the first place, by intellectuals, members of the salaried middle classes, most of whom are one way or another on the public payroll, and self-employed professionals. Consider, for example, those Iraqi intellectuals who in January 1992 called for a broad democratic dialogue and subsequent elections to a parliament or constitutive assembly (*al-Safir*, 6 February 1992), the Tunisian League for the Defence of Human Rights, or the Egyptian Lawyers' Union. This is not to say that democracy has actually become the unanimous demand of intellectuals, let alone a societal demand, throughout the Arab world, or to preclude that the Arab intellectual discourse, currently stressing the priority of democratization, may under certain circumstances, especially in the case of real or supposed external threat, once again put democracy in second place (Labib 1992, 102).

It is notable that political democratization usually goes along with a fairly assertive civil society, including trade unions that enjoy some independence, rather than simply with a private sector of a certain magnitude. All the regimes considered are afraid, or at least suspicious, of too strong and effective a civil society (Makram Ebeid 1992). The measure of associational freedom granted by liberalizing regimes is therefore an indicator of the seriousness of their supposedly democratizing tendencies. In Egypt, Tunisia and Jordan, civil society is certainly more developed than in Syria or Iraq. In Egypt and Tunisia, the change at the top of the regime, in 1981 and 1987 respectively, contributed considerably to removing some of the obstacles to an extended measure of political freedom and participation, and we may assume that without a replacement of incumbent leaderships democratic changes will occur only in exceptional cases. Jordan seems to be exceptional insofar as it witnessed a partial change of its system while its head of state remained. This might be explained by the absence of a regime party in Jordan. Such dominant and privileged, or quasi single parties, as are found in all the other countries considered, are both an obstacle in the way of political liberalization and a power resource for a regime unwilling to share its power with the forces of civil society. In all three cases, Egypt, Tunisia and Jordan, these relatively substantial political changes were preceded by popular unrest or the threat of popular upheaval. Any hope, or expectation, that an enlightened regime would lead its country to democracy without pressure from below would be unfounded.

Economic liberalization and private-sector growth will not necessarily bring about democratization. Democratization, however, does certainly bring about a general increase of private activities, including a growth of the private sector.[13] Democratization is also likely to entail structural changes within the private sector, strengthening the less state-reliant sector which, at the same time, may be more likely to engage in long-term investments rather than in shorter-term commercial or quasi-commercial activities, and thereby enhance development prospects.

Notes

1   I would like to thank my colleague, Helen Tuschling, for her efforts to make my English more readable, and my research assistants Rania Kanj, Hayat Osseiran, and Rola Faour, all graduate students of sociology at the American University of Beirut during the time this article was written, for their help in data collection.

2   The majority of Syria's agricultural co-operatives were service co-operatives; in addition to that there were a limited number of production co-operatives or collective farms. State farms had held some 2 per cent of Syria's cultivable land. Since 1989, the Syrian government has begun to dissolve some of the state farms and production co-operatives. By 1990, the area held by state farms was reduced to some 1.5 per cent of all cultivable land (SAR 1988; 1991).

3   All Syria's statistical data should be regarded with come caution, and should be taken to express trends rather than exact totals. This is particularly so for data on the private sector. There is a large informal sector whose data are neither collected by the Central Bureau of Statistics nor any other data-collecting institution such as the Ministry of Finance or the Ministry of Industry. But even data on the formal private sector are often underestimated, since entrepreneurs, fearing taxation and other cuts from their profits, tend to hide parts of their activities. Different data-collecting agencies end up with diverging data on the same object of analysis – for example, private-sector industrial activities – as a result of different methods on the one hand, and of greater or lesser interest of entrepreneurs in providing correct data on the other (Perthes 1992c, n 21).

4   Gross fixed capital formation (investments) may serve as an example: private-sector investments, in constant prices of 1985, dropped from 6.7 billion LS (35 per cent of all investments) in 1983 to 4.7 billion (52 per cent of the total) in 1990; in current prices private investments increased from 5.9 billion to 21.3 billion LS. Public sector investments dropped from 12.2 billion LS to 4.3 billion respectively, still

increasing in current prices from 11.6 to 19.5 billion LS (SAR 1991, 502f).

5   $-values are calculated on the basis of the free-market rate of the LS.

6   Compare the documentation of parliamentary speeches in Darwish (1990), especially the speeches of Bassam Haddadin and Fakhri Qa'uar, pp 459–65; 484–89.

7   Notably the assistance programme set up by the GCC states after the Gulf War to
support friendly Arab states, particularly Egypt and Syria, will primarily assign
loans to the recipient states' private sectors (*al-Safir*, 12 March 1992).

8   Reasons for this specific weakness of industrial interests may be multiple. It might
be that these less state-dependent elements of the bourgeoisie generally have more
far-reaching demands regarding the reduction of the role of the state. (See
Springborg 1989, 262.) It is conceivable that the competition of private industrialists
with the public industrial sector is more of a threat to the regime's need to maintain
its social basis than the competition (or succession) of private merchants with the
public trade sector: to give up parts of the public industrial sector, or to expose it to
competition, means to give up a resource of patronage; to give up parts of the public
trade outlets and trade monopolies would, however, mean giving up responsibilities
which have become difficult to meet. It might also simply be that merchants and
other elements of the commercial bourgeoisie find it easier to adapt to authoritarian
systems with frequent policy changes and legal insecurity; and that, from the perspective of regime officials, interaction with merchants offers more opportunities for
payoffs. The question deserves further study.

9   Cf. Habib (1990, 375) and Salih (1991, 94), who, however, overemphasizes this
incentive and makes it appear the sole reason for economic restructuring.

10 The regime responded by appointing two further private businessmen, known for
their loyalty and connections to the regime, to the executive, thereby showing the
limits of independence the chamber enjoys.

11 Such as, for instance, the deterioration of educational systems in the wake of austerity programmes, civil war, or war.

12 Richards and Waterbury (1990, 38) suggest that crucial struggles may 'not occur so
much between the state and the forces of civil society that seek to curtail the state as
within the ranks of the state elites themselves.' I would suggest considering these
middle ranks of the state employed as part of a largely state penetrated civil society.

13 This does not deny that other variables, such as the economic pressures suffered by
Jordan and Yemen during and after the Gulf crisis and war of 1990–91, might
impede such developments.

11

Patronage and Solidarity Groups: survival or reformation?

OLIVIER ROY

The modern asabiyya

It is a commonplace to speak of patronage as the usual mode of operation in political life in the Middle East. However, as Jean Leca and Yves Schemeil (1983) have pointed out, it is not specific to the region. What is of interest to us here is not the patronage relation as such, but the nature of its networks, how they relate to the state and to 'what extent they allow a modern state to function. We will consider whether it is merely a vestige of a traditional society, a transition towards a modern state or an obstacle to the emergence of such a state. The cases of Algeria and Tajikistan at the two extremes of the Middle East will provide us with a lead into these issues.

We will begin by distinguishing three types of patronage. First, there is the network that is purely instrumental and temporary. This is built up around one man invested with a certain power and does not survive after he loses this position. Secondly, there is the traditional 'solidarity group' *(asabiyya)*, that is the clan, tribe, village, extended family and so on, whose existence and mode of operation precedes the setting up of a state society and which then dominates the field of politics. This is the case, for example, with the 'tribal' strategy of takeover and management of the state. These groups link themselves to the modern state – which they have sometimes created themselves (for example the Saudi and Afghan royal families) – and use it to their own advantage, while maintaining their cohesion if they are removed from power. This may be described as the Ibn Khaldun model (Leca & Schemeil 1983, 28). Thirdly, there is the modern 'solidarity group', which did not exist prior to the state, or rather which only acquired cohesion from the existence of the state. Such a body is formed in a modern political situation and functions thereafter as a 'solidarity group' according to modes of inter-personal relations identical to those of the traditional *asabiyya*, namely endogamy, patronage, nepotism. Thus it becomes a modern *asabiyya* which administers power to its own advantage, occasionally against the traditional society. This is the Mamluk model.

We are not concerned here with the first type, which is ephemeral, fluctuating and personalized. It has no sociological reality and can be found in widely differing types of political society. What interests us here in particular is the relation between the two other types. The modern *asabiyya* may be the translation of a traditional solidarity group into a new system which changes its mode of operation and survival. Equally, it may refer to entirely new groups which have been created in a state founded on the fragmentation and dissolution of the traditional *asabiyya* (as happened in Algeria).

In the first case, the acquisition of the powers of the state by the *asabiyya* would represent a return to tradition (and indeed its revenge over modernity), but within a modern state system which has been imported and is unable to establish its own roots. Michel Seurat has shown how the image of the modern state may conceal an *asabiyya:* for example, in both the Syrian and Iraqi armies the officer corps (a new *asabiyya*) is itself an expression of a solidarity group which is both traditional and from a minority (from the Alawite sect in Syria and from the town of Takrit in Iraq) and which has used the modern state in order to change the traditional fragmented social structure (ethnic-religious minorities). As Seurat (1989, 131) says: 'The modern state in the Machrek is an asabiyya which has been successful.' In other words, a solidarity group, usually a clan or minority, monopolizes the state and uses it as an instrument of economic exploitation.

Such a state survives by external plunder (either directly as Syria in Lebanon and, for several months, as Iraq in Kuwait; or indirectly, as when Syria uses its power to cause unrest in order to obtain subsidies, particularly from Saudi Arabia), by oil revenues in the case of Iraq, by levies on external trade (the sale of export licences, granting to officials 'commissions' on certain types of income such as drugs, customs duties and technical agencies).

However, this example whereby the modern *asabiyya* becomes rooted in a traditional form of segmented society reveals that the *asabiyya* itself has changed. By the time one faction has taken over the state, it remains only nominally the same. The very process which brought it to power has destroyed the traditional society from which it originated. The modern *asabiyya,* therefore, are no longer an expression of traditional sociability. On the contrary, they lead to the fragmentation of traditional society because of the way the state power allows them to operate, without the safeguards and limitations of a traditional society based on a fine balance of its various solidarity groups. The acquisition of the state by one particular group breaks the symmetry and balances of the traditional society, although it is possible for this equilibrium to be maintained, as in the case of a dynasty of non-tribal origin which successfully keeps itself above the groups – as in Morocco and Jordan.

The state system, therefore, gives the *asabiyya* a power which they did not have previously; indeed it is at the heart of this translation of the traditional

asabiyya into modern factionalism. The traditional *asabiyya* have been fragmented by urbanization, social upheaval and the spread of ideology. They may
reform along different lines, perhaps involving political patronage or economic
exploitation, or they may simply disappear. As we shall see later, in a country
such as Algeria the structures of the traditional society were destroyed by colonization. The modern *asabiyya* therefore are the product of recent history and
the establishment of a new state. The main difference between traditional
asabiyya which reform with the establishment of the state and the new *asabiyya*
is that the former have a legitimacy based on their origin while the latter are in
search of a founding myth and therefore more subject to the risks of having their
legitimacy challenged – as for example the war of liberation for the FLN in
Algeria.

The modern *asabiyya* are a re-formation of group solidarity as a result of the
establishment of the state and the globalization of economic and financial flows.
They represent the reformation of a relationship of traditional solidarity in a
modern situation.[1] While it is still important to know which village a person
comes from and who is married to whom, it is also important to know which
year someone was in the military academy and who studied with which professor of theology. The modern *asabiyya* are not situated in the paternal village, but
in the modern town or the kolkhoz. The militias in Beirut may function in the
same way as the old urban *asabiyya* – the *futuwwa* or brotherhoods of 'bad
boys' who guaranteed order and 'protection' in the areas that were not controlled by the palace – and the parties may operate like networks of clients
around the great notables. Nevertheless, these militias and parties are not simply the
continuation of an old tradition. The stakes that they represent, their links with
international conflicts, the entry of the bazaar into the global economy – all this
means that they are much more than a mere survival of tradition in a modern situation. Even in a traditional society such as Afghanistan, the network that operates around a small local commander – who is himself part of an international
traffic in arms or sometimes drugs – is not the clan that existed in the past but a
reformation of traditional segmented structures around a new political elite and
international flows of wealth.

It can be seen therefore that modern *asabiyya* are not the survival of tribalism
or confessionalism. They may be formed initially on a modern sociological
foundation (the new intelligentsia as opposed to the old families, for example)
and then establish themselves by means of diverse strategies, such as marriage
alliances or the establishment of a political party. This raises a methodological
problem which may help us to understand the differences among the various
Middle Eastern states. There are cases where we can speak of a change from the
traditional to the modern *asabiyya*, for example, Syria, Iraq, Afghanistan, and
Saudi Arabia (the fact that the young princes return with degrees from the
United States does affect the nature of tribal solidarity with the king). But there
are other cases where the traditional society has been fragmented to such an
extent that we can ask whether any of that society remains: this is particularly

the case where there has been a foreign presence, as in Algeria or Tajikistan.

Thus, it is not the vestiges of traditional structures in a modern state that interest us as much as the reformation of solidarity networks in new social and political categories under the guise of tradition. These new networks can in turn have a fragmenting effect on the traditional society and in their own way become instruments of modernization. The state and the modern *asabiyya* thus complement each other.

The disappearance of traditional societies and the retraditionalization of political relations

It seems clear that nowhere in the Middle East is it possible to find a 'traditional society' that is cut off from politics and the state. Traditional solidarity groups that have assumed power have become independent of the place from which they originated. Their legitimacy is undoubtedly based on the memory of an origin which also keeps alive the legend of the group; their method of administering power is undoubtedly based above all on inter-personal relations and patronage. However, this is not simply the vestiges of a tradition in a new political mode; a change has occurred in the way the *asabiyya* are formed.

This change arises first of all from a modification of the traditional structures through their opening up to political activity and the removal of geographical barriers. Another factor is the social upheaval resulting from population transfers, whether for economic or political reasons, combined with the emergence of new elites – for example after the war in Afghanistan, or the revolution and collectivization in Central Asia, or colonization in Algeria. The old political map becomes jumbled up and it is no longer possible to ignore the existence of the state. This situation does not arise because of the emergence of the state, which existed long before (for example the Ottoman state), but from the appropriation by the modern state of areas which until that point had been the domain of local powers (the first of which is certainly the administration of justice, as well as taxation and the use of force). Traditional solidarity groups are obliged to accept this extension of the role of the state and to reform on a less local basis. The centre imposes a new geographical reality which is concentric and not fragmented. Obviously some groups such as distant village communities remain inward-looking, as well as politically and legally autarkic; they resolve internal conflicts themselves and there is a policy of protecting themselves against state intervention. However, such groups become marginalized and put themselves in a weak position. Paradoxically, any 'conservative' strategy, i.e. aiming at the survival of the group, must include an involvement with state activity, otherwise enemy groups will involve themselves first. The extension of the role of the state has destroyed the equilibrium between groups: the group that has been able to relate to the state apparatus immediately gains superiority over the others. This superiority does not stop at the acquisition of individual benefits for its members, but can go as far as a willingness to defeat the opposing group by using the instruments of the state.

What distinguishes the modern *asabiyya* in the Middle East from similar groups which attempt to assume the monopoly of state power in other cultural areas (a 'mafia', single party, *nomenklatura,* body of technocrats and so on) is not the techniques that create, strengthen and perpetuate an esprit de corps by establishing personal links (for example by marriage). In fact any group with hegemonic aims is an *asabiyya* (it is interesting to note that in the republics of the former Soviet Union there has been a vulgarization of the term 'mafia' to apply to any hegemonic group).

In my view what distinguishes the modern *asabiyya* in the Middle East is their tendency towards retraditionalization, in other words to function and to establish themselves – and sometimes even to define themselves – with reference to the codes of the traditional *asabiyya*. This retraditionalization is particularly characterized by the reference to a geographic origin (localism) or by giving a name to the group which is drawn from a traditional repertory. In addition, a new type of notable emerges (for example the president of the kolkhoz) who adopts a traditional method of exercising and manifesting power. If he belongs to a network of modern patronage, he then proceeds to retraditionalize his relationship to this network.

If we consider two countries as different as Algeria and Tajikistan, it is noticeable that the modern *asabiyya* emerge from the virtual disappearance of the sociological structures of the traditional society (village, tribal and even ethnic). However, tradition does not simply disappear in favour of some unknown modernity. Tradition, in the sense of a vision of the world, a system of values and morals as well as personal relationships, has of course not disappeared. It is a platitude to state that in such areas as the position of women, for example, Algeria is more traditionalist than its neighbours, although they are more 'conservative' in the political sphere. The same is true of Tajikistan compared to its Uzbek and Kirghiz neighbours. At the same time, however, a memory remains of the first segmentation, a type of relationship to politics based on local solidarity groups, and this immediately appears to affect the political reformation after independence.

Colonization destroyed the traditional society in both Algeria and Tajikistan (in the guise of sovietization in the latter). The notables were déclassé, sometimes even eliminated, urban migration began, there was a redistribution of landed property, and the appearance of a new dominant culture (new language, written word and schooling) as well as new references involving a marginalization of the vernacular. All these changes have brought forward a new generation which may be nationalist but nevertheless speaks in the language and with the values of the colonizer. Factional debates may be expressed in ideological terms – socialism, democracy, islamism – but the operation of this factionalism rests on different foundations.

The case of Algeria

The modern *asabiyya* in Algeria recruit new members in one specific milieu: that of the former *mujahidin* and the 'sons of martyrs' whose political expression is the FLN. It is therefore a pure product of contemporary history. In the category of the *mujahidin* there is no trace of any transfer of earlier traditional segmentations. Mohammed Harbi (1980, 155ff) has shown that the FLN cadres are quite heterogeneous socially: déclassé and frequently self-educated, they are the product of the colonial fragmentation. But geographical origin has been a factor in the reformation and factionalism in this milieu: the group from the east of the country which supported President Chadli Benjedid is the most powerful faction.

The question that interests us is how the FLN – a political party with an ideological discourse (populism, socialism, statism, arabism, Islam) – has managed to transform itself into a new *asabiyya*. There is a gap between the ideological discourse, which quickly lost all legitimacy, and the overt practice of nepotism and patronage. It is very noticeable that there has been no renewal of the group, which is open only to those who are either former *mujahidin* or the sons of martyrs. And this is what has enabled the ruling class to establish and reproduce itself in a system of new *asabiyya*. For the party is not unified; and the *asabiyya* is not the party itself but the different networks at lower levels such as technocratic *nomenklatura* (the cadres of Sonatrach, the national oil company); the 'mafia' that have grafted themselves on sources of revenue such as ports, import licences and so on; and neo-clannism at the regional level ('localism').

Civil society has given two political reactions to this factionalism and appropriation of the state by the FLN networks. The two universalist discourses focus on Islam, for the Front Islamique du Salut (FIS), and democracy for the other parties. As far as can be seen so far, however, it would seem that all these parties have the same approach as the FLN to the exercise of political power. Alongside the two main democratic parties – the Rassemblement pour la Culture et la Démocratie (RCD) and the Front des Forces Socialistes (FFS) – there are a multitude of small independent parties each centred around one man, one symbol and sometimes a newspaper. (In Tajikistan there is a similar flourishing of personalized newspapers.) These parties put forward a vague programme of pious hopes and strive to appeal to a wide following. However, it is possible to see in them the beginnings of a faction and the formation of a network of personalized solidarity, albeit one without any real focus. They attempt to revive all possible networks in order to establish a potential *asabiyya*, as though their mode of operation were more important than their content (political, sociological, ideological). Such parties exist in the hope of bringing together a large enough membership to be attractive to a regime in search of legitimacy and ready to give the leader of the party a source of income (a prebend), which he could redistribute thereby giving a real existence to the potential group that he has created.

Such intermediaries between the state and society are not new; they are found, for example, in Morocco. What is peculiar to Algeria, is that the networks are totally reformed and without any geographical, clan, or family justification to support them. In such a situation it is necessary to invent a non-political legitimation. For example, in the December 1991 elections, a candidate in Guelma appealed to his old classmates at school to vote for him, as though the fact of having belonged to the same group was enough to form a political network. While solidarity networks of ex-pupils exist everywhere, this is not a strong enough reason to vote for someone in an election. The crisis of political legitimacy has meant that, paradoxically, the appeal to politics is made explicitly by appealing to the establishment of networks which are an end in themselves.

Should we regard this as a failure of politics in an unstable civil society, or is it a sign of the will to reform a civil society?

This illusion of reforming a civil society, borrowing on the myth of the *umma*, is to be found in the political imagery of the FIS although it restricts itself to the Algerian political scene. The discourse of the FIS is above all a discourse that rejects the *asabiyya*, although it must be added that to date our understanding of the party remains superficial and insufficient. Interestingly, when the FIS won the municipal elections in 1990 it was immediately suspected of operating a patronage system in the distribution of housing. Whatever the origin of this story, it is clear that all parties are automatically suspected of operating in this way. In order to understand the situation better we would need to observe the way in which the mosque operates as the centre of a system of influence and distribution. However, it seems clear that the FIS in power would not act very differently from the FLN.

The case of Tajikistan

Almost all political actors in Tajikistan (apart from what we shall call the 'parallel mullahs') have emerged from the old communist *nomenklatura*. They share the same political culture and express their opposition in ideological terms. As in Algeria, however, this ideological discourse is cut off from real problems; it is purely rhetorical. In the same way, the statues of Lenin which the ex-communist regime tries so hard to maintain are purely symbolic, for the reference to marxism and the revolution no longer has any meaning. As in Algeria, the problem facing the different factions is to establish for themselves a group of supporters, to whom these ideological references are no longer meaningful.

Therefore we see the re-establishment of solidarity groups which are based on localism (*mahalgera'i*), that is on a purely geographical basis – the district or even the province – but unable to appeal to a national or even an ethnic base.

The reformation of these groups has nothing to do with monopolizing the state apparatus for the state coffers are empty, and the level of poverty makes the holding of prebends quite meaningless. We may describe the modern *asabiyya*, therefore, as the invention of a new identity, a new solidarity which will appear to be natural, straightforward, non-ideological, and which can therefore operate automatically. In other words, it represents retribalization in the face of a weak state.

Tajiki society is witnessing a process of retraditionalization of a society that was fragmented in the 1920s. The artificial creation of Tajikistan on an allegedly ethnic foundation (the Tajiks speak the Persian language in fact) left the two great towns of Persian culture – Samarkand and Bukhara – in the republic of Uzbekistan. The religious elite in Tajikistan were severely repressed and the traditional rural notables (*bey*) saw the economic foundation of their power disappear. Many indeed were liquidated. When Tajikistan had to become a national entity for the first time in 1929, it had to create a political elite out of nothing (the indigenization of the political apparatus occurred from the 1940s). But the long war against the Basmachis in the 1920s brought about a significant population upheaval. The traditional solidarity groups, therefore, suffered heavy fragmentation. Dushanbe was a village set up as the capital and inhabited by peasants who had been uprooted from the countryside. Finally, collectivization brought the kolkhoz in place of the old village communities and solidarity groups.

Seventy years later Tajiki society appears nevertheless to be very traditional: in a rural society where islamic practice and culture are widespread, the extended family remains the centre of social relations (with early and arranged marriage), and new notables are the centre of economic and political power. Political power is organized around networks of relations which bring together people from the same district who, even if they were actually born in the capital, are regarded as carrying the interests of their solidarity group.

In order to understand this traditionalism we must distinguish two aspects of it. First, there is a part which is a vestige and a memory of the traditional solidarity groups, and secondly there is a part which comes from a reformation of the political arena according to a code and a memory of allegiance which in this substitutes the 'place' for the original solidarity group.

Traditional segmentation left both a terminology and a memory. In Tajikistan, as in Afghanistan, the solidarity group is called the *qawm*.[2] Its use can be enlarged to include any situation where the speaker feels there is solidarity.[3]

In the past every village would have had one or more *qawm*, and each *qawm* had its own mosque and its day of departure for the summer grazing *(aul)*. In the *Farhang-e zaban-e Tajiki* (Dictionary of Tajik), *qawm* is defined as 'the people of a district, locality or neighbourhood who pray in the same mosque under the leadership of an *imam*'.[4] The *qawm* here is defined as a solidarity group attached to one locality, but forming a network since it shares the locality with other groups with which it has a relationship of collaboration or competition. This structure still exists in many villages: thus in the village of Mazar-e Sharif in the Zarafshan valley there are three *qawm* and three mosques. If we consider the names given to the *qawm* it is clear that they have two meanings. Some words refer to a locality but others, more often, refer to a religious pseudo-hierarchy of prestige *(seyyed, sheikh, khwajegan, ghaziha, hajjiha, amirha)* and this in itself is evidence that these 'traditional' *qawm* are themselves the product of an earlier reformation. Nothing remains of the tribe or of the earlier historical period. Apparently, in the past, the hierarchy between these *qawm* was reflected in the choice of marriage partners: a man could not take a wife from a more prestigious *qawm* (for example, a *hajji* could not marry a *ghazi*).

What is the revelance of these divisions today in the political arena? Territorialization and the hierarchy of the *qawm* have suffered from the social upheaval and emergence of new elites arising from sovietization. However, they certainly play a role in the kolkhoz. They appear unexpectedly in the heart of the Communist Party. It is known that the majority of the cadres of the Tajik Communist Party come from the town of Khojent (formerly Leninabad); but it seems that a large number of these cadres come from the *qabileh* (word used by our informant) of the *khwajegan*. It is worth pointing out in this connection that the Turkomen kolkhozs correspond exactly to the former clans (Bouchet 1992).

The idea of a solidarity group being attached to a locality is still important. In Tajikistan it is common to speak of an interconnection between the extended family *(oyla)*, the lineage *(awlad)* over four generations and the locality *(mahal)*. Unlike tribal and clan affiliations, this solidarity is fluid and changes according to the way people live. It may be expanded or reduced according to circumstances and personal choice. People will refer to 'their own' *(khish va tabar)* to refer to a very wide kinship including the side of the wife as much as that of the husband. They will say 'my *qawm*' to refer to a solidarity which goes far beyond kinship, but without either the ability or the desire to define it more precisely. It is clear that the term *qawm* has not disappeared with the system that originally upheld it. It has acquired a new meaning; it is used to describe a specific solidarity group irrespective of its sociological base. This is clearly a reformation, an adaptation of a form of relationship to a different society.

It is here that we find the reformation of traditional segmentation and curiously it is once again around the village mosques which were closed for 70 years that the local segmentation into solidarity groups appears. The basis of these groups may come either from the remnants of a segmentation of traditional *qawm*, or more frequently, from the effect of a social change brought about by the establishment of the kolkhoz. (The two explanations are not contradictory as Bertrand Bouchet has shown in the case of the Turkoman kolkhoz.) The kolkhoz apparatchiks are not bureaucrats as in Russia, but new notables from the region who are creating around themselves new systems of patronage based on access to the goods and the wealth of the kolkhoz. Although it might appear that the kolkhoz is still operating as a collective, in reality it is operating as a clan. The notable of the kolkhoz tends to see it as a traditional solidarity group – clan, tribe, or *qawm* – which integrates into the state system through him, who is thus the interface: this is the model of the *khan* and of the Afghan *malek*. He has access to the land, which is redistributed by renting rather than private ownership, and this enables him to keep the kolkhoz as a place of authority and power. He also has access to fertilizers, fuels and seeds and this enables him to control distribution. Simultaneously, however, he is practising the solidarity of the clan; he uses his influence on behalf of young men who migrate to the town, he supports anyone originally from the kolkhoz who has a position of responsibility in the administration or who is involved in politics. Lavish marriage feasts are an important means of redistribution; on such occasions the notable provides the village with food and drink for two whole days.

But the kolkhoz is not in itself a new *qawm*, for within it there are groups that are excluded or groups that are dominated economically. The groups are distinguished by the mosques: the mosque of the kolkhoz is built and maintained by the administration, its mullah is paid by the kolkhoz. Only a short distance away, however, there is the mosque of the Grand Qazi, the leader of the opposition at the national level who gathers together the minority solidarity groups.

When the struggle for power broke out in Dushanbe in April 1992 it was reflected in the kolkhoz along the lines of the divisions between the new solidarity groups, the result of the process of fragmentation and reformation produced by collectivization.

However, this cannot fully explain why some districts are pro-opposition and others are pro-government, particularly where a district is entirely Tajik and where political position has no connection with ethnic conflict.

In fact, behind the new segmentation at the local level, there is at the national level a reordering of political affiliations according to the district of origin. Political life in Tajikistan cannot be understood without the expression *mahal-gera'i* (localism). According to our informants, however, this is a new word which cannot be found in the dictionary. It describes the political effect of belonging to a 'region' and how the political game has been reformed around this irrespective of the ideological stakes. In fact, by definition, 'localism' cannot be explained ideologically in the way that ethnic solidarity can be translated into nationalist ideology. 'Localism' is a mode of operation but not of legitimization; it belongs therefore essentially to the sub-political level while remaining the key to the political game.

These 'localities' from which the political factions are reformed rarely have any original historical or ethnic characteristic that would explain their solidarity. The feeling of belonging to a homogeneous, local group – compared to the earlier situation where the network of *qawm* divided villages – is, I believe, a result of the restructuring of political life around the administrative territorialization of the Soviet system (although this requires more research). Although the territory has its own economic rationale and administrative and political apparatus, it operates at the macro-political level as a solidarity group joining such or such a political faction on a platform of opposition to other regions, and not in defence of any particular ideological interests.

This localism is extended much further in national politics because Dushanbe is a neutral place; it has not produced a new elite in the way that Tashkent has.

Even people born in the town claim a locality – calling themselves 'the people of Koulab', 'the people of Khojent'and so on.

As we have seen, the district has its own segmentation: the kolkhoz is usually divided, the notion of *qawm* reappears. But there is an identity-seeking aware-ness of belonging to a locality, a district, which no doubt reflects modes of belonging which lost their content after the social and political transformation of the 1920s. The political struggles, the distribution of positions according to place of origin, the idea that wealth is only redistributed to the extent that a dis-trict is linked to the state; all this has strengthened localism, which becomes the rule of the macro-political game.

The modern *asabiyya* are undoubtedly a product of the state, since they arise from an administrative carve-up and use an ideological discourse appropriate for expressing the two significant options for the construction of the state – islamism or secularism. It does not exclude earlier forms of solidarity such as the *qawm* and the tribe, but only allows them either to play a local sub-political role or to link into national politics. The kolkhoz and the mosque are the very places where the traditional *asabiyya* are reformed through the political game led by the state, while the capital becomes the area of political struggle for the modern *asabiyya*, the localist factions.

The state: an optical illusion or a permanent fact?

It appears therefore that we have described two different types of states. First there is the Algerian model where the state remains important since all the *asabiyya* are formed and influenced by the existence of the state. Consequently, there will always be an Algerian state which, however corrupt and bureaucratic, has a certain stability. Then there is the Tajik (or Somali or Afghan) model where the existence of the state will not survive the retribalization.

To what extent has the state created new social strata (for example, bureau-cracy, army, intelligentsia) which only exist because of the state? Alternatively, to what extent has the process of retraditionalization involved locally-based soli-darity groups which are unaffected by or mistrustful of the existence of the state?

In Algeria there is a state apparatus, economic sectors linked to the existence of the state, social strata (especially the new intelligentsia) which exist only because of the state, as well as an army. In Central Asia the collective system survives as well as the apparatus established by the Soviets. Even if these states survive primarily because of the weakness of the opposition, the limited demand for democracy, and the exteriority of civil society, this nevertheless demon-strates that the existence of the state is more resistant to analysis and to events than would have been believed not long ago.

Which legitimizing discourse should these states adhere to? Will they be able to hold on or will they break up in the face of the retraditionalization of political relations implied by the emergence of the new *asabiyya*? Ethnicity and nationalism are the only ways of overcoming neotribalism, for although islamism employs rhetoric against social and tribal segmentation, it cannot control this new segmentation. National sentiments are clear in Algeria and more confused in Tajikistan. However, the reformation of the modern *asabiyya* is not so much a sign of the failure of the state but rather reflects a deep pessimism about a state apparatus which is regarded as incapable of resisting infiltration by networks of solidarity. No one believes that there are civil servants or politicians without allegiances and personal obligations. Even if the idea of public service and incorruptibility is only a myth, at least it is a myth that allows the political process to function. It is clear, however, that this process has been the subject of disappointment and rejection. Looked at this way, the crisis of politics, legitimacy and confidence is not fundamentally different at either of the two ends of the Middle East.

This chapter was translated from the French by Judy Mabro.

Notes

1   For a good analysis of the reformation of networks of influence in a society that has been profoundly changed by the state, the *dawras* in Iran, see Dale Eickelman, *The Middle East: An Anthropological Approach* (Englewood Cliffs, Prentice-Hall, 1981), pp. 197–9.

2. On the *qawm,* see Olivier Roy, 'Ethnies et politique en Asia centrale', in *Revue du Monde Musulman et de la Méditerranée* (January 1992), no. 59–60.

3   Salimi Ayubzad uses *hamqawm* to refer to the Afghan Tajiks in *Cheragh-i ruz,* no. 3 (July 1991), p. 4.

4   The dictionary of the Persian language published by the *Soviet Encyclopaedia* (Moscow, 1969): '*mardom-e yek mahalleh, gozar va ya dehi keh dar yek masjed va az pas-e yek imam namaz mikhanand*'. The equivalences are given as '*tayefeh, qabileh, khalq, mardom*'.

12

Republican Trajectories in Iran and Turkey: a Tocquevillian reading

JEAN-FRANÇOIS BAYART

The comparison of the modernizing authoritarian regimes in Turkey and Iran between the two world wars is a classic of political science. Once we get past the outward appearance of certain reforms undertaken by Mustapha Kemal and Reza Shah, however, it is not certain that this is a valid exercise. First of all, the history leading up to the appearance of each of these leaders differed widely. The political, social and economic organizations of the Ottoman empire and the Safavid or Qajar empires did not have much in common except a profound reciprocal suspicion. In particular, the relationship between *din* and *dawlah* (religion and state) did not assume the same significance in both cases. The Ottoman empire was originally a patrimonial system whose economic ascendancy, in the absence of feudal structures, prevented the formation of a genuine and juridically constituted civil society. It presented itself as a political whole, although the *padishah* heading it still had to come to terms with the religious authority of the *ulama* and the autonomy of the *millet* (communities) governing until the nineteenth century less by coercion than by patronage, thanks to the networks of guilds and religious orders. It was only 'when the empire was subdued by the West and a market society emerged that the bifurcation of state and society occurred: 'No longer the state as society, but the state against society,' writes I. Sunar (1974). In this context, the *Tanzimat* tended to emancipate the power of the sultan and his bureaucracy from the 'checks and balances' which had been curbing them up until then.

The historical course taken by imperial Iran was different. The central Safavid power asserted itself there – even more clearly than was the case in the Ottoman empire where the role of the patrimonial bureaucracy and the army was supreme – by way of the Shi'ite *ulama* brought from the Arab world to codify the rather heterodox faith of the Qizilbash who had placed Shah Isma'il on the throne. Yet again, even more clearly than in the Ottoman empire, the Shi'ite *ulama* acquired an economic and financial power which had no real counterpart among their Sunni peers. They even derived from their establishment in Iraq following the fall of the Safavids and the interlude of Nader Shah's reign (1736–41) a relationship of externality with the political centre something closer in certain respects to the model of Roman Christianity than that of Byzantine and Russian Caesaro-Papistry or the Ottoman model of the *devlet-baba* or father-state (Keddie 1972; Arjomand 1984a; Fischer 1980). Having acquired this autonomy, the Shi'ite *ulama* laboured to preserve it throughout the nineteenth and twentieth centuries, to the point of siding with a constitutional revolution of nationalist inspiration in the years 1905 to 1911 in order to channel it better (Richard 1991b, 120–21 in particular quoting the historian Adamiyat; Lahidji 1988, 133–58). At that time, the *ulama* of the Ottoman empire had lost much of their influence through the *Tanzimat* and also, paradoxically, through the islamic policy of Abdülhamid II (1876–1909), with his heavy reliance on the religious orders.

The respective profiles of the Iranian and Turkish revolutions at the beginning of the century show the signs of these different developments. Both bear the mark of the Russo-Japanese War and its consequences for the tsarist empire. Both convey the rejection of European imperialism and display a desperate attempt at 'moral and intellectual reform' on the part of political formations which know that they are endangered. Both, finally, drew nourishment from a common pool of ideas provided by the writings of the Young Ottomans, the Egyptian Constitutionalists, Sayyid Jamal al-Din Asadabadi al-Afghani and Mirza Husayn Ali Nuri (see, for instance, Cole 1992, 1–26; Keddie 1968; Mardin 1962). However, the Iranian revolution remained profoundly rooted in the traditional actors of the Qajar empire (the *ulama*, the bazaar, the quarter), while the Turkish was secularist from the outset, deeply influenced by nineteenth century European nationalism and the teachings of western philosophy and positivist sociology, and depended on a new actor – the higher civil service – which was Turkish and Muslim but had been living *alla Franca* for several decades.

The modernizing authoritarian regimes of Mustapha Kemal and Reza Shah Pahlavi are not as comparable themselves as may appear at first sight. The nationalist legitimation to which Atatürk and his lieutenants were able to appeal can never be over-emphasized: their service throughout a bitter war of national liberation in which they had taken the initiative to free their country from Christian occupation was beyond question and shielded them from the popular anger which their scandalous reforms aroused, while allowing them to retain within the new regime those elites who initially disputed the direction it was taking and who formed the 'Second Group' within the national Great Assembly. Reza Shah, on the other hand, appeared, not without reason, to be a tool of the British before they deposed him in 1941. And his son, Mohammed Reza, was never to be seen as anything but an American tool until his own downfall in 1979. Moreover, Atatürk revived the constitutionalism of 1876 and 1909, whereas the Pahlavis persistently attempted to conceal the inheritance of the Iranian revolution of 1905–11. Atatürk's regime was certainly authoritarian but he regularly invoked the legitimacy of the national Great Assembly, and overall made a relatively limited use of coercion, by the standards of the fascist west European and Soviet totalitarian regimes to which he was often compared. If we add that Mustapha Kemal did not accumulate personal wealth from the position of power he occupied, while the Pahlavis, father and son, displayed a vast appetite for it, we may certainly doubt that these two cases of authoritarian figures are comparable.

Republic and centralism

On the other hand the two republics, Turkish and Iranian, perhaps deserve to be interpreted in the light of each other, although all the evidence seems to separate them radically. It is not, of course, a matter of comparing political regimes which indeed, as we shall see, cannot be equated: in the first case there is a genuine democratic structure resting on a party system; in the second, an authoritarianism endowed with a strictly circumscribed pluralism, its motive power remaining simple factional strife. But an historical analysis of the genesis of each of these republics yields much insight into the construction of political islamic modernities. In both cases, external constraints have been a deciding factor. Geopolitical constraints, in the first place, arising from the regional context (the insidious conflict between Greece and Turkey; the Iran–Iraq war), the long East–West confrontation, in which Central Asia was one of the major frontiers, and more recent but no less important upheavals as represented by the collapse of the Soviet Union and the war in Kuwait. These lie in the direct line of a history which began at the end of the eighteenth century (in the case of Turkey) and the beginning of the nineteenth century (in the case of Iran), and they nurtured a specific republican imaginary, a rather paranoid character steeped in Jacobin nationalism (in Turkey) or islamic anti-imperialism (in Iran). Above all, they opened the door to the intervention of outside actors who had no hesitation in influencing the trajectory of those republics by means of war, the secret services, terrorism or aid.

Secondly, there were economic constraints in the most classic sense of that term. The strategic choice of the market economy and attachment to the EEC made by Turkey at the beginning of the 1960s, initiated a tendency to democratization, through the medium of conditionality in the matter of human rights, while the pressure of servicing the national debt at the end of the 1970s played a large part in the institutional change and economic liberalization of the neo-Kemalist republic in the first half of the 1980s. Similarly, the necessity of post-war reconstruction, the inability of the quasi-socialist organization of the national economy to adjust to the challenges of the capitalist economic world, and the stagnation of oil prices, led Iran to renew dialogue with western investors, and thus modified the balance of forces within the factional system of the Islamic Republic.

Even more fundamentally, the republican principle itself borrowed from the West both in Turkey and in Iran. Grafting it on comes into the category of that 'historical sociology of the transfer and diffusion' of political modernity described by Bertrand Badie (1986).

None the less, in both cases the weight of these external constraints and borrowings seems less important than that of internal dynamics. This is obvious in the case of Iran, where the setting up of the Islamic Republic was equivalent to a double rejection of external constraints: American influence, and structural adjustment of a rentier economy carried away by the fever of petrodollars, an adjustment upon which the shah had embarked to the great detriment of the bazaar. But in Turkey too the republic was born of nationalist struggle against foreign tutelage, and if the USA pleaded the cause of overtures to democracy in the years 1945–1950, it adjusted easily to the perpetuation of authoritarianism, as its subsequent attitude in Iran suggests.

In both countries, then, the republic seems to be endowed with indisputable internal historicity. We next meet the question of the continuities giving rise to it. In this respect, de Tocqueville's questions can shed valuable light. His interpretation of the French Revolution, which he sees 'emerging as if of itself from the society it was about to destroy', and which he did not think was 'as extraordinary as it once seemed to its contemporaries', is eminently 'continuist', so much so that Albert Hirschman does not hesitate to put it in the category of 'reactionary rhetoric'. In emphasizing that the French Revolution 'was only the outcome of very long travail, the sudden and violent termination of a work over which ten generations of men had laboured', Tocqueville has two clear lines of continuity in mind, neither of them attractive to his liberal spirit.

On the one hand, he sees that 'a great many procedures employed by the revolutionary government had their precedents and examples in measures taken with regard to the common people during the last two centuries of the monarchy', and that at bottom 'the old regime provided the revolution with several of its patterns', the revolution itself adding only 'the atrocity of its genius'. In its cruelty, this diagnosis would apply to Iran and Turkey. The Islamic Republic has been much derided for its return to the methods (and agents) of the notorious SAVAK, and the degree of coercion the new regime has allowed itself has gone far beyond what the Pahlavis thought proper, even though we must take into account a certain relaxation of the severity of the law in rural and small-town areas, so far as problems other than those which are strictly speaking 'islamic' are concerned. Likewise, in Turkey, the functionaries and cadres of the single party of the Kemalist republic embraced the condescending and bludgeoning paternalism of the Ottoman Father-State, summed up admirably by the *Kadro* ideologues in the 1930s: 'Revolution for the people, in spite of the people.'

On the other hand, Tocqueville saw the French Revolution 'augmenting the power and rights of the public authority'. 'If centralization did not perish in the revolution, it was because in itself it was the beginning of that revolution and its emblem.' Nor need we doubt that Iran and Turkey have been concerned not to 'destroy that absolute power, but to convert it.' In Iran, the constitution of 1979 adopted the nationalist creed of the Basic Law of 1906–07, though not without making it rather more rigorous. The non-Muslim religious minorities recognized by the Islamic Republic have a special status under the constitution, giving them the right to collective parliamentary representation but excluding them from the exercise of the highest political functions. Muslims themselves have equal rights based on citizenship, not on ethnic identity. However – and the constitution of 1979 was here moving to greater openness – it is stipulated that 'regional and tribal languages may be freely used in the press and the media, and their literature may be freely taught along with literature in Persian'.[1] Be that as it may, the Islamic Republic has in practice returned to the Pahlavi centralism, using the vehicle of Shi'ism, the confession to which the president of the republic must belong. The place of the Sunni minorities in the new institutions – for the most part Kurds and Baluchis – is thus circumscribed. Both minorities, moreover, stand in a relationship of armed dissidence to the centre: the autonomist Kurdish movements have been repressed by military force from the first months of the revolution, and the Baluchis, with increasing audacity, are waging what amounts to a war of drug trafficking and kidnapping in the south-east of the country. The Azeri question is more complex. We cannot speak of a minority here, since the Azeri Turks have economic control of a good part of Tehran, and have long exercised a prime political influence through the court. Although the independence of post-Soviet Azerbaijan makes some difference to the facts involved in the problem, the prospect of an autonomist Iranian Azeri movement remains unlikely. But during the first months of the revolution, islamic opposition in the shape of Ayatollah Shari'atmadari and the Republican Party of the Muslim People was undoubtedly a way of representing this regional particularism. Olivier Roy goes so far as to suggest that the recent evolution of the Islamic Republic has been to the detriment of the Turkish-speaking elites, and the accession of Hashemi Rafsanjani to the presidency of the republic in 1989 is evidence of Iran re-centring itself around its old Persian-speaking provinces (Roy 1991, 147–8).

None the less, the growth in the power and rights of the public authority – to echo Tocqueville – does not amount simply to the integration of minorities. In its way, the republic has taken up the project of the Pahlavis, and set about constructing a modern state by merely changing the principle of its legitimacy. But it is precisely this change which is important. To the extent that the vast majority of the population is Muslim, the republic has thus given itself the means of resolving the schizophrenia into which western-inspired modernization had cast the country, and of extending the ascendancy of political institutions over society. Bureaucratic normalization has now got the upper hand over revolutionary fervour, and the regime, with fewer and fewer scruples, is taking up the torch of Iranian nationalism and no longer neglects pre-islamic references. The war with Iraq, moreover, immediately mingled the experiences of republicanism and mobilization, whose social effects deserve systematic study. The linking of the provinces to the centre has certainly been made more complex by the increasing power of big regional cities like Tabriz, Isfahan, Shiraz and Mashhad. In the case of the last-named, there is a singular ambivalence in relations between the territorial administration, the *vaqf* of Astan-e Qods – strengthened by its real estate and landed property, the revenues it gets from the sanctuary of Imam Reza and by its direct access to supreme power through the revolutionary guide, Ali Khamene'i, and the foreign minister Ali Akbar Velayati and the bazaar – partly controlled by Afghans, its power augmented by pilgrimage, the opening of the frontier with Turkmenistan, and in all probability the recycling of money from drugs. But in any case, it can hardly be denied today that the Islamic Republic is above all a new avatar of the central Iranian state, whose revolutionary messianism has come to nothing.

The trajectory of the Kemalist republic is an even better example of this point of view. First because it endeavoured to give the ultimate response to the territorial dismemberment of the Ottoman empire and to foreign occupation by reconstituting Turco-Muslim identity. To some extent there had been a forerunner in the islamic approach of Abdülhamid II, which was based on the *tarikat* (sufi brotherhoods), the depositories of demotic Turkish culture. But it was chiefly the ideologues of the Turkish cause – among them many Turcophone intellectuals expelled from Russia and the Balkans by the expansion of the tsarist empire and nationalist revivals – and the Young Turks movement which realized this synthesis. Warmly welcomed by the minorities, the 1908 revolution quickly disillusioned them: it was to remain unwaveringly Turkish and Muslim if only because it was the work of a civil and military bureaucracy consisting by law of Turkish-speaking Muslims. The Committee for Union and Progress embarked on some of the cultural reforms which would be the glory of Kemalism, beginning with the reform of the Osmanli language, which was considerably simplified. During the 1920s and 1930s, the Republican People's Party systematically adopted this 'invention' of Turkish identity as the primordial political identity, making it the definitive cement of the state, and claiming to transcend the human heterogeneity of Anatolia in this way.

Secondly, the establishment of the republic was in the end brought about by that same bureaucracy which had gone on modernizing itself ever since the first half of the nineteenth century, had espoused a way of life *alla Franca*, and having received from Abdülhamid II (too long described as an obscurantist) a particularly effective training system, had taken the reins of power in 1908. It need hardly be said that the Kemalist republic perpetuated this pre-eminence and settled the old rivalry which opposed the centre to the provincial periphery, to the advantage of the former – sometimes at the cost of severe repression, particularly in Kurdish parts of the country. None the less, it institutionalized the subordination of that periphery by tolerating, come what may, the respectful opposition of the 'Second Group' within the national Great Assembly, adopting a multi-party system at the end of the Second World War, and recognizing the

electoral victory of the Democratic Party in 1950. Notwithstanding the corrective military exercises of 1960–61, 1971–73, and 1980–83, the power of this
piece on the political chessboard has since been confirmed, under the changing
colours of the Party of Justice, the Party of the Mother Country and the Party of
the Just Way. It is possible that a new chapter in the history of the republic has
now been opened: unable to crush the guerrillas of the Kurdistan Workers' Party
(PKK) the political class in Ankara, if not the army, is resigned to negotiating
the Kurdish question politically, even if it means opening the Pandora's box of
ethnic-cum-religious identities in Anatolia (Bozarslan 1991, 37–52; von
Bruinessen 1988; Bayart 1978; 1982).[2] But up to the end of the 1980s the republic displayed an entirely Tocquevillian continuity with respect to the imperative
of centralization.

Contrary to appearances, the same is true of its religious policy. Again, the
way for the reforms of Mustapha Kemal had been prepared by the ban on the
powerful *tarikat* of the Bektashi in 1826, the weakening of the *medrese* throughout the reign of Abdülhamid II (who preferred the *tekke* of the religious orders)
and the secularizing memorandum published by Ziya Gökalp in 1916. Atatürk,
moreover, did not separate the state from Islam, in conformity with the French
model of secularism; he definitively subordinated the one to the other by way of
the Office of Religious Affairs (Dumont 1984). In this way he took up the old
scheme of the sultans, always anxious to make the *ulama* subject to them, and
also that of the islamic reformers like al-Afghani and Ziya Gökalp: the making
of religion a state matter in this way was done through its conversion to a positivist ideology as well as by its 'Turkification' (Dumont 1984; Georgeon 1984).[3]
It was this new national and scientistic Islam which appropriated the republican
institutions more and more openly after the victory of the Democratic Party in
1950, and which the ideologues, animated by the spirit of anti-communism,
were anxious to unite with the Kemalist inheritance in the 1960s in order to
struggle better against 'subversion'. Today, most of the pieces on the political
chessboard lay some sort of claim to this 'turco-islamic synthesis', despite their
deep differences: the proto-fascist nationalists of Colonel Turkes, the militants
of Dr Erbakan's Islamic Party, different trends in the Party of the Mother
Country and the Party of the Just Way – all the way to Bülent Ecevit, the former
leader of the Republican People's Party.

The paradoxical invention of modernity

We have reached the point in our argument when the Tocquevillian reading
becomes of great interest again, giving us a better idea of what these continuities
are made of and showing that they go far beyond the mere stakes of centralization and methods of government. For let there be no misunderstanding about the
Tocquevillian problematics. Contrary to appearances, they cannot be reduced to
the condescending and somewhat 'reactionary' establishment of the futility of

the revolutionary drama. They are not a reflection simply on continuity but also on social change. More precisely, their continuist interpretation of revolutionary watersheds does not involve postulating the automatic and exclusive existence of these continuities. History is effectively made up of discontinuities, if only in the minds of the actors in it. This is the entire meaning of the central question of *L'Ancien régime et la Révolution:* 'Is the event in fact as extraordinary as it seemed to its contemporaries at the time?' Tocqueville shared the pre-occupations of what would later be called the history of mentality. Speaking of his search through the eighteenth-century archives, he concludes: 'I found a great many sentiments there which I had believed were born of the Revolution, a great many ideas I had hitherto thought derived from nowhere else, a thousand practices it alone is supposed to have given us; everywhere I found the roots of present society deeply embedded in that old soil.' Similarly, he remarks: 'Let us not be surprised by the wonderful facility with which centralization was re-established in France at the beginning of the century. The men of '89 had toppled the edifice, but its foundations had remained in the very soul of its destroyers, and suddenly it was possible to erect everything on those foundations again and build even more strongly than before.' The enduring nature of the mentality thus explains, to a great extent, those lines of continuity which transcend revolutionary ruptures. But it is blurred by the tumult of events and by 'passion' – a word much used by Tocqueville, who fixes upon the actors in the drama: 'The religious war was only an incident in this great revolution, a prominent and yet fleeting feature in its physiognomy, an ephemeral product of the particular ideas, passions and deeds which preceded it and prepared for it, not the work of its own genius. It was less as a religious doctrine than as a political institution that christianity inspired such furious hatred ... to the extent that the political work of the revolution was consolidated, while its irreligious work was undone ... the French Revolution is ... a political revolution which operated like a religious revolution and took on something of the appearance of one.' In many ways, Tocqueville's work is a meditation on the link between the *courte durée* of the conjuncture and the *moyenne* or *longue durée* of the structure, a meditation which we might describe anachronistically as Braudelian. '[The event] fills the awareness of its contemporaries with its obscuring smoke, but it does not last long; you scarcely see its flame,' writes Braudel, adding: 'Civilizations survive political, social, economic and even ideological risings, which indeed they command insidiously and sometimes powerfully' (1985, 45, 303).[4]

Now the strength of Tocqueville is to suggest the paradoxical nature of this link between the short term and the long term: 'I was convinced that *unknown to themselves*, they had preserved most of the sentiments and customs of the old regime, even its ideas, with the aid of which they had conducted the revolution which destroyed it, and that, *without meaning to*, they had used this debris to construct the edifice of the new society' (my own italics). This is Tocqueville's real lesson to us. Of course there can be no question of simply transferring his interpretation of the French Revolution to the Iranian and Turkish trajectories –

if only, in the latter case, because the concept of civil society, central to Tocqueville's reasoning, seems out of place when applied to the Ottoman empire, and because the phenomena of the mob and of violence, also constituents of the Tocquevillian explanation, are very much of secondary importance in the Kemalist revolution (Mardin 1971). However, we can better understand the paradoxical construction of political modernity in Iran and Turkey if we emphasize the processes of social change and their relationships with the political sphere strictly speaking. We may thus hope to suggest, ironically, that the Turkish Republic is a genuine islamic republic, and the Iranian Revolution was not an islamic revolution.

In Turkey – as we have seen – the electoral dominance of the heirs of the 'Second Group', from Menderes to Özal by way of Demirel, has allowed an official, renovated, scientistic, republican Islam to make its way into the heart of institutions; for instance, since 1982 it has benefited by compulsory religious instruction in both primary and secondary state schools. But at the same time a 'parallel Islam' has developed – to employ the expression of specialists on the former Soviet Union – which has enjoyed wider and wider tolerance since the 1950s. Some of the strands in it are rather conservative (like the powerful Naqshbendi order), even frankly reactionary (like the Suleymanci or the Ticani, who specialized during the 1950s in the destruction of impious busts of Atatürk), or subversive (like the Hareket group, closely related to the Muslim Brothers). None the less, most of the factors in this parallel Islam also convey support for 'civilization' as the ideologues of Kemalism understood it. For instance the Nurcu movement is content to lay claim to 'genuine secularism', that is, complete freedom of thought and religion, without any state control of the intellectual life of the citizens, and altogether quite comparable to the French model which, it should be repeated, is very different from the Kemalist option. For the rest, it does not question any of the great attainments of the republican civil code, even if it puts a socially conservative interpretation on them, and it claims a solid scientistic positivism in which the Koranic justifications retain a decorative function (Dumont 1984, 366ff; Göle 1990; Mardin 1989; Toprak 1981; Algar 1981).[5]

The islamic party led by Dr Erbakan since the 1960s – under the name of the Party of National Salvation until 1980, then after being banned for seven years, under the name of the Prosperity Party (RP) – is very close to this Nurcu movement, whose socio-economic approach it has adopted in its successive programmes. Since the last electoral campaign, the RP has presented itself as the defender of labourers, artisans and small tradesmen threatened by unemployment and interest rates 'contrary to Islam'; it has called attention to ecological threats and the situation of prostitutes, and has not shrunk from defending the position of women, showing a woman not wearing the veil on its posters. The votes it has attracted in its traditional strongholds, central and eastern Anatolia (except for the Kurdish south-east, which has turned away from it because of its alliances with the ultra-nationalists) and, a new phenomenon, in Istanbul, may have been conservation votes or protest votes, but were probably not islamist in the strictest sense.

In any case, the re-islamization of republican institutions operated, during the 1980s, above all by inscribing on the very heart of the state a more moderate and rather contradictory concept of this Turco-islamic synthesis, at the instigation of the army, Mr Özal and his party, ANAP, which was much divided over this question. Inspired by the army, the 1982 constitution aimed to guarantee the depoliticization of Turkish society and consolidate it around a new moral order with strong religious connotations; to enclose it, so to speak, within the magic triangle of family, mosque and barracks (Birtek and Toprak n.d.). Radio and television, the Ministry of Education, the Office of Religious Affairs, the universities, the army itself, were purged in conformity with this orientation – not to mention the harshness of repression against political militants of all shades of opinion and of associations, even cultural associations. But that was to disregard the persistent vigour of the old party system firmly rooted in society for several decades, if not since the second half of the nineteenth century (Vaner 1988; Lewis 1988 part 2; Mardin 1973). This was reconstituted in 1983–87, first in the restrictive forms imposed by the general staff – although their candidate suffered humiliation at the polls – then in the direct continuity of the configuration of the political chessboard of the 1950s to 1970s. Similarly, not enough account was taken of the vitality of 'civil society' which, thanks to migrations both within and outside the country, reformed itself, developed previously unheard-of forms of social struggle (demonstrations by women, homosexuals, ecologists) and moved into the new institutions, most notably by way of the Sufi brotherhood (*tarikat*).[6]

It is possible that the increasing attention these institutions attracted is a particularly conservationist mode of management of modernity, conveying the fears of the 'shop' facing the capitalist transformation of the economy, and also the moral anxieties of the middle classes profiting by it: the religious orders structure the social and sometimes political rise of new actors in the world of business while they comfort groups on the economic defensive. But they do not seem to express the despair and political rejection of those excluded from the system – as has been said, often prematurely, of islamism in Iran and Algeria – any more than they undermine the scientific rationalism of the secular republic by their teaching, as we have seen. Thus they seem to have been experimenting with original responses to the extension of the market economy, going along with it rather than opposing it, and they guarantee the integration into the republic of newly urbanized populations by organizing new networks of clientelism and social mobility, better adapted to the needs of the moment. For instance, it is revealing that the 'progression of Islam' at which western commentators are very ready to take fright – besides the fact that it often proceeds from an optical illusion sustained by the transfer westward of religious practices from eastern Anatolia – goes hand in hand with the economic transformation of the country, and is often a direct product of it. Thus the wearing of the veil has spread because of the development of means of transport and the visits to towns and cities which that transport facilitates. As for the Naqshbendi order, it has managed to take root in various villages in western Turkey where it was previously unknown, through industrialization and the arrival of Kurdish workers who were its adepts (Vergin 1973).[7]

Fundamentally, the very Tocquevillian paradox lies in the fact that the spread and legitimation of Kemalist reforms have been largely brought about by the rising power of their adversaries. The condition of women is a striking example (Petek-Salom Hukum 1983; Göle 1990, 181ff; White 1991). Mustapha Kemal's actions, for which the revolution of the Young Ottomans paved the way, scarcely affected any women at all but those in the urban classes already convinced of the charms of life *alla Franca*. The economic upheavals presided over, successively, by the Democratic Party, the Party of Justice and the Party of the Mother Country, particularly in the countryside, no doubt had more impact in this matter than the voluntarism of the cadres of the Republican People's Party. Similarly, at least for some, the reconstitution of the *tarikat* was a factor of acceptance of the enlightenment, of which the Kemalists had made themselves the positivist heralds. Finally and even more fundamentally, the republic received its definititive legitimation only through the electoral victory of its original opponents: the heirs of the 'Second Group'. Need one say that this paradoxical appropriation of the republic by its adversaries took place at grass roots level, through multiple personal conflicts? Some of these conflicts were channelled into the electoral process, others were settled by violence – and not only in the dark years of general terrorism (Vergin 1973; Vaner 1984; Leder 1979). The 'republic in the village', to echo Maurice Agulhon, was often a republic of hatred.

That being admitted, the awakening of Islam, far from being a danger to democracy in Turkey, can sanction it and consolidate the parliamentary regime, as the parties owing allegiance to catholicism have done in Germany, The Netherlands and Italy, in spite of their initial hostility. Perhaps this hypothesis is over-optimistic in that the 'turco-islamic synthesis' on which the republican edifice now rests is pregnant with a grave contradiction: owing allegiance to Sunni Islam while it destabilizes the Alevi minority (about 20 per cent of the population), which had already been the main target of the 'strategy of tension' conducted at the end of the 1970s by the proto-fascists of Colonel Türkes and the security services (Bayart 1982). At the present time, the 'counter-guerrillas' are encouraging a Sunni-Islamist Kurdish movement, Hezbollah, to engage in armed struggle against the PKK, while the recent textbooks of religious education distributed in state schools give a more negative picture of Shi'ism than before (Bayart 1982; Copeaux 1991). Once persecuted by the Ottoman empire, the Alevi community had welcomed, with relief, the republic which 'deconfessionalized' its condition, and it watched the slow Sunni re-islamization of the institutions after the 1950s with some apprehension. Tomorrow it may be subject to new attacks if the Kurdish question degenerates into inter-ethnic confrontations on a country-wide scale.

But whatever may be the dangers inherent in the resumption of the 'shadow war' conducted by the security against the PKK rebellion, it is not absurd to think that it was the same famous 'turco-islamic synthesis' which authorized the two recent ruptures of the republican trajectory: on the one hand, the attempt to adjust the Turkish economy upon which Mr Özal embarked in January 1980, and which may in time enlarge the social base of the regime, including the Kurdish factor; on the other, the culture and henceforward political recognition of Kurdish specificity. If these two trends were confirmed (and the Kurdish problem at least is one that will not be resolved in a day), the course of the centralization restored by the Kemalist republic would see a notable inversion.

In Iran, the contribution of Islam to the making of a republican modernity has been no less. Not that the Iranian Revolution of 1979 was a true islamic revolution, properly speaking. Certainly popular Shi'ite religious feeling provided it – with its paradigm of the passion of Kerbela – with the main part of its political themes and emotional appeal, although many Shi'ites identified themselves with the 'Safavid Shi'ism' stigmatized by Ali Shari'ati, and many Sunni Iranians took part in the anti-monarchist movement. Moreover, the constitution of the clerical-political factions which took the reins in the new regime and the elaboration of their radical ideology were largely worked out within the religious sphere, throughout the 1960s and 1970s: for instance, through the change in form and to a lesser extent in content of certain *rowzehkhani* in Tehran in the years 1960–63, or on the occasion of the theological and ideological battle that took place in the precincts of the Hoseiniyeh Ershad between 1964 and 1972, most notably setting two of the chief thinkers of the revolution at odds: Shari'ati, mentioned above, and the Ayatollah Motahhari. Then again, there was the departure for Qom and Najaf of a party of theology students from Mashhad after the death of the Ayatollah Milani and the destruction of the *madrasseh* next to the sanctuary of Imam Reza in 1975, or finally the rise to power in the south of Tehran and in other large cities of a new fundamentalist and populist Islam, born of the rural-urban migration, which developed its own networks of associations and prospered all the more easily because the monarchy sometimes showed it favour in order to bring more opposition to bear on the Muslim reformers and the Mojahedin (Chehabi 1990; Richard 1991).

But once we have recognized all this, it is very tempting to paraphrase Tocqueville once more and repeat that the revolution of 1979 was a 'political revolution which operated in the manner, and assumed something of the aspect, of a religious revolution'. The great majority of the clergy kept their own counsel, did not put their support behind the Ayatollah Khomeini's theory of the *velayat-e faqih* (rule of the jurisprudent) and are still concerned to see their destiny linked to that of a regime unable to supply the basic needs of the population. The evolution of that regime remains dependent on the relationship of forces within the clergy and here the weak link in Mr Rafsanjani's apparatus seems to be the Revolutionary Guide with whom he rules in tandem: a simple *hojjat al-Islam*, Ali Khamene'i has not been up to imposing his religious legitimacy on the *ozma* (grand) ayatollahs, and in Qom he sees the menacing figure of his rival Montazeri, removed from the succession to Imam in February 1989, placed de facto under house arrest and courted by the islamic opposition. However, the republic has well and truly passed into its 'Thermidorian' age, and we may recollect that the collegial exercise of authority during the *Directoire* period was characterized by great instability, the unleashing of material appetites under cover of fidelity to the achievement of the revolution, and a good dose of political, democratic and even military adventurism. Factional struggle now looms larger than ideological considerations, and its principal aim is the control of the economic resources by way of the retention or sharing of power. As such it cannot be reduced to a confrontation between 'radicals' and 'moderates'. Many social structures, particularly family networks, straddle that dividing line and forbid us to see Iranian political life, only as a zero-sum game in which every gain by those who claim to be moderate is matched by a loss for those supposed to be radical: both are in a relationship of osmosis rather than externality. Even if Mr Rafsanjani and Mr Khamene'i seem to have chalked up several points since the legislative elections of April 1992, no doubt competition continues in the National Council of Defence, the various security organs and above all in the economic sphere. So far as one can see, the president of the republic controls a large part of the oil revenues through the central bank, as well as bribes from foreign operators thanks to an *ad hoc* commission which sees that they are centralized. Moreover, he himself, with his family and entourage, pursues economic activities, the best known but not necessarily most productive of them being the pistachio-exporting business. The same is true of Mr Khamene'i, who also has at his disposal a considerable percentage of the gifts in cash and gold, whose value it is virtually impossible to calculate, made by ten million pilgrims each year on the tomb of the Imam Reza at Mashhad. But whatever may be the effective control over the currency market exercised by the central bank, which may be thought devoted to Mr Rafsanjani, numerous channels of the autonomous accumulation of power exist in a highly speculative economy: the import-export business, the real-estate market, and the network providing loans without interest, for instance. Factions concurrent with those of the president of the republic and the revolutionary guide thus continue to dispose of their own economic reserves, notably through the bazaar, the religious foundations and the places of pilgrimage. Naturally this is the real stake in the game being played for the great site of the Imam's mausoleum in south Teheran, the development of the sanctuary of Imam Reza at Mashhad, and even more important, the economic reform desired by Mr Rafsanjani. Those described as 'radicals' are perhaps not so much opposed to the principle of that reform as anxious not to see themselves marginalized in the process, even if they can show themselves capable of controlling, in their own interests, the possible privatization of the great foundations they direct, in the manner often noted in sub-Saharan Africa or central Europe. Besides this, the revenues from narcotics, bringing in as rumour has it scarcely less than those from oil, may well be able to contribute to the financing of Iranian political life some day, although nothing suggests they may be doing so now.

We can note, then, that Iranian political society, from both the economic and the religious angles, is now too diversified and complex for anyone to be able to impose as clear a hegemony as that of the Shah in the 1970s. The tendency seems to be an increase in the parcelling out of the system and its evolution towards a neo-corporatist model, if only because the Iranians no longer have access to essential goods and services (housing, cars, travel, education) by these various routes, through the medium of foundations, guilds, and state institutions such as the army or the Revolutionary Guards. In this sense the Islamic republic has proved to be a profoundly modernizing one, having institutionalized the traditional clientelist relations which make up Iranian society, and considerably enlarged the space-time context in which these relations develop. The *hejab*, the subject of many acerbic comments, provides a good example of this point of view if we follow the analysis of Fariba Adelkhah (1991; also, Haeri 1989). The imposition of the veil has been gradual, and was disputed in Iran itself. Today, it gives rise to many practices of innovation in dress which seek, more or less, to circumvent the rigour of the political edict or adapt it to the necessities of modern life, concern for personal comfort, the exigencies of allurement, and last but not least, the ethic of shame and modesty (the *hejab-e darun* or interior *hejab*). By this token it remains one of main points of crystallization of factional struggle and political debate. But its importance lies elsewhere. The main effect of the contrasting practice of the *hejab* has been to extend the access of women to the public sphere: veiled, they can visit pleasure parks or restaurants more easily than before, take part in Friday prayers or various religious meetings in town, or work in public places (although few of them have definitively chosen that path of social emancipation). Whether intentionally or not, the Islamic Republic has transformed the place of women in the social sphere, and done so perhaps better than the Shah's voluntarist policy could. This was not the work of the republic as a regime, although its main leaders have taken note of the role of women in the mobilization of the revolution and have finally recognized them, almost without reservation, as political actors, but of the climate of practices within the republic; women have made sure they did not throw out the baby of their own interests with the monarchical bathwater, and have put their minds to preserving what they gained under imperial rule, for instance, in the domain of conjugal relations, before seeking to extend it.

This fact may be extended to other aspects of Iranian society. Whatever the excesses of the islamic regime, society found room to manoeuvre again and has not ceased to invent its own forms of modernity (Adelkhah 1991; Toussie 1988). Moreover, the clergy had to associate themselves with this work, since they could no longer confine themselves to their relatively comfortable positions as censors of power and change. The clergy became a more or less direct agent of social transformation, moving, for instance, into the media, once regarded as profane, or raising religious shrines to places of cultural and technological modernity, as at Marghad-e Imam and Mashhad. But beyond that, the practices of people active on the Iranian scene go well beyond the islamic problem alone, all the more so because the Iranian Revolution – unlike the Russian or Chinese revolutions, for instance – has never questioned the autonomy of the family unit, endowed with value by religion, or the liberty to engage in business, to which its political base, both popular and of the bazaar, was attached.

At the heart of the republic, then, historical continuity and social change are inextricably mingled. Iran is going through a period of great demographic growth, and under pressure from its young people is withdrawing without futile dramatics from Khomeinist emotionalism, although we must not forget that it gave way to such emotionalism at the old Imam's funeral in 1989. There is no contradiction in this dual attitude. In losing some of its charisma, making itself more of a matter of routine, more 'Thermidorian', the regime is simply exploring a zone of compromise between its initial legitimacy and the social forces bringing with them new dynamics, which do not necessarily reject islamic and revolutionary tenets but do not recognize themselves in those tenets alone. It may be through the domestic cult of the 'martyrs' that we can best see the ambivalence of this relationship of Iranian society to the Islamic Republic. Evidence of family affection for the young people cut off in their prime? Yes, of course. A sign of support for a revolution which may be thought to have gone astray, but which toppled a *taghuti*, a corrupt order? And also, perhaps primarily, the sign of patriotism in the face of Iraqi aggression? Certainly. But as well as these, it is a mark of social distinction, bringing people the respect of their neighbours and allowing access to vital foodstuffs, to air tickets and housing in an economy ravaged by speculation and the 'free market'. A synthesis of the ancestral Shi'ite repertory of Karbala, modern nationalist pride, and strategies for rising in the world or for economic survival, the devotion which the Iranians lavish on the tombs and pictures of their war victims in itself sums up the historic and social density of the Islamic Republic 14 years after it was proclaimed.

As a whole, the politicians responsible are caught in the net of these ambiguous exchanges which blur the dichotomy of 'moderates' and 'radicals': neither one nor the other brings any specific, coherent response to the demands of the actors on the social scene, unless in the form of a distribution of sinecures and services within the framework of neo-corporatist clientelism. In this context, the new economic operators – the entrepreneurs, the *'kravati'* of the bazaar – are undoubtedly the rising force in the country: Muslims, hard workers, devoted to their families, proud nationalists, they are none the less eager to see progress and money, and in a way they form a second wave of 'Rastignacs', to use Bernard Hourcade's expression (Hourcade 1987, 24–8). In any case, they are highly representative of the present face of the Islamic Republic. Regarded in this light, the 1979 revolution can no longer be seen as the revenge of the Shi'ite tradition on a 'modernizing' project conducted too rapidly, a revenge of which Ayatollah Khomeini is supposed to have been the demiurge, nor can it be considered merely the avatar of the centralizing operation. It has been an extremely complex social event, one which put the paradoxical processes giving rise to modernity into gear, or caused them to rebound.

It remains to be seen whether this modernity, simultaneously made up of endogenous innovations and the appropriation of western frames of reference, will make its way towards forms which might be described as 'democratic'. We may doubt it. The Islamic Republic may have enlarged the framework of space and time within which the Iranians develop, and has largely succeeded in transcending urban quarters *(mahalleh)* in the context of exodus from the countryside and the instability of poverty – as witness, among other evidence, the moving of places where religious social events took place, and the disappearance of prominent street leaders who used to rule the fruit and vegetable markets and dictate to the townsfolk on behalf of politicians, the clergy and the bazaar (Richard 1990; Adelkhah 1991a).[8] But on this point it cannot be compared to the Kemalist republic. In the case of Turkey, the political clientelism of a party system took the place of local feeling through the construction of a market economy and the effective practice of universal suffrage, and, to echo Robert Bianchi, it is this party system which, since the 1960s, has brought a corporatist process of the arbitration of particular interests into existence, sometimes in a statist and sometimes in a pluralist manner (Bianchi 1984). In the case of Iran, as we have seen, a neo-corporatist system of the factional type prevails, in the context of a rentier and speculative economy regulated by power networks, and this notable difference certainly militates against the individuation of the citizen's relationship with the state, even if societal forms of 'self-identity' develop in other spheres (Giddens 1991). The great divergence between the two republican trajectories lies here. Thus it is not enough to say that the Kemalist republic is genuinely islamic, or that the Iranian revolution has not been really islamic. It must be added that the one is based on a party system subject to the mandate of the electorate and unable to ensure its complete control of a diversified market economy, while the other is dominated by factions traditionally devoid of partisan organizations worthy of the name, and able to keep control of the revenues from oil, the exchange, and property speculation. On the whole everything else arises from this difference in the relationship of forces between actors and structures within these two republics. It is true, for instance, that the nationalist movement and the advocates of the reform of Islam in Iran have never been noted for the depth or coherence of their democratic convictions, and that this failure to understand the liberal programme has not prepared them to resist the establishment of the dictatorship of the Islamic Republican Party (Chehabi 1990, especially 64ff). But on the other hand we may point out that the Kemalists have sometimes employed rough methods of government, and the Turkish army has never shrunk from correcting the course of democracy. It is the ability of social forces to transform themselves into political forces which constitutes the historical differential between the two systems. Similarly, the 'Özal dynasty' has shown as much greed as the new court of President

Rafsanjani, and the exception embodied by Atatürk in his time should not leave us under any illusions about the abnegation of the Turkish political elites; it is just that the possibilities of straddling positions of power and positions of accumulation are less capable of extensions in a market economy and a competitive political system than in a rentier economy and under an authoritarian regime.

Far be it from me, however, to sing the praises of the neo-liberal problematics of democratization. My purpose is quite different, and partly contradicts any such ideological creed. I think that we can only draw certain provisional conclusions from this swift survey, whose every point might well be scrupulously reconsidered. First, Islam in itself does not have any natural and unequivocal relationship with democracy: the divergence of the Turkish and Iranian republican trajectories are an admirable illustration of that fact. More widely, Islam can be a vehicle of social or political modernity, but it is often such a vehicle 'without meaning to' or 'without its own knowledge', as Tocqueville wrote of the revolutionaries, and Troeltsch of the paradoxical contribution of Protestantism to this same modernity (Troeltsch 1992). Finally, and to use a fashionable expression, the 'world time' of democracy is constantly being screened not through non-temporal cultures (such as Islam or the cultures of Africa and China) but through concrete historical situations: the purpose of democratic engineering is thus immediately limited by the lessons of historical sociology.

This chapter was translated from the French by Anthea Bell.

Notes

1   Article xv of the constitution. See also Richard (1991, 53–78).
2   For the 'Tocquevillian' reading of the process of centralization under the Ottoman empire and the Kemalist republic, I have relied in particular on Lewis (1961); Kazancigil Özbudan (1981); Kushner (1977); Panzac (1988); Mardin (1973) and Mantran ed. (1989).
3   For the development of Ottoman Islam in the nineteenth century, see Keddie (1972, chs 1 & 2); Mardin (1962); Birge (1965); Mantran ed. (1989) and Berkes (1964).
4   Furet (1978) for a convergent but rather different reading of Tocqueville.
5   See also, for an analysis of political Islam in contemporary Turkey, Mardin (1983); Margulies & Yildizoglu (1988) as well as Akin & Karaspan (1988) and Cakir (1992).
6   This concept of 'civil society' is used with reservations, see Bayart (1985b). Following Mardin, historians of Turkey generally consider that the Ottoman Empire had no civil society in the strict sense of the term. The same verdict probably applies to the Kemalist period. However, the political liberalization allowed by the constitution of 1961, and even more the development of the market economy and the social fabric associated with it throughout the following decades, now give some relevance to the idea. On that subject see Bianchi (1984); on the new social struggles, see J.-P.Thieck (1992).
7   We may recall that emigration to Western Europe often goes hand in hand with

intensified religous practice, and possibly with its politicization, see Kastoryano (1988).

8   See also F. Adelkhah 'L'imaginaire économique en République islamique d'Iran' in J.-F. Bayart, ed. *La Réinvention du Capitalisme*. Paris, Karthala, 1994.

9   For a study of these problems applied to the condition of women in the Islamic situation, see Adelkhah (1992).

Bibliography

Abd Allah, Ahmad (1992) 'Dimuqratiyya ala akhaz', *al-Arabi*, Section 111.

Abd al-Fattah, Nabil (1984) *al-Mushaf wa'l-saif*, Cairo.

Abd al-Halim (1979) *al-Ikhwan al-muslimun. Ahdath sana'at al-tarikh*, 3 vols, Alexandria.

Abdel-Khalek, Gouda (1991) 'Economic Liberalization and Democratization in the Middle East', unpublished paper prepared for the Conference on Democratization in the Middle East, Turkish Political Science Association, Antalya, Turkey (14–16 November).

Abdel-Khalek, Gouda, & Tignor, Robert, eds (1982) *The Political Economy of Income Distribution in Egypt*, New York.

Abd al-Majid, Wahid (1990) 'al-Dimuqratiyya fi'l-watan al-arabi (Waraqa khalfiyya)', *al-Mustaqbal al-arabi*, 138.

Abu-Amud, Muhammad Sa'd (1988) 'Sun al-qarar al-siyasi fi'l-huqba al-sadatiyya', *al-Mustaqbal al-arabi* 112, 11 (June), pp. 112–9.

Abu-Hakima, Ahmad Mustafa (n.d.) *The Modern History of Kuwait 1750–1965*, n.p.

Abu Jaber, Kamel, & Fathi, Schirin (1990) 'The 1989 Jordanian Parliamentary Elections', *Orient*, 31, 1, pp. 67–87.

Abu Jabir, Kamil (Abu Jaber, Kamel) (1992) 'al-Bu'd al-siyasi al-ijtima'i li'l-dimuqratiyya wa ma'zaquna al-hadari al-am', *al-Majalla al-arabiyya lil-ulum al-siyasiyya*, 5–6.

Abu'l-Nasr, Muhammad Hamid (1988) *Haqiqat al-khilaf bayn al-ikhwan al-muslimun wa Abd al-Nasir*, Cairo.

Abu-Lughod, Ibrahim (1966) 'Retreat from the Secular Path? Islamic Dilemmas of Arab Politics', *The Review of Politics*, 28, pp. 447–76.

Addi, Lahouari (1992) 'Islamicist Utopia and Democracy' in C. Butterworth & I. W. Zartman (eds.) *Political Islam. The Annals of the Academy of Political and Social Science*, 524 (November).

(1991) 'Peut-il exister une sociologie politique en Algérie?', *Peuples méditerranéens*, 54–5.

Adelkhah, F. (1992) 'Femmes islamiques femmes modernes?', *Pouvoirs*, 62 (autumn).

—(1991a) '"Michael Jackson ne peut absolument rien faire". Les pratiques musicales en République islamique d'Iran', *Cahiers d'études de la Méditerranée orientale et du monde turco-iranien*, 11 (January), pp. 23–40.

—(1991b) *La révolution sous la voile. Femmes islamiques d'Iran*, Paris.

Adil Kamal, Ahmad (1987) *al-Nuqat fawq al-huruf al-Ikhwan al-muslimun wa'l-nizam al-khass*, Cairo.

El-Affendi, Abdelwahab (1991) *Turabi's Revolution, Islam and Power in Sudan*, London.

Ahmed, Akbar S. (1988) *Discovering Islam, Making Sense of Muslim History and Society*, London.

—(1986) *Toward an Islamic Anthropology: Definition, Dogma and Direction*, International Institute of Islamic Thought.

al-Ahnaf, M. (1990) 'L'opposition maghrébine face à la crise du Golfe', *Maghreb-Machrek*, 130 (October–December).

Ajami, Fuad (1983) 'In the Pharaoh's Shadow: Religion and Authority in Egypt' in James P. Piscatori (ed.) *Islam in the Political Process*, London.

Akin, E & Karaspan, Ö. (1988) 'The "Turkish–Islamic Synthesis"', *Middle East Report*, 153 (July–August).

Algar, H. (1981) *The Naqshbandi Order in Republican Turkey*, Berlin.

Ali, Haidar Ibrahim (1992a) 'al-Mujtama al-madani fi misr wa'l-sudan' in Markaz dirasat al-wahda al-arabiyya (ed.) *al-Mujtama al-madani wa dawruhu fi tahqiq al-dimuqratiyya*, Beirut.

—(1992b) *Azmat al-islam al-siyasi: al-Jabha al-islamiyya al-qawmiyya fi'l-sudan namuzajan*, Alexandria.

Amara, Muhammad (1988) 'al-Tayyib wa'l-khabith fi huquq al-insan', *Minbar al-hiwar*, 9.

Amawi, Abla (1992) 'Democratic Dilemmas in Jordan', *Middle East Report*, 153 (July–August).

Amin, Samir (1988) 'Mulahazat hawla minhaj tahlil azmat al-dimuqratiyya fi'l-watan al-arabi' in Markaz dirasat al-wahda al-arabiyya, *Azmat al-dimuqratiyya fi'l-watan al-arabi*, Beirut.

Ammash, Husayn Murhij (1992) *Tajawuz al-ma'zaq. Muntalaqat al-islah al-iqtisadi fi Suriya*, Damascus.

Amnesty International (1990) *Jordan: Human Rights Protection after the State of Emergency*, London.

Anani, Jawad & Khalaf, Rima (1989) 'Privatization in Jordan' in Said El-Naggar (ed.) *Privatization and Structural Adjustment in the Arab Countries*, Washington DC, IMF.

Anderson, Lisa (1992) 'Liberalization in the Arab World', discussion paper for the Mellon Seminar, Near East Department, Princeton University (14 February).

—(1991a) 'Obligation and Accountability: Islamic Politics in North Africa', *Daedalus*, 120 (summer), pp. 95–112.

—(1991b) 'Political Pacts, Liberalism and Democracy: the Tunisian National Pact of 1988', *Government and Opposition*, 26, 2 (spring).

—(1986) *The State and Social Transformation in Tunisia and Libya 1830–1980*, Princeton.

Ansari, Hamied (1986) *Egypt: The Stalled Society*, Albany, NY.

Antoun, Richard (1989) *Muslim Preacher in the Modern World: a Jordanian Case Study in Comparative Perspective*, Princeton.

Arjomand, Said Amir (1992) 'Constitutions and the Struggle for Political Order: a Study in the Modernization of Political Traditions', *European Journal of Sociology*, XXXIII, pp. 39–82.

—(1988) 'Ideological Revolution in Shi'ism' in S.A. Arjomand (ed.) *Authority and Political Culture in Shi'ism*, Albany, NY.

—(1984a) *The Shadow of God and the Hidden Imam. Religion, Political Order and Societal Change in Shiite Iran from the Beginning to 1890*, Chicago.

—(1984b) 'Introduction: Social Movements in the Contemporary Middle East' in S.A. Arjomand (ed.) *From Nationalism to Revolutionary Islam*, London.

Arkoun, Mohammed (1986) *L'Islam, morale et politique*, Paris.

—(1984) *Pour une critique de la raison islamique*, Paris.

Asad, Muhammad (1980) *The Principles of State and Government in Islam*, Gibraltar.

Asad, Talal (1986) *The Idea of an Anthropology of Islam*, Washington, Center for Contemporary Arab Studies, Georgetown University.

Askari, Hossein, Cummings, J.T., and Glover, Michael (1992) *Taxation and Tax Policies in the Middle East*, London.

al-Awwa, Muhammad Salim (1991) 'al-Ta'addudiyya al-siyasiyya min manzur islami', *Minbar al-hiwar*, 20.

Ayalon, Ami (1986) 'Egypt' in H. Shaked & D. Dislon (eds.) *Middle East Contemporary Survey*, VIII, 1983–84, Tel Aviv.

al-Ayari, al-Shadhli (1990) 'Tajribat Tunis ma al-qita'ayn al-amm wa'l-khass wa mustaqbal al-tajriba' in Markaz dirasat al-wahda al-arabiyya, *al-Qita al-amm wa'l-qita al-khass fi'l-watan al-arabi*, Beirut.

Ayubi, Nazih N. (1993) 'Is Democracy Possible in the Middle East?', *European Consortium for Political Research*, Joint Session, Leiden, April (mimeo).

—(1991) *Political Islam. Religion and Politics in the Arab World*, London and New York.

Al-Azmeh, Aziz (al-Azma, Aziz) (1993) 'Islamism and the Arabs' in *Islams and Modernities*, London and New York.

—(1992a) *al-Ilmaniyya min manzur mukhtalif*, Beirut.

—(1992b) *al-Asala wa siyasat al-hurub min al-waqi*, London.

—(1991a) 'Islamic Revivalism and Western Ideologies', *History Workshop Journal*, 32, pp. 44–53.

—(1991b) 'The Discourse of Cultural Authenticity: Islamic Revivalism and Enlightenment Universalism' in Deutsch and Eliot (eds) *Culture and Modernity*, Honolulu.

—(1991c) 'Islam as a Political Category', paper presented to the XVth World IPSA Congress.

—(1991d) 'al-Arab wa'l-dimuqratiyya', *al-Naqid*, 41.

—(1990) 'Utopia and Islamic Political Thought', *History of Political Thought*, XI–i.

—(1989) 'Ba'idan an satwat al-qawl al-dini', *al-Naqid*, 16.

—(1987) *al-Turath bayn al-sultan wa'l-tarikh*, Beirut and Casablanca.

—(1983) *al-Kitaba al-tarikhiyya wa'l-ma'rifa al-tarikhiyya*, Beirut, 1983.

Azmi, Khalid (1989) 'Jam'iyyat rijal al-a'mal al-misriyyin: al-namat al-jadid min jama'at al-masalih fi'l-mujtama al-misri', *al-Fikr al-istratiji al-arabi*, 28, 7 (April), pp. 155–84.

Babeair, Abdulwahab Saleh (1990) 'Contemporary Islamic Revivalism: A Movement of a Moment', *Journal of Arab Affairs*, 9.

Badie, Bertrand (1992) *L'État importé: l'occidentalisation de l'ordre politique*, Paris.

—(1986) *Les deux États. Pouvoir et société en Occident et en terre d'Islam*, Paris.

Baker, Raymond William (1991) 'Afraid of Islam: Egypt's Muslim Centrists between Pharaohs and Fundamentalists', *Daedalus*, 120, 3 (summer).

—(1990) *Sadat and After, Struggles for Egypt's Political Soul*, London and Cambridge, MA.

Bakhash, Shaul (1991) 'Democracy in the Arab World', *Dissent* (summer), pp. 332–60.

Barry, Brian (1983) 'Self-Government Revisited' in David Miller & Larry Siedetop (eds.) *The Nature of Political Theory*, Oxford.

Bates, Robert, & Lien, Donald (1985) 'A Note on Taxation, Development and Representative Government', *Politics and Society*, 14, 1, pp. 53–70.

Bayart, Jean-François (1985) 'L'énonciation du politique', *Revue française de science politique*, 3 (June).

—(1982) 'La question Alevî dans la Turquie moderne' in Olivier Carré (ed.) *L'Islam et l'État dans le monde d'aujourd'hui*, Paris.

—(1978) 'Turquie: la mythologie de l'État national', *Peuples méditerranéens*, 3 (April–June), pp. 113–21.

Baydun, Abbas (1992) 'Ba'ad masa'il al-dimuqratiyya fi'l-fikr al-siyasi al-arabi', *al-Hayat*, 20 June 1992.

al-Bayyumi Ghanim, Ibrahim (1992) *al-Fikr al-siyasi lil-imam Hasan al-Banna*, Cairo.

Beblawi, Hazem, & Luciani, Giacomo, eds. (1987) *The Rentier State*, London.

Becker, Gary S. (1960) 'An Economic Analysis of Fertility' in *Demographic and Economic Changes in Developing Countries*, Princeton.

Beetham, David (1991) *The Legitimation of Power*, London.

Bellin, Eva (1992) 'Tunisian Industrialists and the State' in I.W. Zartman (ed.) *Tunisia. The Economy of Reform*, Boulder, CO, and London.

Bendix, Reinhard (1961) 'The Lower Classes and the Democratic Revolution', *Industrial Relations* (October), pp. 91–116.

Ben Néfissa, Sarah (1992) 'Le Mouvement associatif égyptien et l'Islam. Éléments d'une problematique', *Maghreb-Machrek*, 135 (January–March), pp. 19–38.

Berkes, N. (1964) *The Development of Secularism in Turkey*, Montreal.

Beydoun, Ahmad (1987) 'Des Traditions collectives aux aspirations individuelles' in Dominique Chevallier (ed.) *Renouvellements du monde arabe*, Paris.

Bianchi, Robert (1989) *Unruly Corporatism: Associational Life in Twentieth-Century Egypt*, New York and Oxford.

—(1986) 'The Corporatization of the Egyptian Labour Movement', *Middle East Journal*, 40, 3, 1986, pp. 429–44.

—(1984) *Interest Groups and Political Development in Turkey*, Princeton.

Bill, James (1984) 'Resurgent Islam in the Persian Gulf', *Foreign Affairs*, 63, pp. 108–27.

Binder, Leonard (1990) *Islamic Liberalism: A Critique of Development Ideologies*, Chicago.

—(1978) *In a Moment of Enthusiasm: Political Power in the Second Stratum in Egypt*, London and Chicago.

Biraben, Jean-Noël (1969) 'Essai d'estimation des naissances de la population algérienne depuis 1891', *Population*, 4, Paris.

Birge, J.K. (1965) *The Bektashi Order of Dervishes*, London.

Birtek, F., & Toprak, B. (n.d.) 'The Puzzle of Neo-Republicanism: Contemporary Transformations in State Ideology and the Conflictual Agendas of Neo-Liberal Authoritarianism' (mimeo).

al-Bishri, Tariq (1984) 'al-Dimuqratiyya wa thawrat 23 Yulyu: 1952–1970' in Markaz dirasat al-wahda al-arabiyya, *Azmat al-dimuqratiyya fi'l-watan al-arabi*, Beirut.

Blackbourn, David, & Eley, Geoff (1984) *The Peculiarities of German History: Bourgeois Society and Politics in Nineteenth-Century Germany*, Oxford.

Bon, Frédéric (1979) 'Qu'est-ce qu'un vote?', *L' Histoire*, 2 (June), pp. 105–21.

Bouaouaja, Mohammed (1989) 'Privatization in Tunisia: Objectives and Limits' in S. El-Naggar (ed.) *'Privatization and Structural Adjustment in the Arab Countries*, Washington DC.

Bouchet, Bertrand (1992) 'Le Kolhoze turkmène', *Revue du monde musulman et de la Méditerranée*, 59–60 (January).

Boullata, Issa J. (1990) *Trends and Issues in Contemporary Arab Thought*, Albany, NY.

Boyer, G.R. (1989) 'Malthus was Right After All: Poor Relief and Birth Rates in Eastern England', *Journal of Political Economy*, 97, pp. 93–114.

Bozarslan, H. (1991) 'Turquie: un défi permanent au nationalisme kémaliste', in E. Picard (ed.) *La Question kurde*, Paris.

Brand, Laurie A. (1991) 'Liberalization and Changing Political Coalitions: The Bases of Jordan's 1990–91 Gulf Crisis Policy', *Jerusalem Journal of International Relations*, 13, 4.

Bratton, & Vandewalle, D. (1992) 'Popular Protest and Political Reform in Africa', *Comparative Politics*, 24, 4, pp. 419–42.

Braudel, Ferdinand (1985) *Écrits sur l'histoire*, Paris.

Breuilly, John (1985) *Nationalism and the State*, Manchester.

Brown, L. Carl (1984) *International Politics and the Middle East*, London.

van Bruinessen, M. (1988) 'Between Guerrilla War and Political Murder: the Workers' Party of Kurdistan', *Middle East Report* (July–August), pp. 40–46.

Brynen, Rex (1982) 'Economic Crisis and Post-Rentier Democratization in the Arab World: The Case of Jordan', *Canadian Journal of Political Science*, XXV, 1 (March), pp. 69–97.

Buchanan, Allen (1991) *Secession*, Boulder, CO.

Bul'aras, Abd al-Hayy, & al-Haji, Hisham (1984) 'al-Ittijah al-islami: khilafat tuhaddid bil-inqisam', *al-Mawqif*, 27 (17 November).

Burgat, François (1991) 'Les Islamistes et la démocratie: repères pour une recherche' in Bernabé López García (ed.) *Elecciones, Participación y Transiciones Políticas en el Norte de África*, Madrid, Instituto de Cooperación con el Mundo Árabe.

—(1990) 'La mobilisation islamiste et les élections algériennes du 12 Juin 1990', *Maghreb-Machrek*, 129 (July–September), pp. 5–22.

—(1988) *L'Islamisme au Maghreb*, La voix du sud, Paris.

Burke III, Edmund (1986) 'Understanding Arab Social Movements', *The Maghreb Review*.

Butterworth, Charles (1992) 'Political Islam: the Origins' in C. Butterworth & I.W. Zartman (eds.) *Political Islam. The Annals of the Academy of Political and Social Science*, 524 (November).

—(1987) 'State and Authority in Arabic Political Thought' in G. Salamé (ed.) *The Foundations of the Arab State*, London.

—(1982) 'Prudence vs Legitimacy: the Persistent Theme in Islamic Political Thought' in Hillal Dessouki (ed.) *Islamic Resurgence in the Arab World*, New York.

—(1980) 'Philosophy, Stories and the Study of Elites' in I.W. Zartman (ed.) *Elites in the Middle East*, New York.

Butterworth, Charles, & Zartman, I.W., eds (1992) *Political Islam. The Annals of the Academy of Political and Social Science*, 524 (November).

Cakir, R. (1992) 'La Mobilisation islamique en Turquie', *Esprit* (August–September), pp. 130–42.

Caldwell, John (1982) *Theory of Fertility Decline*, London.

—'Towards a Restatement of Demographic Transition Theory', *Population and Development Review*, 2, 3–4.

Caldwell, John, & Caldwell, Pat (1990) 'Cultural Forces Tending to Sustain High Fertility' in World Bank, *Population Growth and Reproduction in Sub-Saharan Africa*, Washington.

Camau, Michel (1991a) 'Démocratisation et changements des régimes au Maghreb' in Bernabé López García (ed.) *Elecciones, Participación y Transiciones Políticas en el Norte de África*, Madrid, Instituto de Cooperación con el Mundo Árabe.

—ed. (1991b) *Changements politiques au Maghreb*, Paris.

—(1987) *La Tunisie au présent. Une modernité au-dessus de tout soupçon?*, Paris.

—(1984) 'L'État tunisien: de la tutelle au désengagement', *Maghreb-Machrek*, 103, pp. 8–38.

Cantori, Louis J. (1991) 'Political Participation, Consultation and State-Civil Relations in the Middle East', unpublished paper.

Carré, Olivier (1993) *Le nationalisme arabe*, Paris.

—(1991) *L'utopie islamique dans l'Orient arabe*, Paris.

—(1984) *Mystique et Politique. Lecture révolutionnaire du Coran par Sayyid Qutb*, Paris.

—ed. (1982a) *L'islam et l'état dans le monde d'aujourd'hui*, Paris.

—ed. (1982b) *La légitimation islamique des socialismes arabes*, Paris.

—(1978) 'Turquie: la mythologie de l'État national', *Peuples méditerranéens*, 3, (April–June), pp. 113–21.

Carré, Olivier, & Michaud, Gérard (1983) *Les Frères musulmans, Égypte et Syrie (1928–1982)*, Paris.

CERED (1989) *Variables socio-démographiques au Maroc: les interdépendances*, Rabat.

Chamie, Joseph (1981) *Religion and Fertility: Arab and Christian–Muslim Differentials*, Cambridge.

Chatelus, Michel (1984) 'Attitudes Towards Public Sector Management and Reassertion of the Private Sector in the Arab World', paper presented at the Middle East Studies Association of North America.

Chaudry, Kiren Aziz (1991) 'On the Way to the Market. Economic Liberalization and Iraq's Invasion of Kuwait', *Middle East Report*, 170, 21 (May–June), pp. 14–23.

Chehabi, H.E. (1990) *Iranian Politics and Religious Modernism. The Liberation Movement of Iran under the Shah and Khomeini*, London.

Cheriet, Boutheina (1992) 'The Resilience of Algerian Populism', *Middle East Report* (January–February), pp. 9–14.

Chiha, Michel (1957) *Politique intérieure*, Beirut.

Cohen, Amnon (1982) *Political Parties in the West Bank under the Jordanian Regime: 1949–1967*, London.

Cole, J.R.I. (1992) 'Iranian Millennarism and Democratic Thought in the 19th Century', *International Journal of Middle East Studies*, 24, pp. 1–26.

Cole, Juan, & Keddie, Nikki, eds. (1986) *Shi'ism and Social Protest*, New Haven.

Collier, David, ed. (1979) *The New Authoritarianism in Latin America*, Princeton.

Collier, David, & Norden, Deborah L. (1992) 'Strategic Choice Models of Political Change in Latin America', *Comparative Politics*, 24, 2 (January), pp. 229–43.

Cooper, Mark N. (1982) *The Transformation of Egypt*, London and Canberra.

Copeaux, E. (1991) 'L'image des Arabes et de l'islam dans les manuels scolaires d'histoire turcs depuis 1931', *Cahiers d'études sur la Méditerranée orientale et le monde turco-iranien*, no. 12.

Corm, Georges (1993) 'La Réforme économique algérienne: une réforme mal aimée?', *Maghreb-Machrek*, 139 (January–March), pp. 9–27.

Cornelius, Wayne A., Gentleman, Judith, & Smith, Peter H. (1989) *Mexico's Alternative Political Futures*, Center for US/Mexican Studies, University of California at San Diego, Monograph no. 30.

Courbage, Youssef, & Fargues, Philippe (1974) *La Situation démographique au Liban* (2 vols), Beirut.

Craig, Ann L. (1991) *The Mexican Political System in Transition*, Center for US/Mexican Studies, University of California at San Diego.

Crystal, Jill (1990) *Oil and Politics in the Gulf: Rulers and Merchants in Kuwait and Qatar*, New York.

Cuinet, Vital (1896) *Syrie, Liban et Palestine, Géographie administrative, statistique et raisonnée*, Paris.

Dahl, Robert (1971) *Polyarchy*, New Haven.

—ed. (1973) *Regimes and Oppositions*, New Haven.

Dalila, Arif (1990) 'Tajribat Suriya ma al-qita'ayn al-amm wa'l-khass wa mustaqbal al-tajriba' in Markaz dirasat al-wahda al-arabiyya, *al-Qita al-amm wa'l-qita al-khass fi'l-watan al-arabi*, Beirut.

Damascus Chamber of Commerce (1992) *al-Taqrir al-sanawi 1991*, Damascus, Chamber of Commerce.

—(1991) *al-Taqrir al-sanawi 1990*, Damascus, Chamber of Commerce.

Darwish, Sa'id, ed. (1990) *al-Marhala al-dimuqratiyya al-jadida fi'l-urdun: tafasil al-munaqashat wa hukumat al-thiqa*, Amman.

Davis, Eric (1984) 'Ideology, Social Class and Islamic Radicalism in Modern Egypt' in S.A. Arjomand (ed.) *From Nationalism to Revolutionary Islam*, London.

Davis, John (1987) *Libyan Politics: Tribe and Revolution*, London.

Dekmejian, R. Hrair (1985) *Islam in Revolution: Fundamentalism in the Arab World*, Syracuse.

Dessouki, Ali E. Hillal (1991a) 'The Democratization Process in The Arab World: Some Preliminary Remarks', paper presented to the conference organized by the Turkish Political Science Association on Democratization in the Middle East, Antalya, Turkey, 14–16 November (mimeo).

—(1991b) 'L'Évolution politique de L'Égypte: pluralisme démocratique ou néo-autoritarisme?', *Mahgreb-Machrek*, 127 (January–March), pp. 7–16.

Diamond, Larry, Linz, Juan J., & Lipset, Seymour Martin, eds. (1989) *Democracy in Developing Countries* (4 vols), Boulder, CO.

Dirgham, Ahmad (1981) 'Hawla ishkaliyyat al-dimuqratiyya fi'l-watan al-arabi' in Muntada al-fikr wa'l-hiwar (ed.) *al-Tajarib al-dimiqratiyya fi'l-watan al-arabi*, Algiers.

Diyab, Muhammad Hafiz (1987) *Sayyid Qutb. al-Khitab wa'l-idiyulujiyya*, Cairo.

Djaït, Hicham (1988) 'La Deuxième heure', *Réalités*, 11–17 (September)

Donohue, John J., & Esposito, John L., eds. (1982) *Islam in Transition: Muslim Perspectives*, New York.

Duben, Alan, & Behar, Cem (1981) *Istanbul Households – Marriage, Family and Fertility, 1880–1940*, Cambridge.

Duclos, Louis-Jean (1990) 'Les Élections législatives en Jordanie', *Mahgreb-Machrek*, 129 (July–September), pp. 47–73.

Dumont, P. (1984) 'L'Islam en Turquie, facteur de renouveau?', *Les Temps Modernes*, 456–7 (July–August), pp. 352–6.

Dunleavy, Patrick, & O'Leary, Brendan (1987) *Theories of the State: the Politics of Liberal Democracy*, New York.

Dunn, John, ed. (1992) *Democracy. The Unfinished Journey. BC 508 to 1993 AD*, New York and Oxford.

Dwyer, Kevin (1991) *Arab Voices: the Human Rights Debate in the Middle East*, London and New York.

Easton, David (1965) *A Systems Analysis of Political Life*, London.

Economic Science Association in the Syrian Arab Republic (1986) *Nadwat al-thulatha al-iqtisadiyya al-khamisa hawl al-tanmiya al-iqtisadiyya fi'l-qutr al-arabi al-suri*, Damascus, Economic Science Association.

El-Edel, Reda (1982) 'Impact of Taxation on Income Distribution: An Exploratory Attempt to Estimate Tax Incidence in Egypt' in Gouda Abdel-Khalek and Robert Tignor (eds.) *The Political Economy of Income Distribution in Egypt*, New York.

Eickelman, Dale (1986) 'Royal Authority and Religious Legitimacy: Morocco's Elections 1960–1984', in Myron Arnoff (ed.) *The Frailty of Authority*, New Brunswick.

—(1981) *The Middle East: an Anthropological Approach*, Englewood Cliffs.

Eley, Geoff (1992) 'The Social Construction of Democracy in Germany', paper presented to the conference organized by the Social Science Research Council on 'Law, Property and State Power', Istanbul.

Elster, Jon (1988) 'Introduction' in Jon Elster & Rune Slagstad (eds.) *Constitutionalism and Democracy*.

—(1983) *Sour Grapes. Studies in the Subversion of Rationality*, Cambridge.

Elster, Jon, & Slagstad, Rune, eds. (1988) *Constitutionalism and Democracy*, Cambridge.

Enayat, Hamid (1982) *Modern Islamic Political Thought*, London.

Entelis, John (1991) 'The Crisis of Authoritarianism in North African Politics: Islamism, Democracy and the State' in National Academy of Sciences, *After the Transition: Problems of Newly Democratizing Countries*, Washington.

Escallier, Robert, & Signoles, Pierre, eds. (1992) *Changement économique, social et culturel et modifications des champs migratoires internes dans le monde arabe* (2 vols), Tours.

ESCWA (1989) *Demographic and Related Socio-Economic Data Sheets for the Countries of ESCWA*, 6, Baghdad, United Nations.

Esposito, John L., ed. (1983) *Voices of Resurgent Islam*, New York.

Esposito, John L., & Piscatori, James P. (1992) 'Democratization and Islam', *The Middle East Journal*, 45, 3 (summer), pp. 427–40.

Etienne, Bruno (1977) *L'Algérie, cultures et révolution*, Paris.

Fath, Sigrid, & Mattes, Hanspeter, eds. (1992) *Demokratie und Menschenrechte in Nordafrika*, Hamburg.

Farag, Iman (1991) 'La Politique à l'égyptienne. Lecture des élections législatives', *Mahgreb-Machrek*, 133 (July–September), pp. 19–33.

—(1990) 'Les Législatives égyptiennes ou la politique entre clientélisme et citoyenneté', *Égypte/Monde Arabe*, 4/4, pp. 175–6.

Farag, Iman, & Roussillon, Alain (1992) 'Hypothèse totalitaire/hypothèse démocratique, formulations et enjeux du débat sur la démocratisation dans le monde arabe' in *Démocratie et démocratisation dans le monde arabe*, Cairo.

Fargues, Philippe (1990) 'Algérie, Maroc, Tunisie: vers la famille restreinte?', *Population et sociétés*, 248.

—(1986) Un siècle de transition démographique en Afrique méditerranéenne: 1885–1985', *Population*, 2, pp. 1992–14.

Farouk-Sluglett, Marion (1991) 'Iraq: rente pétrolière et concentration du pouvoir', *Maghreb-Machrek*, 131 (January–March).

Farschid, Olaf (1989) '*Hizbiya*: Die Neuorientierung der Muslimbruderschaft Ägyptens in den Jahren 1984 bis 1989', *Orient*, 30, 1, pp. 53–74.

Farsoun, Samih K. (1988) 'Class Structure and Social Change in the Arab World: 1995' in Hisham Sharabi (ed.) *The Next Arab Decade. Alternative Futures*, Boulder, CO.

Fathi, Schirin H. (1990) 'The 1989 Jordanian Parliamentary Elections', *Orient*, vol 31, 1, pp. 53–74.

Ferchiou, Rida (1991) 'The Social Pressure on Economic Development in Tunisia' in I.W. Zartman (ed.) *Tunisia. The Political Economy of Reform*, Boulder, CO & London.

Finley, Moses (1964) *The Ancient Greeks*, London.

Fischer, Michael (1982) 'Islam and the Revolt of the Petite Bourgeoisie', *Daedalus*, 3, 1, pp. 101–25.

—(1980) *Iran: From Religious Dispute to Revolution*, Cambridge, MA.

Fluehr Lobban, Carolyn (1991) 'Islamization in the Sudan', in John Voll (ed.) *Sudan: State and Society in Crisis*, Bloomington, Indiana.

Forstner, Martin (1988) 'Auf dem legalen Weg zur Macht? Zur politischen Entwicklung der Muslimbruderschaft Ägyptens, *Orient*, 29, 3, pp. 386–422.

Foster, G. (1965) 'Peasant Society and the Image of the Limited Good', *American Anthropologist*, 67, 2.

Friedrich, Carl J. (1968) 'Constitutions and Constitutionalism', *The International Encyclopedia of the Social Sciences*, vol 3, New York, p. 318.

—(1950) *Constitutional Government and Democracy*, Boston, MA.

Furet, F. (1978) *Penser la Révolution française*, Paris.

Gaffney, Patrick (1992) 'Popular Islam' in C. Butterworth & I.W. Zartman (eds.) *Political Islam. The Annals of the Academy of Political and Social Science*, 524 (November).

Geertz, Clifford (1973) 'The Politics of Meaning' in *The Interpretation of Cultures*, New York.

—(1964) 'Ideology as a Cultural System' in D. Apter (ed.) *Ideology and Discontent*, New York, pp. 47–76.

Geertz, Clifford, Geertz, Hildred, & Rosen, Lawrence (1979) *Meaning and Order in Moroccan Society*, London.

Gellner, Ernest (1991) 'Civil Society in Historical Context', *International Social Science Journal*, 129 (August), pp. 495–510.

—(1988) *Plough, Sword and Book. The Structure of Human History*, Chicago.

—(1983) *Nations and Nationalism*, Oxford.

—(1981) *Muslim Society*, Cambridge.

—(1967) 'Democracy and Industrialization', *Archives Européennes de Sociologie*.

General Federation of Trade Unions in the Syrian Arab Republic (1987) *al-Taqrir al-amm*, Conference on National Creativity and Self-Reliance.

Georgeon, F. (1986) 'La Politique de l'enseignement en Turquie', *Les Temps Modernes*, 456–7.

Ghabra, Shafeeq (1991) 'Voluntary Associations in Kuwait: the Foundations of a New System?', *The Middle East Journal*, 45, 2 (spring), pp. 199–215.

Ghalyun, Burhan (1992) 'Bina al-mujtama al-madani al-arabi: dawr al-awamil al-dakhiliyya wa'l-kharijiyya' in Markaz dirasat al-wahda al-arabiyya (ed.), *al-Mujtama al-madani wa dawruhu fi tahqiq al-dimuqratiyya*, Beirut.

Ghannushi, Rashid (1991) 'al-Haraka al-islamiyya wa'l-nizam al-dawli', *al-Ghadir*, 14, 15 & 16.

—(1990) 'Ma'alim fi stratijiyyat al-da'wa al-islamiyya', *al-Hiwar*, 19 (autumn).

—(1989a) *Mahawir islamiyya*, Cairo.

—(1989b) 'al-Fikr al-Islami bayn al-mithaliyya wa'l waqi'iyya' in *Mahawir islamiyya*, Cairo.

—(1987) 'Tahlil li'l-anasir al-mukawwina li'l-zahira al-islamiyya bi Tunis' in Markaz dirasat al-wahda al-arabiyya (ed.) *al-Harakat al-islamiyya al-mu'asira fi'l-watan al-arabi*, Beirut.

—(1984) *Maqalat*, Paris.

Giddens, A. (1991) *Modernity and Sef-identity, Self and Society in the late Modern Age*, Stanford.

Gilsenan, Michael (1982) *Recognizing Islam*, London and New York.

Goldberg, Ellis (1991) 'Smashing Idols and the State: the Protestant Ethic and Egyptian Sunni Radicalism', *Comparative Studies in Society and History*, 33.

Goldstone, Jack (1991) *Revolution and Rebellion in the Early Modern World*, Berkeley.

Göle, N. (1990) 'Ingénieurs islamistes et étudiantes voilées en Turquie: entre le totalitarisme et l'individualisme' in G. Kepel & Y. Richard (eds.) *Intellectuels et militants de l'Islam contemporain*, Paris.

Grissa, Abdelsatar (1991) 'The Tunisian State Enterprises and Privatization Policy' in I.W. Zartman (ed.) *Tunisia: the Political Economy of Reform*, Boulder, CO, & London.

von Grunebaum, Gustav E. (1962) *Modern Islam: the Search for Cultural*

Identity, Los Angeles.

Gubser, Peter (1988) 'Balancing Pluralism and Authoritarianism' in P.J. Chelkowski & R.J. Pranger (eds.) *Ideology and Power in the Middle East,* Durham and London.

Habib, Kazim (1990) 'Ta'qib' in Markaz dirasat al-wahda al-arabiyya, *al-Qita al-amm wa'l-qita al-khass fi'l-watan al-arabi,* Beirut.

Haeri, S. (1989) *Law of Desire. Temporary Marriage in Iran,* London.

Halpern, Manfred (1963) *The Politics of Social Change in the Middle East and North Africa,* Princeton.

al-Hamidi, Muhammad al-Hashim (1989) *Ashwaq al-hurriyya. Qissat al-haraka al-islamiyya fi tunis,* Kuwait.

al-Hammami, H. (1989) *Din al-zalamiyya. 'al-Ittijah al-Islami' harakat nahda...am harakat inhitat?,* 3rd edn., Tunis.

Hanafi, Hassan (1982) 'Des Idéologies modernistes à l'Islam révolutionnaire, *Peuples méditerranéens',* 21 (October–December), pp. 3–14.

Harbi, Mohammed (1980) *Le FLN: mirage et réalité,* Paris, Jeune Afrique.

Harik, Iliya, & Sullivan, Dennis, eds. (1993) *Privatization and Liberalization in the Middle East,* Bloomington.

al-Harmasi, Abd al-Latif (1985) *al-Harakat al-islamiyya fi tunis,* Tunis.

Held, David, ed. (1992) *Prospects for Democracy, Political Studies,* XL, special issue, Oxford.

—(1987) *Models for Democracy,* Oxford.

Heller, Mark H. (1990) 'The Middle East: Out of Step with History', *Foreign Affairs,* 59–1, pp. 152–71.

Hendricks, Bertus (1987) 'Egypt's new political map: report from the election campaign', *Middle East Report,* 17, 4 (July–August).

—(1985) 'Egypt's Elections, Mubarak's Bind', *Middle East Report,* 14, 1 (January), pp. 11–18.

Hermassi, Abdelbaki (al-Hirmasi, Muhammad Abd al-Baqi) (1991) 'The Islamicist Movement and November 7' in I.W. Zartman (ed.) *Tunisia: The Political Economy of Reform,* Boulder, CO, & London.

—(1987a) 'al-Islam al-ihtijaji fi tunis' in Markaz dirasat al-wahda al-arabiyya (ed.) *al-Harakat al-islamiyya al-mu'asira fi'l-watan al-arabi,* Beirut.

—(1987b) *al-Mujtama wa'l dawla fi'l-maghrib al-arabi,* Beirut.

—(1984) 'La Société tunisienne au miroir islamiste', *Maghreb-Machrek,* 103 (January–March).

Hermet, Guy, Rose, Richard, & Rouquié, Alain eds. (1978) *Elections without Choices,* London and Basingstoke.

Heydemann, Steven (1992) 'The Political Logic of Economic Rationality: Selective Stabilization in Syria' in Henri Barkey (ed.) *The Politics of Economic Reform in the Middle East,* New York.

Hilal, Ali al-Din, ed. (1986) *Intikhabat majlis al-sha'b 1984: Dirasa wa tahlil,* Cairo.

Hill, Enid (1990) 'Political Issues and Justiciable Questions: Adjudicating the

Constitutionality of Laws in Egypt', paper presented to the annual meeting of the Middle East Studies Association, San Antonio.

—'Egypt's New Capitalism. After Fifteen Years of *al-Intifah*', paper presented to the annual meeting of the Middle East Studies Association, 15–18, Toronto (November).

Hinnebusch, Raymond (1993) 'Syria' in T. Niblock & E. Murphy (eds.) *Economic and Political Liberalization in the Middle East*, London.

—(1990) *Authoritarian Power and State Formation in Ba'thist Syria. Army, Party and Peasant*, Boulder, CO.

—(1985) *Egyptian Politics under Sadat: The Post-Populist Development of an Authoritarian-Modernizing State*, Cambridge.

Hirschman, Albert O. (1973) 'The Changing Tolerance to Income Inequality in the Course of Economic Development', *The Quarterly Journal of Economics*, LXXXVII, 4.

—(1971) *A New Bias for Hope: Essays on Development and Latin America*, New Haven.

Holmes, Stephen (1988) 'Pre-commitment and the Paradox of Democracy' in Jon Elster & Rune Slagstad (eds.) *Constitutionalism and Democracy*, Cambridge.

Hopfinger, Hans (1990) 'Kapitalistisches Agro-Business in einem sozialistischen Land? Syrien versucht neue Wege in der Landwirtschaft', *Die Erde*, 121, pp. 157–76.

Hourani, Albert (1981) *The Emergence of the Modern Middle East*, Berkeley.

—(1967) *Arabic Thought in the Liberal Age, 1798–1939*, London.

Hourcade, B. (1987) 'Les Nouveaux Rastignac', in B. Hourcade & Y. Richard, *Téhéran au-dessous du volcan*, Paris.

Hourcade, B., & Richard, Y. (1987) *Téhéran au-dessous du volcan*, Paris.

Hudson, Michael C. (1991a) 'After the Gulf War: Prospects for Democratization in the Arab World', *The Middle East Journal*, 45, 3 (summer), pp. 407–26.

—(1991b) 'The Middle East under Pax Americana: How New, How Orderly?', paper presented at the annual meeting of the Middle East Studies Association, Washington DC (mimeo).

—(1990) 'The Democratization Process in the Arab World: An Assessment', paper presented to the annual meeting of the American Political Science Association, San Francisco.

—(1980) 'Islam and Political Development' in John Esposito (ed.) *Islam and Development*, New York.

—(1977) *Arab Politics: the Search for Legitimacy*, New Haven.

al-Humsi, Mahmud (1984) *Khitat al-tanmiya al-arabiyya wa ittijahatuha al-takamuliyya wa'l-tanafuriyya: dirasa lil ittijhat al-inma'iyya fi khitat al-tanmiya al-arabiyya al-mu'asira iza al-takamul al-iqtisadi al-arabi 1960–1980*, Beirut.

Huntington, Samuel P. (1984) 'Will More Countries Become Democratic?',

Political Science Quarterly, 99, 2, pp. 193–218.

—(1991) *The Third Wave: Democratization in the Late Twentieth Century,* London.

—(1993) 'The Clash of Civilizations', *Foreign Affairs,* summer 1993.

Husayn, Adil (1984) 'al-Mahaddidat al-tarikhiyya wa'l-ijtima'iyya lil dimuqratiyya', *al-Mustaqbal al-arabi*, 67.

Huwaidi, Fahmi (1992) 'al-Islam wa'l-dimuqratiyya', *al-Mustaqbal al-arabi,* 166, pp. 4–37.

Hyden, Goran (1980) Beyond Ujamaa in Tanzania: *Underdevelopment and an Uncaptured Peasantry,* Berkeley.

Ibrahim, Saad Eddine (1993) 'Crises, Elites and Democratization in the Arab World', *The Middle East Journal,* 47, 2 (spring).

—(ed.) (1989) *al-Ta'addudiyya al-siyasiyya wa'l-dimuqratiyya fi'l-watan al-arabi,* Amman.

—(1988) *al-Mujtama wa'l-dawla fi'l-watan al-arabi,* Beirut.

—(ed.) (1988) *al-Sahwa al-islamiyya wa humum al-watan al-arabi,* Amman.

Ibrahim, Zaynab (1991) 'The Great Flight from Taxes', *al-Ahram al-iqtisadi,* 12, 30, pp. 20–24.

Imam, Samiya Sa'id *(1986) Man yamluk misr?! Dirasa tahliliyya lil-usul al-ijtima'iyya li-nukhbat al-infitah al-iqtisadi fi'l-mujtama al-misri 1974–80,* Cairo.

Ionescu, Ghita, & Gellner, Ernest, eds. (1969) *Populism: Its Meanings and National Characteristics,* London.

Ismael, Jacqueline S. (1982) *Kuwait: Social Change in Historical Perspective,* Syracuse.

Issawi, Charles (1956) 'Economic and Social Foundations of Democracy in the Middle East', *International Affairs* (January), pp. 27–42.

Ittihad al-muhamin al-arab (1991) 'al-bayan al-amm li-ittihad al-muhamin al-arab', Annual Conference, *al-Mustaqbal al-arabi,* 154, 14.

al-Jabiri, Muhammad Abid (1993) 'Ishkaliyyat al-dimuqratiyya wa'l-mujtama al-madani fi'l-watan al-arabi', *al-Mustaqbal al-arabi* (January).

—(1992) 'al-Mas'ala al-dimuqratiyya wa'l-awda al-arabiyya al-rahina', *al-Mustaqbal al-arabi,* 157.

—(1988) *al-Maghrib al mu'asir,* Casablanca.

Jansen, Johannes J. G. (1986) *The Neglected Duty: the Creed of Sadat's Assassins and Islamic Resurgence in The Middle East,* New York.

Jedaane, Fahmi (1990) 'Notions of the State in Contemporary Arab-Islamic Writings' in Giacomo Luciani (ed.) *The Arab State,* London.

El-Kadi, Galia (1990) 'Nouvelles tendances de l'urbanisation en Égypte: Ruptures et continuités', *Égypte/Monde arabe,* 1, 1.

al-Kanz, Ali (1992) 'Min al-i'jab bi'l-dawla ila iktishaf al-mumarasa al-ijtima'iayya', *al-Mustaqbal al-arabi,* no. 158, vol 14.

Kapil, Arun (1991) 'Les Partis islamistes en Algérie', *Maghreb-Machrek,* 133, pp. 103–11.

Karru, Muhammad (1987) 'al-Muthaqaffun wa'l-mujtama al-madani fi tunis', *al-Mustaqbal al-arabi,* 104, 10.

Kasparian, Robert (1991) *L État de la population en 1987,* Beirut.

—(1990) *Enquête sur la famille chrétienne au Liban,* Beirut, Centre d'Études et de Recherches sur l'Orient Chrétien.

Kastoryano, R. (1988) 'Paris–Berlin. Politiques d'immigration et modalités d'intégration des familles turques' in R.E. Leveau & G. Kepel (eds.) *Les Musulmans dans la société française,* Paris.

al-Kaylani, Musa Zayd, ed. (1990) *al-Harakat al-islamiyya fi'l-urdun,* Amman.

Kazancigil, A, & Özubudun, E., eds. (1981) *Atatürk, Founder of a Modern State,* London.

Kazemi, Farhad, & Waterbury, John, eds. (1991) *Peasants and Politics in the Middle East,* Miami.

Keane, John (1988) *Democracy and Civil Society,* London.

Keddie, N.R. ed. (1972) *Scholars, Saints and Sufis. Muslim Religious Institutions in the Middle East since 1500,* Berkeley.

—(1968) *An Islamic Response to Imperialism. Political and Religious Writings of Sayyid Jamal ad-Din al-Afghani,* Berkeley.

Kedourie, Elie (1992) *Politics in the Middle East,* Oxford.

Kepel, Gilles (1984) *Le Prophète et le Pharaon,* Paris.

Kepel, G., & Richard, Y. (1990) *Intellectuels et militants de l'Islam contemporain,* Paris.

Kerr, Malcolm (1963) 'Arab Radical Notions of Democracy', *St Antony's Papers,* 16, London.

Khafaji, Isam (1991) 'al-Burjuazziyya al-mu'asira wa'l-dawla al-mashriqiyya: dirasa muqarina li-Misr wa'l-Iraq', *al-Jadal,* 1.

—(1986) 'The Parasitic Base of the Ba'athist Regime' in Cardri, *Saddam's Iraq. Revolution or Reaction?,* London.

Khalid, Muhammad Khalid (1985) *Difa an al-dimuqratiyya,* Cairo.

al-Khalidi, Salah Abd al-Fattah (1991) *Sayyid Qutb min al-milad ila'l-istishhad,* Damascus and Beirut.

al-Khalil, Samir (1989) *Republic of Fear: The Politics of Modern Iraq,* London and Berkeley.

Khouri, Nicole (1990) 'De la mouvance islamiste en général et des Gama'at Islamiyya en particulier (1970–1985). Essai de lecture sociologique', *Revue Tiers-Monde,* 121 (January–March).

al-Khuli, Lutfi (1981) 'Mulahazat wa ta'qibat hawl al-turuhat al-muta'alliqa bi'ishkaliyyat al-dimuqratiyya fi'l-alam al-arabi' in Muntada al-fikr wa'l hiwar (ed.) *al-Tajarib al-dimuqratiyya fi'l watan al-arabi,* Algiers.

Khuri, Fuad I (1990) *Tents and Pyramids: Games and Ideology in Arab Culture from Backgammon to Autocratic Rule,* London.

Kienle, Eberhard (1990) *Ba'th versus Ba'th: The Conflict between Syria and Iraq,* London.

Kirchheimer, Otto (1969) 'Changes in the Structure of Political Compromise' in F.S. Burin & K. Shell (eds.) *Politics, Law and some Exchanges: Selected*

Essays of Otto Kirchheimer, New York.

Köhler, Michael (1992) 'Islamismus und Autoritarismus in Tunesien', *Konrad-Adenauer-Stiftung Auslandsinformationen* (3 March 1992), pp. 12–24.

Krämer, Gudrun (1993) 'Islamic Notions of Democracy', *Middle East Report*.

—(1992a) 'Islam et pluralisme' in *Démocratie et démocratisation dans le monde arabe,* Cairo, Dossiers du CEDEJ, pp. 339–51.

—(1992b) 'Liberalization and Democracy in the Arab World', *Middle East Report,* 174 (January–February).

—(1987) *Die Wahl zur ägyptischen Volksversammlung vom April 1987,* Ebenhausen.

—(1986) *Ägypten unter Mubarak: Identität und nationales und Interesse,* Baden-Baden.

—(1984) 'Die Wahl zum ägyptischen Abgeordnetenhaus vom Mai 1984' , *Orient* 25, 3, Hamburg, pp. 361–75.

Kusher, D. (1977) *The Rise of Turkish Nationalism 1876–1908,* London.

Labib, Tahir (1992a) 'Ilaqat al-mashru al-dimuqrati bi'l-mujtama al-madani al-arabi', *al-Mustaqbal al-arabi,* 158.

—(1992b) 'Hal al-dimuqratiyya matlab ijtima'i?' in *al-Mawqif,* 1.

Lahidji, A. K. (1988) 'Constitutionalism and Clerical Authority' in S.A. Arjomand (ed.) *Authority and Political Culture in Shi'ism,* Albany.

Lamchichi, Abderrahim (1989) *Islam et contestation au Maghreb,* Paris.

Lapidus, Ira (1992) 'The Golden Age: The Political Concepts of Islam' in C. Butterworth & I.W. Zartman (eds.) *Political Islam. The Annals of the Academy of Political and Social Science,* 524 (November).

—(1987) 'Islam and Modernity' in S.N. Eisenstadt (ed.) *Patterns of Modernity II. Beyond the West,* New York.

Larif-Beatrix, Asma (1987) 'L'Évolution de l'état tunisien', *Maghreb-Machrek,* 116 (April–June).

Laroui, Abadallah (al-Arwi, Abd Allah) (1987) *Islam et Modernité,* Paris.

—(1984) *Mafhum al-dawla,* Beirut.

—(1981) *Mafhum al-hurriyya,* Casablanca.

—(1974) *La Crise des intellectuels arabes,* Paris.

—(1967) *L'Idéologie arabe contemporaine,* Paris.

Laurell, Ana Cristina (1992) 'Democracy in Mexico: Will the first be the last?', *New Left Review,* 194 (July–August).

Laurens, Henry (1991) *Le Grand jeu: Orient arabe et rivalités internationales depuis 1945,* Paris.

Lawson, Fred (1990) 'Libéralisation économique en Syrie et en Irak', *Maghreb-Machrek,* 128 (April–June), pp. 27–52.

Layne, Linda L. (1988) 'Tribu et citoyenneté. Relations primordiales et démocratie dans la Jordanie rurale', *Maghreb-Machrek,* 114 (October–December).

—ed. (1987) *Elections in the Middle East,* Boulder, CO.

Lebanese Family Planning Association (1984) *Family Planning in Rural Lebanon, 1983–1984,* Beirut.

Leca, Jean (1990) 'L'État et société en Algérie' in Basma Khodmani-Darwish (ed.) *Maghreb. Les années de transition*, Paris.

—(1988a) 'L'économie contre la culture dans l'explication des dynamiques politiques', *Bulletin du CEDEJ* (Cairo), 23, pp. 15–60.

—(1988b) 'Social Structure and Political Stability: Comparative Evidence from the Algerian, Syrian and Iraqi Cases' in Adeed Dawisha & I.W. Zartman *Beyond Coercion: The Durability of the Arab State*, London.

Leca, Jean, & Schemeil, Yves (1983) 'Clientélisme et néo-patrimonialisme dans le monde arabe', *Revue Internationale de Science Politique*.

Leca, Jean, & Vatin, Jean-Claude (1975) *L'Algérie politique. Institutions et régime*, Paris.

Leca, Jean, Leveau, Rémy, Djeghloul, Abdelkader, & Kapil, Arun (1991) 'Algérie: Politique et société', *Maghreb-Machrek*, 133 (July–September), pp. 89–111.

Leder, A. (1979) 'Party Competition in Rural Turkey: Agent of Change or Defender of Traditional Rule?', *Middle Eastern Studies*, 15, 1 (January), pp. 82–105.

Legrain, Jean-François (1991) 'La conférence de Téhéran', *Maghreb-Machrek*, 134 (October–December), pp. 124–7.

Lesch, Ann (1989) 'Democracy in Doses: Mubarek Launches His Second Term as President', *Arab Studies Quarterly*, 11.

Leveau, Rémy (1991) 'L'Algérie en état de siège', *Maghreb-Machrek*, 137 (July–September), pp. 116–22.

—(1989) 'La Tunisie du Président Ben Ali: équilibre interne et environment arabe', *Maghreb-Machrek*, 124 (April–June), pp. 4–17.

Leveau, R., & Kepel, G., eds. (1988) *Les Musulmans dans la société française*, Paris.

Levine, Daniel H. (1990) 'Paradigm Lost: Dependence to Democracy', *World Politics*, 40, 3, pp. 377–94.

Lewis, Bernard (1961) *The Emergence of Modern Turkey*, London.

Lewis, John (1964) *Quiet Crisis in India: Economic Development and American Policy*, New York.

Lijphart, Arend (1991) 'Majority Rule in Theory and Practice: The Tenacity of a Flawed Paradigm', *International Social Science Journal*, 129, pp. 483–93.

—(1984) *Democracies: Patterns of Majoritarian Government and Consensus in Twenty-one Countries*, Yale.

—(1977) *Democracy in Plural Societies: A Comparative Exploration*, Yale.

Lipset, Seymour Martin (1960) *Political Man*, New York.

Longueunesse, Elizabeth (1988) 'L'État et syndicalisme en Syrie: Discours et pratiques', *Sou'al*, 8 (February), pp. 97–130.

López García, Bernabé, ed. (1991) *Elecciones, Participación y Transiciones Políticas en el Norte de África*, Madrid, Instituto de Cooperación con el Mundo Árabe.

Luciani, Giacomo (1992) 'Le Nouvel ordre pétrolier arabe', *Maghreb-Machrek*,

136 (April–June).

—(1990a) 'Arabie Saoudite; l'industrialisation d'un État allocataire', *Maghreb-Machrek*, 129 (July–September). pp. 77–93.

—ed. (1990b) *The Arab State*, London.

—(1988) 'Economic Foundations of Democracy and Authoritarianism: the Arab World in Comparative Perspective', *Arab Studies Quarterly*, 10, 4 (autumn).

—(1987) 'Allocation vs Production States: a Theoretical Framework' in H. Beblawi & G. Luciani (eds.) *The Rentier State*, London.

McClelland, David (1963) 'National Character and Economic Growth in Turkey and Iran' in Lucien Pye (ed.) *Communications and Political Development*, Princeton.

McLaurin, R.D., & Jureidini, P. (1984) *Jordan: The Impact of Social Change on the Role of the Tribes*, New York.

MacRae, Donald (1969) 'Populism as an Ideology' in G. Ionescu & E. Gellner (eds.) *Populism. Its Meanings and National Characteristics*, London.

Magnuson, Douglas K. (1991) 'Islamic Reform in Contemporary Tunisia: Unity and Diversity', in I.W. Zartman (ed.) *Tunisia. The Political Economy of Reform*, Boulder, CO.

Mahdavi, Hossein (1969) 'The Pattern and Problems of Economic Development in Rentier States: the Case of Iran' in Michael Cook (ed.) *Studies in the Economic History of the Middle East*, London.

Makram-Ebeid, Mona (1992) 'Kayf yu'addi al-mujtama al-madani dawran fi'l-tanmiya?', *al-Hayat* (18 April).

—(1989) 'Political Opposition in Egypt: Democratic Myth or Reality?', *The Middle East Journal*, 43, 3, pp. 423–36.

—(1988) 'Le Rôle de l'opposition officielle en Égypte', *Maghreb-Machrek*, 119, pp. 52–4.

Markaz dirasat al-wahda al-arabiyya, ed. (1992) *al-Mujtama al-madani wa dawruhu fi tahqiq al-dimuqratiyya*, Beirut.

—ed. (1989) *al-hiwar al-qawmi al-dini*, Beirut.

—ed. (1987) *al-Harakat al-islamiyya al-mu'asira fi'l-watan al-arabi*, Beirut.

—ed. (1984) *Azmat al-dimuqratiyya fi'l-watan al-arabi*, Beirut.

Mantran, R., ed. (1989) *Histoire de l'Empire Ottoman*, Paris.

Mardin, S. (1989) *Religion and Social Change in Modern Turkey: the Case of Bediüzzaman Saïd Nursi*, Albany.

—(1983) 'Religion and Politics in Modern Turkey' in J. Piscatori (ed.) *Islam in the Political Process*, Cambridge.

—(1973) 'Center–Periphery Relations: a Key to Turkish Politics?', *Daedalus* (winter).

—(1971) 'Ideology and Religion in the Turkish Revolution', *International Journal of Middle East Studies*, 2, pp. 197–211.

—(1962) *The Genesis of Young Ottoman Thought: a Study in the Modernization of Turkish Political Ideas*, Princeton.

Margulies, R., & Yildizoglu, E. (1988) 'The Political Uses of Islam in Turkey',

Middle East Report, 153 (July–August), pp. 12–17.

Mayer, Ann Elizabeth (1991) *Islam and Human Rights*, Boulder, CO.

al-Mazrou, Yagob, & Farid, Samir (1991) *Saudi Arabia Child Health Survey*, Riyadh.

Menashri, David, ed. (1990) *The Iranian Revolution and the Muslim World*, Boulder, CO, San Francisco and Oxford.

al-Milaff al-Ihsa'i (1992) *al-Mustaqbal al-arabi*, no. 156, vol. 14, pp. 185–92.

Mimouni, Rachid (1992) *De la Barbarie en général et de l'intégrisme en particulier*, Paris.

Moore, Henry Clement (1991) 'Tunisian Banking: Politics of Adjustment and the Adjustment of Politics' in I.W. Zartman (ed.) *Tunisia. The Political Economy of Reform*, Boulder, CO and London.

—(1990) 'Islamic Banks and Competitive Politics in the Arab World and Turkey', *The Middle East Journal*, 44, 2 (spring), pp. 234–55.

—(1988a) 'La Tunisie: vingt ans de crise de succession', *Maghreb-Machrek*, 126 (April–June), pp. 5–22.

—(1988b) 'Islamic Banks: Financial and Political Intermediation in Arab Countries', *Orient*, 4, 1, pp. 4–57.

—(1986) 'Money and Power: The Dilemma of Egyptian Infitah', *Maghreb-Machrek*, 120 (April), pp. 5–22.

—(1965) *Tunisia since Independence*, Berkeley.

Mottahedeh, Roy (1985) *The Mantle of the Prophet: Religion and Politics in Iran*, New York.

Mouvement de la tendance Islamique (1987) 'Un Point de vue à propos de notre tactique politique pour l'étape actuelle', *Sou'al*, 5.

Munif, Abd al-Rahman (1992) *al-Dimuqratiyya awwalan, al-dimuqratiyya da'iman*, Damascus.

Muntada al-fikr wa'l-hiwar, ed. (1981) *al-Tajarib al-dimiqratiyya fi'l-watan al-arabi*, Algiers.

Mus'ad, Nivin Abd al-Mun'im (1991) 'Jadaliyyat al-istib'ad wa'l-musharaka (muqarana bayna jabhat al-inqadh al-islamiyya fi'l-jaza'ir wa jama'at al-ikhwan al-muslimin fi'l-urdun)', *al-Mustaqbal al-arabi*, 145, pp. 54–74.

Nafi, Hasan (1988) 'al-Idara al-siyasiyya li-azmat al-tahawwul min nizam al-hizb al-wahid ila nizam ta'addud al-ahzab fi Misr', *al-Mustaqbal al-arabi*, no. 112, vol. 11, pp. 72–96.

al-Nafisi, Abdallah Fahd, ed. (1989) *al-Haraka al-islamiyya: ru'ya mustaqbaliyya*, Cairo.

El-Naggar, Said, ed. (1989) *Privatization and Structural Adjustment in the Arab Countries*, Washington DC.

An-Naim, Abdullahi Ahmed (1990) *Toward an Islamic Reformation: Civil Liberties, Human Rights and International Law*, Syracuse.

—(1986) 'The Islamic Law of Apostasy and its Modern Applicability. A Case from Sudan', *Religion*, 16.

al-Naqeeb, Khaldoun Hassan (al-Naqib, Khaldun Hasan) (1991) 'Social Origins of the Authoritarian State in the Arab East' in Eric Davis & Nicolas Gavrielides (eds.) *Statecraft in the Middle East*, Miami.

—(1991) *al-Dawla al-tasallutiyya fi'l-Mashriq al-arabi al-mu'asir. Dirasa bina'iyya muqarina*, Beirut.

—(1990) *Society and State in the Gulf and Arab Peninsula: a Different Perspective*, London (first published 1987 in Arabic, *al-Mujtama wa'l dawla fi'l-jazira al-arabiyya*, Beirut).

Narbeson, John W., ed. (1987) *The Military in African Politics*, New York.

Niblock, T., & Murphy, E., eds. (1993) *Economic and Political Liberalization in the Middle East*, London.

Noble, Paul (1991) 'The Arab System: Opportunities, Constraints and Pressures' in B. Korany & A. Dessouki (eds) *The Foreign Policy of Arab States*, Boulder, CO

North, Douglas (1990) *Institutional Change and Economic Performance*, Cambridge.

Nuwayhid, Walid (1992) 'Ishkaliyyat al-dawla al-arabiyya al-mu'asira al-infisal an al-mujtama', *al-Ijtihad*, 4, 14.

Obermeyer, C. Makhlouf (1992) 'Islam, Women and Politics: The Demography of Arab Countries', *Population and Development Review*, 18, 1.

O'Donnell, Guillermo (1993) 'On the State, Democratization and some Conceptual Problems. A Latin-American View with Glances at Some Post-Communist Countries', *World Development* (August).

—(1973) *Modernization and Bureaucratic Authoritarianism*, Berkeley, Institute of International Studies.

O'Donnell, Guillermo, Schmitter, Philippe C., & Whitehead, Laurence (1986) 'Tentative Conclusions about Uncertain Democracies' in G. O' Donnell, P.C. Schmitter & L. Whitehead, *Transition from Authoritarian Rule. Prospects for Democracy*, Baltimore.

Offe, Claus (1992) 'Capitalism by Democratic Design? Democratic Theory Facing the Triple Transition in East Central Europe', *Social Research*.

Oumlil, Ali (1991) *Fi shar'iyyat al-ikhtilaf*, Rabat.

Panzac, D., ed. (1988) 'Turquie, la croisée des chemins', *Revue du monde musulman et de la Méditerranée*, 50, 4.

Perthes, Volker (1992a) 'Syria's Parliamentary Elections. Remodelling Asad's Political Base', *Middle East Report*, 174, 22 (January–February), pp. 15–18.

—(1992b) 'The Syrian Economy in the 1980s', *The Middle East Journal*, 46, 1, pp. 37–58.

—(1992c) 'The Syrian Private Industrial and Commercial Sectors and the State', *International Journal of Middle Eastern Studies*, 24, 2.

—(1991a) 'A Look at Syria's Upper Class: the Bourgeoisie and the Ba'th', *Middle East Report*, 170, 21 (May–June), pp. 31–7.

—(1991b) 'Syria's Parliamentary Reform and Elections of 1990: Moving from Absolutist to Corporatist Authoritarianism?', paper presented to the annual meeting of the Middle East Studies Association (November 23–6).

— (1990) *Staat und Gesellschaft in Syrien, 1970–1989*, Hamburg.

Petek-Salom, G., & Hukum, P. (1983) 'Après Kemal Atatürk, qu'en est-il de l'émancipation des femmes?', *Peuples méditerranéens*, 22–3 (January–June), pp. 161–80.

Peters, Rudolph (1988) 'Divine Law or Man-Made Law? Egypt and the Application of the Shari'a', *Arab Law Quarterly*, 3, 3 (August), pp. 231–59.

Picard , Elizabeth, ed. (1991) *La Question kurde*, Brussels.

— (1979) 'Clans militaires et pouvoir ba'thiste en Syrie, *Orient*, 20, 1, pp. 49–62.

Piscatori, J.P., ed. (1983) *Islam in the Political Process*, Cambridge.

Przeworski, Adam (1991) *Democracy and the Market: Political and Economic Reforms in Eastern Europe and Latin America*, Cambridge.

— (1988) 'Democracy as a Contingent Outcome of Conflicts' in Jon Elster & Rune Slagstad (eds.) *Constitutionalism and Democracy*, Cambridge.

— (1986) 'Some Problems in the Study of the Transition to Democracy' in G. O' Donnell, P.C. Schmitter & L. Whitehead (eds.) *Transition from Authoritarian Rule. Prospects for Democracy*, III, Baltimore, pp. 47–63.

Puppe, Christine (1985–86) 'Die "Bewegung der Islamischen Tendenz" in Tunesien', unpublished MA thesis, Germersheim.

Ramadan, Abd al-Azim (1982) *Al-Ikhwan al-muslimun wa'l-tanzim al-sirri*, Cairo.

Reed, Stanley F. (1980) 'Dateline Syria: Fin de Régime?', *Foreign Policy*, 39 (summer), pp. 176–90.

Rekhess, Elie (1990) 'The Iranian Impact on the Islamic Jihad Movement in the Gaza Strip' in David Menashri (ed.) *The Iranian Revolution and the Muslim World*, Boulder, CO, San Francisco and Oxford.

Richard, Yann (1991a) 'Les Kurdes d'Iran: révoltes, idéalisme et silence' in E. Picard (ed.) *La Question kurde*, Brussels.

— (1991b) *L'Islam chi'ite. Croyances et idéologies*, Paris.

— (1990) 'Clercs et intellectuels dans la République islamique d'Iran' in G. Kepel & Y. Richard (eds.) *Intellectuels et militants de l'Islam contemporain*, Paris.

Richards, Alan (1993) 'Economic Imperatives and Political Systems', *The Middle East Journal*, 47, 2 (spring).

Richards, Alan, & Waterbury, John (1990) *A Political Economy of the Middle East – State, Class and Economic Development*, Boulder, CO.

Rizq, Jabir (1985) *al-Dawla wa'l-siyasa fi fikr Hasan al-Banna*, Cairo.

Robins, Philip J. (1991) 'Politics and the 1986 electoral law in Jordan' in Rodney Wilson (ed.) *Politics and the Economy in Jordan*, London and New York.

— (1990) 'Jordan's Election: A New Era?', *Middle East Report*, 164–5 (May–August).

Rousseau, Jean-Jacques (1992) *Du Contrat social*, Paris.

Roussillon, Alain (1991) 'Sociologie égyptienne, arabe, islamique, L'approfondissement du paradigme réformiste', *Peuples méditerranéens*, 54–5.

—(1990) 'Entre jihad et el-Rayyan: Phénoménologie de l'islamisme égyptien', *Maghreb-Machrek*, 127, pp. 17–50.

—(1988) 'Sociétés de placement de fonds et "ouverture économique"', *Dossiers du CEDEJ*, 3 Cairo.

Roy, Olivier (1992a) *L'Échec de l'islam politique*, Paris.

—(1992b) 'Ethnies et politique en Asie centrale', *Revue du monde musulman et de la Méditerranée*, 59–60 (January).

—(1991) 'Géopolitique de l'Asie centrale', *Cahiers du monde russe et soviétique*, XXXII, 1 (January–March), pp. 111–50.

Rustow, Dankwart (1988) 'Transition to Democracy' in M. Heper & A. Evin (eds.) *State, Democracy and the Military: Turkey*, London.

—(1970) 'Transitions to Democracy: Toward a Dynamic Model', *Comparative Politics*, 2–3 (April), pp. 337–63.

Ryder, Norman (1983) 'Structure familiale et fécondité', *Bulletin démographique des Nations Unies*, 15, New York.

Saad, Rania (1992) 'Power Struggle within Egypt's Bar Association', *Al-Ahram Weekly* (30 July–5 August).

Sabri Abd Allah, Isma'il (1990) 'Mustaqbal al-dimuqratiyya fi'l watan al-arabi', *al-Mustaqbal al-arabi*, 137, pp. 6–13.

Sadowski, Yahya (1991) *Political Vegetables? Businessmen and Bureaucrats in the Development of Egyptian Agriculture*, Washington DC.

Sa'if Abd Allah (1992) 'al-Mujtama al-madani fi'l fikr al-huquqi al-arabi' in Markaz dirasat al-wahda al-arabiyya, *al-Mujtama al-madani wa dawruhu fi tahqiq al-dimuqratiyya*, Beirut.

—(1988) 'Hawl ba'd mafahim al-dimuqratiyya fi'l-watan al-arabi', *al-Yaqza al-arabiyya*, 40.

Salamé, Ghassan (1993) 'Islam and the West', *Foreign Policy*, 90 (spring).

—(1991a) 'Sur la Causalité d'un manque: Pourquoi le monde arabe n'est-il donc pas démocratique?', *Revue Française de Science Politique*, 41, 3 (June), pp. 307–41.

—(1991b) 'Le Golfe, un an après l'invasion du Kowéit: un pétro-dinar belligène', *Maghreb-Machrek*, 133 (July–September), pp. 3–18.

—(1988) *Nahwa aqd ijtima'i arabi jadid*, Beirut.

—ed. (1987a) *The Foundations of the Arab State*, London.

—(1987b) *al-Mujtama wa'l-dawla fi'l mashriq al-arabi*, Beirut.

Salih, Amani Abd al-Rahman (1991) 'al-Ta'addudiyya al-siyasiyya fi'l-watan al-arabi: dirasa lil namuzaj al-misri wa'l-maghribi', *al-Fikr al-istratiji al-arabi*, 10 (October).

Sandel, Michael (1982) *Liberalism and the Limits of Justice*, Cambridge.

SAR (Syrian Arab Republic) (1991) *Statistical Abstract,* Damascus, Central Bureau of Statistics.

Sartori, Giovanni (1987) *The Theory of Democracy Revisited*, Chatham, NJ.

—(1968a) 'Democracy', *The International Encyclopedia of the Social Sciences*,

4, New York.

—(1968b) 'Political Development and Political Engineering' in John D. Montgomery & Albert O. Hirschman (eds.) *Public Policy*, XVII, pp. 272ff.

—(1962) 'Constitutionalism: a Preliminary Discussion', *American Political Science Review*, 56, 4, pp. 835–65.

Satloff, Robert B. (1986) *Troubles on the East Bank. Challenges to the Domestic Stability of Jordan*, New York.

Sayigh, Yezid (1991) 'Jordan in the 1980s: Legitimacy, Entity and Identity' in Rodney Wilson (ed.) *Politics and the Economy in Jordan*, London and New York.

Sayyid Ahmad, Rif'at (1989a) *Tanzimat al-ghadab al-islami fi'l-sab'inat*, Cairo.

—(1989b) *al-Din wa'l-dawla wa'l-thawra*, Cairo.

al-Sayyid, Ridwan (1992) 'al-Dawla al-arabiyya al-mu'asira wa i'rad al-jumhur anha', *al-Ijtihad*, 4/14.

el-Sayyid, Mustapha Kamil (1991) 'The New Face of Authoritarianism in the Arab World', paper presented to the conference organized by the Turkish Political Science Association on Democratization in the Middle East, Antalya, Turkey, 14–16 November (mimeo).

Scott, James (1976) *The Moral Economy of the Peasant*, New Haven.

Seale, Patrick (1991) 'Asad: Between Institutions and Autocracy' in R.T. Antoun & D. Quataert (eds.) *Syria, Society and Culture and Polity*, Albany.

Seurat, M. (1989) *L'État de barbarie*, Paris.

Shadi, Salah (1981) *Safahat min al-tarikh. Hasad al-umr*, 2nd edn, Kuwait.

al-Sha'ir, Jamal (1988) 'Tajribat al-dimuqratiyya fi'l-urdun' in Markaz dirasat al-wahda al-arabiyya, *Azmat al-dimuqratiyya fi'l-watan al-arabi*, Beirut.

al-Sha'ir, Wahib (1991) 'Tajribat al-Urdun ma al-qita'ayn al-amm wa'l-khass mustaqbal al-tajriba' in Markaz dirasat al-wahda al-arabiyya, *al-Qita al-amm wa'l-qita' al-khass fi'l-watan al-arabi*, Beirut.

al-Shami, Ramadan (1992) 'al-Jaza'ir', *al-Insan*, 2/7, pp.16–28.

Sharabi, Hisham (1988) *Neopatriarchy, A Theory of Distorted Change in Arab Society*, Oxford and New York.

Sharara, Waddah (1980) 'al-Muthaqqafun wa mushkilat infisam al-dawla an al-mujtama' in W. Sharara, *Hawl ba'd mushkilat al-dawla fi'l-thaqafa wa'l-mujtama al-arabiyyayn*, Beirut.

al-Sharif, Kamil (1988) 'al-Sahwa al-islamiyya wa'l-musharaka al-siyasiyya' in Ibrahim (ed.) *al-sahwa al-islamiyya wa humum al-watan al-arabi*, Amman.

—(1984) *al-Fikr al-islami bayn al-mithaliyya wa'l-tatbiq*, Amman.

Shils, Edward (1991) 'The Virtue of Civil Society', *Government and Opposition*, 26 (winter).

Shorter, Fred, and Zurayk, Hoda (1985) *Population Factors in Development in the Middle East*, Washington, The Population Council.

Shukrallah, Hani (1991) 'Democracy and Human Rights in Egypt: Realities, Strategies and Prospects', paper presented at Hearing of Alliance 90/Green Party on Perspectives on the Middle East after the Cold War, Bonn

(September).

Sid Ahmed, Abdelkader (1990) 'Économie islamique, principes et réalités. 'L'Expérience des pays arabes, une première évaluation', *Revue Tiers Monde*, 122 (April–June).

Sivan, Emmanuel (1985) *Radical Islam: Medieval Theology and Modern Politics* (2nd edn. 1990), New Haven.

von Sivers, Peter (1991) 'After the Gulf War: Changes in the Politics and Economies of the Middle East?', unpublished paper.

Skinner, Quentin (1973) 'The Empirical Theorists of Democracy and their Critics: a Plague on Both their Houses', *Political Theory*, I, pp. 287–308.

Sklar, Richard L. (1987) 'Developmental Democracy', *Comparative Studies in Society and History*, 29, pp. 686–714.

Sluglett, Peter, & Farouk-Sluglett, Marion (1990) *Iraq since 1958: from Revolution to Dictatorship*, 2nd edn, London.

Springborg, Patricia (1987) 'The Contractual State: Reflections on Orientalism and Despotism', *History of Political Thought*, 8, 3 (winter).

Springborg, Robert (1990) 'Agrarian Bourgeoisie, Semiproletarians, and the Egyptian State: Lessons for Liberalization', *International Journal of Middle East Studies*, 22, 4 (November).

—(1989) *Mubarak's Egypt: Fragmentation of a Political Order*, Boulder, CO, and London.

—(1986) Intifah, Agrarian Transformation, and Elite Consolidation in Contemporary Iraq', *The Middle East Journal*, 40, 1, pp. 33–52.

Suleiman, Ezra & Waterbury, John, eds (1990) *The Political Economy of Public Sector Reform and Privatization*, Boulder, CO.

Sunar, I. (1974) *State and Society in the Politics of Turkey's Development*, Ankara.

Suwaydan, Ahmad (1980) *Ma'ziq al-amal al-niqabi fi suriya*, Beirut.

Swearingen, Will (1987) *Moroccan Mirages: Agrarian Dreams and Deceptions*. 1912–1986, London.

Taylor, Charles (1992a) *Sources of the Self*, Cambridge, MA.

—— (1992b) *The Ethics of Authenticity*, Cambridge, MA.

Tessler, Mark (1991) 'Anger and Governance in the Arab World: Lessons from the Maghreb and Implications for the West', *Jerusalem Journal of International Relations*, 13, 3, pp. 7–33.

Thabit, Ahmad (1992) 'al-Ta'addudiyya al-siyasiyya fi'l-watan al-arabi: tahawwul muqayyad wa afaq gha'ima', *al-Mustaqbal al-arabi*, 155, pp. 4–20.

Thieck, J.-P. (1992) *Passion d'Orient*, Paris.

Tibi, Bassam (1990) *Islam and the Cultural Accommodation of Social Change*, Boulder, CO.

Todorov, Tzvetan (1993) *On Human Diversity, Nationalism, Racism and Exoticism in French Thought*, Cambridge, MA.

Toprak, B. (1981) *Islam and Politics in Turkey*, Berlin.

Touraine, Alain (1992) *Critique de la modernité*, Paris.

Toussie, H. (1988) 'Anniversaire de la Révolution et Nowrouz', *Cahiers d'études de la Méditerranée orientale et du monde turco-iranien*, 5, pp. 105–17.

Troeltsch, E. (1992) *Protestantisme et modernité*, Paris.

al-Turabi, Hasan Abd Allah (1984) 'al-Shura wa'l-dimuqratiyya: shkalat al-mustalah wa'l-mafhum', *al-Mustaqbal al-arabi*, 75.

TÜSIAD (Turkish Businessmen's Association) (1989) *The Turkish Economy '89*, Istanbul.

Ubaydat, Salim Muhammad (1989) *Athr al-jama'at al-islamiyya al-maydani khilal al-qarn al-ishrin*, Amman

Union of Arab Chambers of Trade, Industry and Agriculture (1991) *al-Taqrir al-iqtisadi al-arabi*, Beirut.

Vandewalle, Dirk (1992) *Popular Protest and Political Reform in Africa*.

—(1990–91) 'The Libyan Revolution After Twenty Years: Part 1 – Evaluating the Jamahiriyah', *USFI Field Staff Reports*, Africa/Middle East.

—(1990) 'Qadhafi's Unfinished Revolution', *Mediterranean Quarterly* (winter), pp. 67–81.

—(1988–89) 'The Prospects for Algeria', *USFI Field Staff Reports*, Africa/Middle East.

—(1988) 'From the New State to the New Era: Towards a Second Republic in Tunisia', *The Middle East Journal*, 42, 4 (autumn), pp. 602–20.

Vaner, S. (1988) 'État, société et partis politiques en Turquie depuis 1902', *Revue du monde musulman et de la Méditerranée*, 50, 4 pp. 87–107.

—(1984) 'Violence politique et terrorisme en Turquie', *Esprit* (October–November).

Vatin, Jean-Claude (1991) 'Crise génératrice, maladie infantile ou faiblesse endogène: le FLN Algérien en fil du temps' in Bernabé López García (ed.) *Elecciones, Participación y Transiciones Políticas en el Norte de África*, Madrid, Instituto de Cooperación con el Mundo Árabe.

Vergin, N. (1973) *Industrialisation et changement social. Étude comparative dans trois villages d'Eregli (Turquie)*, Paris.

Wade, Robert (1990) *Governing the Market*, Princeton.

Waltz, Susan (1991) 'Clientelism and Reform in Ben Ali's Tunisia' in I.W. Zartman (ed.) *Tunisia. The Political Economy of Reform*, Boulder, CO, and London.

—(1986) 'The Islamist Appeal in Tunisia', *The Middle East Journal*, 40, 4 (autumn).

Walzer, Michael (1990) 'The Communitarian Critique of Liberalism', *Political Theory*, 18, 1 (February), pp. 6–23.

Ware, L.B. (1988) 'Ben Ali's Constitutional Coup in Tunisia' in *The Middle East Journal*, 42, 4 (autumn).

—(1985) 'The Role of the Tunisian Military in the Post-Bourguiba Era', *The Middle East Journal*, 39, pp. 27–47.

Waterbury, John (1992) 'Export-Led Growth and the Center-Right Coalition in

Turkey', *Comparative Politics* (January).

—(1991) 'Twilight of the State Bourgeoisies?', *International Journal of Middle East Studies,* 23, 1 (February), pp. 1–17.

—(1977) 'An Attempt to Put Patrons and Clients in their Place' in E. Gellner & J. Waterbury (eds.) *Patrons and Clients in Mediterranean Societies,* London.

White, J.B. (1991) 'Women and Work in Istanbul: Linking the Urban Poor to the World Market', *Middle East Report* (November–December).

Wilson, Rodney, ed. (1991) *Politics and the Economy in Jordan,* London and New York.

World Bank (1990) *Poverty Alleviation and Adjustment in Egypt,* Report no. 8515 EGT, 6/6.

—(1988) *World Development Report,* New York and London.

Worsley, Peter (1969) 'The Concept of Populism' in G. Ionescu and E. Gellner (eds.) *Populism: its Meaning and National Characteristics,* pp. 212–50.

Yashir, Faysal (1992) 'Siyasat al-tashih wa'l-indimaj fi buldan al-maghrib al-arabi', *al-Mustaqbal al-arabi,* 155, 14 (January).

Zamir, M (1985) *The Creation of Modern Lebanon: The Formative Years,* Ithaca and London.

Zartman, I. William (1992) 'Democracy and Islam: "The Cultural Dialectic"', *Annals,* 524 (November), pp. 181–91.

—ed. (1991a) *Tunisia. The Political Economy of Reform,* Boulder, CO, and London.

—(1991b) 'The Conduct of Political Reform' in I.W. Zartman (ed.) *Tunisia. The Political Economy of Reform,* Boulder, CO, and London.

—(1990) 'Opposition as Support of the State' in Giacomo Luciani (ed.) *The Arab State,* London.

—(1987) 'The Military in the Politics of Succession: Algeria', in John W. Narbeson (ed.) *The Military in African Politics,* New York.

al-Zayn, Hasan (1992) 'al-Islam wa'l-dimuqratiyya wa'l-khatar al-mazu'm', *al-Irfan,* 76, 3.

Zaynah, Husni (1992) *al-Dimuqratiyya al-muyassara,* Beirut.

Zghal, Abd al-Qadir (Zghal, Abdelkader) (1992) 'al-Mujtama al-madani wa'l-sira min ajl al-haymana al-idiulujiyya fi'l-Maghrib al-arabi' in Markaz dirasat al-wahda al-arabiyya, *al-Mujtama al-madani wa dawruhu fi tahqiq al-dimuqratiyya,* Beirut.

—(1991a) 'Le Concept de société civile et la transition vers le multipartisme', in Michel Camau (ed.) *Changements politiques au Maghreb,* Paris.

—(1991b) 'The New Strategy of the Movement of the Islamic Way: Manipulation or Expression of Political Culture?' in I.W. Zartman (ed.) *Tunisia, the Political Economy of Reform,* Boulder, CO, and London.

—(1991c) 'Mafhum al-mujtama al-madani wa'l-tahawwul nahw al-ta'addudiyya al-hizbiyya' in *Gramsci wa qadaya al-mujtama al-madani,* Nicosia.

—(1990) 'al-Istratijiyya al-jadida li-harakat al-ittijah al-islami: munawara am ta'bir an al-thaqafa al-tunisiyya?' in Markaz dirasat al-wahda al-arabiyya (ed.), *al-Din fi'l-mujtama al-arabi,* pp. 339–50.

—(1982) 'Western Schools of Thought of the Social Structure and the Middle East' (in Arabic), *al-Mustaqbal al-arabi,* 37, 3, pp. 62–5.

Zubaida, Sami (1989) *Islam, the People and the State,* London.

Zurayk, Hoda (1985) 'Women's Economic Participation' in F. Shorter & H. Zurayk (eds.) *Population Factors in Development in the Middle East,* Washington DC.

Index